# ASPECTS OF LABOR ECONOMICS

NATIONAL BUREAU OF ECONOMIC RESEARCH

*Special Conference Series*

# Aspects of
# Labor Economics

## A CONFERENCE OF THE
## UNIVERSITIES-NATIONAL BUREAU
## COMMITTEE FOR ECONOMIC RESEARCH

A REPORT OF THE

NATIONAL BUREAU OF ECONOMIC RESEARCH, NEW YORK

PUBLISHED BY

PRINCETON UNIVERSITY PRESS, PRINCETON

1962

HD
4901
U5
1960c

Printed in the United States of America
by Princeton University Press, Princeton, N.J.

RELATION OF NATIONAL BUREAU DIRECTORS TO
PUBLICATIONS REPORTING CONFERENCE PROCEEDINGS

Since the present volume is a record of conference proceedings, it has been exempted from the rules governing submission of manuscripts to, and critical review by, the Board of Directors of the National Bureau. It has, however, been reviewed and accepted for publication by the Director of Research.

*(Resolution adopted July 6, 1948, as revised November 21, 1949)*

# Contents

# CONTENTS

# Foreword

THE eight papers in this volume, a sample of current research on problems in labor economics, were discussed at a conference sponsored by the Universities–National Bureau Committee for Economic Research. The scope of the conference was not narrowly limited to a particular problem area or set of areas within the labor field, and the subjects treated in the papers, therefore, are diverse.

Three of the papers, those by Simon Rottenberg, Armen Alchian and Reuben Kessel, and Robert Evans, deal with aspects of market organization or structure. Rottenberg's paper is an economic analysis of the objectives and forms of occupational licensing by states and municipalities and the consequences of such licensing for relative prices, wages, and employment. In a "postscript" Rottenberg applies his analysis to the case of barber licensing in Illinois.

The key postulate in the Alchian-Kessel analysis of monopoly and competition is that public policy toward monopoly in effect, if not in law, puts ceilings on the *pecuniary* income of monopoly organizations, but that competitive organizations are not similarly restrained. Thus, they argue, the price of nonpecuniary income in terms of pecuniary income will tend to be lower and the incentive to substitute nonpecuniary for pecuniary income, therefore, greater for monopolists than for their competitive counterparts. Their paper explores some of the implications of this hypothesis, especially the implication that monopoly is a factor tending to increase discrimination against minority groups of all kinds.

The subject of Evans' study is the always controversial question of the "profitability and viability" of American Negro slavery in the pre-Civil War South. The renting of slaves was fairly common in the antebellum South. Evans has assembled time series on slave rents from original documents in Southern archives. These data together with corresponding data on slave prices and death rates enable him to make new estimates of the rate of return on slave capital. Comparison of these estimates with those on alternative forms of capital indicate that the rate of return on slave capital was approximately equal to that on alternatives. His paper also examines the historical data on slave prices, rents, birth rates, population, and manumissions to see whether they displayed the characteristics of a declining (nonviable) industry.

My paper and that by Melvin Reder both deal with relative (i.e.,

*xi*

percentage) wage differentials among categories of the labor force. The purpose of my paper is to estimate numerically (1) the dispersion among industries of the relative wage effects of labor unions and (2) the extent to which unionism has increased the gross relative dispersion in wages among industries. The purpose of Reder's study is very different: to interpret the findings of recent research on relative differentials among both industries and occupations in the light of economic theory and, particularly, to test competitive theory against these findings.

George Shultz's paper is an investigation and appraisal of the functioning of labor markets in the U.S. as exemplified by the labor market for female clerical employees of Boston banks and insurance companies since World War II. His paper examines the varied reactions of these employers to changes in labor market conditions, the characteristics and supply responses of their employees, and the significance of market intermediaries as suppliers of information to both sides of the market.

The starting point of Jacob Mincer's study is the failure of the "standard" theory of labor supply per head—the familiar "backward-bending" supply curve—to reconcile and explain cross-section and historical data on labor force participation, especially of females. In his attempt to explain these data Mincer has come up with a new and fairly simple theory that is essentially an application of consumption theory to the problem of labor supply. In this theory the amount of work supplied by a family member to the market depends not only on *his* market wage rate (in both its permanent and its transitory aspects), but also on both the permanent and transitory income of the family, the family's asset-debt position, *his* earning power in household production, the prices of market substitutes for household goods, and family tastes. Mincer's tests of simplified versions of the theory against a variety of cross-section data and, less fully, historical data on labor force participation of married women comprise the bulk of his paper.

Abraham Siegel's paper is a study of the morphology of labor protest and, especially, of the interrelations between labor protest and industrialization. On the latter Siegel contrasts his own views with those of Marx and Thorstein Veblen.

The planning committee for the conference included Gary S. Becker, George H. Hildebrand, Stanley Lebergott, H. Gregg Lewis, and Charles A. Myers. Thanks are due to Margaret T. Edgar for her careful final editing of the manuscript, and to H. Irving Forman for preparing the charts.

*Chicago, Illinois*                    H. Gregg Lewis

ASPECTS OF LABOR ECONOMICS

# The Economics of Occupational Licensing

## SIMON ROTTENBERG
### UNIVERSITY OF BUFFALO

ENTRY into certain vocations has been regulated in this country since colonial times. During the early national period, many states required licenses for the practice of law and medicine; but the restraints were eased after about 1820, and by mid-century entry into these professions was open to almost anyone.

The present system of occupational licensing began in the final quarter of the nineteenth century. Since then, states have licensed more and more trades; in 1956, Gellhorn found some eighty occupations that needed state licenses to practice, "exclusive of owner-business."[1]

Municipalities as well as states regulate entry, the number of licensing jurisdictions varying among occupations. Some municipalities license occupations also licensed by their states; some license occupations that are not state-regulated.

The distinction between occupational and business licensing is hard to draw: to license banks is to license bankers; the license for a liquor shop also regulates the shopkeeper. In still other ways, occupational licensing may be indirect rather than direct. In some cases, persons are not licensed but places, things, or uses are. For example, New York City licenses billiard and pool tables, and a person desiring to enter the pool hall trade requires licenses for his tables. In many places weapons must be licensed, and such a license requirement might restrict entry into trades (e.g., bodyguard, watchman) that call for use of weapons. The discussion here, however, is limited to vocational licensing.

To what extent does licensure limit entry into trades? If virtually *all* persons can qualify, the requirement that practitioners be licensed is either a low-cost device for enforcing rules of behavior, or a revenue measure. At the other extreme, the cost of the license may be implicitly infinite, as when licenses are not transferable and there are explicit limitations of numbers, as of taxicabs in some cities or of taverns per-

NOTE: The preparation of this paper was aided by a grant from the Relm Foundation. The paper was written while the author was a member of the faculty of the University of Chicago.
[1] Walter Gellhorn, *Individual Freedom and Governmental Restraints*, Louisiana State University Press, 1956, p. 106.

mitted per police district. Beyond the specified number, *no* person may qualify for entry.

Costs of entry into a trade may be imposed in other ways than by licensure. Hygienic standards for restaurants may require investment in special dishwashing equipment and check entry of those for whom the return would be larger in restaurant keeping than in the next best alternative, *but only if* dishwasher capital costs did not have to be incurred. Similar rules are those requiring licensed funeral directors to maintain large inventories of caskets and laws requiring small coal mines to enforce federal safety standards. In principle, therefore, licensure is not different from other rules that increase costs of entry into occupations.

From the earliest times, licensing statutes and ordinances have been adopted by legislatures on the alleged ground of defense of the public health, safety, and morals. In colonial America, "The people who carried on the Indian trade were, as a class, disreputable and not to be trusted. The most natural solution was to allow only responsible and trustworthy people to engage in this traffic, and, to secure this end, it was enacted that no one should engage in the Indian trade without a license therefor from the colonial governor."[2]

It is true, nevertheless, that (1) when pleas are made to legislatures for new licensing statutes or for amendments that raise standards (costs) for qualifying, they are almost invariably made by practitioners of those trades, not by consumers of their services; and (2) standards are established and examinations conducted by boards of examiners composed of practitioners. The vested interest of the incumbent practitioners in restricting numbers in their trade will be discussed later.

Licenses may be a prerequisite for the practice of a trade or they may only certify as to competence. In the former case only licensed persons may legally practice the trade; in the latter, anyone may practice, but only licensed persons may use some specified occupational title. The Illinois Physical Therapy Registration Act, for example, forbids a practitioner to "hold himself out to the public to be a registered physical therapist unless he is registered by the Department as a physical therapist," but does not "prevent the practice of physical therapy by

---

[2] Thomas K. Urdahl, *The Fee System in the United States*, Madison, Wisconsin, 1898, p. 102.

4

a person not registered under the Act."[3] Such a law may limit entry into a trade if some consumers can be convinced that only registered practitioners are competent.

The enforcement of license laws is vested in the diverse authorities administering the police power of government. Often, however, the real enforcing power lies in the hands of trade associations and trade unions that may maintain inspectors to detect practice by unlicensed persons. They may enforce the laws by direct action or bring cases to the attention of the public authorities. The process of detection and enforcement is costly. Some unlicensed practice will be undetected or "winked at"; a plumbers trade union might "enforce" the licensing law in building construction, but not in building maintenance.

While some licenses are required in the construction industry, the laws fall more heavily on occupations in the tertiary sector of the economy. Within that sector they are concentrated in occupations with high self-employment and in which services are offered to diverse buyers and rendered for short periods. Since the license purports to attest to the quality of the licensed person, it supplies information that, in these occupations, cannot be learned from the experience of continuous and long-period employment. Information obtained from other buyers is presumably more imperfect than that found out more directly.

Only a small proportion of the total labor force is in licensed trades, despite the continuous increase in the number of licensed trades since the turn of the century. Of about 3.8 million persons in the labor force in Illinois, for instance, it is doubtful that more than 275,000 are in trades licensed by the Department of Registration and Education. The numerically important licensed trades, with approximate numbers of licensees in that state are:[4]

| Barbers | 14,500 | Nurses, practical | 7,600 |
|---|---|---|---|
| Beauty culturists | 45,500 | Pharmacists | 8,600 |
| Embalmers | 4,600 | Plumbers | 5,000 |
| Funeral directors | 4,500 | Professional engineers | 15,800 |
| Physicians and surgeons | 15,000 | Real estate brokers | 19,000 |
| Nurses, registered | 60,500 | Real estate salesmen | 14,700 |

Informal evidence is convincing that the licensure laws are administered with intent to produce favorable income effects for practitioners. Complaints against the practice of a trade by unlicensed persons and

[3] *Illinois Physical Therapy Registration Act*, Springfield, 1951, pp. 1-2.
[4] *Annual Report*, Illinois Dept. of Registration and Education, June 30, 1958.

against the checks on entry imposed by licensing laws come not from consumers but rather from people in competitive trades; beauty culturists protest prohibition of their cutting hair by barber licensing laws; drain layers protest limitations imposed upon them by plumber licensing laws; dental hygienists object to constraints imposed upon their permissible activities by dental licensing boards; and osteopaths, chiropodists, chiropractors, and physical therapists complain of their treatment by medical boards. The reasons are obvious. Consumers spend only a small proportion of their income on the services of people in licensed trades and a rise in the prices of these services affects them only slightly, while for tradesmen laws limiting the services they may perform are serious.

In the few cases involving explicit limitation of numbers and in which licenses are transferable (as in some taxicab or liquor dealer cases), monopoly rents produced by limitation can be capitalized and transacted. If the condition of perfect foresight is fulfilled, the buyer pays the seller the full value of expected rents in the transaction price and the buyer derives no monopoly income. If licenses are not transferable or if anyone may acquire a license by meeting stipulated standards, no rents are earned by those who must incur the costs of qualifying. Persons who have entered a trade at a lower cost, however, do receive rents, if they can impose higher costs upon new entrants. Thus incumbents in any trade have the incentive to perpetuate a license requirement and at ever higher standards. Incumbents in unlicensed trades may be expected to promote licensing for new entrants, with entry costs, but only if a "grandfather clause" which licenses incumbents routinely is included. Without that clause incumbents would be required to withdraw from the trade and pay the re-entry costs, thus being deprived of their rents. Gellhorn reports that in a single session of the New Jersey legislature practitioners asked that licensure be required for bait-fishing boats, beauty shops, chain stores, florists, insurance adjusters, photographers, and master painters, and that usually grandfather's clauses appeared in the draft proposals.[5] Each amendment to a licensure law which imposes successively higher entry costs upon new entrants will create new rents for incumbents.

The degrees to which earnings rise and employment declines, because entry has been made more costly, are functions of the elasticities of supply and demand of the relevant trade and of the magnitude of

[5] Gellhorn, *Individual Freedom*, p. 110.

the increase in entry costs. Since monopoly rents produced by a given increase in entry costs for new entrants will be the larger, the more inelastic the demand curve confronting the trade, one would expect that licensure restricting entry will be more common in trades facing inelastic than elastic demands. This can be expressed in the following form: Assume that the cost to incumbents of achieving an increase in entry costs of given magnitude is indifferently distributed among trades and thus equal in all. Assume also that the magnitude of an incremental increase in cost of entry is directly proportional to the costs of lobbying, and so forth, incurred by incumbents. On these assumptions, quasi-rents of given magnitude can be acquired by incumbents the more cheaply, the more inelastic the demand for the services of the trade.

Are there too few people in the licensed trades? Would the economy gain if more were in these trades and fewer in unlicensed trades? In other contexts—as where a maximum price is put on the services of some class of labor which is below the competitive price—insufficiency of resources in the relevant trade is manifested by the failure of the market to clear and the formation of queues on the demand side of the market. Alternatively, if a floor is placed under prices at higher than the competitive price, the market will not clear and queues will form on the supply side. This may be manifested by work sharing through short workweek schedules and by higher relative hourly wages than weekly or annual earnings.

If, however, the license restricts entry by imposing higher entry costs, the market clears and queues do not form, since the numbers entering will cause the return to effort, adjusted for different quantities of entry-investment in licensed and unlicensed trades, to be the same for both. The price of services in the licensed trades will be higher than they would have been if entry into them were free, and it will be higher than the price of services in comparable unlicensed trades; but it will be a price that will clear the market.

Thus in Figure 1, if entry is checked only by increasing entry costs, the supply schedule falls from S to S'; the number employed falls from OA to OB; and the price rises from OC to OD. The market cleared at X before licensing, and clears at Y after licensing.

If entry is checked only by increasing entry costs, and, in addition, a floor (E in Figure 1) is put under prices at higher than the new equilibrium rate, queues will form and work will be nonprice rationed

7

among those who have entered, since supply OF will exceed demand OG, at that price.

If entry is checked not only by increasing entry costs but also by absolutely limiting the number who may enter, there will also be

FIGURE 1

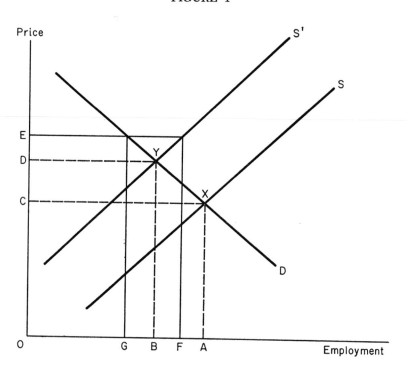

queueing and rationing, but only if the number to which entry is limited is smaller than the number at which the market will clear; here entry will be rationed among those who aspire to enter.

Thus in Figure 2, the supply schedule would be SS if entry were perfectly free and license entry costs were not imposed; S′S′, if license entry costs were imposed; S′XS,″ if they were imposed and, in addition, an absolute numerical check is made effective at the number OA. The price OE will prevail and, at that price, OB would enter, if the numerical check had not been set at OA. AB, therefore, is the number excluded by the entry-rationing rule. If, of course, the numerical limit were established at OC (or any other number larger than OD), the

8

numerical check would be irrelevant, and there would again be neither queues nor any other form of nonprice rationing.

What is the specific nature of the checks on entry imposed by licensing statutes? The licensing "industries" produce, to a certain extent, homogeneous products because unions and associations have drafted model laws and lobbied for them—with some success. An

FIGURE 2

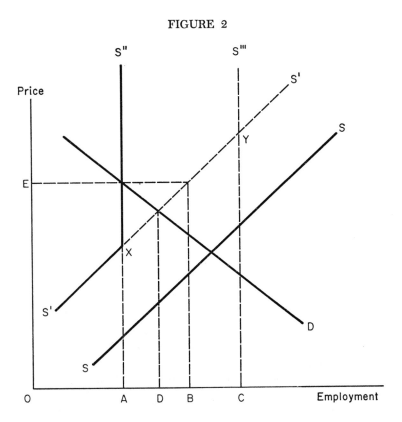

examination of the experience of a single state, therefore, has something to tell about the practice of all states. In Illinois the following different kinds of checks are imposed by licensing laws: age, general schooling to specified standards, trade or professional schooling, apprenticeship, and examination. For example, the Funeral Directing and Embalming Law limits the practice of funeral directing to registered funeral directors. Requirements for registration are that the applicant be at least twenty years old and a citizen of Illinois, of good moral character and temperate habits, be certified as a registered embalmer and have

9

passed an examination. For the prior qualifying test for registration as an embalmer, requirements are to be at least twenty-one years old and of good character, to have completed one academic year in an approved college or university, to be a graduate of an approved school of embalming (at least nine months' course), to have been apprenticed to a registered embalmer in Illinois for at least one year, to have passed an examination and be "properly protected against communicable diseases."[6]

This is not an uncommon set of qualifying rules. Each rule separately will check entry to a trade, either by imposing explicit costs or implicit costs. For instance, requirement of general or professional schooling at specified standards imposes tuition and foregone income costs during the period of schooling. These higher entry costs in the licensed trade cause the supply curve of labor to fall and the price of services of labor in the trade to rise. The return to effort in a licensed trade, adjusted for the relative costs of entry, will be the same as in unlicensed trades, but only if, at each possible price of labor, new entrants are fewer than would have been attracted to it in the absence of higher entry costs. On the principle that people distribute themselves among employments in ways that make net advantage equal in all, the latter outcome can be expected. If, with higher entry costs, the supply curve did not fall, the price of labor would not be higher and the yield to effort (adjusted for entry costs) would be lower in licensed than in unlicensed trades. When the qualifying rules impose entry costs, employment in the licensed trade is rationed by price.

An example of nonprice rationing rules is the previously mentioned requirement of a specified age. The result is the same as in the case of price-rationing rules, except that the age composition in the trade will be different from what it would be if entry were free. The age requirement will demand a higher price to attract a given number of new entrants (i.e., the supply schedule will fall), because some entrants to the licensed trade will have acquired skills with experience in other employments while "waiting" to meet the age limit. In addition, their opportunity costs will have risen; they will have better alternatives than they would have had if they had been permitted to enter the trade at an earlier age. As before, the adjusted return to effort will be the same in all trades, licensed and unlicensed. The number employed in the licensed trade will be smaller than if entry into it were free, if

---

[6] *Illinois Funeral Directing and Embalming Law*, Springfield, 1956.

the demand schedule for labor in the trade is negatively sloping; numbers employed will be unaffected only if the demand schedule is perfectly inelastic.

If there is an explicit numerical check on entry (as when the number of licenses is limited), if licenses are not rationed by price, and if licenses are nontransferable, a different result from those of the foregoing cases ensues. The number in the trade will be less, the price of labor of the trade will be higher, just as in the other cases, but the return to effort will be higher than in other trades. Sufficient additional numbers cannot be transferred to the trade to wipe out the real differential in it because of the constraint on the number of entrants permitted. If, however, the number of licensees is equal to or greater than the number who would have made their way into the trade, if there were no licensing, none of these consequences follow and the licensing becomes nonrestrictive and irrelevant. If licenses are transferable, even in the case of explicit numerical checks, there will be no difference between the case of numerical checks and the other cases, and the return to effort (adjusted for entry costs) will be the same in all trades.

In trades where licensing checks are imposed on new entrants but not on incumbents, the return to effort will be higher for incumbents than in other trades because of their freedom from the additional costs of entry, but it will not be higher for new entrants who do incur these costs. Since only incumbents earn quasi-rents from checking entry by imposing new costs of entry, it is to be expected that there will be successive demands for making entry costs higher. Each generation of entrants will seek to make entry more costly for succeeding generations. That process was noted above: legislatures are not only continuously confronted by requests of unlicensed trades that they be licensed but also by requests of licensed tradesmen that qualifying standards for their trades be raised. Usually, legislatures are offered a package which includes blanket exemption from the new costs of those already practicing the trade.

The history of Illinois barber licensing is a case in point.[7] In 1909, a law was passed requiring that a person not then practicing barbering would have to serve an apprenticeship or attend a barber school and pass an examination to be licensed to practice. A 1927 law specified that only those who had completed eight grades of school could qualify

[7] Smith-Hurd, *Illinois Annotated Statutes*, Chap. 16 3/4, "Barbers, Historical Note."

to become apprentices. A 1929 amendment required both six months' barber schooling and an apprenticeship for a license. Further rises in standards followed: 1937, age standards; 1939, entry only to citizens and aliens who had filed intention to be naturalized; 1947, the course of instruction in barber school lengthened from six to nine months; 1951, completion of ten years of school for enrollment as a student barber.

If foresight is perfect, the rejection rate (the ratio of failures to numbers examined) will be zero. If the rejection rate is positive, and if the qualifying standards are honestly applied and not used as a covert strategy for hiding explicit numerical entry checks, it is because foresight is less than perfect.

Less than perfect foresight is a necessary condition for the existence of gains from licensing (through use of increased entry costs). Incumbents free of entry costs imposed on new entrants gain by increased income. The gain is equivalent to that accruing to the sellers of transferable licenses after the capital value of the licenses has risen. In both cases, the gain is produced by lack of foresight. If the market had been estimated correctly there would be no rise in transferable license capital values. If the behavior of legislatures had been estimated correctly, entrants would have crowded into the trade before higher costs of entry had been imposed, so that earnings would have been lower in the prelicensing period and higher in the postlicensing period, but equal to adjusted earnings in other similar trades over the long run. In conditions of uncertainty, the more shrewd estimate correctly the probability that higher entry costs will be required of new entrants and take advantage of the lower entry costs, while the less shrewd underestimate the probability. If there is overestimation of the probability, too many crowd into the trade, and returns fall below those in comparable employments.

The larger the cost of entry relative to the current value of the expected income from a trade, compared with other trades, the smaller will be the number who enter; therefore, the magnitude of the entry cost imposed by licensing is an index of the power of the license to check entry. The larger the relative cost of entry and, therefore, the higher the price of labor in the trade, the larger is the incentive to engage in unlicensed practice. Aspirants will seek to be illegally licensed—as by buying passing grades on examinations—if the cost is less than the cost of acquiring the information necessary to pass the examination.

Why do licensing arrangements usually check entry by imposing entry costs rather than in other ways, say, by explicit numerical checks? The answer is that the costs can be defended on grounds that standards are being raised and consumers are being protected against the consequences of error. Pleas can be made for the public interest. Explicit numerical checks must be defended on grounds of external diseconomies; too many taxis, racing for customers, will cause accidents on the streets, or too many taverns will cheapen liquor and increase drinking. Legislatures appear to consider adverse third-party effects less plausible than higher standards as grounds for licensing for most trades.

Costs of entry imposed by licensing are of diverse classes. Some who gain from increased entry costs for others are indifferent to the nature of the costs and interested only in their aggregate magnitude. Others gain only if costs are increased by requiring that *their* services be bought by aspirants in order to qualify for entry. For example, owners of colleges of embalming and teachers in them prefer that all prospective registered embalmers be required to enroll in such colleges, that the course of instruction to be taken be for longer rather than shorter periods, and that the whole cost of entry be spent for embalming college instruction. Some evidence of this attitude is found in attempts to monopolize the required services by owners of barber schools, who oppose the teaching of barbering in public vocational schools and prisons.

The age composition of persons in licensed trades can be expected to be different from that in similar unlicensed trades, and the mean age in licensed trades is higher. New entrants to the labor market, making their first occupational choices, choose indifferently between free-entry occupations with low earnings and positive entry-cost occupations with high expected earnings, so long as the yield to effort, adjusted for entry costs, is the same in both. If the rules for rationing licensed employments among first-job choosers are indifferent to age, new entrants into licensed and unlicensed trades will be random with respect to the age of new entrants to the labor market. But where entry into the licensed trades is postponed by age or educational qualifications for admission, the age of entry of first-job takers into licensed trades will be higher than into similar unlicensed trades.

*13*

There will be little movement between the two kinds of trades during the middle years of working life. Once having entered a licensed trade, the licensee will be reluctant to leave. The skills and knowledge which the licensing requirements compelled him to acquire are specialized to the licensed trade and will yield income to him only in that trade. Outmigration from licensed trades will be low also among those in a licensed trade who entered the trade when entry was free or when the cost of entry was lower than that currently prevailing. They will earn quasi-rents in that trade, but they will earn no rents in any other. In-migration to licensed trades of unlicensed tradesmen in their middle years will also be low for two reasons. Where the acquisition of a license requires full-time schooling or apprenticeship, income is fore-gone. Since earnings of persons in their middle years are higher than for younger men, the cost, in foregone income, of training for entry into the licensed trades will be higher. Furthermore, the period of payoff for investment in training will be shorter for older men than for younger.

The mean age of retirement from licensed trades will be higher than from similar unlicensed trades. The cost of retirement is the loss of earnings that would have been received, if retirement had been postponed. Since licensing, by checking entry, causes earnings to rise, this cost will be higher in licensed than in unlicensed similar employ-ments. Aggregating these components—higher age of entry into licensed trades and of exit from them, and small net movements between licensed and unlicensed trades—produces a higher mean age in licensed trades.

### Postscript on Barber Licensing in Illinois

I propose now to examine licensure in the barber industry with special reference to the State of Illinois. Forty-seven of the old forty-eight states license barbers.

Barber examining boards are almost always composed of practi-tioners. Some years ago Chicago proposed to license barbers munici-pally (state licensing has been in effect since 1909). The barber trade unions and associations opposed municipal licensing, unless the city examining board be composed of barbers but, failing the mayor's con-sent, the licensing ordinance was not adopted.

It is evident that barbers desire to use licensure to restrict entry.

One of the vice presidents of the Barber's Union (Journeymen Barbers, Hair Dressers, and Cosmetologists) wrote in the union journal:[8]

> While the barber boards, barber schools and the International Union are separate organizations, there is much in common between them. We are particularly pleased to see the Barber Boards of 47 States giving heed to the law of supply and demand. Good schools and well-trained students are necessary for future progress of the barber profession, but too many schools and too many students . . . can stop progress and shatter the hopes of the future. . . . Operators of schools and colleges should put teaching and sufficient training ahead of accumulating dollars. . . . This cannot be done if students do not have sufficient practice on the chair. Too many students mean too many poorly trained students and too many poorly trained students mean too many cut-rate barbers. The law of supply and demand must be heeded if we are to continue to hold our present price structure and go forward to make our profession what it should be.

The union's president enumerated the achievements of the union in its seventy-two year history: "established individual health requirements for practitioners, shop sanitation standards, professional educational requirements, educational programs calling for practical training, examinations, apprenticeship terms, State license laws. . . ." All these achievements have the effect of limiting numbers in the trade. There is a network of organizations through which the restrictive strategy is made effective. These include the state barber associations, which are the legislative arm of the union, a National Association of Barber Examiners, a Barber Schools Association, and associations of employing and self-employed barbers.

In Illinois the number of barbers has been declining relative to total and active population. The census of 1950 counted fewer barbers (males in the occupational class, "barbers, beauticians, and manicurists") than did the 1920 census.

|  | *Illinois* | |
|---|---|---|
|  | *Census Count* | |
| *Barbers per 1,000:* | 1950 | 1920 |
| Total population | 1.4 | 2.0 |
| Active population | 3.2 | 4.9 |

[8] *Journeyman Barber*, Nov. 1958, pp. 395, 397.

The relatively diminished number of barbers is not conclusive proof that licensing has checked entry. It may simply be evidence that barbering is a declining industry and that others perform the services formerly done by barbers. It may also be evidence of technological progress, as the invention of electric hair clippers, which caused a given demand schedule for barber services to be transformed into a fallen demand schedule for barbers.

The demand for barber services seems to be somewhat inelastic. While the invention of the safety razor produced a good substitute for barber shaving services, there does not seem to be a good substitute for haircutting services. Some degree of elasticity is produced by the possibility of diminishing the frequency of haircuts as prices rise, and the do-it-yourself movement can make some progress. Indeed the union is aware of the threat posed by do-it-yourself. The president of the union wrote:[9]

> Certain manufacturing interests and supply dealers . . . have aided and abetted the so-called 'Do-It-Yourself' slogan. They have advertised and sold to the general public hair cutting sets, cosmetics and other supplies used in barber and beauty shops. The International Union [is] . . . opposed to the 'Do-It-Yourself' program. We believe that the manufacturers of products used in barber and beauty shops should sell directly to those shops—not disperse to drug and department stores for over-the-counter sales. . . . When manufacturers advertise . . . that the general public can perform these services, they are in competition with our people. . . .

Some elasticity is probably introduced by employment of unlicensed barbers. It would be difficult for them, however, to operate in street shops, and most unlicensed barbering is probably confined to itinerants who cut hair out of sight of licensing board inspectors.

The cost of entry into the occupation, in the absence of licensing requirements, would be low. The legislative representative of the union estimated in 1958 that the cost of equipping a one-chair barber shop was $1,500.[10] Another estimate puts entry costs at $1,000 per chair for a three-chair shop and less per chair for larger shops where plumbing and electrical installation overhead can be distributed over a larger number of chairs.[11]

[9] *Ibid.*, June 1958, p. 197.   [10] *Ibid.*, April 1958, p. 127.
[11] Interview with proprietor of Moler Barber School, Chicago.

The Illinois barber licensing law requires annual renewal of licenses. The flow of new entrants into the trade seems to be insufficient to compensate for deaths and retirements, so that in Illinois the stock of licensed barbers has declined somewhat, as shown in the next tabulation.[12]

| Year | New Barber Licenses as Percentage of Renewed Licenses | Sum of New and Renewed Barber Licenses |
|------|------|------|
| 1950 | 4.41 | 14,822 |
| 1953 | 3.33 | 14,993 |
| 1956 | 2.80 | 14,748 |
| 1958 | 2.87 | 14,484 |

The price of barber services in Chicago has risen relatively in recent years. The Bureau of Labor Statistics sample for measuring price changes for barber services consists of two union shops, one in the central city and one outlying. Only one item—male haircuts—is priced, once each quarter. The prices since December 1952 have been:

| | |
|---|---|
| December, 1952 to June, 1955 | $1.50 |
| September, 1955 to March, 1959 | 1.75 |
| June, 1959— | 2.00 |

Since some barber services are sold in Chicago at less than the union rate, the BLS price is not accurate, but no better index is available. The "all-items" BLS consumer price index for cities rose by 10 per cent from 1952 to July, 1959.

The Illinois barber licensing law is sufficiently comprehensive to make it appear unlawful for any person to shave himself, if he is not a licensed barber. The law reads, in part (paraphrased):[13] It is unlawful for any person to practice barbering without a certificate of registration as a registered barber. Anyone of the following constitutes the practice of barbering: to shave or trim the beard or cut the hair.

A barber committee (three barbers, each licensed for at least five years) must consent to the following standards before they can be applied by the state government: ascertain the fitness of applicants for licenses; prescribe rules for examining applicants; establish standards for barber schools; establish standards of prior education for admission

[12] *Annual Reports*, Illinois Dept. of Registration and Education.
[13] *Illinois Barber Law*, Dept. of Registration and Education, 1959.

to barber schools; conduct hearings on license revocations and suspensions.

The law requires student barbers to have certificates of registration; to qualify they must be sixteen and one-half years old, be U.S. citizens, and must have completed two years of high school. Apprentice barbers must also have certificates of registration. Qualifying standards require seventeen and one-fourth years of age; successful completion of a course of study in a recognized barber school (1,872 hours completed in not less than nine months); passing an examination in the primary theory and practice of barber science and art, including anatomy, physiology, skin diseases, hygiene and sanitation, bacteriology, barber history and law, pharmacology, electricity and light, haircutting, shaving and shampooing, massaging, and implements. No barber shop may employ more than one apprentice for each registered barber it employs. The period of apprenticeship must be at least two and one-quarter years.

Requirements for the certificate as a registered barber (the barber license) are: age, nineteen and one-half years; completion of the period of apprenticeship; success in a second examination covering scientific scalp and facial treatments for cosmetic purposes, use of creams, lotions, and other preparations in conjunction with galvanic, faradic, and high frequency electricity, ultra violet radiation, vibratory appliances, barber shop management, ethics, salesmanship, standardized services, advanced haircutting and shaving technique (including scientific finishing and artistic grooming), and professional courtesy.

The law also defines standards for recognized barber schools with respect to curriculum, teaching staff, location, etc.; establishes standards of practice for barbers; and provides for the three types of licenses for barber teachers—theory, practice, and joint theory and practice.

It is clear from a mere recital of the law that it imposes entry costs of some magnitude, and that consumers searching for a qualified person merely to cut hair must pay for a tie-in package of many other skills superfluous for this purpose. Presumably, most people seek haircutting rather than scalp care services in barber shops. A recent issue of a barber's magazine suggests that incumbents do not know "barber science" well, unless they know whether the discovery of bacteria is credited to Louis Pasteur, whether Vitamin D is effective against scurvy, whether proteins contain traces of phosphorous, and whether arrector muscles pass from the surface of the true skin.[14]

[14] *Master Barber and Beautician Magazine*, January 1958.

The barber case exhibits a common characteristic of occupational licensing: by requiring longer periods of schooling than is objectively required for the learning of skills and knowledge relevant to the practice of the craft, things relevant to other crafts are also learned. The system defines high minimum standards for practitioners. It raises (albeit unnecessarily) the mean quality of legal practitioners (when quality is measured by the sum of knowledge commanded) and diminishes the dispersion about the mean. Put otherwise, it diminishes specialization in skill acquisition and (somewhat less certainly) specialization in the exercise of skill, by insisting that all practitioners be qualified in many disciplines.

It should be noted parenthetically that, while licensing causes the mean quality of *legal* practitioners to rise, by excluding those at the lower part of the qualitative range who could have practiced legally in the absence of a licensing statute, it does not necessarily cause the mean quality of the relevant service to rise. Whether it does or not turns on the behavior of consumers of the service after the trade has been licensed, who in the absence of licensing would have employed the qualitatively low tradesmen who sold their services at correspondingly low prices. If consumers substitute for low-quality barbers, who are now not permitted to practice, the haircutting services of their wives, the qualitative mean falls; if they substitute the services of higher-quality barbers, the qualitative mean rises. If both occur, as is likely, the outcome is an arithmetic consequence of the magnitudes of opposite movements.

Barber licensing laws are more restrictive in some states than in others. Both the Barbers' Union and the Master Barbers' Association oppose reciprocity of licensing among the states.[15] This is a rational policy for them, for, if reciprocity prevailed, people would enter through the widest door, and high entry costs in some states would be vitiated by low costs in others.

In addition to restricting entry into the trade, barbers also fix prices for their services either directly or by lobbying for state minimum-price laws for barber services. Fourteen states have such laws. It is reasonable to surmise that the fixed price is higher than a price determined by the demand and the (restricted) supply schedules. If the higher price is secured by price fixing rather than by imposing still higher entry costs, it may be either because the cost of pursuing price-fixing strategy

[15] *Journeyman Barber,* October 1957, p. 293; and June 1958, p. 197.

is lower than the cost of the latter, or because practitioners are impatient to have higher prices and seek to avoid the long run during which higher entry costs check new entrants.

The additional numbers who may be attracted to the barbering trade by the higher prices may be prevented from entering by the imposition of additional entry costs. Alternatively, when prices for barber services are fixed at levels above what would be determined by the intersection of the demand and supply schedules, there will be an excess of supply. Demand will then be rationed among incumbents in the industry. Hypothetically, the rationing could occur by having employing barbers choose among licensed barbers. But any barber unemployed as a result of this rationing process would be able to establish his own firm (i.e., to employ himself in an own-account business), since there are no legal restraints on establishing new barber shops, and the cost to already licensed barbers of entry into the industry is low. Therefore, the excess supply would cause demand to be rationed by the choices of consumers among barbers who present themselves for employment. The result would be an average less-than-full workweek in the barbering trade.

The specification and enforcement of a minimum price does not mean that barber services will be uniformly priced in all establishments. In some, prices higher than the minimum will be charged, and the products offered for sale will be of higher quality than those in lower-priced establishments. The same variation in prices and product quality will obtain in the absence of minimum price enforcement. The effect of minimum pricing is to cut off products at the lower range of the qualitative hierarchy and to cause consumers who would have bought them to turn to substitutes.

# Method and Substance in Theorizing About Worker Protest

ABRAHAM J. SIEGEL

MASSACHUSETTS INSTITUTE OF TECHNOLOGY

THE main purpose of this paper is to outline a unifying analytical framework for the varied probings into work and its discontents—a span of theory which, for want of a conventional label, I have called "worker protest theory."

## A Framework for Theorizing About Worker Protest

The totality of theorizing about worker protest must be viewed as an interlocking structure of hypotheses and generalizations of varying scope and compass. We have no single theory of protest, for men have asked no single question nor viewed the phenomenon of protest from any one vantagepoint.

Worker protest like "the wage" is a cryptic shorthand for a generic around which our theorizing turns. It is neither necessary nor possible for an analytical framework to enumerate all the elements into which our general substantive focus may be parsed, to detail their almost limitless variability and interrelatedness, or to specify the complete array of questions (and answers when and if found) in which they may play a part. The analytical framework is more like the road map than the detailed aerial photograph of an area. The analytical mapping of the main possible routes of worker protest theory and their intersections which I outline here has served as a useful guide for my own early curiosities about this field of theory and has whetted many more.

### ELEMENTS OF WORKER PROTEST THEORY

Two major lines of inquiry have dealt with these general questions: What are the sources of worker protest? What are the consequences of worker protest? The first broad question seeks to explain and account for worker protest; the second is concerned with its effectiveness in generating change, and probes the significance of its role in affecting or explaining something else. A third general question is implicit in the first two: What is the nature of worker protest? All three questions have generally involved static and dynamic considerations, and it is therefore appropriate to append to each the phrase, "at a given point in time and over time." In addition to this time horizon, each question involves an analytical context—a domain within which "ifs" are sought and to which "thens" apply. Finally, each question involves its dramatis personae—a delineation of who protests and to or against whom.

We have thus as the basic ingredients of worker protest theory: (1) the sources of protest; (2) the nature of protest; (3) the impact of protest; (4) an analytical time horizon; (5) an analytical context; and (6) the relevant parties. Before illustrating the possible diversity of scope and compass in theorizing about worker protest within this framework, I comment briefly on each of these elements and further elaborate the second.

### 1. Sources of Protest

Protest derives from a source. It is a response to dissatisfactions and discontents which stem (or are seen as stemming) from some tension-creating relationship or burdensome experience. Protest gives testimony to a conscious gap between the worker's view of "what is" and "what should be," for deprivation is always measured against a matrix of expectation.[1] The feeling that "whatever is, is right" may coexist with abject poverty, rigorous physical hardships, submission to absolute tyrannical authority, but it is incompatible with protest. Formulation and expression of a complaint is dependent upon the prerequisite cognizance of aberration from some normative mold. The deviation may be vaguely apprehended or precisely pinpointed. It may be real or imagined. The dimensional extent of the "grievance gap" may vary; its size may range from almost total to relatively trivial discrepancy vis-à-vis the normative standard of reference.[2] Discontent, in any case, in

[1] This way of thinking about sources of protest is broad enough to encompass any taxonomy of causes of conflict we may care to detail. It comprises, for example, the traditional distinction between "issues" and "problem" disputes, where the former refer to conflict over basic disagreements—about power or income sharing, over group survival, etc.—and the latter to conflict over the interpretation or minor modification of such basic agreements already negotiated or accepted.

[2] The immediate points of friction generating discontent may be the same in two situations. The ultimate source of the grievance, however, because the view of the source involves a prognosis as well as a diagnosis of the irritating affliction, may be seen differently in different instances. An employer's unwillingness to meet a wage demand may be consistent with several views of the source of dissatisfaction. The source may be seen as lying in the system and eradicable only with its demise in the wake of revolution; or it may be seen, in the context of an otherwise generally acceptable situation and in the light of one or another rationally articulated criterion, as an unjustified intransigence on the part of the employer but of transient

22

the sense of some such grievance gap constitutes the first element of protest theory. In any organization and in all industrial societies there are continuing (although not equally important) sources of irritation and potential conflict. Over time, these grievance gaps will change with variations in either the "what is" or the "what should be." Significant shifts in the yardstick of the "what should be" will reshape satisfactions and dissatisfactions; marked changes in the "what is" may disturb established norms and redefine new reference points.

## 2. *The Nature of Protest*

A description of the nature of protest involves four basic components: the manifestations of protest; the direction of protest; the structure of protest; and the magnitude of protest.

MANIFESTATIONS OF PROTEST. Protest is the communication[3] of discontent through some overt demonstration or expression. These manifestations of discontent are the instrumentalities which serve at one and the same time as indicators of tension and as intended generators of change. They are simultaneously the symptoms of worker discontent and the means resorted to for assuaging discontent.

The forms for expressing discontent are many. The strike, of course, is one of the most common. But there may be recourse as well to retreat from industry and return to rural ties, machine breaking, riots, petitions, absenteeism, personnel turnover, restriction of output, boycotts, grievance filing—all focused within the world of work; or in the larger society, political action, racial, religious, or ethnic antagonisms, wife beating or drunkenness. The list is far from exhaustive.[4] For within each of the forms listed we can find a subarray of variety. The strike, for example, may be walkout or sit-down; restriction of output on the job may involve slowdowns, rigid adherence to work rules, dilution of quality considerations or sabotage; political action may involve pressure politics and lobbying or the creation of independent parties.

---

significance and amendable by recourse to an orderly demonstration of protest pressure leveled narrowly and specifically at this limited "injustice."

[3] The social theorist is, of course, primarily interested in the socially communicated and socially relevant expressions of discontent, i.e., expressions which impinge in some fashion on the structure and functioning of the body social, political, or economic. Unperceived and undiscovered expressions of discontent, the isolated hurling of rocks into an empty sea from a clifftop, for example, are difficult to incorporate in any theorizing about sources, nature, or impact of protest.

[4] For a detailed classification, see A. Kornhauser, R. Dubin, and A. M. Ross, eds., *Industrial Conflict*, New York, McGraw-Hill, 1954, p. 14.

DIRECTION OF PROTEST. Discontent will impart to its protest expression a directional dimension. Protest of the present may look either to the past or to the more or less immediate future as a normative guide. Backward looking protest is defensive. The "what is" is found wanting with reference to the "what has been" and is fought off. Forward looking protest is more aggressive. The "what is" is projected into the "what could be" and is fought for. The former is essentially a conservative or retrogressive response to recent violation of tradition; the latter a reformist or radical expression of the desire to depart from tradition.

To the direction of desired change there also attach a distance and a rate. There will be some greater or lesser degree of change desired which defines, so to speak, the extent of travel toward yesterday or the envisaged tomorrow. In addition, there will be a greater or lesser rate of travel which the worker may regard as minimal to escape or correct abuses of today. How much of the present is acceptable is inversely related to how far and how fast from the present the worker would depart.

STRUCTURE OF PROTEST. The manifestations of discontent may be expressed individually or collectively.[5] The structure of protest describes the character of its collectivization. It describes the institutional conformation of the organizational vessel in which discontent is coagulated and through which it is given expression. The organizational configuration of protest, too, has no fixed anatomy. Protest may be loosely organized or tightly disciplined. There may be a host of competing would-be "proprietors" and organizers of protest or we may find at another time or place, a few coordinated, centralized, and legitimized agencies of protest organization. Organizational structure may be ephemeral and short lived or highly institutionalized and firmly entrenched and, in the latter instance, may be worker-, employer- or state-designed.

MAGNITUDE OF PROTEST. The magnitude of protest refers to the aggregation of overt protest manifestations. Because of the varieties mentioned earlier, such aggregation confronts us with an obviously difficult problem in addition. The magnitude of overt protest manifestations, incidentally, may or may not be positively related to the aggregate of discontent, i.e., the sum total of individual grievance gaps referred to under manifestations of protest, some or many of which may remain latent or be barred from overt expression by suppression.

---

[5] For an early perceptive discussion of this distinction see Carleton H. Parker, *The Casual Laborer and Other Essays*, New York, Harcourt, Brace, and Howe, 1920.

## 3. *The Impact of Protest*

Protest will be aimed at effecting change in one or several rules in the highly complex web of rules[6] which relates worker to work process, employer, and the state. Or it may be directed at effecting small or major changes in the process or procedure of rule-making itself.[7] Or it may focus on a combination of these. The impact of protest refers to the effectiveness of protest, i.e., to the manner in which the relevant conflict or disagreement is resolved. The extent to which the rules or rule-making procedures are or are not revised in the desired direction of the protesting workers measures the effectiveness or ineffectiveness of their protest.

## 4. *The Analytical Time Horizon*

This refers simply to the point or span of time encompassed in our generalization. Some questions and proposed answers will be concerned with a short or intermediate span of time; others will deal with behavioral patterns and courses of evolution over much longer and, occasionally, even millennial periods.

## 5. *The Analytical Context*

The range within which we have generalized will describe the limits of transferability of our theory. The context of analysis refers to the range, within which sources are detected, and to the site of protest impact. The points at which protest manifestations are directed will vary. The site of protest may thus involve a job, a work group, a plant, a company, an industry, or a society. A theory about one or several aspects of worker protest may thus posit some proposition which is offered as valid for *one* industry in the United States, for example, or it may be wrought in broader contextual configurations, i.e., offered as valid for *all* industries in the United States, for one industry whatever the nation, for all industries whatever the nation, and so on.

---

[6] For an elaboration of this concept see John T. Dunlop, *Industrial Relations Systems*, New York, Holt, 1958, Chapter 1; or Clark Kerr, Frederick H. Harbison, John T. Dunlop and Charles A. Myers, "The Labour Problem in Economic Development," *International Labour Review*, March 1955; or Clark Kerr and Abraham Siegel, "The Structuring of the Labor Force in Industrial Society: New Dimensions and New Questions," *Industrial and Labor Relations Review*, January 1955, pp. 163-164.

[7] For a typology of rule-making procedures see Kerr and Siegel, "The Structuring of the Labor Force . . ." pp. 165-167.

## 6. The Relevant Parties

Since we have confined our focus to worker protest, the outside limits of permissible acting (protesting) parties is described by our conception of the labor force. Which specific components of the labor force play a central role in analysis again depends on the contextual scope of the theory we seek to evolve. Marx made the initially simple distinction of designating owner-employer and everyone else who either was or was soon to become a "worker" and spun his theory in these terms. More than a century later it is evident that theorizing about worker protest may turn on many other distinctions in our cast of characters, for the Marxian polarization is marred and mangled in the overlapping network of worker and employer, managed and managers, which has subsequently emerged in the bureaucratization of industry and the proliferation of possible dimensions of the labor force. In most theories concerning protest, worker refers to the arbitrarily delimited group of wage earners below some given level of managerial or supervisory personnel in the hierarchy of managed and managers.[8] But there may also be theories concerned with conflict between one group of "managers" and another (the line and staff disagreements), between one group of workers and another (skilled versus unskilled production workers), and so on.[9]

## The Potential for Review and Revision of Theory Provided by the Framework

In this conception of the boundaries of worker protest theory we are free to put many questions, to relate these to others which bear most directly upon them, to shift our glance from one level of theory to another. We try to find confirmations and reinforcements for our theorizing or, where we note contradictions and inconsistencies, we are encouraged to search for reconciliation. If we find too limited an analytical context for a hypothesis we want to explore and compare in broader horizons, we enhance transferability of generalization by unleashing a few of the variables impounded in our *ceteris paribus* pound and let them roam in a *mutatis mutandis* world. We close in on excep-

[8] See for example, the way in which this distinction is drawn in Frederick H. Harbison and Charles A. Myers, *Management in the Industrial World*, New York, McGraw-Hill, 1959, pp. 3-20.

[9] A taxonomy of many such potential levels for theory is found in Wilbert E. Moore, "The Nature of Industrial Conflict," in *Industrial Conflict and Dispute Settlement*, Industrial Relations Centre, McGill University, 1955, pp. 4-9.

tions we note by seeking out alternative strategic factors or, this failing, by bringing the order of generalization down a notch or two, adding an additional level of theory thereby but perhaps gaining new insights simultaneously. There is, in brief, the prod to continual refinement and synthesis in this welter of generalization. And new or newly found experiential evidence, new curiosities, new or modified policy needs make this an ongoing perpetual process. In this section I want simply to suggest by illustration the paths we are free to pursue in this adventure of learning more about worker protest.

Three different levels of analysis were selected. Each, in turn, is part of a set of questions which deals primarily with one of the three major questions at the beginning of the preceding section.

1. The first set of questions and answers incorporates all three issues, but the formulation somehow always seems to give an added emphasis to the impact and consequences of worker protest—perhaps because many of the authors engaged in generalizing at this broad level were concerned with fashioning social tracts in the guise of social theory. I am referring, of course, to that heritage of curiously fascinating and conflicting admixture of restrained or explosive polemic, implicit or patent advocacy, muddied metaphor, mild expressions of faith, fiery depositions of dogma, and occasional flashes of brilliant insight, which make all the rest so much easier to take and which we have called "theories of the labor movement."

2. The second set of questions involves a shorter time horizon, analysis ranges within much narrower confines, and the primary concern is a search for sources of worker unrest. "Human relations research in industry" is an awkward but communicative reference to the level of theory I have in mind here.

3. The third set of questions deals with one specific aspect of one of the components of the nature of protest and its evolution over time. I have chosen to comment on those researches which have sought to trace out "the natural history of the strike" as illustrative of the range of theory which is possible here.

### The Rise and Fall of Worker Protest in "Theories of the Labor Movement"

In an earlier paper Clark Kerr and I examined the traditional theorizing about labor organization. This involved an enumeration of authors and a description of their works, which we included in our discussion of theories of the labor movement.[10] Mark Perlman has still another but quite similar listing in his recent effort to examine this range of theory.[11] For my purposes it is not essential to get universal agreement on who gets counted as "theorist of the labor movement"; for I propose to discuss here only a sample grouping of such theories, and it is enough to say simply that I have included in my own version of what gets counted here that theorizing which encompasses much, i.e., that level of theory where time horizons are long, contexts wide, and substantive focus broad.

Theorizing about worker protest at this general level must frequently be inferred from a more inclusive range of traditional theorizing about labor organizations; and, in fact, the latter is often only implicit in what is more directly put as a theory of economic development. What we find essentially in each is some pattern of protest which reflects an underlying set of assumptions concerning the relation of the working out of the industrialization process (although most traditional theories of the labor movement focused almost entirely on development cost in a liberal capitalist mold), the concomitant development of discontent and its protest expression, and the management and manipulation of this protest. Broad theories of worker protest and of industrial development are contingent upon each other. Each protest pattern hinges upon (1) a measure of disparity between a postulated set of material and psychological needs or demands and what in fact is actually forthcoming and accrues to the worker in industrial society; and (2) a set of corollary views concerning the resultant changes in the magnitude of worker protest and of its impact. Together these assertions delineate the pathways of protest over time; they mark out the ebb and flow of protest and its attendant steady, waning or increasing potential for effecting change.

I have chosen to comment here on the similar protest patterns derived from a reading of Marx and Veblen. Other groupings of theorists of the labor movement afford modified and, in the case of Selig Perlman,[12] quite different protest patterns. The Marx-Veblen mappings which I outline here, however, are illustrative of the mode of theorizing about worker protests at this level and of the leeway and direction

[10] Kerr and Siegel, "The Structuring of the Labor Force . . .", pp. 151-159.

[11] Mark Perlman, *Labor Union Theories in America*, Evanston, Row, Peterson, 1958.

[12] Selig Perlman, *A Theory of the Labor Movement*, New York, Augustus M. Kelley, 1949 reprint of the 1928 edition.

which our analytical framework affords, both in the evaluation of validity and contemporary relevance of theory cast in this broad context and in the formulation of alternative tentative hypotheses.

PROTEST MAPPINGS[13]

The simple diagrammatic format of Figure 1 was chosen to summarize the corollary views in Marx and Veblen concerning the evolution of protest magnitude and impact over time. The abscissa in this figure is a time scale in developmental or "industrial" time units. Different

FIGURE 1

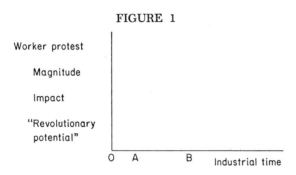

points along the time axis represent different stages of industrial development. Preindustrial time lies to the left of the origin. The progress from industrially undeveloped to mature industrialization is measured by moving out to the right. At point O the society is essentially a nonindustrial society. At point A it is in the incipient stages of industrial growth. At point B it is a relatively developed industrial society. For the purposes of the argument below it is not important to define any single precise unit of measurement to provide us a continuum of degree-of-industrialization gradations; my interest will focus primarily on the distinction between the society at point A in industrial time—the early phases of the industrializing society—and that at point B—the relatively developed industrial society. For this distinction, reference to a number of criteria (all interrelated) can provide us with a rough but adequate range about points A and B and permit us to discern the relatively undeveloped from the relatively developed industrial society.[14] It is

[13] The protest mapping concept and the mappings discussed here are variations on a theme outlined in an unpublished manuscript by Kerr and Siegel, "Industrialization and the Changing Nature and Impact of Worker Protest."

[14] I have in mind the criteria generally utilized to evaluate relative degrees of industrial development:

(1) Relative importance of different productive activities—which may be gauged

easy enough to ascertain, for example, that Britain of the late eighteenth–early nineteenth century, Japan of the late nineteenth century, Russia in the early twentieth century, and India or China today would each be situated somewhere around point A and that each of these today, with the exception of India and China, would lie at or near point B.

Along the ordinate I will plot the ordinarily sensed rather than the specifically cardinally defined estimates of the magnitude of overt worker protest and a related mapping of the impact (or effectiveness) of worker protest. These are admittedly impressionistic plottings, but I feel that they do no severe injustice to the Marx-Veblen mapping or vision of how magnitude and consequences of worker protest vary over industrial (in their own context, capitalist industrial) time.

*The Marx-Veblen Protest Mappings*

The Marxian and Veblenian analyses of industrial development and labor organization present essentially the same protest mappings and may be represented as in Figure 2. The first two figures plot the magnitude and impact of protest, respectively. These elements of protest have already been defined. The third figure plots what may be termed the "protest potential for massive change" and requires brief explanation. What I have in mind here is a probability estimate of the likelihood that protest *if* effective will involve severe, drastic, sharply discontinuous change in the prevailing distribution of power, income, or

---

by occupational distribution by branch of production; the proportion of gross national product deriving from agriculture, industry, etc.; the balance of development (multiple-industry development or not).

(2) Relative capitalization—which would be measured by the amount of real capital per head and reflected in the nature of the method and organization of production; the extent of division and specialization of labor and economies of scale which are related to the roundaboutness of method of production.

(3) Output, income, investment, welfare incomes—output and income per head (absolute levels and rates of increases); the proportion of expenditures on food and necessities to total expenditures; ratio of investment to GNP and direction and nature of investment; level of medical care available, standards of nutrition, housing and sanitation; amount of child labor used.

In addition, (4) degree of urbanization may serve as a partial indicator of degree of industrialization and (5) a variety of demographic estimates (e.g., rate of increase in population, fertility and mortality rates, expectation of life) will reflect changes in economic growth.

An alternative approach for arriving at similar judgments about such a classification could involve using the criteria described by Rostow in his delineation of stages of growth. Point A would correspond to his society in the process of "take-off"; point B to his "maturing society" or "high mass-consumption" stages. See "Rostow on Growth," *The Economist*, August 15 and 22, 1959, pp. 409-416 and pp. 524-531.

status in the society. "Revolutionary potential" may be another way of expressing this imminence or remoteness of massive, extremely rapid, or radical change, which effective protest will imply at any point in industrial time.

FIGURE 2

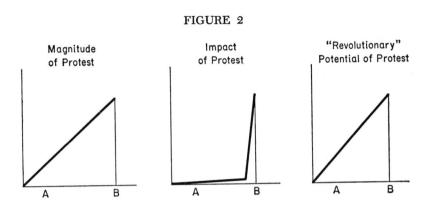

MARX.[15] These courses charted for the magnitude, impact, and likelihood of revolutionary change summarize the following assertions in Marxian analysis:

1. With the creation of an industrial work force begins the expression and accumulation of worker discontent.

2. As the society moves from incipient to mature (capitalist) industrial development, the accumulating unrest continues to mount.

3. The increasing magnitude of protest continues to be frustrated. The impact or effectiveness of protest is at best trivial and minuscule; protest thus not only "massifies" but also intensifies and gains in combative, revolutionary, explosive potential as industrialization proceeds.

4. The revolutionary potential peaks in the neighborhood of point B, i.e., in the relatively mature stages of industrial development and culminates in swift and massive rejection of the prevailing social, political, and economic institutional arrangements.

5. The proletarian revolution reconstitutes an alternative classless

[15] For an overview of the Marxian analysis of labor organization in capitalist industrial society, see: Karl Marx and Friedrich Engels, "Manifesto of the Communist Party" in *A Handbook of Marxism*, New York, International Publishers, 1935, pp. 30ff; Karl Marx, *Capital*, New York, Modern Library, 1936; "Wage-Labour and Capital" in *Selected Works*, Moscow, Cooperative Publishing Society of Foreign Workers in the U.S.S.R., 1956, Vol. I; V. I. Lenin, *What Is to Be Done*, New York, International, 1929, pp. 31-118; and A. Lozovsky, *Marx and the Trade Unions*, New York, International, 1935.

"good society" in which the sources of worker discontent (and, as a consequence, all worker protest) are eliminated.

The Marxian assumptions and deductions which account for the particular shape these patterns assume are briefly as follows:

1. As the society develops industrially, as the use of machinery and division of labor are extended, the size of the "proletariat" expands. More and more members of the society assume a common role in the productive process. In the developed society the polarization of classes is complete. We find society comprising on the one hand, the proletariat, and on the other, the bourgeoisie.

2. With the creation of the industrial labor force its protest begins. The source of initial discontent lies in the disruption of tradition, and the direction of protest is backward looking. The protest is not unified or disciplined. It manifests itself in riots, machine breaking, and in efforts "to restore by force the vanished status of the workman" of the past.

3. Protest continues to mount, and its manifestations are expressed in increasingly unified and organized fashion.

The source of discontent as we move further from A lies more and more in the unmitigated and increasing immiseration of the proletariat in the face of increasing development. Accumulation of wealth at one pole is matched by "accumulation of misery, agony of toil, slavery, ignorance, brutality, mental degradation, at the opposite pole. . . ."[16] Fluctuations and crises in production make his existence even more precarious.

Concomitantly, developing industrialization facilitates the emergence of a common class ideology and the capacity to organize. Not only are more and more members recruited into the ranks of the proletariat but their commonality is promoted by improved communication and transportation facilities which permit dissemination of ideas, of action programs, and hence of growing class consciousness; by political education gained in political organization in bourgeois alliances; by physical concentration of masses of workers in industries and cities. There are increasing collisions over the class distribution of the national dividend, but to little avail. The result is an "ever-expanding union of the workers." Organization of the worker grows "stronger, firmer, mightier."

[16] *Capital*, p. 709. There is in addition, the psychological immiseration found in the degradations of the Juggernaut of capital (*ibid.*, pp. 708-9) and in the ever-widening social gulf between proletariat and capitalist class.

4. The consequence of "disciplined, united, and organized" but hitherto ineffective and frustrated protest is revolution. The point in industrial time at which the series of "veiled civil wars" between the classes proceeds to the point where "that war breaks out into open revolution" and where the violent overthrow of the bourgeoisie lays the foundation for the sway of the proletariat is a point within the B range of development. Only in the mature society have all the antecedent prerequisites for maximum protest impact and for successful revolution been met. In the stages of developed "monopoly and imperialist capitalism" the explosive peak is reached. Unrest becomes impossible to contain within the bounds of the prevailing structure of society. The massive potential of the cumulatively intensified discontent is hurled against the old order, the proletarian revolution is under way and "the expropriators are expropriated."[17]

5. The drastic reconstitution of society eliminates the basic sources of prior worker discontent and ushers into being a protestless order, whose internal structure harbors no "inner contradictions," no latent or overt worker unrest.

VEBLEN.[18] Veblen's protest mappings are essentially similar to the Marxian, but they are much more hedged about with qualifications and possible alternative routes and are premised on quite different (although not entirely disparate) grounds.

[17] There are some qualifications attached to these general courses predicted for protest which reflect growing apprehension about their general validity. Engels, for example, complains about the British "bourgeois proletariat" which does not behave in accord with the projected pattern. He elsewhere shifts from the formal position which accounts for the coming social revolution as resulting from the increasing pressure of the capitalist strait jacket upon the increasingly miserable proletariat to a position that social revolution will result as a consequence of increasing pressure of successful, working class movements—successful, i.e., in *decreasing* misery—upon the capitalist employers who "fire the first shot," take recourse to violence in the attempt to crush the proletariat's advances, and are in turn overwhelmed and expropriated. Lenin, too, is aware of deterrents in the paths of the plotted courses. Essentially, however, the formal analysis and prognosis is never rejected by either Marx, Engels, or Lenin. Not until Stalin's era do we find a rejection in practice if not in preachments of many of the assumptions of the inherited dogma.

[18] See Thorstein Veblen, *The Theory of Business Enterprise*, New York, Scribner, 1904, Chapters II, III, IX and X, pp. 5-65, 302-400; and *Absentee Ownership and Business Enterprise in Recent Times*, New York, Huebsch, 1923. For some interesting commentaries on Veblen: Joseph Dorfman, *Thorstein Veblen and His America*, New York, Viking, 1934; J. A. Hobson, *Veblen*, New York, Wiley, 1937; Paul T. Homan, "Thorstein Veblen," in *Contemporary Economic Thought*, New York, Harper, 1928; and W. C. Mitchell, *Lecture Notes on Types of Economic Theory*, New York (Augustus M. Kelley), 1949 (mimeo), Vol. II, pp. 218-252.

Veblen's theory of the labor movement is as firmly imbedded in his analysis of a "liberal capitalist" system as is Marx's. Veblen sees the origins of modern labor organization in the hiatus between the dominant institutions of corporate capitalism and those which the prevalent technical environment "requires" for the fulfillment of communal advantage and optimal material well-being.

Veblen's analysis of modern capitalism proceeds in a pageantry of colorful, emotive contrasts and neatly demarcated dichotomies. The forces of communal "serviceability" are dramatically pitched against the contaminating and the disserviceable elements. The "savage" society, handicraft industry, the machine process, impersonal mechanistic cause-and-effect habits of thought, industrial employment, production of goods and the underlying population stand in contrast to the barbarian society, corporate capitalism, teleological and anthropomorphic metaphysics, pecuniary employment, production of profits, conspicuous waste and consumption, captains of business or of finance, absentee ownership, the vested interests. Workmanship, the parental bent, idle curiosity, industrial emulation, serviceability, and improved material welfare find expression in the first array; acquisitiveness, getting something for nothing, pecuniary emulation, waste, sabotage, and disserviceability are emphasized by the latter.

The core of the conflict in modern capitalist society arises from the *de jure* institutional incompatibility with the *de facto* technological environment. Modern society is characterized technically by the machine process, institutionally by absentee (i.e., absent from the actual productive and industrial process) ownership. The institution of absentee ownership finds its rationale and sanction in the contemporaneously anachronistic structure of legal and political ideologies of the handicraft era. The institution of natural property rights is buttressed and perpetuated by those vested business and financial interests whose habituation is primarily a pecuniary one, and who live by seeking and getting something (profit) for nothing (no productive activity). The captain of business or of finance is essentially concerned with the production of profits. The *de facto* existence, however, of the modern machine technology and its productive potential for eliminating material want render obsolescent the *de jure* institutional prescriptions and pecuniary habituations. The machine process imparts to all engaged in the industrial employments a matter-of-fact, cause-effect orientation. Removed from any connection with direct pecuniary motivations, imbued with the sense of workmanship, skeptical of the conventional received doctrines of natural property rights, resentful of the inequalities which arise in the environment dominated by business ideology, propelled by growing recognition of the waste and sabotage of production (restriction of output) perpetuated by business pecuniary proclivities, the "underlying population" (Veblen's industrial labor force) finds its entire habits of thought recast and diverging from those of the business interests. The discipline of the mechanically standardized industrial system tends toward dissent from now archaic and disserviceable received principles. The polarization of society into business versus industry crystallizes into an intolerable impasse. The "labor movement" in Veblen is the consequence of this growing disposition to dissent from received tradition and a reflection of the drift away from the habituation to outgrown capitalist institutions. The fountainhead of organized dissent is the technician and the skilled worker but the "underlying population" joins in the revolt given direction by this corps of leaders. The general strike, "a conscientious withdrawal of efficiency . . . for such time as may be required to enforce their argument," is the weapon which can abolish absentee ownership and free the productive forces of society from the restrictions of pecuniary vested interests in the subsequent guild socialist organization of a collective, cooperative, "Soviet of technicians" order. That order marks the victory of social habits of thought and action in touch with the "generically human" and creative propensities of man—the propensities to construct and to seek out knowledge guided by the concern for the survival and enhanced satisfaction of humanity's material wants.[19]

[19] This very brief summary of the generalized protest pattern is an extreme oversimplification of the Veblen argument. As mentioned earlier, Veblen is rarely specific in his description of a unilinear trend and almost always qualifies his assertions with possible alternatives. In his later writings, especially, Veblen emphasized more and more the possibility that the "obsolescent" institutions, the "imbecile" institutions, i.e., outmoded sanctions and habitual arrangements, would resist "reasonable" adjustment, persist because they have become rationalized, and assert a coercive prescription upon behavior which the "veiled interests" seek to preserve, and lead ultimately to the suicidal decay of civilization because of their essential disserviceability to society. Thus he is ever skeptical, for example, of the revolt of the "underlying population" and castigates the behavior of the American AFL trade unions insofar as they fail to go beyond the effort to "adapt, construe, recast earlier working arrangements with as little lesion to received preconceptions as the new exigencies and habits of thought held by them will permit." He emphasizes the role of militarism, nationalism, and of patriotism in effectuating the persistence of the imbecile institutions. "Imperialistic nationalism" and "habituation to warlike ideals" can lead to the "sterilization of revolutionary socialism." Veblen mentions the increasing misery (both in degree and volume) which is the outcome of the

*Alternative Protest Mappings*

Marx and Veblen were concerned with generalization of the most widely transferable sort. Each had what he felt to be a model of the industrial world. In 1960, extrapolation of British or American experience no longer suffices as the relevant context for analysis of comparable scope and generality. The roads to industrialism are many, and general assertions about patterns of protest over industrial time must encompass a vastly wider range of experience and history.[20] We know in advance that any generalization encompassing industrial and industrializing society will be hazardous at best. Gerschenkron has made the point that the Marxian generalization which suggested that the "industrially more developed country presents to the less developed country a picture of the latter's future" could be valid only as a half-truth, because it tends to conceal differences in the industrial development of backward countries as compared with the industrialization process which already advanced countries have undergone. The shift from industrial backwardness to industrial maturity will, in the course of its evolution, present to the developing society different challenges dependent upon a variety of possible differences in its character. And the late-comers in industrial development, he maintains, faced with different problems, may apply institutional instrumentalities and provide ideological incentives for which no counterpart may be found in the history of the established industrial societies.[21]

In view of the heterogeneous nature of the industrialization process, Gerschenkron's assertion is indisputable. The heart of his thesis, as I see it, is however only a caution against seeing in the detail of any one country the detail of the entire world at a comparable point in industrial time. And it is a caution which the contemporary disciples even more than the original theorists of the labor movement have too often tended to neglect. It is not, I think, a prohibition of "thinking big." For there remains that half of the generalization which is truth (or an approximation to it) which we must seek out for clues to similarities

---

capitalist system of ownership but minimizes the role of increasing misery as a factor making for reasoned class consciousness and the replacement of the present scheme with one more advantageous to the majority. The disposition for dissent of Veblen is less "rational" and more "cause-effect" in tenor than that of Marx.

[20] For a development of this theme, see Kerr, Dunlop, Harbison, and Myers, *Industrialism and Industrial Man*, Harvard University Press, 1960.

[21] Alexander Gerschenkron, "Economic Backwardness in Historical Perspective," in *The Progress of Underdeveloped Areas*, Bert F. Hoselitz, ed., University of Chicago Press, 1952.

in general drifts and evolutionary patterns, if we are to retain even a shred of faith in the potential usefulness of theory for action. The Gerschenkron assertion does not per se suggest a futility in comparative analysis or the impossibility of the relevance of the same basic forces in shaping the histories of similar (not identical) and, therefore, comparable contextual units. This is, after all, the essence of generalizing at any level, however narrow or limited its range. The essence of his warning is, rather, a justification of conceptualizing a framework for analysis such as this. Both make us cognizant of levels of theory, of multilinearities interwoven in the similarities, and of the multiple tactical procedures we may employ in coming to grips with—and hence continually revising—the future as history.

What general protest mappings, then, do the histories of industrialization viewed from a contemporary vantage point suggest? I have used as a springboard for grasping at such theoretical straws the rather crude technique of comparative statics. Two "snapshots" of worker protest, each separated from the other by a substantial lapse of industrial time, are first outlined and then compared for whatever suggestions they may contain to permit us to arrive at some tentative chartings of the course of worker protest over industrial time. The first view is a composite of worker protest in the society at point A in our protest charts. It is a portrait whose general features reflect the character of worker protest in a large number of countries still in this incipient stage of industrial time and the character of past protest configurations in countries now industrialized but that, at one point of chronological time in the past, occupied a comparable position in industrial time. The second view is a description of worker protest in the society which is relatively mature industrially—a composite characterization of worker protest seen in the contemporary developed societies (stage B in Figure 1).[22]

1. WORKER PROTEST IN THE INITIAL STAGES OF INDUSTRIALIZATION. The transition to industrialism involves social as well as technical revolution.[23] Incipient industrialization generally precipitates an initially

[22] I have avoided extensive footnote documentation in these bits of portraiture simply to avoid cluttering up the next pages with a large number of citations culled from a perusal of histories of both industrialized and industrializing nations and commentaries on them. References bearing on general aspects of worker protest which I regard as basic pegs on which to hang speculation have already been noted in the first section above.

[23] For an interesting conjecture about the consequences of a conceivable "fully automatic factory" type of industrialization of the future which might sever this

amorphous, volatile protest whose source derives in part from the disruption of tradition inherent in the creation of a nonagricultural work force. It is nothing new to point out that the recruitment of an industrial work force frequently entails the destruction and recreation of institutional arrangements—changes in economic goals and incentives, decay of old skills and retraining for new, disintegration of traditional patterns of reward and punishment, urbanization and the concentration of population in the new industrial centers, disruption of the traditional mode of work and reorientation to novel methods of production and conditions of work discipline. All involve adjustments which are more or less coercively, more or less smoothly, more or less rapidly effected in the transition from preindustrial to industrial society, from the traditional to the newly emergent cultural arrangements. The disruptive impact of the transition to industrialism will depend upon the specific rate and character of the industrialization process and upon the sociopolitical and ideological milieu in which it is initiated and which restrains or exaggerates its excesses, protects or neglects the welfare of the newly created nonagricultural work force. Industrialization, however, irrespective of the soothing or irritating additives which may be administered in the process, is generally sufficient per se to constitute a "great transformation" which arouses a host of protest reactions as the traditional patterns give way to the disruptive force of encroaching industrialization.[24]

---

initial tie between social and technical changes, see the discussion by David Riesman, "Some Relationships between Technical Progress and Social Progress," *Explorations in Entrepreneurial History*, Vol. IV, 1953-54, pp. 131-146. The complete automaticity of production, it is argued, by not involving human beings who must be "reformed," does not involve the disruption of old values and modes of life of the populace (vis-à-vis production), and therefore no initial protest obstacles which industrialization efforts of the past and present confronted or still confront in the transitional stage.

[24] Karl Polanyi finds the root source of subsequent worker protest not in the industrialization process per se but in the specific organizing principle which sparked its development in capitalist England, i.e., the all-encompassing self-regulating market mechanism of the economic liberal philosophy. To be sure, the transitional hardships may have been aggravated by the "satanic mills" pinpointed by Polanyi. Yet the industrial revolution initiated by the first five-year plan in the socialist ethos of twentieth-century Russia did not manage to escape the protest consequences of the significant social transformation which the industrialization process per se evoked. The forms of protest differed as did the forms of labor organization which sought to control and channel this protest, but the essence of the protest was clearly a reaction to the transition to industrial society. There are few historical exceptions to this generalization. See Karl Polanyi, *The Great Transformation*, New York, Farrar & Rinehart, 1944.

The break with traditional society patterns is difficult to absorb under the smoothest of transitions. The shock is frequently compounded by the harsh circumstances encountered in the incipient stages of industrialization. The initial shift from the agricultural to the non-agricultural sector will be effected under the aegis of recruitment practices involving both push and pull factors. Where recruiting techniques involve either open and forceful coercion (enclosures, compulsory labor drafts, etc.) or indirect coercion (tax levies, e.g.), and where the village economy has not completely collapsed, i.e., where lack of immediate subsistence is not the most compelling push factor, the compulsory disturbance of family life and of village ties will weigh heavily in the subsequent accretion of hardships which may accumulate to create personal disorganization, frustration, and discontent in the new industrial worker. Where the recruitment procedure uses the lure of high wages, the anticipation of the high wage may be cut into quite deeply by the labor jobber's share of the contractual remuneration. Even where the ties to the old are negligible—and there is increasing evidence that urban-rural ties have been overstressed—the expectational gloss will be marred by the harsh realities of industrial employment and of urban living. Housing conditions are generally deplorable, sanitation measures at a minimum, recreational, educational, associational or leisure facilities nonexistent. In earlier industrialization processes, the relentless, routinized discipline, the long hours, the impersonality of the factory mark a drastic reversal of the work pattern of the countryside left behind. The search for guaranteed employment (if that was the motivation for leaving the rural area) may be disappointed by a glutted labor market, by temporarily arrested investment of the vagaries of an autonomous market mechanism. The early transitional rootlessness of those separated from close familial or extended familial association, of the only partially committed industrial workers, may be emphasized by the presence of ethnic discrimination or by the absence of civil or political rights.

The direction of discontent vacillates. The old rhythm is disrupted and commitment to the new is only partial; or, if complete, only partially digested. The accumulation of mass frustrations, of hardships, and tensions vents itself in "chaotic stirrings of misery"; this is the period of amorphous, inchoate, and volatile restlessness, the period of experimentation, the "seeding time" of ideas and organization. It is the period of vacillation between nostalgia for the old halcyon days and of vigorous assertion to rights and privileges, to improvements in material welfare and status in the new industrial society.[25] To this "defensive-offensive" wavering, there may be added a flavor of resentment which may be either internally or externally directed in the quest for rapid economic development and improvement.[26]

It is the period of competing radical appeals, and there are expectations that the totality of society can be sharply transformed by the elimination of one or another root evil which is specified as responsible for prevailing discontent and hardship. The envisaged change, whatever the direction aimed for, is big rather than partial; and its attainment is seen as imminent with the successful demolition of the offending practice of institution. The distressing effects of the present are erased and what is left is either unmarred tradition or the glorious new world of the future.

The structure of organization collectivizing the discontent in this early period is often as fluid and as uncoordinated as the directional aspirations of discontent are still ill-defined or inarticulate. The very inarticulateness of the new industrial worker (often completely illiterate) tends to encourage agitational arousing of latent subsurface dissatisfactions and restlessness, which remain unexpressed, or redefinition, articulation, and interpretation of the unrest that is expressed.[27]

[25] In an unpublished manuscript Reinhard Bendix points up this admixture of traditionalist and radical worker ideology in the transition from agricultural to industrial society in England. "Much of the complexity [of his preceding survey] derives from the juxtaposition of traditionalism and radicalism. Every harking back to the 'good old days' contained an element of radical protest against industry and its spokesmen. And every assertion of political rights and every violent outburst was made legitimate, in the eyes of the workers, by reference to the ancient rights of Englishmen under the Constitution." The phenomenon is discernible, with varying degrees of emphasis on the traditionalist and radical or revolutionary aspects, in virtually all such transitions. The impact and the role of early agitational direction, the rate and tangible returns of industrial development, the social and political background of the nation, the degree of the new worker's alienation from the traditional background will help determine the direction in which the balance may be thrown.

[26] The nationalisms of Italy, Germany, and Japan, of Russia and China, of the Middle East and Southeast Asia, of Africa and Latin America are all members of the same family to the extent that nationalist sentiment is aroused and harnessed in the emulatory appeal for industrial development.

[27] This articulation of protest on behalf of the worker may come from middle-class intellectuals within the country, and in currently developing areas may derive as well from international sources (e.g., international labor organizations, the Communist party, other already structured labor movements, etc.). Another indirect but significant form of pressure may stem from the leaders of the traditional society on behalf of the tribesmen in the industrial sector.

Many competing "leaders" are likely to be seeking proprietorship of the workers' malcontent; and it is not uncommon to find in this phase an uncoordinated multitude of competing organizations, "localized, atomized, factionalized," springing up simultaneously in the attempt to channel and direct the expression of discontent. Even where there are general unions, they are weak and unstable. The tactics of these organizations are still groping and experimental. Goals may be limited to eliminating momentary, local, specific grievances; or they may emphasize grandiose schemes and social miracles, "hit-and-run," once-for-all solutions which promise unlimited revolutionary consequences in the vision of the self-regulating utopia persisting eternally after the elimination of the designated root of the evils of society. The organizational ties and the sites at which redress of discontent is sought are as frequently political as they are industrial. There will be vehicles as varied as the goals or tactics but the organizational nuclei do not persist. They are temporary, short lived, loose, and ephemeral. They disintegrate in the wake of failure and re-form in the next wave of enthusiasm or frustration. Poorly financed, they rarely concentrate on the perpetuation of the organization or the association.

The concomitant manifestations of this initial unrest and loosely structured protests are virtually everywhere similar in nature. There will be retreats from the present to the past.[28] There will be machine breaking, "wildcat," "lightning," "unofficial" strikes, spontaneous demonstrations, sporadic riots, violence, mass petitions and manifestos, nihilistic striking out, blind revolt—"desperate reaction to intolerable distress"[29]—all mingling in contemporary underdeveloped societies with the repeated urgings to get on with development in a hurry—which flare up, spread rapidly, explode, and fade only to make way for renewed uprising.

[28] The earlier literature on economic development is replete with illustrations of the oft-encountered hurdle to successful industrialization which urban-rural migration constitutes. There are situations, to be sure, where such retreat is completely cut off and others, where it is not, in which the retreat may be tentative rather than permanent because the rootless worker may be caught between the upper and nether millstones of privation and hardships of the new society and the inability of a disintegrating village economy to reabsorb such workers in large numbers. As we indicated earlier, more recent studies seem to minimize this uncommittedness and, in fact, stress the problems of overcommitment in contexts of vast under- and unemployment.

[29] G. D. H. Cole, *A Short History of the British Working Class Movement*, London, Allen and Unwin, 1948, p. 58.

2. WORKER PROTEST IN THE RELATIVELY DEVELOPED INDUSTRIAL SOCIETY. Sources of discontent and of industrial conflict do not disappear in the industrially developed society. The nature and extent of the grievances, however, are different from those of the early transitional period. Many of the earlier dissatisfactions have been eliminated or mitigated. The transitional flux of the initial shift from agriculture to factory with all of its concomitant social disruption is in good part removed from the scene. Shifts are no longer "from one way of life to another but from process to process within one way of living."[30] The usufructs of industrial developments have generally permitted some improvement in hygienic and housing conditions, a diminution of initial physical hardships and deprivations, a variety of concessions yielded to or wrested by the industrial worker. Important changes in the political rules of the game may be an achievement of the past and permit more effective and therefore less frustrating action in the sphere of economic and social reforms. Or where civil and political rights have not been achieved by the worker (either in society at large or in the sphere of production), an autocratic welfare policy may have succeeded in reducing the explosive potential of accumulated dissatisfaction by paternalistically bestowing some economic and social reforms, or both. There will still remain the inevitable sources of discontent arising from (1) the opposition of interest between managers and managed, from (2) the remaining gap between limited means of want-satisfaction on the one hand and desires on the other, and from (3) the need to adapt distribution of income or power in some fashion to changed conditions within the dynamic and complex industrial society.[31] The translation of these discontents into action, however, differs in the developed society in contrast to the expression of discontent in the transitional society.

The direction of protest in the developed society has also changed. The nostalgic and the traditionalist, directing protest backward where they existed, are of greatly diminished consequence. Within the new society, the successor generations of workers are attuned from the start

[30] This would apply to the transitional consequences of twentieth-century "automation," heralded by so many as the second Industrial Revolution. The technical aspects of automation may well involve "revolutionary" changes, insofar as "control" is added to "power." The social consequences, however, are likely to be not sharply discontinuous.

[31] See Kerr, "Industrial Conflict and Its Mediation," *American Journal of Sociology*, November 1954, pp. 230-234; and Moore, "The Nature of Industrial Conflict," pp. 1-15.

to the new patterns of reward and punishment, of mode of work, methods of production, conditions of work discipline. The sought-for change from the total situation of the present is generally pragmatically partial rather than total. Concomitantly, although the degree of urgency and immediacy may remain high in attempts to effect limited, specific change, such urgency with respect to massive and fundamental institutional leaps into the past or the future is greatly attenuated. The protest of the developed industrial society appears in and of the framework of that society to a far greater extent than did the protest of the incipient industrialization stage. And most of this is a consequence of intermediate improvement and of mitigated and changed discontents which the successful maturation of economic growth has permitted, albeit only after earlier conflicts over the distribution of its attendant benefits; in lesser part it is attributable to the significant change which has taken place with the passage of industrial time in the structure of protest.

The organizational structure of worker protest in the developed society has become centralized, formalized, legitimized, and viable. It is cohesive, and there are far fewer overlapping and competing organizations asserting jurisdictional privileges in identical protest terrain. Organization is well financed, there is paid and often self-perpetuating leadership, there is concern with the survival and continuity of organization per se. Functions are more clearly established and recognized, tactics and ends more closely considered. It should be made explicit that when I speak of organization I do not refer exclusively to the traditional trade union or labor movement–labor organization of, for, and by the worker. In the "open" societies, this is, more or less, the case. But labor organization, in the sense of structuring a web of rule whereby the role of the labor force vis-à-vis the work process and society at large is defined, does not always result in a relationship in which the worker via his own organization participates effectively in industrial rule making, rule changing, or rule enforcement. The organizational forms which claim the proprietorship and control of worker protest may be cast in alternative molds. The state may organize trade unions or monolithic political parties in the name of the workers; but these in fact are essentially agencies of the state. It may devise a corporative order which comprises a state-organized or -controlled labor front. It may capture worker-initiated organizations. Similarly, employers may build a variety of paternalist forms of organization or, in combination with the state, join in fashioning official government "harmony" organizations. The role of the worker implicit in each of the various forms of labor organization is, of course, significantly different. In any event, however, in the developed industrial society, we find some mode of structured labor organization (whether worker-, employer-, or state-designed) which has succeeded in assuming some direction or control over worker protest or in suppressing it. Organization has become institutionalized, bureaucratized, and stabilized. A legitimatized vehicle for protest expression or containment has been fashioned.

The change in the organizational structure of protest is accompanied by a revision in the overt manifestations and expressions of discontent. In the developed industrial society, protest expressions are stripped of many of the inchoate and volatile characteristics of earlier protest. They tend to become more rational, predictable, and stylized. Sporadic riots, violence, explosive outbursts are replaced by more peaceful varieties of collective bargaining, joint consultations, or political bargaining. Strikes may take place, but if so, they are different from those of the past. "Yesterday they were battles; today few of them are more than protest demonstrations."[32] Sporadic and spontaneous strikes give way to the new-fashioned strike which has become "enlightened, orderly, bureaucratic"—almost chivalrous in its tactics and cold-blooded in its calculatedness. It is the tool of rationalized rather than desperate revolt, of disciplined rather than impulsive dissatisfaction. Structured organization has evolved bounds and constraints upon the characteristic choice or availability of protest expression. In the case of bona fide worker-initiated organization which has matured with the passage of industrial time, we find a greater willingness to discuss, to bargain, to compromise, to proceed more cautiously and gradually. The organization is no longer an illegal conspiracy but an accepted social institution. There has been successful moderation of some earlier dissatisfactions, and real reform. Leaders are concerned with survival and perpetuation of the organization, with its finances, with its internal discipline and stability. The characteristic choice of protest expression will be molded, in addition, by the state's intervention and elimination from the realm of the legitimate certain modes of protest. Where parliamentary reins of government have been assumed by a labor party, there may be further constraints which worker organization imposes upon the choice of protest manifestation. Even the

[32] K. G. J. C. Knowles, *Strikes—A Study in Industrial Conflict*, Oxford, Blackwell, 1952, p. 4.

"enlightened" strike may be frowned upon as a legitimate protest technique. In the case of employer or state-designed organizational vehicles—because the essence of their strategic function has been from the beginning the calculated harnessing of worker protest—we find that, whatever the mode of organization legitimatized via a combination of coercion and concession, the magnitude and revolutionary potential of worker protest in the society are both held in tow. Protest manifestations that are allowed are directed through channels provided by the state or employer. The specific channels developed for expression of discontent serve as legitimatized safety valves, which direct and manipulate worker discontent toward minimizing explosiveness and serious social disruption—an achievement made feasible only in the permissiveness of economic growth. There will be some discontent remaining unresolved and uncontrolled and finding expression in manifestations other than the directed and legitimatized: absenteeism; personnel turnover or "striking with the feet," where the ordinary strike is unavailable; restriction of output, when the latter alternatives may be removed by compulsory labor direction; rank and file rebellions via unsanctioned strikes, and so on. But, in contrast to the early stages of the transition to industrialism where most protest expression was of this illegitimate-in-the-eyes-of-the-society variety, in the developed industrial society only a relatively small portion of discontent finds outlet in such manifestation.[33]

[33] These composites of worker protest, because they are conglomerate sketches, are types rather than replicas, and a by-product is the inevitable presence of individual exceptions. (See Howard Becker, "Constructive Typology in the Social Sciences," *Through Values to Social Interpretation*, Duke University Press, 1950, pp. 93-127.) If we scan the universe from which the "typical" views were sketched, we find, however, that we need not ransack the historical evidence to provide illustrative instances of the types. It is rather for the exceptions that we must dig deep. Two atypical instances, for example, of the view of unstructured protest coinciding with early industrial development are the Danish and the Japanese experiences. In Denmark, where the rate of development was slow enough to minimize the rigors of a more rapid rate of industrialization (but not too protracted to create frustrations of expectations concerning the benefits of industrialization), where the industrial labor force was recruited in part from skilled artisans already accustomed to urban dwelling and inured to the discipline of industrial workshops, and where the survival of the guild system beyond the middle of the nineteenth century left an extremely significant legacy of organizational propensity, the lag between the beginnings of industrialization and the structuring (in this case via worker initiated trade unions) of protest was minimized. In Japan, the structuring of organization and of protest was assumed from the very start by the employer and the state. Independent worker-initiated organization was repressed, and paternalist organization of the dependent worker's protest was simply the traditional vehicle which was ensconced in the new industrial context. And France and Italy come to mind as exceptions

What inferences about the dynamics of worker protest magnitude, impact, and revolutionary potential are to be drawn from these static composites of protest?

I suggest a general mapping, which is significantly different from the Marx-Veblen generalizations, shown in Figure 3. The dashed line represents the "Russian model" variant of the generally similar patterns sketched.

FIGURE 3

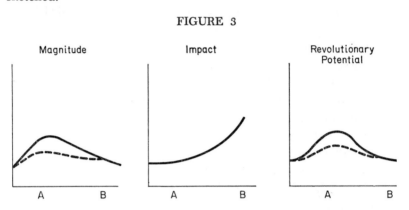

The alternative mappings assert that: (1) the magnitude of protest manifestations will rise in the earlier stages of industrial development but will have peaked and begun to diminish at a point in industrial time before the mature industrial society, point B; (2) the effectiveness of worker protest will have proceeded along a generally upward trajectory throughout industrial time (which is tantamount to the assertion that many of the sources of discontent will be gradually alleviated over industrial time); and (3) the revolutionary potential of protest will, in light of the paths described for (1) and (2), have peaked similarly at some point before the mature stage of industrialism and will be declining.

Marx (and to a lesser extent, Veblen) saw increasing misery unrelieved by industrial growth as a significant source of accumulating worker discontent and of mounting revolutionary ardor. The revised mappings take account of the recorded capacity to improve absolute levels of living with increasing industrial development. Marx (and again to a lesser extent, Veblen) saw an inflexibility in the rule-making relationship involving workers, employers, and state, and in turn projected a

to many of the features of worker protest described as typical of the relatively developed industrial society.

protracted period of completely ineffective or only trivial protest impact. In the face of sheer, intolerable distress and frustration, that minimal impact finally vented itself in an explosive revolutionary outpouring when finally, in the mature stages of growth, workers had garnered the organizational might to undertake the expropriation of the expropriators successfully. The revised mappings take account of the recorded flexibilities and of the concessions seized or ceded throughout the process of industrialization and growth and of the conservatizing effects of contemporary "unified and disciplined" worker organization. Structured organization in the face of visible gains already achieved and of continuing gains to be shared in the future has served in the mature industrial society more often as a threat *to* rather than *of* revolution and massive change.

The historical record is clear on the potential and the actual benefits of economic growth—so clear, in fact, that most of the two-thirds of the unindustrialized world is now clamoring for industrialization. In the early stages, incipient industrialization has yet to pay off. It is not surprising to find that, with no alternative purchase price for the proprietorship of early protest, those early organizers of protest with no responsibility for either the initiation or the direction of industrialization can only promise jackpot gains, which lie at the end of a quick once-for-all fundamental change in the organization of society. At the same stage, those early organizers of protest, who happen also to be the responsible initiators and directors of development, will try to devise various suppressing devices to keep it from upsetting the developmental apple cart too soon and will have been substantially, although not completely, successful in these attempts if "take-off" is followed by maturation of growth. The more advanced industrial society will have permitted gradual reform and improvement. In the cases where industrialization has advanced or will have advanced in the Russian model of centralized-state initiation, direction, and coordination of growth, the labor organizational arms of the state will have been permitted to put increasing emphasis on consumption as against production activities. They may have been accorded increasing degrees of latitude in adjusting local grievances, etc., as the need for restraining such proclivities diminishes with succeeding industrialization. And in the democratic advanced industrial society with free labor movements, the earlier and cumulative reforms and improvements will have altered similarly the appeal required for the successful "merchant of discontent." Cole's description, drawn from late nineteenth-century Britain but generally applicable to mature industrial societies, provides a clear picture of this revised appeal:

> The appeals which had roused the workers in the thirties and forties would have made no impression on their successors in the latter part of the century. . . . In the great industries, the workers had ceased to be a ragged and starveling mob, easily aroused, either by a Feargus O'Connor or a James Rayner Stephens, or by some one of the many "Messiahs" who sprang up in the early years of the century. They had acquired a status, and in many cases a little "stake in the country," if only to the extent of a few pounds in the "Co-op" or a house in process of being bought through a Building Society.
>
> No longer were mass uprisings, huge sudden revolts bred of despair and spreading like wildfire none knew how, likely or even possible. Strikes had become, for the most part, orderly movements, prepared for in advance and conducted by organised bodies and under duly constituted leadership. The orators of the Social Democratic Federation had thundered revolution in vain; the evolutionary Socialism of the I.L.P. made a far greater appeal. But even this did not rouse the mass; the I.L.P. set itself to win over the individuals one by one. Socialist propaganda had become far less an appeal to the emotions and instincts, and far more an appeal to reason. O'Connor had been hot as hell; Sidney Webb was always cool as a cucumber.[34]

I should stress that these alternative mappings are not intended as predictions but only as projections in relevant contexts. They do not assert that all societies will attain mature industrialization and that these protest mappings will have come to prevail everywhere, but only that, in those societies that have or will have reached the stage of relatively mature industrialization, we shall find that these mappings have generally prevailed. And perhaps the key explanation in the end will be attributed to Marx and his dire predictions after all. "Managerial elites" the world over, whatever their character and in whatever industrializing societies, will have been forewarned by Marx of the possible consequences of too protracted and rigid an inflexibility in the initially autocratic rule-making processes in industry. In the knowledge also that the message has not escaped the worker's eye either they will have, on this account, dramatically revised the Marxian projections for

---

[34] Cole, *A Short History of the British Working Class Movement*, pp. 269-270.

the magnitude, impact, and revolutionary potential of worker protest in industrial society by demonstrating a "coerced preference" to share rather than lose *in toto* income, power, or status.

Let me conclude this section with a much briefer set of comments on each of the two other levels of theory I have chosen to illustrate the leeways and guideposts afforded by the analytical framework.

SOURCES OF WORKER PROTEST IN HUMAN RELATIONS RESEARCH IN INDUSTRY

I have elsewhere described the features of this range of theory concerned with worker protest:

> . . . human relations research in industry is generally confined to the "social system" of the factory—or even more narrowly, the small group—and [focuses on] the relations existing among its parts. . . . Explanations to account for industrial unrest are sought *within* the organizations in which men work. Finally, human relations policy proposals aiming at the amelioration of conflict are similarly directed almost exclusively within the establishment and emphasize the strategic significance of leadership styles, communication patterns, work flows, participation, etc., in effecting cooperative industrial relations.[35]

The point may simply be noted here.

If we compare these human relations researches with the analysis of the traditional theorist of the labor movement we get a striking contrast in tone, temper, and context of research. The traditional theorist of the labor movement imparts a flavor to his work which is big and lusty; we are always confronted with wide-ranging strategic factors within immense social contours. The human relationist's concerns look almost weak and wispy if we put them alongside these millenarian tales of manifest destiny and triumphs of the "good society." His gaze rarely wanders beyond the narrow confines of his plant or work group, and what he sees are little troubles in little places amendable by little treatments. No images of the broad reconstruction of societies here; only the concern with restoration of the internal collaborative environment of the plant. No references to big or even little economic and political pressures which churn up mounting frustrations; in almost complete oblivion to the larger world of industry and society, the

---

[35] Abraham J. Siegel, "The Economic Environment in Human Relations Research," *Research in Industrial Human Relations: A Critical Appraisal*, Conrad M. Arensberg *et al.*, eds., New York, Harper, 1957, pp. 86-87.

human relationist roots out unrest in faulty face-to-face relations or communications patterns in the plant.

Our framework of worker protest permits and encourages all levels of analysis. Moreover, it stresses the need to relate one unit of analysis to another. It suggests that broad generalization of the "theory of the labor movement" type will be only vaguely suggestive of strategic factors and will have to be broken down, so to speak, to take account of exceptions in less sweeping levels of generalization to round out and close in on valid analytical perception. What it calls into question concerning the minuscule context of the human relationist's level of analysis, in which he seeks to discover and explain sources of unrest, is whether he can put his finger on any or enough strategic factors to permit theorizing at all. The environmentalist critique of human relations research grows out of a unified perception of worker protest theory and has turned basically on the appeal to open the analytical door a bit wider to take account of more than proximate, internal variables in explaining worker motivations, attitudes, and behavioral patterns. It has asserted that findings adduced within the plant will have extremely limited, if any, transferability. The criticisms may have been extreme and harshly put but have spurred among human relationists increasing recognition of the need to post no impermeable barriers in the search for strategic explanatory variables.[36]

To this extent, the usefulness of human relations research in having called attention to and rectifying the earlier disregard by others of internal work-group relations and in advancing our knowledge in the areas of learning theory, social perception, and role theory is even further enhanced.

### NATURAL HISTORY OF THE STRIKE

Concern with sources and consequences of worker unrest has been supplemented by a variety of studies concerning one or another aspect of the nature of unrest. Manifestations of protest have been widely studied, and perhaps the most carefully and exhaustively reviewed is the strike. Studies focused on the nature of the strike have included precisely the same kind of separating into components carried out in this study for the more inclusive phenomenon, worker protest, in an

---

[36] See, for example, the recent reconsiderations of appropriate analytical levels in human relations research in William F. Whyte, *Man and Organization*, Homewood, Illinois, Irwin, 1959; and in Leonard R. Sayles, *Behavior of Industrial Work Groups*, New York, Wiley, 1958.

effort to get at more knowledge of the strike. Strike theory is again illustrative of the accretions to knowledge permitted by thinking in terms of interlocking webs and strands of theory.

Numerous authors have sought to describe and explain the changing patterns of frequency, magnitude, and duration of the strike over time.[37] Most of them have dealt with annual strike data for a country or several countries and attempted to find and interpret patterns of aggregate strike activity over time in industrial society. There have been few disputes over the facts concerning the withering away of the strike and, even surprisingly and quite unlike the debates over human relations theories, few basic disagreements over interpretation to explain the facts. Explanations have been carefully conceived and generally valid but have been supplemented and modified by related notches of theory and thereby enriched.

In noting exceptions to the natural history of the strike at different industry levels, for example, Kerr and I proposed what is, in effect, a supplementary strand of theory where the strategic variables seemed to be something quite different from those pointed to in dealing with aggregate strike data.[38] And pulling the reins just a bit tighter on relevant analytical context and confining it solely to the coal mining industry, Gaston Rimlinger has further refined our knowledge and sharpened our thinking about strike theory.[39]

## Concluding Comments: Problems and Prospects in Worker Protest Theory

This paper has been neither an effort to enumerate all possible levels of generalization about worker protest, nor to review and evaluate in careful detail any one or several levels of theory, nor to innovate or

[37] See for example, K. Forchheimer, "Some International Aspects of the Strike Movement," *Bulletin of the Oxford University Institute of Statistics*, January 1948, pp. 9-24, and September 1948, pp. 294-304; and *idem*, "Some International Aspects of Strikes," *Bulletin of the Oxford University Institute of Statistics*, September 1949, pp. 279-286; Alvin H. Hansen, "Cycles of Strikes," *American Economic Review*, December 1921, pp. 616-621; Arthur M. Ross and Donald Irwin, "Strike Experience in Five Countries, 1927-1947: An Interpretation," *Industrial and Labor Relations Review*, April 1951, pp. 323-342; Knowles, *Strikes—A Study in Industrial Conflict*; and Arthur M. Ross and Paul T. Hartman, *Changing Patterns of Industrial Conflict*, Harvard University Press, 1960.
[38] Kerr and Siegel, "The Interindustry Propensity to Strike—An International Comparison," *Industrial Conflict*, pp. 189-212.
[39] Gaston V. Rimlinger, "International Differences in the Strike Propensity of Coal Miners: Experience in Four Countries," *Industrial and Labor Relations Review*, April 1959, pp. 389-405.

propose with all the proper credentials any new theorizing about worker protest. I have sought rather to stress a way of looking at the relation of method and substance in theorizing about any substantive area. This is an approach that points up the innumerable problems which beset those who would venture into the future (or for that matter, into an interpretive accounting of the past), but that points up as well the progress made and the enormity of the still unmined veins in this range of theory.

I had indicated at the outset that the conception of a framework is a matter of taste. Perhaps the choice here can be explained by two reasons:

1. The framework has the chastening effect of urging caution in claiming universality for generalizations and serves as a continuing reminder that the answers we propound are vitally shaped by the questions we have asked and the limits we have imposed on where we look for them.

2. Equally important, however, it permits free-swinging, wide-ranging speculation which, though recognized in advance as undoubtedly half-truth, still provides guides and clues for further exploration or follow-up theoretical refinement.

In this breadth of permissible peregrination and in the concomitant recognition of diversities in theoretical compass, we are spared from smashing against the Scylla of speculating for eternities and ubiquities, unaware of the many smaller worlds for theory to be reconciled and related to the broad-brush generalizations, and at the same time, may avoid foundering on the Charybdis of the comfortable case study or its near equivalent, the spuriously precise and completely manageable but not always relevant unit for analysis.

## COMMENTS

ELLIOT J. BERG, Harvard University

In this very suggestive paper Abraham Siegel sets down some ways of looking at worker protest—how and why it arises, the factors determining its intensity and form, how it develops over time. I should like to focus my comments on one aspect of Siegel's analysis—that pertaining to the sources of worker protest. Why does worker protest arise in industrial society? Discussion of this question will involve some consideration of (1) the analytic framework of the paper and (2) the substance of the analysis.

1. Why should the social theorist interested in protest movements single out one particular group for theoretical treatment? Workers, however defined, are a highly significant social and economic group, and this is one reason for moving them to the center of the theoretical stage. It is, furthermore, necessary to demarcate the scope of analysis somehow; as Siegel shows, there is a sufficiently vast range of questions pertaining to workers as a group. But aside from this, do industrial workers have some special role in society, some peculiar status which justifies special analytic attention? Or are workers—defined, let us say, as wage earners below some given point in the hierarchy of skill, income, and authority—simply one of a number of groups to whom no special theories of social protest apply?

Most theorizing about worker protest does in fact assign to workers a special status in industrial society. For most labor theorists, it is this special status that justifies inquiry into labor protest rather than into social protest in general. Worker protest is a useful and appropriate subject of analysis, not only because relations between managers and the managed are of basic importance in industrial society, but also because there is something unique in the worker's situation.

This is of course clear in Marx and Veblen, as Siegel shows so well. For Marx, labor protest is the inevitable consequence of the development of capitalist society. The worker rises up because he is caught in increasing misery and insecurity, trampled under the capitalist Juggernaut. For Veblen, similarly, the worker is special—but in his view for psychological rather than for economic reasons. Exposure to the discipline of the machine process encourages in industrial wage earners the development of matter-of-fact, that is, rational, thinking. They begin to glimpse the possibilities of what science, the machine, and an efficient ordering of society might bring. They become ripe for change.

More recent attempts to use the concept of worker protest have followed in this tradition; they too make workers particularly prone to protest by virtue of their position in industrial society. In some of the joint writing of Clark Kerr, John Dunlop, Frederick Harbison, and Charles Myers, for example, it is argued that wage earners in industrial society live in a state of perennial latent protest arising from the frustrations implicit in being governed by a web of rules they usually have little to do with making.[1]

All of these theories of protest are open to a common criticism: in all of them social protest originates and evolves differently for workers than for other groups in society. For Marx and Marxists there was, until the Maoist revisionism of recent times, little consideration of the potentials of peasant protest. For Veblen, it is habitual exposure to the machine process that separates industrial workers (and engineers) from other men. Kerr and his associates make the implicit assumption that industrial workers suffer frustrations which are qualitatively different from those suffered by other groups.

Furthermore, all three of these theories rest on empirical propositions—the Marxian on increasing misery, the Veblenian on psychological transformation, the Kerr *et al.* analysis on a definition of the industrial worker as in perpetual semi-revolt. The first two, as Siegel shows, are simply not in accord with the facts now, in most parts of the world. For the last, there is no convincing evidence that industrial wage earners are, per se, subject to greater frustrations than other social groups.

2. What are the causes or sources of worker protest in Siegel's analysis? First, he defines one general source: the existence of a grievance gap, a gap between what is and what might be. But he then treats two general cases in which sources of discontent are discussed in rather different terms. In early industrialization, discontent and protest arise from the disruptive effects of the recruitment process—the process, that is, of securing the transfer of labor from traditional subsistence-production oriented villages to industrial employment. The shocks and hurts of the recruitment process in its early stages are apparently—though not made altogether definite—a source per se of labor protest. In mature industrial society also there is worker discontent, though it arises not from entanglement of the wage earner in a web of rules, but from the clash of interests between managers and the managed and from the continuing gap between the wants of wage earners and their incomes.

Questions arise from this formulation. With respect to the sources

---

[1] See their article, "The Labour Problem in Economic Development," *International Labour Review*, March 1955. It should be noted that the views on worker protest expressed in this article have been considerably revised in later writings of the Inter-University group. Cf. their *Industrialism and Industrial Man*, Cambridge, Mass., 1960.

of protest during early industrialization, it is hard to accept the view that the disturbances arising from the recruitment process are sources per se of protest, at least if protest is to be used in any meaningful way. Early industrialization may tend to create stresses which give rise to discontent on the part of new wage earners. But this discontent need be significantly intense, as Siegel implies elsewhere in the paper, only if a relatively large "grievance gap" develops. And there is no a priori reason why such a gap should develop.

It does appear to be true that in some of the now industrialized countries worker discontent "peaked" during the period of early industrial development. The process of recruiting the initial labor forces in many countries was characterized by the existence of strong "push" factors—overpopulation, rural misery, radical changes in land tenure. Entry into industrial employment presented many disadvantages. Aside from submission to unaccustomed discipline, wage differentials in many cases did not make industrial employment particularly inviting; in late eighteenth-century England the money income of the agricultural laborer who retained some rights on common land in his village was probably not much lower than the average wage income obtainable in the new mills and factories. While it is not certain that even in these conditions the recruitment of early labor forces was as difficult as the received doctrine on this matter would have us believe,[2] sources of discontent were real and widespread.

For the currently industrializing parts of the world—as Siegel notes—recruitment into paid employment is less clearly a source of protest. In much of the underdeveloped world, entry into industrial employment presents tremendous advantages in comparison with village life. The climate of managerial and government opinion everywhere now tends to soften the transition for new workers. Governments everywhere borrow—usually with the help of the I.L.O. and visiting experts—factory acts and labor codes based on those existing in the industrial countries.

More important, income distribution tends, in most of the underdeveloped world, to shift in favor of industrial wage earners. In most poor countries with large subsistence sectors the wage earning labor force is, as a group, a kind of aristocracy. The average annual per

---

[2] Cf. Morris D. Morris, "The Recruitment of an Industrial Labor Force in India, with British and American Comparison," *Comparative Studies in Society and History*, April 1960, pp. 305-328.

capita income of an unskilled wage earner in those countries is almost always far in excess of the average money income of peasant farmers in the subsistence sector.

It is, of course, difficult to compare relative living levels of the peasant in subsistence sectors with those of the wage earner in town, because great differences in styles of life are involved. But there can be little doubt that the trading of village life for industrial wage earning is by no means repugnant to rural people in the poor countries even where, as in most of Africa and parts of Latin America and Asia, there is little rural overpopulation squeezing men from the villages.

A final factor mentioned by Siegel should be underlined. In much of the currently industrializing world the entry into paid employment need not and frequently does not involve a permanent commitment to paid employment. Many wage earners retain ties with their villages throughout the period of early development. In some cases, particularly in Africa, widespread use of migrant labor permits men to have the best of both worlds (though some critics argue it is the worst of both worlds). While at some stage in development migrancy must give way to permanent or semipermanent commitment, it provides an easy road over the difficult period of early industrialization.

All of this suggests that there is no necessary reason to expect a large grievance gap among the wage workers of countries currently beginning their industrialization. Early industrialization in the modern world of itself is not a cause of worker protest. And if worker protest on a significant scale is not a necessary feature of the process of early industrialization, there is even less reason for it to appear in mature industrial societies. Siegel seems to be saying this when he describes the sources of protest in mature industrial economies, for here he emphasizes conflicts of interest and income distribution problems. In this sense, he puts worker protest theory back into the context of a general theory of social protest. In the advanced economy the sources of protest are no longer essentially specific to labor; protest arises because of gaps between income and desires, and because the national income cannot be divided to every group's satisfaction.

Once the source of social protest is located in grievance gaps and clashes of economic interest, then the elaboration of a theory of worker protest must necessarily be part of a general theory of social protest. For the same factors that explain worker protest should explain peasant revolts and movements of lower middle-class anger like Poujadism. The way is open, too, for consideration of one set of factors omitted by Siegel—the role of short-run cyclical factors in protest movements. In the short run, economic historians have shown us, the price of bread is probably the greatest single influence on the curve of worker protest. These are matters on which the economist with a penchant for social theory can say a great deal.

GASTON V. RIMLINGER, Rice University

The paper states its objective to be the provision of a "unifying analytical framework for the varied probings into work and its discontents. . . ." I shall begin by directing my comments to two interrelated aspects of this objective: first, I shall consider the kind of unification the paper achieves; and second, I shall examine the structure of the analytical framework it presents. A third question on which I shall comment briefly is the usefulness of the framework presented.

1. My first questions are: What does Siegel want to unify analytically and how does he do it?

The framework he presents is intended to unify for purposes of analysis a fairly broad area of study, an area designated by the label worker protest. It covers a wide sector of what is usually treated in the context of labor history, labor theory, industrial relations, or just plain labor problems. The worker protest area, as Siegel points out, covers a great variety of individual and collective patterns of behavior. Worker protest has many different causes, a multiplicity of fairly vague dimensions, and a host of possible consequences. The paper implies that, as an area of analysis, worker protest is essentially similar to other more familiar areas, such as, for instance, the area of wages. We might agree that a concept like wages is not free from ambiguities, but it does not appear to be nearly so elusive as the concept of worker protest.

However, the fact that worker protest is a bit elusive and the fact that it covers a great variety of behavior patterns merely emphasize the necessity for some framework that provides *analytical unity*. The provision of such a framework, in addition to the designation of an area susceptible to analytical integration, would be an important contribution not only to the study of labor problems but to social science. Although in my estimation the present paper does not meet the qualifications of an ideal analytical framework, it does provide helpful guidance for steps in that direction. In the brief space allocated to my discussion, I shall not dwell on some of the valuable insights of the paper but will concentrate mainly on its shortcomings in achieving the difficult task of constructing an over-all framework to serve effectively as a step toward generalized theoretical formulations of labor protest.

As I see it, analytical unity requires at least two conditions: first, the major aspects of a problem have to be classified into a manageable number of variables; and second, the variables chosen for this purpose must conceivably be relevant for some common, general, theoretical formulation of the problem. If the variables chosen are not conceivable components of a general theoretical explanation, they almost necessarily will fail to show the interrelationships between various aspects of the problem studied. If one cannot readily conceive how the variables may be theoretically interrelated, I do not see how one can speak of an effective analytically unifying framework.

Does Siegel's approach fulfill the two conditions just mentioned? It seems to fulfill the first condition, that is, he divides the general phenomenon into a reasonable number of variables. I am referring here to variables which Siegel treats under "elements of worker protest theory." More specifically, I have in mind the following: the sources, nature, and direction of protest; and also the structure, magnitude, impact, and the parties to protest. I am not sure that this approach meets the second condition. No effort is made to show in what way these variables are visualized as essential and interrelated parts of some general theoretical formulation. They seem to be mainly labels put on certain categories of empirical phenomena without any attempt to explain their potential significance in a network of causal interrelations. The unity they impart to the study of protest is mainly descriptive. It is an external rather than an analytical kind of unity. I have the feeling that these categories were chosen for a description of specific aspects of protest, rather than for their direct relevance from an analytical point of view.

2. I want to shift now to my second area; the structure of the analytical framework presented in the paper. This deals mainly with the question of how the various parts of the framework do in fact relate to each other. What is Siegel's "framework for theorizing about worker protest"? So far as I can tell, it is a generalized description of the phenomenon of worker protest in terms of his elements of worker protest theory.

My first observation on this framework is that these ingredients are a rather mixed bag. Some of them as, for instance, the magnitude or impact of protest, are elements which a protest theory ought to explain. Other ingredients, like the "analytical time horizon," are arbitrarily chosen by the investigator. Moreover, this particular ingredient does not describe the protest phenomenon but the framework.

My second observation is that although this framework provides us with certain descriptive categories, all of these categories are essentially static. In Siegel's words: "The analytical framework is more like the road map than the detailed aerial photograph of an area." But protest is a dynamic phenomenon. It is influenced very decisively by historical legacies acting as lags and by new ideas acting as leads. The framework fails to stress these dynamic aspects.

My third observation on the framework concerns the absence of some mechanism relating the variables to each other. It seems to me that the major purpose of an analytical framework is to orient us toward cause and effect relationships. It ought to suggest how the variables may interact with each other. Or, a framework should show at least the degree to which different variables are compatible with each other. Siegel assumes that there are significant relationships between his elements. But he does not spell them out in his framework. The relationships between protest ingredients and other factors are presumably not to be introduced until the framework is applied to particular situations. They are not part of the framework.

This brings me to my fourth observation on the framework, which relates to the relevance of the chosen ingredients. I indicated a moment ago that from the point of view of analytical unity one should be able to view the selected ingredients as parts of some general theory. At this point, with reference to the framework, my concern is whether the ingredients presented are necessary and sufficient for analyzing the protest phenomenon. To put it more directly: How do we know that these are the elements we really want to stress for analytical purposes. We may intuitively sense that Siegel's elements of worker protest theory are meaningful for analysis, but unless we have in mind at least some theory of protest, we cannot determine their relevance. Nor do we know what other important variables have been left out of the framework.

3. I turn now to the third area of my comments: the usefulness of the framework presented. Regardless of what I have said up to now about the internal structure of the framework, what really matters is its usefulness as a tool of analysis. This usefulness is best tested by examining how the author himself applies his framework to a given problem.

Siegel translates the views of Marx and Veblen into the terms of his framework. His main concern is with their explanation of protest and with the development of the protest movement in the course of industrialization. Marx clearly furnishes the better case for the application of the protest framework, because, I think, he has an analytically unified and dynamic system. In other words, Marx provides a mechanism for relating Siegel's protest ingredients to each other. In Marx the elements of protest are interacting with each other and with a system of authority represented by capitalist-dominated industrial society. Marx has a system which makes it possible for Siegel to relate to each other such "protest elements" as the magnitude, the impact, and the revolutionary potential of protest. And these ingredients in turn are related to structural changes in the organization of protest.

Having examined the Marxian system in the light of the analytical framework, Siegel finds the Marxian model inadequate as an explanation of the development of protest during industrialization. He then proceeds to give us another explanation in the form of "alternative protest mappings." These alternative protest mappings depict the evolution of protest during industrialization, described in the vocabulary of Siegel's analytical framework. But the explanation of this evolution, it seems to me, draws at least as much on Marx's analysis as it does on Siegel's framework. The protest mappings introduce dynamic relationships into the framework. This is done by way of reinterpreting the Marxian model in the light of more recent historical experience. With Siegel as with Marx, the stage of industrial development becomes an important factor in determining various elements of protest. Other important variables introduced at this point are the amount or rate of change taking place, and the sociopolitical structure of the industrializing society.

The whole section of the paper dealing with protest during industrialization is quite interesting. We might agree or disagree in varying degrees with some of its generalizations, or we might point to factors that were not adequately considered. But that is not the heart of the matter. The important question is: To what extent does the analysis depend on the framework provided earlier? Or, more generally, how much does an acquaintance with this framework assist us in understanding and explaining protest during industrialization, or in any other period? I should say that the framework furnishes a set of questions which help us organize our data. We can apply these questions to different times and places for purposes of comparative analysis. In this respect, such a framework holds its greatest promise. All this is certainly very useful for purposes of exploration. Beyond that, however, the framework is useful only if we have some reason for organizing our data into the particular empirical categories it provides. And that depends, as I argued earlier, on our general theoretical preconception of the protest phenomenon. Thus, the very least that must be said for Siegel's framework is that it constitutes a systematic approach to a complex phenomenon. Apparently, this is what Siegel tried to achieve in his paper. He states that he is chiefly interested in developing a "way of looking" at the question. Further development and refinement of the framework are possible and are desirable in order to enhance the value of the framework as an analytical tool.

# Labor Force Participation of Married Women: A Study of Labor Supply

JACOB MINCER

COLUMBIA UNIVERSITY AND NATIONAL BUREAU OF
ECONOMIC RESEARCH

## Introductory: Statement of the Problem

ON the assumption that leisure time is a normal good, the standard analysis of work-leisure choices implies a positive substitution effect and a negative income effect on the response of hours of work supplied to variations in the wage rate. An increase in the real wage rate makes leisure time more expensive and tends to elicit an increase in hours of work. However, for a given amount of hours worked, an increase in the wage rate constitutes an increase in income, which leads to an increase in purchases of various goods, including leisure time. Thus, on account of the income effect, hours of work tend to decrease. In which direction hours of work change on balance, given a change in the wage rate, cannot be determined a priori. It depends on the relative strengths of the income and substitution effects in the relevant range. The single assumption of a positive income elasticity of demand for leisure time is not sufficient to yield empirical implications on this matter.

An empirical generalization which fills this theoretical void is the "backward-bending" supply curve of labor. This is the notion that on the average the income effect is stronger than the substitution effect, so that an increase in the wage rate normally results in a decreased amount (hours) of work offered by suppliers of labor. Extreme examples of such behavior have been repeatedly observed in underdeveloped countries. On the American scene, several kinds of empirical evidence apparently point to the same relationship:[1] the historically

NOTE: Research reported in this paper was supported, in part, by a grant from the Social Science Research Council. Data from the 1950 Survey of Consumer Expenditures were made available on punch cards by the Bureau of Labor Statistics. For encouragement and helpful comments I am indebted to Dorothy S. Brady, Gary S. Becker, Zvi Griliches, Mark Leiserson, Phillip J. Nelson, Elliot Zupnick, and to members of the Columbia University Workshop in Labor Economics.

[1] The pioneering works of research and interpretation in this area are well known. See: Paul H. Douglas, *The Theory of Wages*, Macmillan, 1934; John D. Durand, *The Labor Force in the U.S.*, Social Science Research Council, 1948; Clarence D. Long, *The Labor Force under Changing Income and Employment*, Princeton University Press for National Bureau of Economic Research, 1958.

declining work week in industry; historically declining labor force participation rates of young and old males; an inverse relation between wages of adult males and labor force participation rates of females by cities in cross sections; an inverse relation between incomes of husbands and labor force participation of wives, by husbands' incomes, in budget studies. Similar phenomena have been reported from the experience of other modern economies.

The secular negative association between the length of the work week, participation rates of males, and rising real incomes is clearly consistent with the backward-bending supply curve.[2] Whether this is also true of cross-sectional data on males is a question which has as yet received little attention. Superficially, the cross-sectional behavior of females seems similarly capable of being rationalized in terms of a backward-bending supply response, or at least in terms of a positive income elasticity of demand for leisure. Such views, however, are immediately challenged by contradictory evidence in time series. One of the most striking phenomena in the history of the American labor force is the continuing secular increase in participation rates of females, particularly of married women, despite the growth in real income. Between 1890 and 1960 labor force rates of all females fourteen years old and over rose from about 18 per cent to 36 per cent. In the same period rates of married women rose from 5 per cent to 30 per cent, while real income per worker tripled.[3]

The apparent contradiction between time series and cross sections has already stimulated a substantial amount of research. The investigation reported in this paper is yet another attempt to uncover the basic economic structure which is, in part, responsible for the observed relations.

The study starts from the recognition that the concepts of work, income, and substitution need clarification and elaboration before they can be applied to labor force choices of particular population groups, in this instance married women. The resulting analytical model, even though restricted to two basic economic factors, seems capable of explaining a variety of apparently diverse cross-sectional behavior patterns. It also, in principle, reconciles time series with cross-section behavior, though further elaboration is needed for a proper explanation

[2] For a rigorous statement, see H. Gregg Lewis, "Hours of Work and Hours of Leisure," *Proceedings of the Industrial Relations Research Association,* 1957.

[3] Based on Long, *The Labor Force,* Table A-6; and *Employment and Earnings,* Bureau of Labor Statistics, 1960.

of the former. The empirical focus of the paper is a reinterpretation of old cross-section materials, and an investigation of newly available data generated by the 1950 BLS Survey of Consumer Expenditures.

## Conceptual Framework

### WORK

The analysis of labor supply to the market by way of the theory of demand for leisure time viewed as a consumption good is strictly appropriate whenever leisure time and hours of work in the market in fact constitute an exhaustive dichotomy. This is, of course, never true even in the case of adult males. The logical complement to leisure time is work broadly construed, whether it includes remunerative production in the market or work that is currently "not paid for." The latter includes various forms of investment in oneself, and the production of goods and services for the home and the family. Educational activity is an essential and, indeed, the most important element in the productive life of young boys and girls. Work at home is still an activity to which women, on the average, devote the larger part of their married life. It is an exclusive occupation of many women, and of a vast majority when young children are present.

It is, therefore, not sufficient to analyze labor force behavior of married women in terms of the demand for leisure. A predicted change in hours of leisure may imply different changes in hours of work in the market depending on the effects of the causal factors on hours of work at home. Technically speaking, if we are to derive the market supply function in a residual fashion, not only the demand for hours of leisure but also the demand for hours of work at home must be taken into account. The latter is a demand for a productive service derived from the demand by the family for home goods and services. A full application of the theory of demand for a productive service to the home sector has implications for a variety of socioeconomic phenomena beyond the scope of this paper.

### FAMILY CONTEXT

The analysis of market labor supply in terms of consumption theory carries a strong connotation about the appropriate decision-making unit. We take it as self-evident that in studying consumption behavior the family is the unit of analysis. Income is assumed to be pooled, and total family consumption is positively related to it. The distribution of consumption among family members depends on tastes. It is equally important to recognize that the decisions about the production of goods and services at home and about leisure are largely family decisions. The relevant income variable in the demand for home services and for leisure of any family member is total family income. A change in income of some family member will, in general, result in a changed consumption of leisure for the family as a whole. An increase in one individual's income may not result in a decrease in *his* hours of work, but in those of other family members. The total amount of work performed at home is, even more clearly, an outcome of family demand for home goods and for leisure, given the production function at home. However, unlike the general consumption case, the distribution of leisure, market work, and home work for each family member as well as among family members is determined not only by tastes and by biological or cultural specialization of functions, but by relative prices which are specific to individual members of the family. This is so, because earning powers in the market and marginal productivities in alternative pursuits differ among individual family members. Other things equal (including family income), an increase in the market wage rate for some family member makes both the consumption of leisure and the production of home services by that individual more costly to the family, and will as a matter of rational family decision encourage greater market labor input by him (her). Even the assumption of a backward-bending supply curve would not justify a prediction of a decrease in total hours of work *for the particular earner*, if wages of other family members are fixed.

Recognition of the family context of leisure and work choices, and of the home-market dichotomy within the world of work, is essential for any analysis of labor force behavior of married women, and perhaps quite important for the analysis of behavior of other family members, including male family heads. For the present purpose of constructing a simple model of labor force behavior of married women it will be sufficient to utilize these concepts only insofar as they help to select and elucidate a few empirically manageable variables to represent the major forces of income and substitution contained in the market supply function.

## WORK CHOICES

Let us consider the relevant choices of married women as between leisure, work at home, and work in the market. Income is assumed to have a positive effect on the demand for leisure, hence a negative effect on total amount of work. With the relevant prices fixed, increased family income will decrease total hours of work. Since the income effect on the demand for home goods and services is not likely to be negative,[4] it might seem that the increased leisure means exclusively a decrease in hours of work in the market. Such a conclusion, however, would require a complete absence of substitutability between the wife and other (mechanical, or human) factors of production at home, as well as an absence of substitution in consumption between home goods and market-produced goods. Domestic servants, laborsaving appliances, and frozen foods contradict such assumptions. Substitutability is, of course, a matter of degree. It may be concluded therefore that, given the income elasticity of demand for home goods and for leisure, the extent to which income differentially affects hours of work in the two sectors depends on the ease with which substitution in home production or consumption can be carried out. The lesser the substitutability the weaker the negative income effect on hours of work at home, and the stronger the income effect on hours of work in the market.

Change in this degree of substitutability may have played a part in the historical development. At a given moment of time, the degree of substitutability is likely to differ depending on the content of home production. Thus substitutes for a mother's care of small children are much more difficult to come by than those for food preparation or for physical maintenance of the household. It is likely, therefore, that the same change in income will affect hours of market work of the mother more strongly when small children are present than at other times in the life-cycle.

While family income affects the total amount of work, the market wage rate affects the allocation of hours between leisure, the home, and the market. An increase in the real wage rate, given productivity in the home, is an increase in prices (alternative costs) of home production as well as of leisure in terms of prices of wage goods. To the

---

[4] Fragmentary cross-sectional data on food preparation at home indicate a negligible income elasticity. The demand for other home goods and services (including care of children, and their number) may be more income elastic.

extent of an existing substitution between home goods and wage goods such a change will lead to an increase in work supplied to the market. Again, the strength of the effect is a matter of the degree of substitution between wage goods and home production.

In a broad view, the quantity of labor supplied to the market by a wife is the fraction of her married life during which she participates in the labor force. Abstracting from the temporal distribution of labor force activities over a woman's life, this fraction could be translated into a probability of being in the labor force in a given period of time for an individual, hence into a labor force rate for a large group of women.

If leisure and work preferences, long-run family incomes, and earning power were the same for all women, the total amount of market work would, according to the theory, be the same for all women. Even if that were true, however, the *timing* of market activities during the working life may differ from one individual to another. The life cycle introduces changes in demands for and marginal costs of home work and leisure. Such changes are reflected in the relation between labor force rates and age of woman, presence, number and ages of children. There are life-cycle variations in family incomes and assets which may affect the timing of labor force participation, given a limited income horizon and a less than perfect capital market. Cyclical and random variations in wage rates, employment opportunities, income and employment of other family members, particularly of the head, are also likely to induce temporal variations in the allocation of time between home, market, and leisure. It is not surprising, therefore, that over short periods of observation, variation in labor force participation, or turnover, is the outstanding characteristic of labor force behavior of married women.

To the extent that the temporal distribution of labor force participation can be viewed as a consequence of "transitory" variation in variables favoring particular timing, the distinction between "permanent" and current levels of the independent variables becomes imperative in order to adapt our model to family surveys in which the period of observation is quite short.

## An Econometric Model for Cross Sections

### "PERMANENT" LEVELS OF VARIABLES AND AREA REGRESSIONS

The simplest specification of a labor-market supply function of married women to which the theoretical considerations lead is:

$$m = \beta_p \cdot y + \gamma w + u \ (1)$$

where $m$ is the quantity of labor supplied to the market, $y$ is a "potential permanent level" of family income[5] computed at a zero rate of leisure and of home production, $w$ is the wife's full-time market wage or market earning power, and $u$ reflects other factors or "tastes." Since family income so computed is a sum of market earning powers of family members plus property income, we may write $y = x_p + w$, where $x_p$ stands for the permanent level of income of the family which does not include earnings of the wife. For empirical convenience we shall identify $x_p$ with income of the husband. This creates some inaccuracy, to the extent that contribution to family income of family members other than head and wife is important.

It is useful to rewrite equation 1 in terms of income of the husband since most data relate labor force behavior of wives to incomes of husbands. Indeed, the use of observed family income in empirical study of the supply relation would be inappropriate. Instead of serving as a determinant of labor force behavior, it already reflects such decisions. Substituting for $y$ into (1):

$$m = \beta_p \ (x_p + w) + \gamma w + u = \beta_p x_p + a w + u \ (2)$$

Since $a = \beta_p + \gamma$, equation 1 can be estimated by means of equation 2.

In equation 1 parameter $\beta_p$ represents the effect of "permanent" family income on the wife's market labor input, keeping her market earning power constant; $\gamma$ represents the effect of the wife's market earning power, keeping family income constant. The theoretical expectation is that $\beta_p < 0$ and $\gamma > 0$.

The statement of the hypothesis $\beta_p < 0$ in equation 2, when applied to cross sections is: Given a group of women with the same market earning power, and tastes for leisure assumed independent of husbands' earning power, there will be, on the average, a negative relation be-

[5] The definition of "permanent" and "transitory" components of income follows that stated by Friedman in his consumption theory. Permanent income is income in the long-run sense, measuring income status or normal income position. Transitory income is the difference between current and permanent income. See Milton Friedman, *A Theory of the Consumption Function*, Princeton for NBER, 1957.

69

tween husbands' income and hours of market work of wives.[6] This is so because, in this statement, a higher income of husband means a higher family income and, on the assumption that leisure is a normal good, this implies a lesser total amount of work of the wife, at home and in the market.

On the assumption that, in cross sections, productivities of women in the market are unrelated to their productivities in the home, $w$ measures the relative price of labor in the two sectors. In equation 1 $\gamma$ is therefore a pure substitution effect, hence a positive number reflecting the attractive power of the wage rate in pulling women into the labor market. Parameter $a$ in equation 2 is a relative price effect not compensated by a change in income. The question of its sign can be stated as follows: Given a group of women whose husbands have the same earning power, what is the effect of a difference in the female wage rate on hours of work on the market? Clearly, a higher wage rate will shift women from the home sector and from leisure to the market sector. However, since in this case family income increases as a result of the increase in the wives' earning power, *total* hours of work will tend to decrease. Whether hours of work in the market will increase or decrease depends on whether the job shift from home to market adds more hours of work to the market sector than is subtracted from it by a possibly increased consumption of leisure. Whether the net outcome is a positive or negative sign of $a$ is, therefore, an empirical question. It is certainly incorrect to predict that the income effect of the wage rate on market work exceeds the substitution effect by analogy to the backward-bending supply curve. The two substitution effects involved in this comparison are quite different; the strength of substitution between wage goods and leisure time has no bearing on the strength of substitution between home production and wage goods. If anything, one would intuitively expect the latter to exceed the former.

Equation 2 was specified in terms of long-run magnitudes, such as earning power of husband and wife which also implies a long-run concept of hours of work on the left-hand side. Such specification is inappropriate for most empirical data in which individual families report current annual income and labor force participation of the wife during a survey week, or her work experience during a year. One set

---

[6] To the extent that women with strong tastes for leisure tend to seek out rich husbands, the true income effect (keeping tastes fixed) is overestimated in cross sections.

of data, however, is usable without adapting the model to the distinction between "permanent" and current magnitudes: These are area statistics which were heavily utilized by Douglas and Long mainly because of the absence of more detailed disaggregations. Even with such data currently available, which are much richer on the individual level, the area averages have special advantages for the purpose of estimating the coefficients of equation 2. First, the data provide information on average earning power of employed females, which can be used as a proxy for $w$. The second and basic merit of the community averages is that they can be interpreted as approximations to the long-run or permanent levels of the relevant variables.[7] Given that the age and family-type mix in different communities is rather similar at a given time,[8] average income and labor force figures could be considered equivalent to average magnitudes over the life-cycle, when secular trends in population and income are disregarded. At any rate, these averages are free from short-run "transitory" deviations of individual incomes from their normal levels. However, the community averages contain a transitory deviation common to the whole group. In other words, some areas may at a given time be below or above their normal levels of economic activity. The labor force response to such a transitory deviation should be clearly distinguished from the response to an individual difference in a group. Abnormally low or high levels of economic activity in a community create different employment opportunities, and, broadly speaking, cyclical variations in wage rates. On that account, rational timing of market work would be pro-cyclical. On the other hand, a cyclical decline means a loss in husbands' incomes and employment which may induce an opposite labor force response of wives. The controversy centering around the "added worker hypothesis"[9] is a debate about the net outcome of these two different forces for groups over the business cycle. Responses to individual short-run income variations *within* a group at a given time are motivated

[7] This strategy has been employed with some success in the analyses of consumption behavior. See Margaret G. Reid, "Consumption and the Income Effect" (unpublished manuscript); also R. Eisner, "The Permanent Income Hypothesis: Comment," *American Economic Review*, Dec. 1958, pp. 972-980.

[8] Labor force rates by cities, standardized for age, differ negligibly from unstandardized ones.

[9] According to that hypothesis, the labor force increases in depressions because unemployment of the main breadwinner induces other family members to seek employment. See W. S. Woytinsky, *Additional Workers and the Volume of Unemployment in the Depression*, S.S.R.C., 1940. For a critical analysis see Long, *The Labor Force*, Chapter 10.

by only one of the forces, since the cyclical level is fixed for the whole group. Knowledge of this response to transitory income of the family provides, by itself, no answer to the question posed by the "added worker" controversy.

Table 1 provides estimates of the coefficients of equation 2 as well as coefficients for the equation expanded to include 5 independent

TABLE 1

AREA REGRESSIONS OF LABOR FORCE RATES OF MARRIED WOMEN,
ALL NORTHERN STANDARD METROPOLITAN AREAS OF 250,000
OR MORE POPULATION IN 1950

| | INDEPENDENT VARIABLES | | | | | |
| | $X_1$ | $X_2$ | $X_3$ | $X_4$ | $X_5$ | $R^2$ |
| | (thousands of dollars) | | | (per cent) | | |
|---|---|---|---|---|---|---|
| Regression coefficients | −0.62 | +1.33 | +0.12 | −0.41 | −0.24 | 0.62 |
| and standard errors | (0.21) | (0.11) | (0.27) | (0.53) | (0.61) | |
| Regression coefficients | −0.53 | +1.52 | | | | 0.51 |
| Elasticities at means | −0.83 | +1.50 | | | | |

NOTE: See text for description of independent variables.
SOURCE: *U.S. Census of Population 1950*, Vol. II, *Characteristics of the Population*, Tables 86, 88, 183; Special Report, *General Characteristics of Families*, Table 41; and Gertrude Bancroft, *The American Labor Force, Its Growth and Changing Composition*, New York, Wiley, 1958, Table D-11.

variables. The regression analysis was restricted to 57 largest Standard Metropolitan Areas (population, 250,000 and over) in the North. It was felt that the SMA approximate labor markets more properly than cities. Southern areas were excluded because of the desire to exclude color differentials, which need to be studied separately. The dependent variable is the labor force participation rate (in per cent) of married women with husband present during the census week early in 1950. $X_1$ is the median income in 1949 of male family heads, wife present; $X_2$ is the median income of females who worked 50 to 52 weeks in 1949. These are the empirical proxies for $x_p$ and $w$ in equation 2. Three independent variables were added to help in the interpretation. Since areas differ by educational composition, which may affect as well as reflect tastes for market work or for its continuity, this variable was represented by the per cent of population age 25 and over with completed high school education or more ($X_3$). The position of the community relative to its normal levels of economic activity (group transitory) was represented by the male unemployment rate ($X_4$). Finally, to take care of the more important differences in demand for work at home, the per cent of families with children under 6 years of age was represented by ($X_5$).

The coefficients in Table 1 are informative: Judging by the coefficient of determination ($R^2$), the male income ($X_1$) and female wage rate ($X_2$) variables alone explain a half of the observed variation in labor force participation rates among areas in 1950. The effect of husbands' incomes is negative,[10] as theoretically expected. The effect of wives' earning power is positive, and indeed stronger than the effect of income. This result is quite suggestive with regard to time series, though not directly applicable.[11] The introduction of a measure of educational level ($X_3$) into the equation attenuates the wage rate effect somewhat, though not significantly in a statistical sense. Unemployment ($X_4$) is seen to have a discouraging effect on labor force participation. This appears to be a contradiction of the added worker hypothesis, though the information is not sufficient to yield statistical significance.[12] Finally, the presence of small children ($X_5$) has an effect in the expected direction, though again statistical significance is lacking.

ADAPTATION OF THE MODEL TO ANALYSIS OF FAMILY SURVEYS

When labor force behavior (reported for a week or for the preceding year) of wives is related to current income of husbands in family surveys, the observed relation is a compound of two effects which it is important to distinguish: the responsiveness of labor force behavior (1) to husbands' long-run income positions, and (2) to current deviations of that income from its normal level.[13]

[10] This stands in contrast to Long's finding that the negative relation between earnings of males and labor force rates of females, by areas, which was observed by Douglas and Long in other census periods, seems to have vanished in 1950. Such an impression, however, is based on a gross regression between the two variables and is not confirmed, when the other relevant variable, the female wage rate, is included in the equation. Table 1 indicates no basic change in the structure of the labor force relation between 1940 and 1950: A comparable two-variable regression in 1940 showed an income elasticity of $-0.91$ and a wage rate elasticity of $+1.26$. The change in the *gross* regression from negative to positive is due to a larger positive intercorrelation between male and female earnings in 1950 ($r = +.8$) than in 1940 ($r = +.4$).

[11] See section on cross sections and time series, below, for a discussion of time series.

[12] For a further discussion of the "added worker" question, see section on secular and cyclical effects of transitory components, below.

[13] For present purposes, a similar distinction between current and "permanent"

How the two factors, if distinct, may affect empirical results is easily discernible: Assume, for example, that, other things equal, wives' market activities are geared to long-run or permanent income, and are not affected in quantity or in timing by current deviations from it. Compare two groups of families, standardized for other characteristics, and with the same observed distribution of husbands' incomes in each. If differences among incomes are purely transitory in one group, and of a lasting nature in the other, an inverse relation between income of husband and participation of wife will be observed in the second group, but not in the first. Exactly the opposite result is obtained if we assume that wives respond to transitory, but not to permanent income. More generally, the observed negative relation will be steeper in the first group, if labor force behavior is more responsive to transitory than to permanent levels of income, and conversely if it is more responsive to permanent levels. Thus, survey observations may yield slopes of varying steepness in different bodies of data, depending on the differential responsiveness of labor force behavior to the two components of income, and on the extent to which the current income variation in the observed groups is "made up" of the two components.

A basic question, at this point, is whether a response to transitory income does exist at all. It is not obvious that temporal variation in family income makes it worthwhile to change the timing of market activities of wives. Such a hypothesis, however, may be derived from several considerations:

According to the simplest version of consumption theory, the absolute income hypothesis, current consumption responds to changes in current income. Hence, as income declines, leisure declines, and work increases. If the temporary change in family income, say a decline, is due to a change in employment (of head), and the family finds itself with an excess amount of "leisure," an attempt is made to restore equilibrium by increased market work of the wife. This is particularly likely, if unemployment is not general, and if the husband to some extent helps out at home.

This theory does not explicitly recognize distinctions between consumption responses to short-run and long-run income variation. Such a distinction is basic to the permanent income theory. According to that

---

levels of the female wage rate is not formally introduced. Short-run variations in it, or rather in employment opportunities, are largely a matter of industry differences among communities. We may assume that such differences are much less important in family surveys than in area comparisons.

theory, aggregate family consumption is determined even in short periods by long-run levels of family income. Adjustment between planned consumption and income received in the short period of observation (current, or measured income) takes place via saving behavior, that is, via changes in assets and debts. However, if assets are low or not liquid, and access to the capital market costly or nonexistent, it might be preferable to make the adjustment to a drop in family income on the money income side rather than on the money expenditure side. This is so because consumption requiring money expenditures may contain elements of short-run inflexibility such as contractual commitments. The greater short-run flexibility of nonmoney items of consumption (leisure, home production) may also be a cultural characteristic of a money economy. Under these conditions, a transitory increase in labor force participation of the wife may well be an alternative to dissaving, asset decumulation, or increasing debt. One useful empirical implication of this hypothesis for labor force behavior is that it should be inversely related to the level of family assets, both in the life-cycle and in the short-run sense.

The proper interpretation of survey data, therefore, requires a specification of transitory income $(x_t)$ in addition to permanent income $(x_p)$ which was included in equation 2. The model becomes:

$$m = \beta_p \cdot x_p + \beta_t \cdot x_t + a \cdot w + u \ (3)$$

Two avenues are open for empirical utilization of equation 3. One is an attempt to estimate the coefficients, particularly the new coefficient $\beta_t$. Another is the exploration of the implications of equation 3 for observable relations in various bodies of survey data. Both approaches are used. In both cases the major substantive interest is focused on the relative sizes of $\beta_p$ and $\beta_t$, as well as on those of $\beta_p$ and $a$.

Equation 3, if correct, points out two major reasons for the difficulties in understanding the usual cross-sectional findings.[14] No information is available on the extent to which current income represents long-run income. When labor force rates of wives are classified by characteristics of husbands, little or no information is given on characteristics of wives. Since the newly available data from the 1950 BLS Survey of Consumer Expenditures are less deficient in these respects, we turn first to them for an empirical analysis.

[14] Comprehensive summaries of census findings are provided by Gertrude Bancroft, *The American Labor Force, Its Growth and Changing Composition*, New York, Wiley, 1958, and by Long, *The Labor Force*.

## BLS Survey of Consumer Expenditures

The more systematic testing of the analytical model (equation 3) and estimation of its parameters, particularly of $\beta_t$, the coefficient of transitory income, were made possible by cards especially prepared by the Bureau of Labor Statistics from its 1950 Survey of Consumer Expenditures. The cards contain information on economic and other characteristics of individual earners cross-classified by a number of such characteristics of the urban consumer units of which they are members. In what follows, employment status of wives is related to income and work experience of husbands, roughly standardized by age, education, and family type.

For the purpose of this study, the data were restricted to white husband-wife families, excluding units of which heads were self-employed or not gainfully occupied. The excluded population subgroups are known to exhibit differential patterns of labor force behavior. Separate analyses and comparisons are therefore required. The resulting homogeneous sample contained 6,766 consumer units. It was stratified by age and education of head, as well as by presence or absence of young children in the younger age group.[15] The 12 strata so obtained (shown in Table 2) were in turn subdivided into units with heads working full time year-round, and heads not fully employed during the year. Whenever analytically convenient, these subgroups within strata were merged.

The first three columns in Table 3 provide information on average labor force responses of wives to empirical approximations of the permanent levels of the independent variables given by weekly earnings of fully employed heads and by weekly earnings of employed wives. The female labor force rates[16] (column 3) can be interpreted as such response only within each of the four age-family type groups. Differences between groups are influenced by life-cycle phenomena.

Within each of the age-family type groups, except the first, average labor force behavior of wives is consistent with the findings in the area regression. That is, the positive effect of the female wage rate outweighs the negative effect of heads' income power. Indeed, the positive

[15] Preschool children are not important numerically in the older age groups. Unfortunately, time and budget considerations did not permit more detailed stratifications.

[16] Strictly speaking, these are employment rates, that is, the proportion of wives who were employed at any time during the survey year. Labor force rates are, therefore, somewhat underestimated.

TABLE 2

STRATIFICATION AND SAMPLE SIZES OF
HUSBAND-WIFE URBAN CONSUMER UNITS, 1950 BUREAU OF
LABOR STATISTICS DATA

|  | Education of Head | | |
|---|---|---|---|
| Age of Head | Elementary (8 years or less) | High School (9-12 years) | College (13 years or more) |
| Less than 35, oldest | 139 | 747 | 283 |
| child less than 16 | 75 | 216 | 119 |
| Less than 35, no | 55 | 258 | 45 |
| small children | 15 | 59 | 43 |
| 35-54 | 851 | 1,308 | 618 |
|  | 287 | 280 | 139 |
| 55 and older | 491 | 232 | 117 |
|  | 221 | 113 | 25 |

NOTE: Upper figures for each group refer to family units with heads working full time year-round. Lower figures refer to units with heads working less than a full year.

TABLE 3

LABOR FORCE RATES OF WIVES OF FULLY EMPLOYED HEADS, BY HEADS' AGE,
EDUCATION, INCOME, AND BY WIVES' WEEKLY EARNINGS

|  |  | Heads' Earnings per Week (dollars) | Wives' Earnings per Week | Wives' Labor Force Rate[a] | |
|---|---|---|---|---|---|
| Heads' Age | Heads' Education | (1) | (2) | Average (per cent) (3) | When Head Earned $2,000-$3,000 (per cent) (4) |
| Less than 35, | Elementary | 62.5 | 41.2 | 27 | 19 |
| oldest child | High school | 71.6 | 44.2 | 23 | 27 |
| less than 16 | College | 83.6 | 47.1 | 18 | 36 |
| Less than 35, | Elementary | 63.3 | 44.7 | 62 | 62[b] |
| no small | High school | 66.7 | 46.3 | 69 | 65 |
| children | College | 80.1 | 50.5 | 69 | 83[b] |
|  | Elementary | 70.0 | 41.1 | 31 | 37 |
| 35-54 | High school | 79.5 | 45.9 | 33 | 45 |
|  | College | 115.3 | 52.4 | 38 | 56 |
|  | Elementary | 65.8 | 38.6 | 16 | 21 |
| 55 and older | High school | 85.6 | 41.1 | 20 | 38 |
|  | College | 122.5 | 58.1 | 23 | 38[b] |

SOURCE: 1950 BLS data.
[a] Husbands employed full time year-round.
[b] Based on less than 20 observations.

wage rate elasticity must be more than twice as large as the negative income elasticity since, moving from lower to higher education and income levels in each group, the per cent increase in wives' weekly earnings is less than half the per cent increase in husbands' earnings. Over the life cycle as a whole, this excess of the wage rate elasticity over the income elasticity is not so great, since the young group with small children exhibits what seems to be a stronger negative income effect or a weaker positive wage rate effect, or both. The theoretical likelihood of such behavior of units at the time when small children are present was discussed before.[17]

Differences in labor force behavior between the age-family type groups are caused largely by life-cycle differences in family responsibilities. The low rates in the open-ended oldest age group probably reflect retirement age, as well as effects of larger property income and of greater contributions to family income by members other than head and wife. This is supported by the fact that the percentage difference between full time earnings of heads and total family income increases after age 35 despite the declining labor force rates of wives.[18]

The last column of Table 3 suggests a response of labor force behavior to transitory components of income. At the same low current earnings of husbands ($2,000-3,000 in this illustration), labor force rates of wives increase with the heads' education, hence with their permanent income. The increase in rates is much more pronounced at the fixed income level than for the group averages. Clearly, the higher the education of the head, the larger the (negative) difference between the fixed current income figure and his expected or long-run income position. In other words, in column 4, negative income transitories increase as we move from lower to higher education levels of heads in each age-family type group. To sum it up, figures in column 3 reflect the fact that, in each age group, the discouraging effect of husbands' normal earning power is more than outweighed by the positive effect of the female wage rate. The latter effect is augmented in column 4 by the negative transitory components of husbands' income exerting an additional push into the labor market.

More evidence on the influence of transitory components of family income on wives' labor force behavior is provided in Table 4. Rates for

[17] See section on Work Choices, above.
[18] See Table III in the author's "Labor Supply, Family Income, and Consumption," *Proceedings of the 1959 Annual Meeting of the American Economic Association, American Economic Review*, May 1960, p. 577.

TABLE 4

LABOR FORCE RATES OF WIVES, BY EARNINGS AND EMPLOYMENT OF HEADS

| | EDUCATION OF HEAD | | | | | | | | |
| | ELEMENTARY | | | HIGH SCHOOL | | | COLLEGE | | |
| | Heads' | | Labor Force Rates of Wives | Heads' | | Labor Force Rates of Wives | Heads' | | Labor Force Rates of Wives |
| AGE OF HEAD | Earnings | Weeks[a] | | Earnings | Weeks[a] | | Earnings | Weeks[a] | |
|---|---|---|---|---|---|---|---|---|---|
| Less than 35, oldest child less than 16 | $3,253 | 52 | 27% | $3,724 | 52 | 23% | $4,346 | 52 | 18% |
| | 2,329 | 38 | 33 | 2,772 | 40 | 30 | 2,527 | 41 | 39 |
| | −29 | −27 | +22 | −26 | −23 | +30 | −42 | −21 | +117 |
| Less than 35, no small children | 3,291 | 52 | 62 | 3,467 | 52 | 69 | 4,166 | 52 | 69 |
| | 2,407 | 38 | 66 | 2,385 | 39 | 73 | 1,902 | 32 | 88 |
| | −27 | −27 | +6 | −31 | −25 | +6 | −54 | −39 | +28 |
| 35-54 | 3,636 | 52 | 31 | 4,135 | 52 | 33 | 5,996 | 52 | 38 |
| | 2,395 | 36 | 44 | 2,871 | 39 | 49 | 3,442 | 42 | 52 |
| | −37 | −31 | +42 | −30 | −25 | +48 | −43 | −20 | +37 |
| 55 and older | 3,420 | 52 | 16 | 4,450 | 52 | 20 | 6,370 | 52 | 23 |
| | 1,792 | 28 | 27 | 2,139 | 30 | 27 | 2,950 | 34 | 16 |
| | −47 | −44 | +68 | −52 | −42 | +35 | −46 | −35 | −30 |

SOURCE: 1950 BLS data.

NOTE: Upper figures for each age-family group refer to heads who worked full time year-round; figures on second line refer to heads who worked part period or part time, or both; figures on third line for each group are the percentage difference between upper and lower lines.

a Weeks paid for.

wives are higher when heads did not work a full year than when they did, in each of the 12 population groups except in the oldest with highest education level. The higher labor force rates in the second line for each group may have been expected in view of the lower annual earnings of heads. However, the differences between earnings within each group are of a quite different nature than those between groups. To the extent that the family units within each group have been made homogeneous by the stratification, income differences within them are of a transitory nature.

The extent to which the families within each group are homogeneous with respect to normal earnings of husbands can be inferred from the third line for each group. If the wage rate (weekly earning rate) were the same for the heads who were not fully employed as for those who were, the percentage "loss" of time worked (weeks not employed) would account for, and would exactly equal, all of the "decline" in the year's earnings. It is clear from Table 4, that (transitory) differences in weeks worked rather than (permanent) differences in wage rates account for the overwhelming part of the differences in the year's earnings between the 2 subgroups, particularly in the strata with elementary and high school education. In the college stratum, however, almost half of the drop is accounted for by permanent differences— the relative decline in earnings is almost twice as large as the relative decline in weeks worked. The heterogeneity of the group with respect to permanent income is not surprising: it lumps people with one year of college together with highly trained professionals.

Table 4 not only shows the existence of a negative labor force response to transitory income, but also suggests orders of magnitude of the elasticity. For each group ratios of percentage difference in labor force rates to percentage difference in earnings and to percentage difference in weeks worked provide rough alternative estimates of this elasticity. These estimates, shown in the last two columns of Table 5, generally exceed the estimate of the elasticity with respect to permanent income levels derived from the area regression (Table 1). A more rigorous test for the hypothesis that the labor force response to transitory income is stronger than the response to permanent income is developed in a procedure (Table 5) which also yields numerical estimates of the elasticities.[19]

[19] The elasticity estimates are equivalent to estimates of regression coefficients of equation 3 stated in terms of logarithms of its variables. They are used for purposes of comparability. In the following discussion the same symbols are used for elasticities as for slopes, but the distinction is made explicit in the text.

TABLE 5

GROSS AND PARTIAL REGRESSION COEFFICIENTS OF LABOR FORCE
RATES OF WIVES ON EARNINGS AND WEEKS WORKED BY HEAD

| AGE OF HEAD | EDUCATION | SLOPES[a] | | | ELASTICITY ESTIMATES OF: | | | Alternative Elasticity Estimates[b] of $\beta_t$ | |
|---|---|---|---|---|---|---|---|---|---|
| | | $b_{mz}$ (1) | $b_{mz.e}$ (2) | $b_{me.z}$ (3) | $\beta_p$ (4) | $\beta_t-\beta_p$ (5) | $\beta_t$ (6) | (7) | (8) |
| Less than 35, oldest child less than 16 | Elementary | −0.132 | +0.035 | −0.327 | +0.04 | −0.61 | −0.57 | −0.79 | −0.82 |
| | High school | −0.604 | −0.503 | −0.347 | −0.80 | −0.75 | −1.55 | −1.19 | −1.33 |
| | College | −0.520 | −0.423 | −0.453 | −1.02 | −1.26 | −2.28 | −2.76 | −5.60 |
| Less than 35, no small children | Elementary | −0.460 | −0.438 | −0.071 | −0.22 | −0.05 | −0.27 | −0.24 | −0.22 |
| | High school | −0.246c | −0.188c | −0.210c | −0.09 | −0.15 | −0.24 | −0.19 | −0.24 |
| | College | −0.624 | −0.577 | −0.190c | −0.35 | −0.14 | −0.49 | −0.51 | −0.77 |
| 35-54 | Elementary | −0.623 | −0.568 | −0.124 | −0.68 | −0.20 | −0.88 | −1.14 | −1.35 |
| | High school | −0.511 | −0.433 | −0.535 | −0.61 | −0.81 | −1.42 | −1.61 | −1.92 |
| | College | −0.086 | −0.338 | +0.915 | −0.54 | +1.21 | +0.67 | −0.86 | −1.85 |
| 55 and older | Elementary | −0.402 | −0.346 | −0.139 | −0.73 | −0.43 | −1.16 | −1.45 | −1.50 |
| | High school | −0.205 | −0.254 | +0.213 | −0.56 | +0.53 | −0.03 | −0.67 | −0.83 |
| | College | −0.092 | −0.143 | +0.326 | −0.40 | +0.71 | +0.31 | +0.66 | +0.85 |

SOURCE: 1950 BLS data.

[a] $b_{mz}$ = slope of regression of labor force rate (per cent) on earnings of head (thousands of dollars).

$b_{mz.e}$ = slope of regression of labor force rate on earnings of head, keeping weeks worked constant.

$b_{me.z}$ = slope of regression of labor force rate on weeks worked, keeping earnings of head constant.

[b] Based on Table 4: Ratios of percentage difference in labor force rates to percentage difference in earnings (col. 7), and to percentage difference in weeks worked (col. 8).

c Not significantly different from zero, under a 5 per cent level.

After merging the two employment groups, in each of the cells, a simple and a 2-variable regression of labor force rates of wives on the year's earnings of husbands and on weeks worked by him yielded the gross and partial slopes listed in Table 5. The slope ($b_{mx}$) of the gross regression of wives' labor force rates on husbands' earnings (column 1) combines the effects of permanent and of transitory income. The partial slope of the same relation ($b_{mx.e}$ in column 2) keeps the number of weeks worked by the head constant. It, therefore, approximates the response to heads' normal earning power, rather than to their current income. Finally, $b_{me.x}$ (in column 3) represents the response to weeks worked by heads, keeping their total earnings constant.

The sign of the slope $b_{me.x}$ (column 3) provides a test for the difference between the strengths of the two income effects on labor force behavior of wives.

If the distinction between permanent and transitory income did not matter, a change in weeks worked by heads, with total earnings constant, would produce no labor force response. This hypothesis is rejected by the data. All slopes in column 3 are statistically significant, except those in the young group without small children. This exception is plausible: the stage in the life cycle represented by this group, namely the period between marriage and first child, is usually short, and during that time most of the wives are employed anyway; thus, there is very little scope for variations in timing of employment within that stage.

Now a decline in weeks, keeping total earnings constant, means a corresponding amount of increase in earning power, which is offset by a transitory loss of income of the same amount. The change in the permanent component of income is expected to bring about a *decrease* in labor force participation. The same change of the transitory component in the opposite direction is expected to stimulate an *increase* in market activities. The direction of the net outcome depends, therefore, on which income effect is stronger. Indeed, the negative sign of $b_{me.x}$ provides evidence that the effect of transitory income outweighs the permanent income effect!

An estimate of the labor force response to transitory income (coefficient $\beta_t$ in equation 3) is obtained as follows: The partial regression $b_{me.x}$ measures the arithmetic difference in labor force rates of wives due to the equal (but of opposite sign) differences in permanent and in transitory components of income. Converting the arithmetic difference in labor force rates into a percentage difference (using rates of wives with fully employed husbands as base, column 3 in Table 3), and dividing it by the percentage difference in income, that is, by $(1/52 \times 100)$ we obtain the estimate of the difference $(\beta_t\text{-}\beta_p)$ in elasticity terms.[20] This estimate is shown in column 5 of Table 5.

The slope $b_{mx.e}$ which serves as an approximation of the response to permanent income $(\beta_p)$ is next converted into an elasticity at the mean by the usual procedure[21] using the averages in Table 4. The estimate is shown in column 4 of Table 5. The sum of column 4 and column 5 in Table 5 provides an estimate of the response elasticity to transitory income $(\beta_t)$, which is shown in column 6. These estimates of transitory income elasticity in column 6 resemble the alternative estimates in columns 7 and 8, though they are somewhat smaller.

Looking at the sizes of parameter estimates in Table 5, we find perhaps most meaningful for purposes of comparisons with aggregates those in the modal population group (age 35-55, high school education). The estimate of the elasticity with respect to permanent income $(\beta_p)$ in it is not very different from the corresponding estimate in the area regression (Table 1). The estimate of the transitory elasticity $(\beta_t)$ is more than twice as large.

The estimates vary among population subgroups in a roughly systematic way: Response to permanent income is weaker the higher the educational level of heads 35 years of age and older. Responses to transitory income differ in a similar way. An opposite pattern is discernible in the young groups with small children. In the young but childless groups the magnitudes are either small or statistically unreliable.

It is difficult to say how much substance could be assigned to these differentials, given all the necessary qualifications—about the rata and the estimating procedure. As previously mentioned, small income elasticities in the childless groups are theoretically plausible. But they may also be produced by the arithmetic of elasticities, since levels of partici-

[20] $\dfrac{e}{m}.b_{me \, . \, x}$, where $e$ is number of weeks worked by the heads, measures the percentage change in labor force rate per 1 per cent increase in weeks employed, keeping husbands' income constant. But a 1 per cent rise in $e$, as stated in the text implies a 1 per cent rise in transitory income $x_t$, *and* a 1 per cent decline in permanent income $x_p$. Hence: $\dfrac{e}{m}.b_{me \, . \, x}$, in elasticity terms.

[21] Elasticity at the mean of $y$ with respect to $x$ is equal to the slope of the regression of $y$ on $x$, multiplied by the ratio of the mean of $x$ to the mean of $y$.

pation are high in these groups. The weakening response to transitory income with rising education level in the groups with family heads over 35 years old is consistent with the hypothesis that the availability of assets obviates the need for offsetting temporary income change by means of labor input.

The differential extent to which transitory components in heads' incomes are offset by family labor input in the various population groups is shown in Table 6. In each stratum the regression slope of

TABLE 6

ESTIMATES OF FRACTION OF NEGATIVE TRANSITORY INCOMES OF HEADS, WHICH IS OFFSET BY FAMILY LABOR INPUT

| Age | Education | $b_{ye}$[a] | $b_{xe}$[b] | $1-\dfrac{b_{ye}}{b_{xe}}$ |
|---|---|---|---|---|
| Less than 35, children under 16 | Elementary | 18.7 | 39.1 | 0.52 |
| | High school | 27.4 | 51.2 | 0.47 |
| | College | 33.2 | 60.5 | 0.45 |
| Less than 35, no small children | Elementary | 13.4 | 43.8 | 0.69 |
| | High school | 23.1 | 47.1 | 0.51 |
| | College | 32.4 | 60.1 | 0.46 |
| 35-55 | Elementary | 42.1 | 56.8 | 0.26 |
| | High school | 32.4 | 60.8 | 0.47 |
| | College | 46.7 | 75.1 | 0.38 |
| Over 55 | Elementary | 40.6 | 54.6 | 0.25 |
| | High school | 45.1 | 54.1 | 0.17 |
| | College | 54.9 | 62.3 | 0.12 |

SOURCE: 1950 BLS data.

[a] $b_{ye}$ = slope of regression of family income (dollars) on weeks worked by head.

[b] $b_{xe}$ = slope of regression of heads' income (dollars) on weeks worked by head.

family income (before tax) on weeks worked by heads was divided by the regression slope of heads' earnings on weeks worked by them. This ratio measures the loss in family income relative to the loss in husbands' earnings due to one week's loss of employment. The per cent by which the numerator is smaller than the denominator measures the extent to which a change in head's income was offset by an opposite change in income of other family members.[22]

The results in Table 6 show that the absorption of negative transitory components of heads' income declines with increasing education after

[22] "Loss" and "change" are only figures of speech in a cross-section analysis.

age 35, and with advancing age in each education group. This absorption is, of course, a net effect of all earners, not just the wife, and is consistent with the hypothesis on alternatives to dissaving.

## Census Surveys

Decennial censuses and current population reports of the Census Bureau are the major sources of empirical knowledge about labor force behavior of various population groups. The cross-sectional information on labor force rates of married women is usually contained in one-way or, less frequently, two-way classifications of these rates by variables such as: current or preceding year's income of husbands or of family, education, occupation, age, presence and age of children, color, location, and so forth. These gross relations between labor force rates and the classifying variables are manifold and bewildering. A literal reading of such relations as separate effects of the particular classifying variables is confronted with puzzling differences among various sets of cross-sectional data and leads to apparent contradictions with time series. The purpose of the empirical analysis in this section is to explore the extent to which the economic model presented in this paper (equation 3) is capable of rationalizing some of the observed patterns. Alternatively, this exploration can be viewed as a set of additional tests of the model and of hypotheses concerning sizes of its parameters.

In order to apply equation 3 to the observable gross relations let us deduce the implications of the model for such relations. Starting with the observed gross relation between husbands' income and wives' participation rates $(b_{mx})$, it can be shown that:[23]

$$b_{mx} = [\beta_p \cdot P + \beta_t \cdot (1\text{-}P)] + a \cdot b_{wx} \ (4)$$

Specifically, the observed elasticity is a sum of two terms. The first term (in brackets) is an average of permanent $(\beta_p)$ and transitory $(\beta_t)$ income elasticities weighted by the ratio $(P)$ of permanent income variance to current income variance. Since both elasticities are negative, this term is negative. The second term is a product of the

---

[23] From $m = \beta_p \cdot x_p + \beta_t x_t + aw + u$, where the variables are measured as deviations from their means,
$$\Sigma mx = \beta_p \cdot \Sigma x_p \cdot x + \beta_t \cdot \Sigma x_t \cdot x + a\Sigma wx + \Sigma ux$$
Assuming that $x_t$ is independent of $x_p$ and of $u$, and dividing by $\Sigma x^2$:
$$b_{mx} = \beta_p \cdot P + \beta_t \cdot (1\text{-}P) + ab_{wx},$$ where $b_{mx}$ is the least squares regression of $m$ on $x$, $b_{wx}$ the least squares regression of $w$ on $x$ and $P$ the ratio of variance of $X_p$ to the variance of $X$. Elasticities replace slopes and relative variances replace variances when the original model is specified in logarithms.

female wage rate elasticity ($a$) and the elasticity of wives' earning power with respect to current income of husband ($b_{wx}$), that is, of the rate at which a difference in wage rates of wives is associated with a difference in income of husbands. The second term is expected to be positive. It must, therefore, be smaller in absolute size than the first, in order to yield the usually observed negative relation between labor force rates of wives and incomes of husbands, by husbands' current income brackets. This is true for two reasons: $b_{wx}$ is small, thereby weakening the positive effect of the wage rate; and $\beta_t$ is substantially stronger than $\beta_p$, thereby augmenting the negative effect of (permanent) income. That the regression of earning power of wife on income of husband is rather weak is indicated by several sets of data. According to Table 3, the elasticity coefficient is 0.4 to 0.5, by income averages of education groups within age groups. A similar figure was computed from a Census cross-classification of median occupational full-time wages of husbands and wives in 1956.[24] Another computation, which applies full-time average incomes of education classes of males and females[25] to a cross-classification of husbands and wives, by educational background,[26] produced an elasticity coefficient of about 0.5. The inverse regression of the same variables produced an elasticity coefficient of 0.7. Strictly speaking, these are estimates of $b_{wx_p}$ and $b_{x_p w}$ respectively, the regressions with permanent incomes. The term in equation 4 is the regression of *current* income on wives' wage rate ($b_{wx}$) which is likely to be weaker than $b_{wxp}$.[27]

When the wage rate of wife is kept fixed, the second term in equation 4 vanishes, and

$$b_{mx.w} = \beta_p \cdot P + \beta_t \cdot (1\text{-}P) \quad (4a)$$

If the absolute size of $\beta_t$ is, in fact, greater than that of $\beta_p$, the observed regression $b_{mx.w}$ is steeper than the "long-run" coefficient $\beta_p$, so long as the variance of current income exceeds the variance of permanent income ($P < 1$). Also, the negative size of $b_{mx.w}$ increases the smaller $P$, that is the greater the contribution of transitory components to the current income variance.

---

[24] Published as Table 2 by Richard N. Rosett in "Working Wives: An Econometric Study," *Studies in Household Economic Behavior*, Yale University Press, 1958, p. 85.

[25] *Current Population Reports*, P-60, No. 27, April 1958, Table 20, p. 37.

[26] *Current Population Reports*, P-20, No. 83, Aug. 1958, Table C, p. 2.

[27] Indeed, a reasonable assumption that $X_t$ is independent of $w$, yields

$$b_{wx} = b_{wx_p} \cdot P, \text{ since } \frac{\Sigma\, wx}{\Sigma\, x^2} = \frac{\Sigma\, wx_p}{\Sigma\, x^2_p} \cdot \frac{1}{P}$$

Looking next at the regression on $w$, and assuming the $X_t$ is independent of $w$, we find the expression for the gross relation between wives' earning power and labor force rate is:[28]

$$b_{mw} = \beta_p \cdot b_{x_pw} + a \quad (5)$$

It is clear from equation 5 that the observed gross wage rate elasticity of labor force participation ($b_{mw}$) underestimates the true elasticity ($a$), because of the negative first term on the right-hand side. It must be positive, however, if $/a/ > /\beta_p/$, and closer to $a$ than to zero, if our previous estimates are roughly correct.

Implications 4 and 5 can be simultaneously put to a test, if labor force rates of wives are cross classified by husbands' income and by a measure of wives' earning power. One such cross-classification in census data provides the opportunity. Table 7 is a two-way tabulation of labor force rates of wives in survey week of March 1957, by income of husbands in 1956 and education level of wife. We use the latter as an index of wives' earning power, assigning to it average full-time incomes of females in these education classes. Empirical results are consistent with the theory.

(1) A comparison of equations 4 and 4a indicates that $/b_{mx.w}/ > /b_{mx}/$. That is to say, the decline in participation associated with increasing income should be stronger when $w$ is held constant than when it is not. Rates of decline are, in fact, more pronounced in the inside columns of Table 7 than in the left-hand marginal column.

(2) The gross relation of participation rates and earning power (measured by education) of wives is positive and strong. This has been repeatedly observed in census data.[29]

(3) When income of husbands is held fixed, the increase in participation with increasing wage rate of wives is stronger than when it is not. Rates of increase are more pronounced in the inside rows of Table 7 than in the left-hand marginal row.

(4) The systematic differences between rows and columns in Table 7 are indicative of the influence of income transitories. From left to right, successive columns correspond to income distributions of groups

[28] Multiply equation 3 by $w$, sum over all values, and divide by $\Sigma w'$:
$$\Sigma mw = \beta_p \cdot \Sigma x_p w + \beta_t \cdot \Sigma x_t w + a \cdot \Sigma w^2$$
and
$$b_{mw} = \beta_p \cdot b_{x_pw} + \beta_t \cdot b_{x_tw} + a, \text{ and if } X_t \text{ is independent of } w:$$
$$b_{mw} = \beta_p \cdot b_{x_pw} + a$$

[29] See Long, *The Labor Force*, pp. 94-96, and Bancroft, *The American Labor Force*, pp. 65-69.

with higher education and occupation levels. Research in income distribution and consumption[30] indicates that $(1-P)$, the relative importance of transitory components in the income variance, increases with education and occupation level. Equation 4a, therefore, predicts steeper

TABLE 7

LABOR FORCE RATE OF WIVES, BY OWN EDUCATION, BY INCOME OF HUSBANDS, URBAN AND RURAL NONFARM, MARCH 1957

(per cent)

| INCOME OF HUSBANDS IN 1956 | Total | Elementary School | High School | | College | |
| | | | 1-3 Years | 4 Years | 1-3 Years | 4 Years and Over |
|---|---|---|---|---|---|---|
| Total | 30.4 | 26.3 | 29.9 | 31.6 | 35.5 | 39.4 |
| Under $1,000 | 33.5 | 25.6 | 38.4 | 48.7 | n.a. | n.a. |
| $1,000-1,999 | 29.8 | 24.7 | 27.1 | 42.8 | n.a. | n.a. |
| 2,000-2,999 | 36.7 | 30.3 | 34.6 | 47.0 | n.a. | n.a. |
| 3,000-3,999 | 36.3 | 31.0 | 34.4 | 38.8 | 54.1 | n.a. |
| 4,000-4,999 | 32.3 | 24.7 | 33.5 | 33.4 | 43.5 | n.a. |
| 5,000-5,999 | 29.1 | 24.4 | 26.1 | 28.6 | 41.9 | 50.0 |
| 6,000-6,999 | 27.1 | 19.3 | 20.8 | 28.1 | 35.1 | 40.8 |
| 7,000-9,999 | 20.7 | 16.0 | 16.2 | 21.4 | 22.1 | 24.7 |
| 10,000 and over | 11.5 | n.a. | n.a. | 8.5 | 9.5 | 18.3 |
| Median full-year incomes of females, by education | | $2,408 | $2,583 | $3,021 | $3,440 | $3,809 |

SOURCE: Labor force rate, *Current Population Reports*, P-50, No. 81, p. 2, Table 2. Median full-year incomes of females, *Current Population Reports*, P-60, No. 27, p. 37, Table 20.
n.a. = not available.

slopes at higher education levels, *provided* $/\beta_t/ > /\beta_p/$. The increase in slopes by columns is clearly visible in Table 7. The systematic differences by rows are, of course, a reflection of the same phenomenon.

(5) A numerical check on the previously estimated parameters showed them to be rather surprisingly good: Using estimates of $\beta_p$ from Table 1, $\beta_t$ from the modal class in Table 5, a value of 0.8 for $P$,[31] and of 0.4 for $b_{wx}$, equation 4 predicts an average 3 per cent (negative) difference in participation rates of wives for a 10 per cent (positive)

[30] See the marginal propensities and income elasticities in H. S. Houthakker, "The Permanent Income Hypothesis," *American Economic Review*, June 1958, p. 401. Also my "Study of Personal Income Distribution," unpublished Ph.D. dissertation, Columbia University, 1957.

[31] Friedman's estimate of 0.85 relates to family incomes. The value for husbands' incomes is probably somewhat smaller. The calculations are not sensitive to modest differences in assumptions.

difference in current incomes of husbands. This is a good approximation to the actual slope in the marginal column of Table 7.

At the same time, equation 5 predicts an average increase of about 2 per cent in labor force rates of wives for a 10 per cent increase in wives' earning power. This is, again, a remarkably good approximation to the actual value in the marginal row of Table 7.

Equation 4 provides an insight into the nature of bias involved in interpreting the observed gross relation between labor force rates of wives and income of husbands as the "true" income effect. It does not provide a unique answer as to whether such gross regressions under-estimate or overestimate the true income effect. Given the notion that the response to transitory income is stronger than that to permanent income, the expression indicates that the negative elasticity is over-estimated on account of the variability of transitory components in current income ($P < 1$), but a contrary bias is produced by the positive intercorrelation between husbands' income and wives' wage rate.

Since $b_{wx} = b_{wx_p} P$ on the assumption that $x_t$ is independent of $w$, it follows from equation 4 that the closer the independent variable approximates a permanent income concept, the flatter the gross relation between it and the labor force rate. This is true for two reasons: the negative term in equation 4 decreases, and the positive term increases. It is for these reasons, roughly speaking, that the slope of the relation between labor force rates of wives and education level of husbands,[32] or family rent,[33] is close to zero.[34]

Several other behavior patterns observed in census data can be analyzed in terms of the model presented here.

Labor force rates of wives reported in a survey week, by occupation of husbands, are roughly inversely related to average incomes of husbands in these occupations. However, at the same low income brackets of husbands, participation rates reverse their ranks: they are higher at higher occupational levels[35] (as measured by income). These are effects of transitory components of income of the same kind as shown

---

[32] See, for example, *Current Population Reports*, P-60, No. 27, April 1958, Table F.

[33] Tabulations of the 1940 Census indicate a weak negative slope. The 1950 BLS data used here show a zero or even slightly positive slope.

[34] When $P = 1$ is put into equation 4, it becomes $b_{mx_p} = \beta_p + a \cdot b_{wx_p}$. With the orders of magnitudes of our estimates, $b_{mx_p}$ is close to zero.

[35] See Table F in *Current Population Reports*, P-60, No. 12, also exhibited and discussed by H. P. Miller, *Income of the American People*, pp. 88-89, and by Bancroft, *The American Labor Force*, p. 124.

in column 4 of Table 3, where the classification is by education of husband.

Another set of data which suggests a response to temporary income change are classifications of labor force rates of wives by labor force status of husband and by his age. Not being in the labor force is more likely to be a short-run phenomenon for younger husbands (education, temporary disability, etc.) than for older ones. Table 8 shows a strong labor force response in the younger groups and none in the group over

TABLE 8

LABOR FORCE RATES OF WIVES, BY AGE AND LABOR FORCE STATUS OF HUSBANDS

| | Employment Status of Husbands | | | | | |
| | 1954 | | | | 1955 | |
| Age of Husbands | Employed | Unemployed | Not in Labor Force | Employed | Unemployed | Not i Lab Forc |
| --- | --- | --- | --- | --- | --- | --- |
| 14-24 | 26.3 | 26.6 | 55.3 | 29.2 | 32.0 | 60.( |
| 25-44 | 27.3 | 30.7 | 54.9 | 27.4 | 42.3 | 44.; |
| 45-64 | 29.5 | 34.0 | 27.3 | 31.3 | 35.2 | 28.( |

SOURCE: *Current Population Reports.*

45. The fact that the response to labor force status of husband is stronger than the response to his employment status is also reasonable in view of the short observation period (survey week).

The relation between "transitory" income variability and observed labor force behavior can also be detected by varying the length of the observation period. Extending the period of observation means reducing the importance of transitory income components, hence reducing the negative slope of the income-labor force relation.

In Table 9 a comparison is made between work experience of wives by income level of husbands and by periods of observation. Columns 1 and 2 present the long-run (since marriage) work experience of married women, with husbands and children present, classified by income of husbands as reported at the time of the survey (1955). Over the long run for which the work experience is reported income differences were undoubtedly smaller, but in the same direction.[36] The income-labor

[36] It can be shown that, in general, the correlation between current and permanent income is:

$$r(x,x_p) = \sqrt{P} + r(x_t,x_p) \cdot \sqrt{1-P}$$

This is always positive, with the exception of the case when a negative $r(x_t, x_p)$ exceeds in absolute value the ratio $\sqrt{\dfrac{P}{1-P}} = \dfrac{\sigma(x_p)}{\sigma(x_t)}$

force relation which is strongly negative for the short observation period (column 3) vanishes in the long period[37] (columns 1 and 2). To repeat the previous argument, this does not mean that the response to permanent income is zero. The permanent elasticity ($\beta_p$) which is negative is just about offset by the positive wage rate elasticity ($a$),

TABLE 9

WORK EXPERIENCE OF WIVES, BY INCOME OF HUSBAND, OBSERVATION PERIOD, AGE, AND PRESENCE OF CHILDREN

| | WORK EXPERIENCE SINCE MARRIAGE[a] | | LABOR FORCE RATE IN SURVEY WEEK, 1956[b] | | | |
| | *Age, 25-35* | *Age, 18-40* | | | | |
| | *With Children* | | | *Age 20-44* | | |
| INCOME OF HUSBAND IN 1955 (dollars) | Average Number of Years at Work (1) | Average Number of Years at Work (2) | All (3) | *With Children of Age:* | | No Children (6) |
| | | | | Less Than 6 (4) | 6-18 (5) | |
| less than 3,000 | 2.67 | 2.24 | 38.1 | 22.4 | 54.6 | 59.0 |
| 3,000-4,000 | 2.61 | 2.49 | 30.4 | 16.7 | 39.0 | 61.0 |
| 4,000-5,000 | 2.71 | 2.63 | 29.6 | 15.8 | 38.5 | 62.6 |
| more than 5,000 | 2.68 | 2.64 | 24.0 | 11.1 | 35.9 | 56.5 |

[a] From article based on "Growth of American Families Study," *Milbank Memorial Fund Quarterly*, July 1959, Table 5, p. 291.
[b] Based on *Current Population Reports*, P-50, No. 73, Table 9.

even though the effect of the latter is attenuated by the fact that wives' earning power usually rises less than half as fast as that of husbands' when moving up the permanent income brackets of husbands.

Since columns 1 and 2 report for women with children, and column 3 pertains to all women of a similar age group, the latter were further subdivided by presence and age of children for clearer comparison. The contrast between the long-period and the short-period relation is, indeed, stronger for the more appropriate comparison of columns 1 and 2 with columns 4 and 5, rather than with column 3. Moreover, the breakdown by presence of children reveals a phenomenon, previously suggested, and repeatedly observed in census data:[38] When small

---

[37] The age span in cols. 1 and 2 obscures somewhat the interpretation of results in Table 9. A comparison of cols. 1 and 2 indicates, however, that the quantitative effect is not strong enough to affect the conclusions.
[38] See *Current Population Reports*, P-50, No. 39, Table 6. Also Durand, *The Labor Force in the U.S.*, pp. 91-92.

children are present the observed negative relation of labor force rates with income is stronger than when they are absent (column 6). Considerations of substitutability between care of children and wage goods and services are consistent with such findings. According to the theoretical argument, the positive wage rate effect ($a$) is weaker and the negative income effect ($\beta_p$) is stronger the lesser the substitutability between wife's labor at home and goods and services obtainable in the market. This is likely to be the case when small children are present.

## Implications

### CROSS SECTIONS AND TIME SERIES

If the orders of magnitude of the parameter estimates of equation 3 are roughly correct, there is no real contradiction between findings on labor force behavior of married women in cross-sections and in time series. The impression of a contradiction is due to the way cross-sections have been looked at, in terms of gross relations between income of husband and labor force participation of wife. Such gross comparisons yield results (slopes or elasticities) which are sensitive both to the existence of transitory components in income and to the covariation of wives' earning power with husbands' income. The transitory components accentuate the negative effect of income. In their absence, the cross-sectional negative relation would hardly be noticeable. If, in addition, the positive relation between husbands' and wives' incomes were stronger than is usually observed in cross-sections, a positive rather than negative relation would be found between labor force rates of wives and incomes of husbands, even at a point of time.

Thus, if equation 3 is projected onto time series, two facts intervene which convert the negative income relation in cross-sections into a positive secular relation: (1) short-run transitory components of income are not relevant to long-run developments, and (2) the female wage rate has risen over time at least as fast as the male rate.

It is of some interest, at this point, to inquire how much of the quantitative change over time can be "explained" by the use of the supply function estimated from the recent cross sections.

The appropriate equation for this purpose is equation 1,

$$m = \beta_p y + \gamma w + u \text{ where } \gamma = a - \beta_p$$

and $y$ is family income computed as a sum of earning powers of husbands and wives. The estimated equation is (from Table 1):

$$m = -0.53y + 2.05w \quad (6)$$

In Table 10 actual secular changes in labor force rates of married women are compared with changes predicted by equation 6. The data used for the comparison are not exactly appropriate. They cover the

TABLE 10

ACTUAL AND "PREDICTED" SECULAR CHANGES IN LABOR FORCE
RATES OF MARRIED WOMEN, 1890-1959

|  | 1889-1919 | 1919-29 | 1929-39 | 1939-49 | 1949-59 |
|---|---|---|---|---|---|
| Changes in full-time[a] earnings of males (dollars) | 685 | 878 | 328 | 561 | 562 |
| Changes in full-time[b] earnings of females (dollars) | 386 | 504 | 252 | 585 | 576 |
| Changes in family[c] earning power (dollars) | 1,071 | 1,382 | 580 | 1,146 | 1,138 |
| Expected changes in labor force rates | +2.2 | +3.2 | +2.1 | +6.0 | +5.7 |
| Actual changes[d] in labor force rates | +4.4 | +2.7 | +2.1 | +7.8 | +8.4 |
| Expected as per cent of actual changes | 50% | 119% | 100% | 77% | 68% |

[a] In 1949 prices. SOURCE: Long, *The Labor Force*, Table 17, p. 118; and *Survey of Current Business*.
[b] In 1949 prices. SOURCE: Long, *The Labor Force*, Table C-8, p. 356.
[c] Sum of first and second lines.
[d] SOURCE: Long, *The Labor Force*, Table A-6, p. 297.

whole United States population, rather than white urban families for which equation 6 was estimated. The historical trend for the latter is steeper than for the aggregate. On the other hand, secular improvements in the census reporting system, urbanization, and decline in homework for pay which was easily overlooked by interviewers and respondents, lend an opposite bias to the census data. The latter bias is probably strongest in the earliest period, for which the relative discrepancy between actual and estimated is largest (1889-1919 in Table 10). The "fit" since 1919, which is on the whole surprisingly good, shows an interesting trend: the early decade is "overexplained" by equation 6, and the per cent of actual changes "accounted for" by equation 6 declines over time. Implicit in this finding is a suggestion that the negative income elasticity has been decreasing over time,[39] or that the positive wage rate elasticity has been growing over time. Both developments are consistent with the theory underlying the analysis in this paper: they are to be expected, if the degree of substitutability between home production and wage goods has been historically increasing.[40]

This historical change can also be viewed as an omission in equation 6 of a set of relative prices, which are fixed in cross sections. These are relative prices of commercial performance of household tasks. A secular decline in such prices relative to other consumer prices means that the secular increase in opportunity costs of work at home is *underestimated* by equation 6.

On the other hand, it cannot be assumed that productivity in the home remained constant while productivity in the market increased over time. To the extent that productivity in the home increased with the growth of productivity in the market, the female wage rate *overestimates* the increase in the relative price of female labor among its alternative uses. However, in the face of a small family income elasticity of demand for home production and with secularly rising incomes, the growing productivity at home meant a decline of hours of work at home. This, in turn, was likely to mean a shift toward market activities.[41] Thus, to the extent that the increase in $w$ over time overestimates the change in relative prices, a positive effect toward market work is exerted (in a residual fashion) via income effects on home production and leisure.

---

[39] This is consistent with an observed secular flattening of gross income-labor force slopes in cross sections.

[40] See discussion under Work Choices.

[41] To take an extreme illustrative example, if growth of productivity was as rapid in the home as in the market, and the income elasticity of demand for home production close to zero, $w$ would measure nothing else but the decline of hours of work at home. In other words, the income elasticity of hours of work at home would be $-1$. Since the negative income elasticity of total hours of work is surely less than unity, a shift toward market work is clearly implied.

The evaluation of the relative importance of these factors in bringing about the results shown in Table 10 is not undertaken here.[42] It requires a fuller theoretical development and empirical specification of the model presented in this paper.

SECULAR AND CYCLICAL EFFECTS OF TRANSITORY COMPONENTS

The consideration of labor force responses to actual or expected "transitory" changes may have some relevance to historical changes. Educational and occupational trends may put more young married women into the labor market while their husbands acquire formal training or experience on the job and family income is temporarily low. The trends toward early marriages and greater longevity generate prospects of long-lasting reduction in homework after the children are grown. Such expectations may motivate women toward more education and training and induce higher labor force rates throughout the life cycle. The spread of contractual commitments (insurance, installment buying, etc.) to lower income groups may make the adjustment of money income to expenditures more compelling than the adjustment of expenditures to money income.

Analysis of cyclical changes in labor force participation of married women requires an assessment of the effect of transitory changes in income as well as of cyclical change in the female wage rate. The first effect is negative: a decline in employment of head, hence in family income, induces (or temporarily prolongs) labor force activities of wives. On the other hand, cyclical changes in female wage rates or of employment opportunities favor the shifting of market activities to periods of prosperity. The income factor is stressed by the proponents of the "added worker" hypothesis. The employment opportunity is stressed by its opponents. Empirical data do not show any definite cyclical patterns in labor force behavior.

If, for the analysis of work choices of wives, we define the wage rate somewhat more broadly to include employment opportunities, it can be shown that the estimated parameters in equation 3 indeed predict an almost complete cancellation of the two opposing tendencies, hence the absence of pronounced cyclical patterns. Define the wage

[42] But see the very interesting data and hypotheses presented by Long, *The Labor Force*, Ch. 7.

rate as an expected magnitude, that is, a product of the actual wage rate and the probability of being employed. If employment in the community drops by $p$ per cent and actual wage rates remain unchanged, the expected wage rate drops by $p$ per cent. Since the loss of family income is due to the loss of employment, its decline is also $p$ per cent on the average. But with the same per cent decline in $w$ and $x$ (ex ante family income), the net outcome depends, according to equation 3, on the comparative strengths of the negative transitory income elasticity $(\beta_t)$ and the positive wage rate elasticity $(a)$. According to our empirical estimate $(a = +\ 1.5$ in Table 1, $\beta_t = -1.4$ in the modal group, Table 5) the net effect is negligible. Even if a slight margin in favor of the wage rate is likely, the difference is not clear enough to yield discernible patterns.

While the parameter estimates predict no clear-cut cyclical patterns of labor force participation of married women in the aggregate, they point to differential patterns of subgroups depending on employment experience of husbands. In families whose heads have become unemployed, the relative decline in family income is much stronger than the relative decline in the "expected" wage rate of the wife. In such families, therefore, labor force rates of wives are likely to increase in recessions. In all other families, incomes are relatively stable but wage-rate expectations decline somewhat. The likely result in these families is a slight decrease in labor force rates of wives.

These conclusions are confirmed by a recent study[43] of the 1958 recession experience, based on a subsample of the Census Current Population Survey. According to this study, 21.6 per cent of the wives of unemployed husbands increased their labor force participation during the recession period, 16.8 per cent decreased it, and 61.6 per cent did not change. At the same time, 11.1 per cent of the wives of employed husbands increased their labor force participation, 16.6 per cent decreased it, and 72.3 per cent did not change.

[43] Arnold Katz, "Cyclical Unemployment and the Secondary Family Worker," Board of Governors, Federal Reserve System. The paper was presented at the meeting of the Econometric Society, December 1960, in St. Louis, Missouri.

In his paper, Katz presents additional evidence in favor of our hypothesis that families may maintain consumption levels through labor force adjustments to transitory income changes, and that for married women the response to such income changes is quite pronounced. He shows, for example, that a wife's labor force adjustment to her husband's unemployment is more extensive when this idleness is less anticipated.

FAMILY INCOME DISTRIBUTION AND CONSUMPTION[44]

Analysis of economic factors influencing labor force behavior of married women carries a direct implication that family income composition and distribution, consumption behavior, and labor supply are intimately related problems. Decisions of family members about work are related to family income in an ex ante sense and are reflected in the ex post total money income of the family. The labor supply function here presented is an analytical bridge between the distribution of personal income (of family heads, for example) and the distribution of total money income of the family. The income effect on market labor supply, both in its long-run and transitory senses, implies a reduction in income inequality when moving from personal incomes (of heads) to family incomes. The wage-rate effect implies an increase in inequality, since incomes of husbands and market earning powers of wives are positively related. For particular population groups observed, the more prevalent the transitory components in heads' incomes, and the weaker the association between the wage rates of the family members, the greater the equalizing effect of labor supply on family income distribution—and conversely.

With respect to consumption behavior, it is clear that the analysis of economic adjustments to changes in family income must include adjustments in the composition of consumption, particularly between the "visible" items (money expenditures) and the "invisible" ones such as leisure and home production. This is an apparent adjustment, on the money income side, of the money income–money expenditures equation, and is an alternative to adjustment on the expenditure side or in asset position, or both. The three alternatives have distinct implications for a money economy.

Finally, in studying factors affecting family consumption, it is not sufficient to look at sociodemographic characteristics of the family head in order to add explanatory variables to income or to gauge the permanent income of the family. For short-period observations the knowledge of employment status and labor force behavior of family members is of primary importance.[45]

[44] For a more detailed discussion and empirical evidence, see my paper "Labor Supply, Family Income, and Consumption," *American Economic Review*, May 1960, pp. 574-583.
[45] A time-series consumption function based on such data is presented by the author in "Employment and Consumption," *Review of Economics and Statistics*, February 1960, pp. 20-26.

# COMMENT

CLARENCE D. LONG, The Johns Hopkins University

During the last half-century, there has been an enormous increase in the labor force participation of married women. Even now, however, at any given time two of three wives are at home, in school, in institutions, or playing bingo with other wives, and are therefore unwilling or unable to work. Whether various economic and social forces will bring more of these wives into the labor force is an absorbing economic question, especially since wives are the majority of adult women and form the largest source of additional gainful labor. The economic forces that have aroused most attention have been those centering around income or wages. Real incomes have been rising in most western nations. Do these rising incomes have the effect of bringing more wives into the labor force or of driving out some of those now working?

On this question there has been a confusion of evidence, especially as between moment-of-time and over-time relationships. Moment-of-time studies have been of two sorts: One sort, among different localities such as cities or metropolitan areas, have usually shown that the higher a locality's per capita income, adjusted to adult-male equivalents, the lower the labor force participation rates of its females, including those in ages in which most women are married. The other sort, among different income groups in the same locality, have shown even more uniform tendency for husbands in higher income groups to have smaller proportions of wives in the labor force.

On the basis of these moment-of-time relationships, one might expect that a great rise of real incomes over time would have resulted in a notable decline in the tendency of wives to work. On the contrary, the labor force participation of wives has not only failed to decline, it has risen enormously—perhaps sixfold from 1890 to 1960.

What has been the cause of this apparent contradiction between the inverse behavior at a moment of time, and the positive behavior over time? Various studies, including my own,[1] have attributed it to the difference between static factors at a moment of time and dynamic factors over time, the latter including (1) declining burden of house-

[1] Clarence D. Long, *The Labor Force under Changing Income and Employment*, Princeton University Press for National Bureau of Economic Research, 1958, pp. 97-140.

work due to fewer children, better appliances, more outside services for the home; (2) declining hours of work in office and factory jobs, so that more women could perform a dual function of wage earner and wife or mother; and (3) the opening up of new job opportunities for women. Other dynamic forces were also explored: rising wages and improved education of females, relative to males; and the push and pull of young and older males who were, on net balance, leaving the labor force.

My study even attempted some simple statistical illustrations of how these various dynamic factors may have contributed to the inflow of wives into the labor force. But it did not attempt to set up a rigorous analytical model, because the factors seemed too numerous, the relationships among them too complex and changing, and their statistical measurement too inadequate to permit us to fit them into any mathematical framework. Thus, the contradiction between the over-time positive relation and moment-of-time inverse relation was not fully or precisely reconciled.

This gap Jacob Mincer now undertakes to fill by demonstrating that the same model can explain both moment-of-time and over-time relationships.

Most recent investigations into the relation of labor force participation to wages recognize that wages exert both income and price effects on willingness to work. Under the income effect, higher wages should, other things equal, cause the worker to take some of the higher income in the form of more leisure and therefore less labor force participation. Under the price effect, the same wage rise also raises the price or cost of leisure to the worker; his enjoyment of leisure is marred by the thought of how much earnings he is foregoing, so that he is tempted to work more rather than less.

Which effect triumphs? Ever since Lionel Robbins wrote his article on the elasticity of demand for income in terms of effort,[2] economists have recognized that the outcome cannot be predicted on theoretical or a priori grounds, but depends on the relative preferences of individuals as between real income and leisure and thus can only be determined by empirical investigation. Most empirical investigations of moment-of-time relationships do, however, indicate that the income effect has triumphed over the price or substitution effect, and that

[2] "On the Elasticity of Demand for Income in Terms of Effort," *Economica*, June 1930, pp. 123-129.

higher earnings have been associated with lower labor force participation.

Mincer's model adds two novel features to the analysis of the relationship between income and labor force participation.

First, he points out that the choice is not a mere two-way choice between leisure and paid work, but a three-way choice between leisure, paid work, and unpaid housework or family chores. The outcome of this three-way choice will be a family decision. And this family decision will depend on husband's income, wife's earnings, relative desires for market goods, home goods, and leisure; substitutability of market goods for home goods (as whether a wife can buy a washing machine or pay a commercial laundry to take over that part of housework). Mincer simplifies this problem by setting up a model, in which the labor force participation of wives depends on incomes of husbands, earnings of wives, and other factors or tastes.

Second, he makes use of Milton Friedman's consumption theory, namely, that people adjust their consumption expenditures, not to their current incomes (the absolute-income hypothesis) but to their permanent incomes. A family whose head normally earns $10,000 a year tends to spend on consumption, say, $8,000 a year. If the regular income of the family head should drop temporarily to $5,000, the family will continue to spend $8,000 because it has geared its spending and living habits to what it regards as its long-run income and is unwilling to adjust its scale of living to temporary fluctuations in income. But where does it get the wherewithal to pay for the $3,000 excess of consumer spending? It may make up this excess in two broad ways: either by drawing on past savings or future credit—assets of various kinds; or by having some member of the family enter the labor force. Young and poorly educated families may not have much savings or credit; for these, the only alternative may be increased labor force participation of son, daughter, or wife. Mincer's hypothesis is that the labor force participation of the wife may be greater, the smaller the permanent income of the husband, and the smaller the current income in relation to the permanent income.

Having set up his hypothesis, Mincer tests it against a variety of moment-of-time data.

1. Cross-section data, from a number of standard metropolitan areas.

2. Newly available data of the Bureau of Labor Statistics' Survey of Consumer Expenditures in 1950, in which the labor force participation

of wives was classified by age, education, and income of family head, and by wife's earnings, with separate labor force participation rates given for wives whose husbands earned currently much less than when fully employed.

3. Census sample data for March 1957, in which the labor force rates of wives were classified by education of wives (as broadly reflecting their earning power), stratified by husbands' income groups in 1956.

4. Census sample data on long-run work experience for wives (since marriage), by income group of husband in 1955, and short-run labor force rates by the same income groups.

The results of these moment-of-time studies are as follows:

First, he finds, as others have, that wives' labor force participation rates respond negatively to husband's incomes: the more husbands earn, the less wives work. But he finds, in addition, that wives' labor force participation rates respond positively to wives' earning power: the more the wife is capable of earning, the more likely she is to work. Moreover, the wives' positive elasticity with respect to wives' earnings is about double their negative elasticity with respect to husbands' income.

Second, his findings support his hypothesis that wives are more apt to work if husbands' current earnings were below permanent earnings; and that the response of wives' labor force to so-called transitory income is stronger than to permanent income—in fact more than double. Given a period long enough for transitory elements to disappear, the inverse relationship seemed to disappear also, because the strong positive elasticity with respect to wives' earnings more than offset the remaining weak negative elasticity with respect to permanent income of husbands.

Third, the response of labor force to income, both permanent and transitory, is weaker the higher the educational level of family heads over 35—presumably because better educated family heads have other assets which make it unnecessary for wives to work if income is low. Higher-income husbands tend to have higher-earning wives, but the relationship is a weak one.

Mincer, having tested his econometric model against moment-of-time data, is now ready to use it to explain why the labor force participation of wives has grown enormously with income since 1890. For this purpose he uses changes from one census year to the next in full-time earnings of males, in full-time earnings of females, and in family earnings (the sum of the male and female earnings). Full-time and not current earnings are used, because over long periods the problem of transitory incomes is supposed to be not relevant. Inserting these earnings changes into his equation derived from moment-of-time data, he estimates what the change in labor force rates of wives will be from one decade to the next and then compares this predicted change with the actual change recorded from the census data.

The results are noteworthy. For each interdecennial comparison, his model predicts increases in wives' labor force participation. Thus, Mincer observes, there is no apparent contradiction between the findings of the labor force behavior of married women in cross-section and time series. The impression of a contradiction derives from the way the cross-section has been looked at, in terms of gross relations between income of husbands and labor force participation of wives. The gross inverse relation at a moment of time is due largely to two factors: (1) the existence of transitory components in income—without them the cross-sectional negative relationship will hardly be noticeable; and (2) the weak covariation of wives' earning power with husbands' income, a weakness which nullifies the strong tendency of wives' labor force rates to be positively associated with their own earnings. Over long periods of time, the transitory component is largely absent and the female earnings rise as much as male earnings (if not more). This combination, of a big rise in female earnings, and a strong positive relationship between wives' labor force participation and their own earnings, more than offsets the weak income relation with husbands' permanent income.

So much for the description of what Mincer has undertaken to do. Now for an appraisal of his success.

As to moment-of-time relationships, Mincer has proved his case fairly well. I find reasonably convincing his evidence that: (1) transitory-income influences are stronger than permanent-income influences in explaining labor force participation; (2) wives' labor force participation is positively related to wives' own potential earnings, and is stronger than the negative income elasticity; and (3) the wives' earnings, while varying with husbands' earnings, do not vary nearly as much, so that in moment-of-time data the positive wage-rate elasticity of wives is largely cancelled out, leaving the negative income effect triumphant. The evidence that he has amassed rests on data that are independent enough in source and rich enough in classification to establish his hypothesis rather convincingly.

As to his studies over time, he has made something of a case: that the rise of labor force participation of wives has been due to the greater upward pull of their own rising earnings over the downward pull of their families' rising incomes, especially since full-time wages of females have gone up faster than those of males.

A number of features of the study suggest, however, that more is needed than two variables—earnings of husbands and of wives—to explain the labor force behavior of wives in the long-run periods.

For one thing, the equation does not predict the over-all changes fully but only four-fifths of the rise. This underprediction need not be very disturbing; on the contrary, it would be suspicious if Mincer could fully explain the entire rise in labor force of wives for 70 years by only two variables. In view of the many other factors which could help explain this rise, it is perhaps a virtue of his equation that it leaves some room for their impact.

For another thing, the equation does not predict decade movements very accurately. For the three-decade changes between 1890 and 1920, it is far off indeed. (However, since the census labor force data were slightly undercounted in 1890 and 1920 and greatly overcounted in 1910, Mincer was doubtless justified in bypassing the decade-to-decade movements in the first 30 years and merely studying the whole change from 1890 to 1920. But even that change is twice as great as his equation predicts.) For the next decade, 1919-29, the equation overpredicts the actual change by a fifth. For 1939-40 and 1949-59, it underpredicts the actual changes by wide margins. Only in 1929-39, a decade of depression—when, incidentally, transitory income, ignored in this equation, might have been expected to operate—was the prediction exactly right.

Next, the study does not take account of one of the most interesting developments of those decades—the behavior of the labor force of Negro women. Yet, Negro wives show the same inverse labor force income relationship as white wives at a moment of time, and the wages of Negro women have probably risen not only more rapidly than those of Negro men, but also more rapidly than those of white women. I have the impression that employment opportunities for Negro women have also improved relatively. Yet the labor force participation rate of Negro females has declined since 1900 and especially since 1930. The case of Negro women provides a severe challenge to an econometric model which attempts to unify the explanation of moment-of-time and over-time behavior. A model which purports to explain dynamic increases also carries the obligation of explaining dynamic decreases. I think the data are available for such a study, at least since 1940. In any event, the case of Negro wives calls for discussion.

In addition, although Mincer indicates that the possession of young children makes the labor force–income relationship at a moment of time more steeply inverse, his model over time makes no allowance for the decline of young children relative to the number of wives. This would presumably help explain why his model does not predict the full rise in labor force participation of wives.

Finally, the study does not take advantage of the existence of recent annual data to test the year-to-year changes in labor force participation of wives against the year-to-year changes in husbands' incomes and wives' earnings, and using, of course, both permanent and temporary incomes. If Mincer does not feel that the annual statistics of labor force and earnings are adequate for such a test, his discussions should at least point out the statistical and analytical difficulties.

On the whole, this paper impresses me as first-rate. The ideas are fertile, the analysis stimulating, the empirical applications resourceful, especially with regard to the cross-sectional data. I do not regard the case as proven. Before Mincer can be said to have fully demonstrated the usefulness of his model in resolving the apparent contradiction between inverse cross-sectional behavior and positive dynamic behavior, he will have to carry out further empirical investigation: First, separate investigation of the labor force behavior of Negro wives both at a moment of time and over time. Second, further cross-sectional analysis of wives' behavior before 1950. Third, an analysis of wives' labor force behavior in detailed localities, for example rural and urban areas or individual cities of the United States and of other countries. Fourth, an analysis of wives' labor force behavior over time, by age, education, and number of children, or presence and absence of children. Fifth, an analysis of labor force behavior from one year to the next, to test the flexibility of the model, especially the functional relationship of the labor force to transitory income.

Until these further studies are made, however, this study must remain as I find it now: not really an empirical explanation of the dynamic behavior of the labor force participation of wives, but an idea for such future investigation. On the basis of this idea, a scholar with an appetite for hard work would be justified in launching an extensive inquiry into the dynamic behavior of labor force of wives. I hope it will be Mincer who does it. In any event, we should be grateful to him for a careful and imaginative piece of work.

# A Nonunion Market for White Collar Labor

GEORGE P. SHULTZ

UNIVERSITY OF CHICAGO

THIS is a report on the labor market for female clerical employees of banks and insurance companies in Boston. The research is part of the broad effort to appraise the operation of labor markets in the United States so that their strengths and limitations as wage-determining and labor-allocating devices are better understood, and so that policy suggestions can be based on a firm factual foundation.

More specifically, study of a white collar labor market serves these purposes: (1) The field is important for its own sake, since this occupational group is large and growing, and there has been little previous wage research in the white collar field.[1] (2) The conditions that prevail here offer important contrasts to those encountered in many recent wage studies, which have concentrated on collective bargaining in manufacturing industries. Orme Phelps, for example, has suggested the importance of concentrating on differentiation if research is to be relevant to the whole labor force rather than only to manufacturing or to unionized situations.[2] (3) Studies of nonunion labor markets can contribute to efforts to isolate the effects of unions on wages. For the most part, studies of the impact of unions have proceeded without

NOTE: The research reported here was conducted by the author in collaboration with Irwin L. Herrnstadt and Elbridge S. Puckett when all three were associated with the Department of Economics and Industrial Relations Section, Massachusetts Institute of Technology. The research was completed in 1956 and reported in summary fashion at the Tenth Annual Meeting of the Industrial Relations Research Association (September, 1957) in a paper entitled "Wage Determination in a Non-Union Labor Market." The present paper draws freely on the earlier one, while reporting the research results in greater detail. Carol Fernstrom provided editorial assistance and help in preparation of the tables and Douglass V. Brown valuable comments on the manuscript.

The research received financial support from the Sloan Research Fund of the School of Industrial Management and from the Industrial Relations Section, Massachusetts Institute of Technology.

I thank my colleagues for their help on the research and Massachusetts Institute of Technology for financial support of the project.

[1] Subsequent to the date of the Conference on Labor Economics, a study of the clerical labor market in Madison, Wisconsin, became available. The findings of this more recent study are strikingly similar to those reported here. See Eaton Hall Conant, "Wages and the Behavior of Firms and Workers in a Clerical Labor Market," University of Wisconsin, Ph.D. Dissertation, 1960.

[2] Orme Phelps, "A Structural Model of the United States Labor Market," *Industrial and Labor Relations Review*, April 1957, pp. 402-423.

the benefit of extensive information about nonunion labor markets in the United States today. (4) Nonunion labor markets predominate in the United States, and it is important to understand how they work as a basis for decisions on a wide range of economic issues. As an example, much of the discussion of the wage-push inflation question assumes that wage changes are transmitted almost automatically from one sector of the economy to another, from the union to the nonunion sector, without reference to particular labor market conditions. Knowledge about the mechanisms of a market such as the one under review can test this assumption.

The pages that follow present a description of the research approach, methods, and sources of data; information about employment and wages in the field during the period studied; an analysis of the reaction of the firms studied to their labor market; information on the characteristics and market behavior of their employees; a view of the role of various market intermediaries in this situation; and general conclusions.

## Research Methods and Sources of Data

The limited research resources available for this study were spread over both the demand and supply sides of this labor market in order to obtain a comprehensive view and draw together two areas of theory and research that are too often treated separately: wage studies focusing on demand conditions and collective bargaining on the one hand, and, on the other, labor force and labor mobility analysis.

Concentration on one type of industry makes it possible both to trace a broadly identifiable set of demand conditions through the wage policies and actions of a related group of firms and to get an understanding of the labor market behavior of employees in the industry and of the labor supply conditions facing the firms. Limited research resources and a desire for fairly comprehensive information led to concentration on the banking and insurance industry groups and on female clerical workers as areas for research.

The data in Table 1 show both the strength and weakness of this selection. The banking and insurance industries are quantitatively significant in the Boston area and clerical employment dominates these industries, but other industries employ even larger numbers of clerical workers. The sample of employees interviewed as part of the research was drawn from those employed by banking and insurance firms and

## TABLE 1

### CLERICAL WORKERS BY INDUSTRY, SEX, AND PROPORTION OF INDUSTRY EMPLOYMENT, BOSTON METROPOLITAN AREA, 1950

| Industry | Employment | | | Industrial Distribution of Clerical Workers | | Clerical Workers, by Proportion of Industry Employment | |
|---|---|---|---|---|---|---|---|
| | All Workers | Male Clericals | Female Clericals | Males | Females | Males | Females |
| Construction | 53,113 | 728 | 1,442 | 1.3% | 1.3% | 1.4% | 2.7% |
| Manufacturing | 262,010 | 14,944 | 21,960 | 26.9 | 20.3 | 5.7 | 8.4 |
| Transportation, communication and other public utilities | 77,741 | 7,621 | 13,729 | 13.7 | 12.7 | 9.8 | 17.7 |
| Transportation | 48,725 | 5,501 | 2,708 | 9.8 | 2.5 | 11.2 | 5.6 |
| Communication | 14,974 | 751 | 9,086 | 1.4 | 8.4 | 5.0 | 60.7 |
| Other public utilities | 14,042 | 1,369 | 1,935 | 2.5 | 1.8 | 9.7 | 13.8 |
| Wholesale and retail trade | 200,968 | 9,259 | 19,621 | 16.7 | 18.1 | 4.6 | 9.8 |
| Finance, insurance and real estate | 53,242 | 5,228 | 21,724 | 9.4 | 20.0 | 9.8 | 40.8 |
| Banking and other finance | 17,247 | 3,365 | 7,589 | 6.0 | 7.0 | 19.5 | 44.0 |
| Insurance and real estate | 35,995 | 1,863 | 14,135 | 3.4 | 13.0 | 5.1 | 39.3 |
| Business and repair services | 24,872 | 927 | 2,763 | 1.7 | 2.5 | 3.7 | 11.1 |
| Personal services | 55,090 | 601 | 2,226 | 1.1 | 2.1 | 1.1 | 4.0 |
| Professional and related services | 104,931 | 1,692 | 13,346 | 3.1 | 12.3 | 1.5 | 12.8 |
| Public administration | 54,556 | 13,852 | 9,400 | 25.0 | 8.7 | 25.4 | 17.2 |
| Other[a] | 28,430 | 612 | 2,212 | 1.1 | 2.0 | 2.1 | 7.8 |
| Total | 914,953 | 55,464 | 108,423 | 100.0% | 100.0% | 6.1% | 11.9% |

SOURCE: *1950 United States Census of Population, Massachusetts*, Bulletin P-C 21, Department of Commerce, Bureau of the Census, pp. 277-278.

[a] Includes agriculture, forestry and fishing, mining, entertainment and recreation.

therefore may not represent the supply side of the whole market for clerical workers in Boston. We are dealing here, then, with a submarket, a part of the general market for clerical employees.

Basic descriptive and statistical information about the Boston area and about banking and insurance is available from state and federal government sources and from various private financial services. These data provided the general background for our more detailed research. The detailed study is based for the most part on information supplied by 13 banks and insurance companies in the area and by 158 of their employees.[3] Most of the data were collected in 1954, 1955, and 1956, though some use is made of information referring to later years. Each of these firms supplied a list of its female, nonsupervisory employees, from which 15 in the case of large firms and 10 in the case of small firms were drawn at random. Tables 2 and 3 provide data on the size of firms in the study compared with all banking and insurance establishments in the area.

Each firm was asked for a wide range of factual information about its operations, particularly with respect to wage and employment matters. While the information obtained from the firms varied considerably in both quality and quantity, it was sufficient in every case to be useful and, in some cases, was voluminous and most helpful. On the basis of this information interviews were held with individuals in each firm in an effort to obtain judgments on policy questions and interpretations of the data collected from their firm.

Each employee was interviewed privately by a member of the research group and was assured that the responses were confidential. Most interviews took place at the respondent's home, but some were conducted at other convenient places such as an office in the Massa-

---

[3] The 13 firms were selected to assure that each would have a significant number of female clerical employees and that the unit studied would be responsible for its own policies. This led to elimination of all firms with fewer than 100 employees in all and those with home offices outside the area. The total possible number of firms was thus reduced from some 674 (including 417 offices of insurance agents) to 27, accounting for 54 per cent of the employment. These 27 firms were then separated by size (more and less than 750 employees) and by industry (banking, life insurance, and insurance other than life). Two large firms and 3 small ones were then selected from each industry, though 2 of the smaller firms were later dropped from the study. In one case, the firm decided to shift its operations to a suburban location just as the study was getting under way and preferred not to be involved simultaneously in a move and a study of employment problems. In the other case, the firm decided not to be involved in the study, apparently because of reluctance to permit interviews with a random sample of its employees. Where there was any choice in selecting firms, it was made at random.

chusetts Institute of Technology or a downtown coffee shop. The company cafeteria of one firm was used, and the quality of the interviews obtained there indicated that the results were not biased because of the location. Each employee was asked for considerable demographic and household information and for a fairly detailed work history. The

TABLE 2

Total Banking and Insurance Establishments in Boston and Brookline (A) Compared with Firms Having Home Offices in Boston or Brookline and Employing More Than 100 People (B), September 1953

| | Establishments in A | | Firms in B | | |
| Industry | Number of Units | Number of Employees | Number of Units | Number of Employees | Employees in B as Per Cent of Total in B |
|---|---|---|---|---|---|
| Banking | 90 | 9,739 | 14 | 8,354 | 86% |
| Insurance | 584 | 27,998 | 13 | 12,211 | 44 |
| Life | 47 | 10,932 | 5 | 6,921 | 63 |
| Other than life | 120 | 11,981 | 8 | 5,290 | 44 |
| Agents | 417 | 5,085 | 0 | – | – |
| Total | 674 | 37,737 | 27 | 20,565 | 54%a |

a Excluding agents, this is 63 per cent.

interviews were conducted informally, with interviewees encouraged to talk freely, but in areas relevant to the study.

Information was also obtained from interviews with representatives of private employment agencies, private clerical schools, public and parochial high schools, and from the Massachusetts Employment Service. These interviews focused on the scope of the placement activities of these organizations and the ways in which the counsellors worked with employers and those seeking work.

*General Information About the Area and Industry*

The period 1948-56 was one of generally full employment for clerical workers in the Boston area, as in most other areas of the United States, though the situation in Boston eased perceptibly in 1949 and 1954. Reports on job openings listed by the State Employment Service (SES), voluminous newspaper advertisements for clerical help, the testimony of employment managers, high school guidance counsellors and other observers, and data on employment and the number of commercial-

TABLE 3

BANKING AND INSURANCE FIRMS WITH HOME OFFICES IN BOSTON OR BROOKLINE, EMPLOYING MORE THAN 100 PEOPLE COMPARED WITH FIRMS STUDIED, 1953

| Industry | Firms in Area (100 or more employees) | | | | Medium-Sized Firms (100 to 749 employees) | | | | Large Firms (750 or more employees) | | | |
|---|---|---|---|---|---|---|---|---|---|---|---|---|
| | All Firms | Number Employed | Firms Studied | Number Employed | All Firms | Number Employed | Firms Studied | Number Employed | All Firms | Number Employed | Firms Studied | Number Employed |
| Banking | 14 | 8,354 | 5 | 4,745 | 11 | 2,456 | 3 | 547 | 3 | 5,898 | 2 | 4,198 |
| Insurance | 13 | 12,211 | 8 | 9,028 | 7 | 2,001 | 4 | 1,070 | 6 | 10,210 | 4 | 7,958 |
| Life | 5 | 6,921 | 4 | 6,329 | 3 | 971 | 2 | 379 | 2 | 5,950 | 2 | 5,950 |
| Other | 8 | 5,290 | 4 | 3,126 | 4 | 1,030 | 2 | 691 | 4 | 4,260 | 2 | 2,435 |
| Total | 27 | 20,565 | 13 | 13,773 | 18 | 4,457 | 7 | 1,617 | 9 | 16,108 | 6 | 12,156 |

course graduates seeking work each year all confirm this general characterization of employment conditions. More particularly, this was a period of rising employment in the finance sector of the Boston economy, reflecting the dominant theme of growth in demand for their services experienced by the great majority of firms, including 11 of the 13 covered in this study.

Estimates made by the U.S. Bureau of Labor Statistics show that employment in finance rose by about 12 per cent between 1951 and 1956. In contrast, the rate of increase in nonfarm employment in the Boston area was about 4 per cent and in manufacturing employment was about the same in 1956 as it had been in 1951.[4] Moreover, personnel turnover among clerical workers is high, as the young girls who make up the bulk of employees move into and out of the labor force as well as among jobs. Even a firm with stable clerical employment, on the average, will constantly need to attract new employees.

Data compiled by the BLS indicate that clerical rates of pay in the Boston area rose by about 55 per cent between 1948 and 1956, a gain larger than for production workers in the manufacturing industries of Massachusetts and of Boston.[5] The year-by-year increases in clerical rates are shown in Table 4. Note that the rate of increase was smaller between 1949-50 and 1954-55 than for other yearly intervals.

The wage structure for office occupations in banks and insurance companies is broadly the same throughout the country, as shown in Table 5. In addition, as Chart 1 indicates, the structure of rates has been stable in Boston from 1948 through 1958. These facts may be accounted for in part by the broad similarity of the basic occupational skills used by firms in office work. While a given job tends to have a somewhat wider content in a small firm than in a large one, and the employee in the small firm probably develops more job knowledge

[4] *Employment and Earnings*, Bureau of Labor Statistics, Annual Supplement, June 1957, p. 81.
[5] Average weekly earnings of production workers in manufacturing in the Boston area rose by about 21 per cent between 1951 and 1956 compared with a 32.4 per cent rise in the standard weekly salaries of women office workers in finance, insurance, and real estate between the same years in the area. Over the entire period, 1948 to 1956, average weekly earnings of manufacturing production workers in Massachusetts rose by about 40 per cent. The rise for women office workers in the Boston area for the same period was 54.6 per cent. Production worker percentages were computed from data appearing in *Ibid*, p. 127 and the May, 1954 issue, p. 110. The wage concept used is not strictly comparable with that for the computations of changes in wages for women office workers. The differences in magnitude of movement are great enough, however, to substantiate the general statement made in the text.

TABLE 4

STANDARD WEEKLY SALARIES OF WOMEN OFFICE WORKERS IN THE FINANCE,
INSURANCE, AND REAL ESTATE DIVISION IN BOSTON,
JANUARY 1948 TO SEPTEMBER 1956

| Item | Jan. 1948 | Jan. 1949 | Jan. 1950 | Mar. 1951 | Apr. 1952 | Mar. 1953 | Mar. 1954 | Apr. 1955 | Sep 195 |
|---|---|---|---|---|---|---|---|---|---|
| Index[a] (1953=100) | 77.1 | 80.9 | 84.0 | 90.0 | 95.3 | 100.0 | 104.9 | 107.8 | 119 |
| Per cent of increase | 1948 to 1949 | 1949 to 1950 | 1950 to 1951 | 1951 to 1952 | 1952 to 1953 | 1953 to 1954 | 1954 to 1955 | 1955 to 1956 | 194 to tc 19. |
| | 5.0 | 3.8 | 6.9 | 5.9 | 5.0 | 4.9 | 2.8 | 10.6 | 54. |

NOTE: Salaries are based on the following selected jobs: Bookkeeping-machine operators, class B; comptometer operators; file clerks, class A and class B; order clerks; payroll clerks; key-punch operators; office girls; secretaries; general stenographers; switchboard operators; switchboard operator-receptionists; tabulating-machine operators; general transcribing-machine operators; and typists, class A and class B. Since data were not collected for secretaries, key-punch operators, and tabulating-machine operators in 1948, 1949, and 1950, data for those years are based on the 12 other jobs. Data for comparable jobs were used to make the link between 1950 and 1951.

[a] In computing the indexes and percentage increase, the average weekly salaries for each of the selected occupations for each year were multiplied by the average of March 1953 and March 1954 employment in the job. These weighted earnings for individual occupations were then totaled to obtain an aggregate for each year. Finally, the ratio of the aggregate for a given year to the aggregate for the base period (March 1953) was computed and the result multiplied by the base year index (100) to get the index for the given year. There were changes in the minimum size of establishments covered between January 1950 and March 1951 (26 to 21) and between April 1952 and March 1953 (21 to 51), and no adjustment was made in the data to make average weekly earnings comparable for all periods. The use of constant employment weights, however, eliminates the effect of changes in the proportion of workers represented in each job included in the data.

that is strictly organizational in nature, the basic skills involved are easily identifiable, commonly used, and transferable from one firm to another. This does not mean, however, that individual performance on a given job is uniform; indeed, substantial quality differences appear to characterize work on these jobs.

This uniformity of job content helps to explain the clustering of rates of pay for particular jobs. For example, 80 per cent of the establishments employing inexperienced typists in Boston in the winter of 1957-58 and having a specified minimum hiring rate fell within a 30 per cent rate range; 60 per cent of the establishments fell within a 12½ per cent range. Furthermore, some of this dispersion is explained by

TABLE 3

COMPARISON OF WAGE STRUCTURES IN THIRTEEN CITIES, OFFICE OCCUPATIONS OF WOMEN IN FINANCE, WINTER 1957-58

(in numbered rank of occupation in salary structure)

| Cities | Bookkeeping-Machine Operators, Class B | Accounting Clerks, Class B | File Clerks, Class B | Key-punch Operators | Secretaries | Stenographers, General | Switch-board Operators | Typists, Class A | Typists, Class B |
|---|---|---|---|---|---|---|---|---|---|
| Northeast | | | | | | | | | |
| Boston | 7 | 6 | 9 | 5 | 1 | 2–4 | 2–4 | 2–4 | 8 |
| Newark-Jersey City | 7 | 6 | 9 | 3 | 1 | 2 | 4 | 5 | 8 |
| New York City | 5–7 | 5–7 | 9 | 5–7 | 1 | 3 | 2 | 4 | 8 |
| Philadelphia | 6 | 7 | 9 | 5 | 1 | 2–3 | 2–3 | 4 | 8 |
| South | | | | | | | | | |
| Atlanta | 5 | 7 | 9 | 6 | 1 | 3 | 2 | 4 | 8 |
| Baltimore | 7 | 6 | 9 | 4 | 1 | 2–3 | 5 | 2–3 | 8 |
| Dallas | 7 | 5–6 | 9 | 5–6 | 1 | 2 | 3 | 4 | 8 |
| North Central | | | | | | | | | |
| Chicago | 5 | 7 | 9 | 6 | 1 | 2–3 | 2–3 | 4 | 8 |
| Cleveland | 6 | 5 | 9 | 7 | 1 | 3 | 4 | 2 | 8 |
| Minneapolis-St. Paul | 7 | 4 | 9 | 6 | 1 | 3 | 2 | 5 | 8 |
| West | | | | | | | | | |
| St. Louis | 6 | 7 | 8–9 | 3–5 | 1 | 3–5 | 2 | 3–5 | 8–9 |
| Los Angeles-Long Beach | 7 | 6 | 9 | 4 | 1 | 2 | 3 | 5 | 8 |
| San Francisco-Oakland | 7 | 6 | 9 | 5 | 1 | 2 | 3 | 4 | 8 |

SOURCE: *Wages and Related Benefits*, Bureau of Labor Statistics, Feb., 1959.

## CHART 1

Bk = Bookkeeping machine operator, B   TA = Typist, A
FC = Clerk, file B                     TB = Typist, B
St = Stenographer, general             AC = Clerk, accounting, B
Sw = Switchboard operator, general     KO = Key-punch operator
                                       Se = Secretary

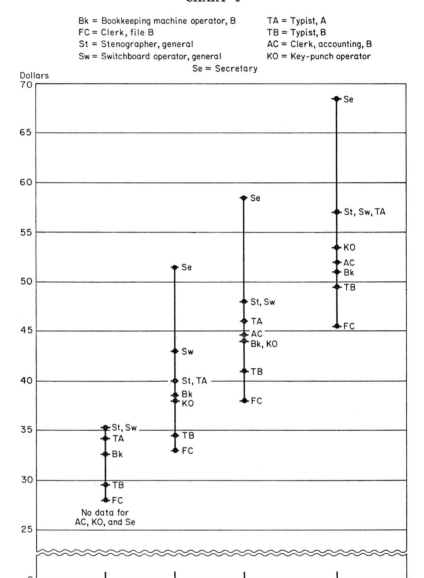

dispersion in scheduled weekly hours. Table 6 shows that weekly hours are shorter in finance than in most other industries. In finance, most workers are on a 36¼- or 37½-hour week. These differences in hours of work tend to offset the differentials in weekly rates of pay by industry

TABLE 6

SCHEDULED WEEKLY HOURS OF OFFICE WORKERS IN BOSTON, BY INDUSTRY,
WINTER 1957-58

(per cent of employment)

| INDUSTRY | 35 | Under 40 HOURS | | | Totalᵃ | 40 | Over 40 |
|---|---|---|---|---|---|---|---|
| | | 36¼ | 37½ | 38¾ | Totala | 40 | Over 40 |
| All Industries | 8 | 10 | 25 | 8 | 66 | 34 | 1 |
| Manufacturing | 9 | 2 | 15 | 9 | 36 | 63 | 2 |
| Public utilities | 3 | — | 55 | — | 58 | 42 | — |
| Wholesale trade | — | 8 | 31 | 4 | 51 | 49 | — |
| Retail trade | 12 | 7 | 19 | 6 | 78 | 22 | — |
| Finance | 9 | 22 | 28 | 11 | 94 | 6 | — |
| Services | 19 | 6 | 13 | — | 56 | 43 | 1 |

SOURCE: *Wages and Related Benefits*, BLS, Feb., 1959.
ᵃ Includes weekly schedules other than those shown separately.

group, so that, on an hourly basis, finance would move up in the
community wage structure, and the width of the band of rates for
particular jobs would be narrowed (see Table 7). Nevertheless, the
weekly take-home pay in finance is relatively low.

TABLE 7

EEKLY PAY FOR WOMEN IN OFFICE JOBS IN BOSTON, BY INDUSTRY, WINTER 1957-58

(dollars)

| cupation | Manu-facturing | Non-Manu-facturing | Public Utilities | Whole-sale Trade | Retail Trade | Finance | Services |
|---|---|---|---|---|---|---|---|
| okkeeping, class B | 61.00 | 54.00 | — | 62.50 | 52.00 | 51.00 | — |
| counting clerks, class B | 60.50 | 55.50 | 62.00 | 59.00 | 51.50 | 52.00 | 60.00 |
| le clerks, class B | 50.50 | 46.00 | 48.50 | 49.50 | 44.50 | 45.50 | 48.50 |
| y-punch operators | 59.50 | 56.00 | 62.00 | 63.50 | 53.00 | 53.50 | — |
| cretaries | 74.50 | 70.50 | 85.50 | 74.50 | 69.50 | 68.50 | 66.00 |
| enographers, general | 64.00 | 59.50 | 64.50 | 67.50 | 55.50 | 57.00 | 55.50 |
| itchboard operators | 66.50 | 56.50 | 67.00 | 63.50 | 55.00 | 57.00 | 49.00 |
| pists, class A | 57.00 | 60.00 | — | 72.00 | — | 57.00 | 61.50 |
| pists, class B | 54.00 | 50.00 | 50.50 | 55.00 | 49.00 | 49.50 | 48.50 |

SOURCE: *Wages and Related Benefits*, BLS, Feb., 1959.

Comparison among areas of weekly wages for women office workers in finance shows that Boston ranks about tenth among thirteen cities for which data are available (Table 8). However, weekly hours are sharply lower in Boston than in most cities,[6] so that on an hourly basis Boston would move up to about the middle of the distribution.

## UNIONIZATION

The employee groups involved in the study were not unionized in 1956, nor were there any serious attempts to unionize them in the post-World War II decade on which this study concentrated. From time to time, general statements about white-collar organizing drives were issued from a federation headquarters or the office of a national union, but nothing concrete took place in Boston banking and insurance offices. By the winter of 1957-58, the only industry group in which a high proportion of office workers was organized was public utilities (switchboard operators are classified as office workers, and most telephone company employees in Boston are members of independent unions). For all industries, 15 to 19 per cent of office workers were employed in establishments where their occupations were covered by collective bargaining agreements.[7] White-collar labor, then, may be characterized as a nonunion labor market.

## SERVICE-RENDERING INDUSTRIES

Banking and insurance firms are essentially service rendering rather than goods producing in their functions. It is characteristic of these firms that, while wage costs are small in relation to the total amount of money handled, they are large in relation to the cost of the service rendered. Firms use, as one measure of their own effectiveness, ratios of labor cost to total costs and such ratios are often used by public examiners. Thus, wage rates, as a central element in wage costs, are of far more than passing importance to banks and insurance companies.

Operating policies tend to reflect the responsibility as trustees for large amounts of the public's money, which is exercised by these firms.

---

[6] U.S. Bureau of Labor Statistics, *Wages and Related Benefits, Nineteen Labor Markets, 1957-58*, BLS, Bulletin No. 1224-20 (issued Feb. 1959), p. 55.

[7] The individual industry percentages were: manufacturing, 20-24; public utilities, 75-79; wholesale trade, 15-19; retail trade, 10-14, and services, 0-9. The survey did not have sufficient coverage to warrant separate presentation of data for finance, insurance, and real estate, but information collected in the course of this study suggests that finance falls in the 0-9 per cent group. The all-industry percentage for plant workers was 70-79 (*ibid.*, p. 48).

TABLE 8

WAGE LEADERSHIP AMONG THIRTEEN CITIES, OFFICE OCCUPATIONS OF WOMEN IN FINANCE, WINTER 1957-58

(in numbered rank of city in payment of wages)

| City | Bookkeeping Machine Operators, Class B | Accounting Clerks, Class B | File Clerks, Class B | Key-punch Operators | Secretaries | Stenographers, General | Switchboard Operators | Typists, Class A | Typists, Class B |
|---|---|---|---|---|---|---|---|---|---|
| **Northeast** | | | | | | | | | |
| Boston | 10 | 9 | 9–10 | 9–10 | 12 | 11 | 11–12 | 7–8 | 7–8 |
| Newark-Jersey City | 7 | 6 | 6 | 5–6 | 6 | 6 | 6 | 6 | 6 |
| New York City | 2–3 | 5 | 3 | 4 | 2 | 4 | 2 | 5 | 4–5 |
| Philadelphia | 8 | 8 | 9–10 | 8 | 10 | 9 | 10 | 7–8 | 9 |
| **South** | | | | | | | | | |
| Atlanta | 6 | 11–12 | 11 | 12–13 | 9 | 8 | 7–8 | 11 | 10–11 |
| Baltimore | 13 | 11–12 | 13 | 9–10 | 11 | 13 | 13 | 12 | 13 |
| Dallas | 12 | 10 | 12 | 12–13 | 7 | 7 | 7–8 | 9–10 | 10–11 |
| **North Central** | | | | | | | | | |
| Chicago | 1 | 1 | 1–2 | 1 | 1 | 1 | 1 | 1 | 1 |
| Cleveland | 2–3 | 2 | 1–2 | 5–6 | 4 | 5 | 5 | 2–3 | 2 |
| Minneapolis-St. Paul | 9 | 7 | 7–8 | 11 | 8 | 10 | 9 | 13 | 7–8 |
| **West** | | | | | | | | | |
| St. Louis | 11 | 13 | 7–8 | 7 | 13 | 12 | 11–12 | 9–10 | 12 |
| Los Angeles-Long Beach | 4–5 | 4 | 5 | 2 | 3 | 2 | 4 | 4 | 4–5 |
| San Francisco-Oakland | 4–5 | 3 | 4 | 3 | 5 | 3 | 3 | 2–3 | 3 |

SOURCE: *Wages and Related Benefits*, BLS, Feb., 1959.

These organizations are touched throughout with the public interest, and there is a long history of regulation by state and federal governments to remind management of its obligations. The impact on wage policy of these public interest and regulatory aspects of banking and insurance businesses may be indirect and somewhat elusive, but—particularly for firms writing policies required by law, as workmen's compensation or automobile liability insurance—the direction of pressures is clear. The atmosphere within which many of the firms work out their wage policies can be summed up: money held in trust must be handled conservatively; increases in costs must be justified in terms of public service rendered at the minimum possible cost.

Despite many broad similarities in their immediate environment and operating problems, firms in this sector also vary in important respects. Some are stock companies and others mutual companies; the public's stake in the efficiency of their operations varies; some are quite small in size and others are huge in the scale of their operations; the markets they serve vary in rate of growth, number of competitors, and in other ways. While all variations have implications for their operations in the labor market, this is a market characterized on the demand side by firms touched with the public interest and accustomed to moving slowly and conservatively on matters affecting costs of operations.

## The Firms and Their Wage and Employment Policies

William Bowen,[8] at the beginning of his summary of the findings of certain labor market studies, states, ". . . perhaps the most dominant theme of these studies . . . is their emphasis on the diversity of ways in which individual firms react to changes in the 'scarcity' of labor." The elements of this diversity and how various courses of action develop may be expressed in general terms before turning more specifically to the findings of this study.

[8] William G. Bowen, *The Wage-Price Issue: A Theoretical Analysis* (Princeton University Press, 1960), pp. 94-95. His full discussion runs from pp. 93-103. The labor-market studies on which he relies and from which I, too, have drawn are: R. A. Lester, *Hiring Practices and Labor Competition*, Industrial Relations Section, Princeton University, 1954; idem, *Adjustments to Labor Shortages; Management Practices and Institutional Controls in an Area of Expanding Employment*, Industrial Relations Section, Princeton University, 1955; Charles A. Myers and George P. Shultz, *The Dynamics of a Labor Market*, New York, Prentice-Hall, 1951; and Lloyd G. Reynolds, *The Structure of Labor Markets; Wages and Labor Mobility in Theory and Practice*, New York, Harper, 1951.

## MODEL OF A FIRM'S RESPONSE TO CHANGES IN ITS
### LABOR MARKET CONDITIONS

It may be useful to start with the growing consciousness of the firm that it has problems on its hands as it faces a tightening labor market. The firm's need for labor may be growing rapidly, as it was for many of the firms included in this study. Even without growth in demand, employment of a labor force characterized by high turnover means that hiring is a constant activity. Let the labor market tighten and problems appear for the firm, particularly at the hiring level. If the firm is accustomed to paying low rates for the labor it hires and to a market where jobs are scarcer than people, it is likely to view with alarm the gradual rise in the rates it pays.

Growing consciousness of the problem leads to increased effort to deal with it. A personnel department is formed with responsibilities for policy as well as for routine employment. Information is sought about rates paid by other firms and the methods they use to deal with the problem. Many of these methods may substitute for, or at least provide an important complement to, increases in wage rates—advertising, visits to high schools, more careful employment interviewing, and other means. The tastes of present and prospective employees may be cultivated by provision of special features in working conditions. Quality standards may be changed, at least on certain jobs, and efforts may be made to see how part-time help can be used or used more effectively. These measures serve to enlarge the labor pool from which the firm draws. It may be necessary also to reorganize jobs. To some extent capital expenditures for laborsaving equipment may be substituted for labor where there is great and apparently lasting scarcity in a particular occupation. The personnel department is the prime originator and administrator within the organization of this nonwage response.

The firm may also be forced to change its wages, especially as its competitors' demands on the market increase. Strategies may vary, depending in part upon employment needs and success with nonwage appeals. The firm may decide to be a wage leader, hoping to attract a high quality of applicants; conversely, it may plan on high turnover and low quality as a result of lagging wages, in favor of hoped-for lower costs.

In deciding on the relative weight to put on nonwage and wage forms of adjustment, there are a number of factors to be borne in mind.

As Bowen states,[9] "the basic economic appeal of these non-wage forms of adjustment is that they may permit a rather subtle yet a profitable form of wage discrimination." Thus, a wage increase at the hiring level is visible and will have an impact on the balance of the wage structure. Within limits, this is not true for many nonwage methods of adjustment. In addition, the firm may consider the reversibility of its actions should market conditions change. It is much easier to reduce buying effort than to cut wages. The responses of a firm to variations in labor market conditions, then, are likely to be quite diverse. Wages are an important element of response but are far from the only one.

## COMPANY PERSONNEL POLICIES

The emergence and development during the decade following World War II of explicit personnel policies in the firms studied and of organizational arrangements for administering them is one of the clear findings of this study. The general tightness of the labor market, following an era in the 1930's and early 1940's when the supply of labor was generally ample and when the job security offered by banks and insurance companies gave them a preferred position in the labor market, not only influenced wage levels and wage policies, but also precipitated a complete re-evaluation of personnel policies. With the exception of two of the smaller firms, one or more of the following changes were evident in all the firms studied.

1. Advent and expansion of personnel departments. In several of the smaller firms where the need for personnel departments had never been felt, additional resources were allocated to the tasks of procuring and maintaining an adequate labor force. In the case of one company, too small to bear the cost alone, a personnel department was set up to serve two companies which were related in a financial and geographic sense. In all the companies, personnel problems were accorded more attention at the policy-making level. In some cases, specific responsibility devolved upon a man also engaged in other policy problems. In other cases, especially in larger firms, a man of policy-making calibre was given the status of a high company official and the full-time job of organizing the personnel function in the firm.

2. New methods of recruiting labor. With the exception of one of the larger firms, the pre-world War II practice had been to rely on walk-in applicants to fill the company's personnel needs. Reliance on walk-ins

[9] Bowen, *The Wage-Price Issue*, p. 96.

and informal channels of recruitment now proved insufficient and was supplemented by more active efforts to find workers and to impress them with the merits of working for the particular company. The larger firms developed active recruitment efforts for members of high-school graduating classes and, in some cases, combined this recruiting with opportunities for part-time work in the last part of the senior year. Smaller firms increased sharply their use of employment agencies and, to a somewhat lesser extent, their use of newspaper advertising.

3. Cooperation with other companies. The tradition had been to regard wage and other personnel practices as confidential within the firm and among firms. This policy of secrecy was scrapped, and all the firms are now involved in efforts to develop a common pool of information about the labor market.

4. Expansion of the labor pool from which employees are drawn. The larger firms, especially, formerly relied exclusively—and still rely primarily—on high-school graduates as the source of labor. But hiring standards have been relaxed in various ways. Firms that had employed only single girls relaxed that policy (one personnel manager mentioned that "we even hired a sailor's wife"). In five firms, conscious effort was made to identify jobs suitable for handicapped persons and to find people to fill these jobs, an effort described as having quite satisfactory results. In at least three cases, jobs were set up for part-week and part-day employment. In two cases, a so-called "following" of workers has been developed to help meet seasonal needs for extra workers.

5. Increased cultivation of employee tastes. Although the physical appearance of the offices of the firms studied seemed much more pleasant in some cases than in others, all the firms emphasized their working conditions in employment interviews, contrasting them with the less "nice" working conditions and fellow employees in "trade" and "factories." A company-financed dance at a prominent hotel may help promote this notion. Other efforts include the maintenance of subsidized cafeterias and the adjustment of working hours to ease the burdens of traveling to and from work. Of course, where some special condition exists, such as the existence of a new air-conditioned building, that fact is called to the attention of prospective employees.

6. Efforts to deal more effectively with grievances. These efforts are in part preventive. Ten of the firms have developed formal wage structures, in seven cases through use of job evaluation. Training programs for supervisors have been designed to develop an appreciation of com-

123

pany policies and of the employees' view of the organization. The beginnings of formal grievance procedures were apparent in two or three companies, but this development did not appear to have gone very far.

7. Substitution of capital for labor. Dictating machines and large typing pools are widely used, although the consequent depersonalizing of work relationships has caused problems in some instances. Only the higher executives seem entitled now to the well-rounded secretary. The period of this study preceded widespread installation of modern electronic computers to perform clerical tasks in offices such as those studied. These laborsaving devices have doubtless been welcomed in part because they ease personnel requirements.

8. Changes in the quality of labor expected. There are two dimensions to the "quality" problem. On the one hand, the tightness of the labor market has an impact on hiring standards, as expressed in such variables as intelligence, technical skill, and personal appearance. On the other, discipline is affected, and expectations about individual performance are altered. The discipline dimension of quality is especially obvious to firms whose wages are on the low side of the market. In one such case, the wage position of the firm was shifted in part to give supervisors a stronger hand in insisting on good performance, including low absenteeism and promptness.

These changes in personnel policies are related more or less directly to the tightness of the labor market. Increased turnover, increased difficulty in filling vacancies, and knowledge by the companies that their employees could readily obtain jobs elsewhere were all factors underlying the changes. In response to these pressures, the firms invested in a variety of nonwage appeals to new employees and in organizational arrangements to implement these appeals. They approached the labor market with increased sophistication and buying effort.

### WAGE STRATEGIES

Increased buying effort did not relieve banks and insurance companies of the necessity of increasing wage rates, for clerical rates in the Boston area rose by about 55 per cent between 1948 and 1956. Except for the two smallest firms in the sample studied, the primary emphasis in company wage policy was on the hiring rate for inexperienced workers. The great majority of accessions were at that level, reflecting policies of promotion from within, the location of turnover, the concentration of employment on routine jobs, and the nature of the largest increment in the labor pool—each year's high school graduates.

In general, the approach of firms to increases in hiring rates was conservative. Within the firm the burden of proof fell largely on those individuals who advocated an increase. The success of these companies in preventing an explosive upward movement of hiring rates is suggested by the fact that their rates were just above the minimum wage at the time when the minimum was raised to 75 cents and later to $1.00 per hour. Indeed, three companies decided on rate increases in anticipation of the minimum wage change, which thus performed a sort of mopping-up function in this labor market. Nevertheless, as will be developed below, the wage changes studied here were made primarily in response to labor supply problems.

The focus of pressures about hiring rates was on individuals in the personnel department. These were the people making contacts with high schools and employment agencies. They interviewed applicants, trying to attract them by the "net advantages" of working for the firm; they received the complaints of operating departments about the poor quality of labor hired and complaints from outside the firm about any inadequacies of their hiring rates. For the most part, the personnel department took the initiative in proposing changes in pay scales or in arranging systems to make the initial rates to be offered more flexible. They were forced to develop their case and argue it through a top management that almost universally took a "show me" attitude. Even if the personnel department did not make policy, it played a strategic role in initiating, administering, and often suffering with policy.

Data on minimum hiring rates were collected for a period of nine years, 1947-55. In six of the nine years at least 10 firms reported their minimum hiring rates. At most, the top rate in a given year was 12 per cent higher than the bottom rate and, generally, the band was under 10 per cent. In some cases, predominantly for firms in the low end of the band, the minimum hiring rate was the bottom of a range within which hiring could take place. The purpose was to give more flexibility in bidding for labor, and the effect was to narrow the actual band of rates. In part, the narrowness of the band reflects the fact that the large firms included in this study were points of reference in wage surveys for all the firms studied. In general, the larger the firm, the broader the coverage of wage comparisons it made (Table 9).

Small firms, which hired against specific openings for the most part,

125

TABLE 9

ELEMENTS OF RECRUITING AND WAGE POLICIES, THIRTEEN COMPANIES

| Company Size | Primary Source of Labor | When Recruit | Primary Knowledge of Market Condition | Range of Comparison | Formal or Informal Structure | Job Evaluation | Promotion from Within |
|---|---|---|---|---|---|---|---|
| L | A | A | A | B | B | B | A |
| L | A | A | A | D | A | A | A |
| S | A | A | C | B | B | B | A |
| S | B, D, E | B | C | B | B | B | A |
| L | A | A | C | B | A | A | A |
| L | A, D, E | B | B | D | A | A | A |
| S | B, C, E | B | A | B | A | A | A |
| S | B, E | B | B | D | A | B | A |
| L | A | A | B | D | A | A | A |
| L | A | A | B | A | A | B | A |
| S | B, C | B | B | A | A | A | A |
| S | B | B | B | A | A | A | A |
| S | B, C, D, E | B | B | A | A | B | A |
| Totals | A=7, B=6, C=3 D=3, E=5 | A=6 B=7 | A=3, B=7 C=3 | A=4, B=5 C=0, D=4 | A=10 B=3 | A=7 B=6 | A=13 B=0 |

KEYS:

| | |
|---|---|
| L=large | A=high school |
| S=small | B=private agency |
| | C=S.E.S. |
| | D=walk-ins and referrals |
| | E=advertising |

When Recruit: A=spring B=against openings

Primary Knowledge of Market Condition: A=own survey B=regular survey (BLS, FRB, NOMA, etc.) C=informal contacts

Range of Comparison: A=key firms in own industry B=key firms in own and other industries C=all finance D=market

Formal or Informal Structure: A=formal (specified rate ranges) B=informal

Job Evaluation: A=yes B=no

Promotion from Within: A=yes B=no

126

tended to follow market movements. Small and large firms seeking a high quality of help generally made rate changes on an analytic basis. They had established a desired position for themselves and, on the basis of wage survey information, sought to maintain that position. Firms with a low wage–low quality strategy, however, tended to demand more than wage-survey evidence for a change in their rates, in part because of distrust of the survey results. They looked for evidence in their own experience with recruiting and turnover to supplement the findings of wage surveys.

Most of the larger firms engaged in heavy recruiting efforts in the spring, trying to hire "our share of this year's crop" of high school girls. If a large firm missed out on this market, it would tend to have personnel difficulty for the balance of the year. As a result, the very structure of labor supply forced upon the firm an analytical problem. It was necessary to anticipate in policy on hiring rates what the so-called "going rate" would be. Firms could still pursue varying wage-quality strategies, but even the firm with the low wage strategy apparently could not afford to be very far off the pace. Interviews with recruiters from such firms are full of references to adverse comments, made by high school guidance counsellors, about their rates of pay.

Two general observations stand out most clearly from the interviews with management people. The first is the conviction that significant quality differences exist in this labor supply and that the average quality hired will be related to the firm's place in the wage structure. The wage-quality relationship seems to take shape over a period of time. Firms with lagging wages may not at first notice much difference in the number and quality of applicants, but they do notice a difference in their ability to hire these applicants. They could fill their openings without raising the wage but only by lowering hiring standards. A firm that is contracting its employment could, therefore, lag in wages for some time without feeling much effect. On the other hand, an expanding firm with jobs opening up at higher skill levels must attract a relatively high percentage of promotable girls. Firms in such a position seem to find a high wage strategy of critical importance in their ability to select the kind of work force they desire.

The other general observation concerns the power of labor supply forces as these forces appeared to the firms. The changes in hiring rates in all these firms were unquestionably responses to tight labor supply conditions. As one personnel director put it, "We have to at least keep up with the salaries of the other banks and insurance companies. Everyone is howling for girls and the kids are not dumbbells. They go where they pay more." This is not to overlook the importance of nonwage appeals. Rather, a hiring rate above a certain minimum seemed to be a necessary, though not a sufficient, condition for successful recruitment. In some cases firms established a "going-rate" policy that did not wait on specific indicators of recruiting trouble. In other cases, the firm's policy of waiting for adverse experience of its own before changing rates provided an almost steady stream of internal evidence that low wages and labor supply troubles are related.

Another important aspect of wage policy involves the structure of wages in the firm. The point has already been made that the firms moved during the post-World War II decade toward more formal wage structures and, in about half the cases, to a job evaluation system of some sort (Table 9). The reasons for this development did not seem to differ much from those found elsewhere: the inequities and chaos that can develop within firms from a random and uncontrolled rate structure; the procedural difficulties of making rate comparisons without some sort of plan; the stimulation of War Labor Board and Wage Stabilization Board regulations; and the general tendency to imitate what is being done elsewhere. Underlying these general reasons in the firms studied, two others appeared to be important. Emphasis on hiring rates led to a tendency for compression in the wage structure unless this problem was dealt with explicitly. Compression, as experienced by a number of the firms, was deplored because faithful employees with limited mobility were apparently being neglected with a generally bad effect on morale, including the morale of their immediate supervisors. In addition, since jobs throughout the wage structure have many common elements among firms, people can move readily to good alternative employment. These problems are forcefully expressed in an internal memorandum on wage policy distributed in 1951 to the top management of one of the firms studied.

The financial problems of these groups [in jobs above the hiring level] have an adverse effect on the morale of all members at nonsupervisory levels as well as on the managers with whom they discuss their affairs. These groups have relatively long service with a low turnover ratio. In general, they have acquired skills which are valuable to the Company and they constitute the backbone of our nonsupervisory office force. They have roots in the Company and have little desire to seek employment in new fields.

We are thus beginning to be a training school which furnishes skilled employees to other industries. For example, we are hiring semi-skilled Burroughs machine operators in the range from $30 to $35.21 per week. After six months to a year, these girls as skilled operators can earn $40 a week or better in other industries. We have verified these rates with Burroughs. Several girls have proved it for us by leaving for better paying jobs.

A job evaluation and job classification system, if approved by the Government and adopted by the Company, could enable us to price our wage rates competitively. It would permit us to re-classify employees who have successfully learned skills in the Company.

At the present time, the Personnel Department has notice of fifteen to twenty girls who are considering jobs in other companies. Many of these girls do not easily make the decision to quit. They feel that there are many advantages in working for us; they have many personal ties in the departments where they now work. Cost of living and merit increases, plus notice that the Company is actively seeking a plan which will permit wage adjustments, will persuade many girls in this situation to remain with the Company.

In summary, the wage strategies pursued by firms could all be classed under the general heading, "pay whatever the market forces you to pay," but this was interpreted in different ways by different firms. The differences in approach apparently were related to differences in size, type of business, and immediate employment trends. The dimensions of difference were the quality of help desired, as related to position in the community wage structure, and the extent to which the firm tried to anticipate or follow general rate changes.

EXCERPTS FROM THE EXPERIENCES OF INDIVIDUAL FIRMS

*A Prominent Insurance Company*

This firm's employment of clerical help increased moderately between 1945 and 1950 but then rose sharply, by about 20 per cent, between 1951 and 1953. Employment at the end of 1950 was below the level of a year earlier, but this reflected inability in the last half of the year to get the quality of help desired rather than a slowing down of the firm's need for additional people. Traditionally the firm maintained individual rates with no over-all plan for the wage structure. The hiring rate was consistently among the lowest for the firms surveyed in this study.

The organization began to change during World War II and, by the end of the war, the employment department had been expanded to a small personnel department with its main emphasis on recruiting activities. The firm occupies a prominent building, and in the immediate postwar years was able to fill the bulk of its jobs from a steady stream of walk-in applicants. Gradually, however, the firm was forced to seek other sources of labor. This need was dramatized for the firm by the end of 1950 in the form of many unfilled vacancies. In 1951, the personnel department was again reorganized and one of the important operating men was given the full-time job of personnel director, a post at the policy-making level with access to the firm's top management group.

His early efforts to move the firm's hiring rate to a higher position in the community wage structure were rebuffed. Concern within the firm for the impact on other rates of changing the hiring rate forced him to present an over-all plan for the firm's wage structure. The arguments against it ran: "we can't make rapid increases in clerical rates when our policy holders pay fixed premiums"; and "turn-over is high among our employees for reasons unrelated to wage rates." Arguments such as these prevailed for several years but eventually gave way, as an accumulation of evidence led to a rather dramatic shift in wage policy.

The evidence behind the policy shift was of several types. Quantitative information on personnel shortages was kept. Interviews with job applicants nourished the suspicion that the walk-in applicants were increasingly people who had been "picked over" by other firms. Operating supervisors complained about low quality and the increasing difficulty of maintaining standards for attendance, punctuality, and tidiness. Efforts to recruit actively in the high schools met with only fair success. Company recruiters reported remarks of high school guidance counsellors, such as, "Why should they go to you when they can get more somewhere else?" An analysis was made of turnover which showed that one-fourth to one-third of voluntary quits were connected directly or indirectly with unfavorable wage comparisons. This percentage exerted considerable leverage in a period of labor shortage.

Finally, an extensive and detailed wage survey was made for the firm by an outside group, and its results were expressed in the rate changes in the new wage policy.

For this firm conditions in the labor market forced a broad reconsideration of company personnel policy, including wage policy, on a somewhat reluctant management. The personnel director of the firm is careful to point out that "money isn't everything" and that the changes made were far more extensive than a simple change in the hiring rate. Nevertheless, there is no doubt that wages were an essential part of the over-all package of "net advantages" this firm was selling to its employees, and that satisfactory sales were most difficult to achieve without a relatively attractive hiring rate.

*Another Large Insurance Company*

This firm experienced slow growth in permanent clerical employees in the decade following World War II but did expand considerably its use of part-time workers to meet seasonal needs. Personnel work at the company had been carefully organized during World War II and the activities were in the hands of responsible men in the firm. The firm's over-all wage-quality strategy was more carefully thought through than in most of the other firms, and it illustrates an important strategy alternative.

The firm consciously pursued a policy of paying a little below what it regarded as the market rate, knowing that the average quality of its people might suffer somewhat as a result. Its experience showed, however, that some good-quality girls came there "by chance," so that enough promotable material usually was available to the firm. Where this was not the case, it did not hesitate to hire from outside the firm. An effort was made to organize most jobs so that they required little training. On the whole, the firm felt that others paying high rates had a higher average quality than they could use fully and were really wasting money.

The firm participated in wage surveys made by other firms in the area but relied primarily on surveys made by the Bureau of Labor Statistics on the grounds that BLS surveys were broader and more systematic. It did not change rates, however, on the basis of survey results alone. The survey helped to decide how much to change, but a change was not made unless the firm's own experience suggested the need for it. A primary indicator was "bleeding" in the rate ranges.

*131*

When they found that they could recruit a high proportion of girls only at the hiring rate reserved for "exceptional" people, a need for a change in the rate range was indicated. In addition, the firm recorded such indicators as the number of interviews per hire, the turnover, and the number of unfilled vacancies. The personnel people were a little suspicious of their own figures on unfilled vacancies and felt that perhaps the vacancies were not really there—until loud complaints came from department managers. The same could be said about quality standards for new people. At any rate, they relied heavily on indicators from the firm's own experience before grudgingly moving the wage rate up.

*A Large Bank*

This firm ranks among the larger and more rapidly growing employers of clerical labor in the area. To fill its large accessions each year, the firm has turned to and relied primarily on the supply of labor entering the market each year from high schools. Its well-organized personnel department makes numerous visits to high schools each year to persuade teachers, high school guidance counsellors, and students that this bank is a good place to work.

In the view of the personnel department, the firm's large-scale and aggressive recruiting demanded a hiring rate slightly above average. In addition, the timing of the firm's hiring made it difficult for the firm to await adverse experience of its own before changing its rates. It was deemed essential to make a large proportion of the yearly accessions out of the group graduating each year from high schools. Thus, the firm felt it necessary to follow an anticipatory and analytical approach to wage changes.

The firm estimated each year the labor requirements of major firms in the area and the number of high school graduates who would be looking for clerical work. On the basis of these estimates and a "feeling" of what was happening to wages as seen by other employers, employment agencies, and high school guidance counsellors, the firm decided upon the rate range with which it would enter the market. The objective was to appear in a leadership role. This wage policy was aggressively supplemented by other nonwage appeals and by efforts to bring girls into the firm before graduation on a part-time basis.

In addition to general efforts to keep costs down, two types of restraining forces were operating in this case. First, there are only a few really large firms recruiting in the Boston area high schools, and they feared that really aggressive bidding for the high school graduates would only run up the price. This possibility was discussed among personnel people and no doubt served to moderate the forces of competition. The other restraining force was the problem of maintaining an equitable internal wage structure in the firm. Rapid increases in hiring rates would mean either increases all along the line or growing discontent among longer-service employees. Such a situation, it was felt in this firm, could easily lead to unionization of these employees, an outcome clearly viewed as most undesirable.

All in all, however, the firm was a wage leader both in timing and level. Its wage policy illustrates an adaptation to the structure of supply on which it drew in a period of labor shortage.

*A Small Bank*

This firm employed a little over 100 people in 1956 and had experienced a slow growth in the decade following World War II. Consequently, it hired only a small number of people each year. Its hiring rate was consistently about average among the firms covered by the study, and turnover was the lowest of any firm included in this study. Adjustments in rates were made from time to time on the basis of wage survey material collected by large employers and made available to those who cooperated in the survey. The firm relied almost entirely on internal recruiting, using its own employees as its best sources of information and advertisement. It had no personnel department and no labor supply difficulties and was, to a certain extent, a little bewildered by all the shouting about labor shortages.

## Patterns of Job Choice Among Clerical Workers

Information about employer personnel policies and wage decisions was supplemented by study of the labor force activities of a sample of clerical workers. Work histories were collected by interviews with 158 employees of the thirteen firms studied, each at the time on the payroll of a bank or insurance company. The names were drawn at random from lists supplied by the firms, with 10 names selected from each small firm and 15 from each large one.

As shown in Table 10 those interviewed were predominantly under twenty-four years of age, single, and residents of households headed by parents, guardians, or other relatives. A significant minority, one-

## TABLE 10
### STATISTICAL DESCRIPTION OF THE SAMPLE

|  | Number | Percentage |
|---|---|---|
| AGE DISTRIBUTION | | |
| Under 20 | 33 | 20.9 |
| 20–24 | 64 | 40.5 |
| 25–34 | 32 | 20.3 |
| 35–59 | 29 | 18.3 |
|  | 158 | 100.0 |
| MARITAL STATUS | | |
| Single | 117 | 74.0 |
| Married | 33 | 20.9 |
| Widowed, Separated, or divorced | 8 | 5.1 |
|  | 158 | 100.0 |
| HOUSEHOLD CHARACTERISTICS | | |
| Head of household | 27 | 17.1 |
| Not head of household | | |
| With parents, guardians or other relatives | 106 | 67.1 |
| With husband | 25 | 15.8 |
|  | 158 | 100.0 |

fourth to one-third, were over twenty-five years of age and had important responsibilities for maintenance of the household.

ORIENTATION TO CLERICAL WORK AND CONFIDENCE IN ITS AVAILABILITY

These 158 people had held jobs in 411 firms since leaving school and 343 of these jobs (83 per cent) were in clerical work. Of them, 122 had held jobs exclusively in clerical occupations since leaving school. In contrast, before leaving school, 80 per cent of these individuals had held nonclerical jobs, for the most part, in retail sales in stores or service work in drugstores, ice cream parlors, or similar establishments. The interviews were full of unsolicited adverse comments about jobs in trade and service industries and, to a less extent, about jobs in factories (see Appendix A for examples).

The experience of those interviewed in making job shifts fostered confidence in the ready availability of work (Table 11). About 80 per cent of the job shifts were voluntary. An increase in salary was associated with three-fourths of the shifts when the worker stayed in the labor market. In 60 per cent of the cases the individual spent less than two weeks between jobs, and 85 per cent of the individuals had

## TABLE 11

PERCENTAGE DISTRIBUTION OF REASONS FOR LEAVING JOBS

| Reasons for Leaving | Current Age of Worker | | | | Total Reasons |
|---|---|---|---|---|---|
| | Under 20 | 20–24 | 25–34 | 35–59 | |
| INVOLUNTARY | | | | | |
| | 7.1 | 23.1 | 13.6 | 20.9 | 18.3 |
| VOLUNTARY, REMAINING IN LABOR MARKET | | | | | |
| Salary and opportunity to advance | 21.4 | 18.3 | 22.3 | 17.4 | 19.4 |
| Nonsalary economic advantages | 0 | 1.9 | 1.0 | 6.1 | 2.9 |
| Working conditions | 7.1 | 8.7 | 8.7 | 4.3 | 7.1 |
| Personal relationships | 21.4 | 14.4 | 19.4 | 8.7 | 14.6 |
| Type of work | 25.0 | 17.3 | 16.5 | 9.6 | 15.1 |
| Other | 10.7 | 5.8 | 8.7 | 5.2 | 6.9 |
| VOLUNTARY, LEAVING LABOR MARKET | | | | | |
| Marriage and pregnancy | 0 | 1.0 | 2.9 | 8.7 | 4.0 |
| Return to school | 7.1 | 2.9 | 2.9 | 6.1 | 4.3 |
| Change of husband's residence | 0 | 3.8 | 0 | 3.5 | 2.3 |
| Other | 0 | 2.9 | 3.9 | 9.6 | 5.1 |
| Total reasons | 8.0 | 29.7 | 29.4 | 32.9 | 100.0 |

NOTE: More than one answer possible per person per job.

### DESCRIPTION OF CATEGORIES

Salary and opportunity to advance, consideration of salary or a chance for promotion.

Nonsalary economic advantage, consideration of job security and fringe benefits of various sorts.

Working conditions, preferences with respect to the number of working hours, days of work, and the type of physical plant.

Personal relationships, the social satisfactions derived from working in a firm, including those related to the nature of supervision, type of co-workers, and the presence of friends.

Type of work, for which workers indicated dissatisfaction with the inherent nature of the work they were performing.

never spent more than one month out of a job while still in the labor market. For about 20 per cent of the job shifts, a new job had been lined up by the individual before she left the old job.

METHODS OF LOCATING JOBS AND ACQUIRING JOB INFORMATION

The sources by which those interviewed located jobs are shown in Table 12. The outstanding fact shown by this table is the importance of market intermediaries and sources of information which tend to expose the job applicant to knowledge of a range of job alternatives. The most important channels of information were schools and private

TABLE 12

SOURCES BY WHICH JOBS WERE LOCATED

| SOURCE OF JOB | PERCENTAGE DISTRIBUTION | | | | | |
|---|---|---|---|---|---|---|
| | Age of Workers at Time of Study | | | | Total Sources | Number of Job Sources |
| | Under 20 | 20–24 | 25–34 | 35–59 | | |
| Schools | 21.0 | 16.3 | 15.0 | 12.4 | 15.5 | 67[a] |
| Private employment agencies | 10.5 | 10.2 | 15.9 | 16.5 | 13.4 | 58 |
| State employment service | 5.3 | 3.4 | 3.7 | 4.1 | 3.9 | 17 |
| Newspaper advertisements | 0 | 15.0 | 20.6 | 7.4 | 12.3 | 53 |
| Common awareness | 8.8 | 8.8 | 7.5 | 9.1 | 8.6 | 37 |
| Girl friend | 31.6 | 23.8 | 15.9 | 19.8 | 21.8 | 94[b] |
| Relatives, family friends, and contacts | 21.0 | 16.3 | 16.8 | 19.0 | 17.8 | 77[c] |
| Company recruiters | 0 | 3.4 | 9.3 | 9.1 | 2.5 | 11 |
| Other | 1.8 | 2.7 | 3.7 | 7.4 | 4.2 | 18 |
| Total sources | 13.2 | 34.0 | 24.8 | 28.0 | 100.0 | |
| Number of jobs | 57 | 147 | 107 | 121 | | 432 |

NOTE: More than one answer possible per job and per person.
[a] High School in 32 cases.
[b] Friend worked at the firm in 59 cases.
[c] Relative or family contact worked at the firm in 57 cases.

employment agencies, and if the State Employment Service and newspaper advertisements are added, these channels were the means by which individuals found almost half the jobs identified in this study. As in the case of industrial labor markets, friends and relatives were also prime sources of job information, accounting for about 40 per cent of the jobs identified. Nevertheless, the importance here of relatively well-organized channels of information for locating jobs stands in sharp contrast to findings in industrial labor markets.[10]

Studies of industrial labor markets have shown the typical industrial worker to be poorly informed about job alternatives, even when in the process of changing jobs. In this study, too, the majority of workers did not seem well informed or thoughtful in their labor market behavior. In about one-third of the job shifts identified in this study the person interviewed knew almost nothing about the job before applying and knew only the general type of work involved in another 40 per cent of the shifts. In about one-fourth of the cases, however, the person knew about the general salary levels at the firm and about some aspects of the working conditions before making application.

In about two-thirds of the cases, the individual had no specific knowledge about jobs other than the one taken at the time of the job shift. In about one-fourth of the job shifts, however, the individual made more than one application, indicating she had explored alternatives to some degree. Three-fourths of those interviewed, when asked the additional question whether they knew of any places using clerical help which they considered "good" or "bad" places to work, identified firms other than their own and gave explicit reasons for the good or bad evaluation. A significant minority, perhaps one-fourth to one-third, of these clerical workers, then, possessed some knowledge of job alternatives when they made job shifts, and a somewhat greater number had enough knowledge about other firms to make a loose judgment about the desirability of working at these other firms.

FACTORS IN JOB CHOICE

An effort was made in the interviews to identify in a general way the preference structure of these clerical workers. They were asked why they had left earlier jobs, what had led them to choose their present

---

[10] From a study of the San Francisco Bay area labor market, Malm also noted the sharp contrast between channels of recruitment for manual and clerical workers. He studied employer recruiting practices and covered a wider range of industries and sizes of firms than this study does. High schools were not as important as they appear to be here, but formal channels do predominate in the case of clerical workers. F. Theodore Malm, "Recruiting Patterns and the Functioning of Labor Markets," *Industrial and Labor Relations Review*, July 1954, pp. 507-525.

The study of clerical workers in Madison, Wisconsin, also found formal channels to be of great importance in that labor market. Eighty per cent of the jobs on which workers reported were located through market intermediaries, with the Public Employment Service playing an important role. See Conant, "Wages and Behavior of Firms and Workers," p. 117.

positions, their satisfactions and dissatisfactions in their current jobs, and what they considered to be the characteristics of "good" and "bad" places of employment. Here, too, the general picture obtained is not very different from that identified in other studies. Individuals vary in what they want from a job and, in all cases, they consider more than the financial side. In only a minority of job shifts were salary and other nonsalary economic attributes of a job singled out as the primary reason for taking the new job.

The picture for job terminations, however, is somewhat different. Two-thirds of the individuals who left jobs did so voluntarily and stayed in the labor market. Reasons given for leaving were, in about one-third of the cases, dissatisfaction with salary or other economic attributes of the job, in 45 per cent, unsatisfactory personal relationships on the job or dissatisfaction with the type of work. Of the 158 women interviewed, 60 said they intended to leave the firm for which they were working; more than half, 34, gave as the reason dissatisfaction with their current salary or with their chances for increases in salary. In describing good and bad places to work, about 40 per cent of the 158 specified economic advantages as identifying a good job, though only 18 per cent cited that reason in identifying bad jobs.

The picture of employee behavior that emerges in this labor market seems broadly consistent with the belief of firms that raising wages and improving working conditions were essential to attract and retain employees. Almost half the jobs taken by the sample of workers studied were located through reasonably well-organized information pools. These pools provide their users with knowledge of a range of job alternatives and with rough standards for evaluating salaries. A significant minority of girls, about 20 per cent, knew about jobs other than the one they accepted and had at least a general idea of the economic dimensions of jobs applied for. To be sure, most of the workers made no pretence to a systematic exploration of the job market. But in many instances some market intermediary did that for them and, in a substantial minority of instances, workers conducted some search on their own.

This study suggests that financial incentives play a significant role in the preference structure of these clerical workers, although within a strong framework of other job objectives. It is apparent that these girls place a high value on their working environment and on the status of the work they do. Most of them seem to have rejected consciously factory work or selling, where many of them had earlier experience on part-time jobs, thus narrowing their range of job choice. Within this range, however, a substantial minority, again about 20 to 25 per cent, emphasized salary and general financial considerations in their reasons for leaving and taking specific jobs, their notions of what makes for a good or a bad job, and their intentions about their current job.

In a tight labor market, where firms are struggling to attract workers and avoid turnover, the behavior of this minority of workers can have a significant impact. The initial job choices and subsequent movements of these workers punish the low-wage firm and encourage those employers who maintain salaries in line with or above their competitors in the labor market.

## Role of Market Intermediaries

Because market intermediaries appeared to play an important role here as sources of job information, both to firms seeking employees and to workers seeking jobs, their methods of operation were also studied, with emphasis on high school placement activities.[11] The information about private employment agencies is limited, since these organizations were reluctant to provide desired information. Interviews were held with nineteen high school counsellors engaged in placement activities—fourteen associated with high schools in principal Boston suburbs and five with the Boston school systems, both public and parochial.

### APPROACH TO PLACEMENT ACTIVITIES

High schools vary considerably in the amount of effort devoted to placement activities and in the sophistication of their approach. In general, however, the view was widespread that satisfactory placement in jobs was a growing responsibility of the schools. The approach of individual guidance counsellors varied somewhat in the degree of control assumed. In some cases, the approach was rather authoritarian: the counsellor tried to place an individual girl on a particular job without giving her much information about alternatives. The more prevalent view, however, was that girls should get from the initial placement process some skill in ways of finding jobs. Thus, at some schools girls

[11] The Public Employment Service apparently did not play an important role here. In contrast, a study in Madison, Wisconsin found there that it is a principal channel of job information for clerical workers. See Conant, "Wages and Behavior of Firms and Workers," pp. 119-122.

were told about a number of jobs, occasionally given a list of firms to visit, and were urged to supplement basic information available at the school with the kind of information obtainable only on the job site.

### ACQUISITION OF INFORMATION AND ITS DISPERSAL

Every counsellor interviewed was convinced that the market for clerical help was extremely tight. Many more companies than ever before were taking the initiative in contacting high schools, and placement people were frequently unable to recommend anyone to fill particular vacancies. As one of them expressed it, "We have many more calls for jobs than we have girls to fill them."

As a result of their contacts with firms, guidance counsellors accumulated much information about available job openings and the basic employment terms for them. In some schools, the information about openings was posted on a bulletin board; in others, guidance counsellors talked over a range of possible alternatives with individual girls. Information filtered out through teachers in the business courses and through discussions among the girls themselves. As one man noted, "The girls talk a lot among themselves about salaries and when jobs in firms paying lower salaries are offered, they refuse them." The result, it seemed, was that enough information became generally available to set a sort of salary norm for a particular year.

Some placement officers were much more aggressive than others in feeding information back to firms and in commenting critically about low rates. Ten of the nineteen interviewed volunteered comments about such action, as this typical statement: "I won't send a girl to a place like that because they exploit girls by paying them too low. They tell me the girls aren't worth it, but I say if you want them you'll have to pay it, because they can get it somewhere else." Many small firms call in for help and say in effect, "You know the salary schedules; tell me what I should pay and I'll pay it." Thus, the information collected at the high schools moved out to the demand as well as to the supply side of the market.

All the schools emphasized their desire to place the better girls in what were considered the better jobs, as rewards for better than average performance in the classroom. Better jobs were not defined exclusively in terms of better pay, but pay appeared to be one obvious attribute. The result of this process was to sort out the labor supply according to a quality dimension and to provide a broad association in the placement process of quality and pay. Some quotations may help give the flavor of this aspect of placement activities: "My goal is to give the better job to the better girl. If good jobs don't come in, then I'll take the initiative and shop around for them." "I tell the outstanding kids to hold out for the better job; I tell them you ought to get a top-notch job. Don't be in too much of a hurry. Hold off. Talk it over with us. We'll interpret the significance of a job offered to you."

## PRIVATE AGENCIES

The information obtained about private employment agencies is not sufficient for a detailed statement about their operations. These agencies are apparently concerned primarily with placement into the high-paying jobs requiring definite skills and experience. Their concern about their reputations with employees as well as employers led them to avoid handling poor openings. They seemed willing to tell an employer when his rate was below that offered by others, a fact confirmed by statements made in interviews with employer representatives. Employers pointed out, in addition, that the agency's fee is roughly proportionate to the rate of pay on the job.

One employer related the following incident, implying that it illustrated a frequent pattern of events:

We phone the agency asking for a girl and saying that the pay is $40 a week. The agency claims it cannot get a girl unless the pay is $45. So we say if she is good we might pay $45. Let her come in and we'll see. Then the agency runs an advertisement that it has a job paying $45. This attracts girls to the agency, which tells them that that job has been filled but there is another that pays less, although the exact amount will be determined when the girl applies for the job. The result is the agency causes the employer to make a tentative offer of $45 and this figure has raised the girl's expectations, as does the suggestion by the agency that the employer is willing to bargain. In addition, girls look at the ads and get the idea that $45 is something to shoot at for a job like this.

## SUMMARY

In general, the information obtained from high school guidance counsellors tends to confirm the impression of employers and, to a lesser extent of employees, that the counsellors play an important role in this market. They appear to have some direct influence on selection of jobs

*141*

for the best girls. They counsel girls not to take the first job offered but to look around, though they deplore the extent to which this advice is ignored. From the standpoint of their effect on the labor market, the most important of their activities is their almost automatic acquisition of information. This information, which becomes available at the time of year when most hiring takes place, is widely shared on both sides of the labor market. Even if girls do not make a systematic search of job alternatives, the process of pooling and sharing information tends to perform that function for them. Thus, the placement activities of high schools improve the operation of this labor market.

## Conclusions

A tight market for female clerical workers in Boston banks and insurance companies during the post-World War II decade has been identified. The reactions of a group of firms and their employees to that labor market and the role played in it of various market intermediaries, especially high school guidance counsellors, have been described. Five points of special interest emerge from the study.

1. The supply side of the market is characterized by the addition each year of a large group of workers flowing from high schools into jobs. Most of the large firms and some smaller ones wish to attract a share of this group. The resulting focus of competition among firms at a point in time and at common locations has led to ready wage comparisons and has increased the upward pressure on wages. Some firms followed a policy of raising their rates in anticipation of this competitive struggle. Firms with lagging rates of pay felt the pressure most strongly, of course, often hearing about their position in the community wage structure directly from the guidance counsellors and feeling the impact of labor shortages in the form of a lower average quality of applicants. The structure of supply created more of a "market place" than is usually found and, in turn, the operation of the market place added knowledge to and improved the operation of that labor market.

2. Formal channels for finding out about job openings were more important for the clerical workers covered in this study than is apparently the case for manual workers. In particular, high school guidance counsellors play an important role in the placement of high school girls in initial jobs. Perhaps the most important function of the counsellors was their assembly of information about the market, which flowed to

both the supply and demand sides of the market. This information-pool role is worthy of note now, when the number of people coming out of high schools each year will be increasing rapidly. High schools can help individuals find satisfactory jobs and improve the operation of labor markets in the long run by helping individuals understand better the process of finding a job.

3. The responses of firms to that tight labor market were diverse. As in other studies, much more than a simple wage response was found. The firms were able to moderate the impact of labor scarcity on wages by increasing their buying effort, lowering their quality standards, and broadening their sources of labor supply. These devices are a parallel in the labor market to efforts by firms to differentiate their goods and services for sale in the product market. Many of these nonwage responses are reversible and their use injects an element of flexibility in a firm's adjustments to changing labor market conditions.

4. Most of the workers studied made no systematic search of job alternatives as they shifted from one employer to another, and many of them were uninformed about alternatives that might be open. Nevertheless, a substantial minority of workers did appear to be reasonably well informed and willing to move to jobs with better pay and comparable working conditions. In a tight labor market the leverage of such a group can have an important impact on the wage policies of firms. The impact, while concentrated on jobs at the hiring level, extends throughout the wage structure and reduces the monopsony power of firms over employees with long service and skills specialized to the firm. This extension operates through internal comparisons and the impact on morale of what appears to employees and their supervisors as inequitable treatment.

5. This market does not, of course, operate in isolation, free of the forces at work in the economy generally or in the Boston area. Nevertheless, its responses to these forces operate through a mechanism with a basically internal orientation. The changes in personnel policy and in wages made by the firms were stimulated by their own conditions of labor supply. Certainly, then, one cannot expect economic events in other industries and locations to have an automatic effect on this labor market. If the event affects the demand for or supply of clerical workers in Boston, as did the expansion of government offices in Boston resulting from the upsurge of activity during the Korean conflict, then a response here may be expected.

*143*

In the post-World War II period, the study of labor markets has led gradually to a shift in attitude toward them on the part of labor economists. Research has revealed the complexities—the barriers that often impede the flow of people to jobs of their choice, the extent of ignorance about alternative employment opportunities, and the broad range of motives to which people respond in their labor force activities. If the initial reaction to the findings of research was disenchantment with a stripped-down model of the labor market drawn from economic theory, subsequent reflection has led to a more sophisticated view. In this later effort some of the classic works have turned out to be valuable, after all. Charles A. Myers, for example, quotes with approval from the works of Marshall and Hicks, who "analyzed with great insight the operation of labor markets, as distinct from product markets."[12] And Myers notes, referring to the United States, that "personal and institutional factors undoubtedly did impede movement in certain local labour markets and at particular times; but the broad waves of movement did correspond to those suggested by the theoretical model."[13] The effort now is to use the richness of empirical detail on hand—with economic theory as a guide, but not a master—to distinguish among the many types of situations under which the price of labor is determined. This study of a white-collar labor market may be portrayed, then, as one piece of data in this broad effort.

## Appendix

EXCERPTS FROM EMPLOYEE INTERVIEWS

A. Reasons for Working:

I guess I just wanted to feel independent.

I had to—your mother supports you long enough and then you have to go to work. I didn't have anyone but myself to support when I started working; I guess that I just didn't like the idea of "hanging around" when everyone else is working.

Well, I wasn't going to college . . . you just don't go to school for twelve years and then hang around . . . you got to have money. I can't say to my mother I won't work and you got to support me.

---

[12] Charles A. Myers, "Labor Market Theory and Empirical Research," in John T. Dunlop, *The Theory of Wage Determination*, London, MacMillan, 1957, p. 317.
[13] *Ibid.*, p. 326.

It's not fair and I want to work. I guess every girl does. She wants to have clothes and buy things she wants . . . and you meet people. . . .

When you graduate from high school you can do three things; you can go to college, get married, or go to work. I didn't go to college or get married, so I went to work.

I need the money to help out at home. I wouldn't stay at home and loaf. I'd be very bored.

Well, I didn't have to . . . but I was excited about getting a job and having my own money . . . it was just the natural thing to do.

Money is the main reason: I have to live and I can't live off my parents forever. I think that when you work there are more things that you can do . . . you're independent . . . anyway, eventually everyone has to go out and work. It's good to know some kind of work in case some day you really have to work.

The first time I went to work it was just for kicks, you know something to do . . . after I graduated from high school there was nothing to do but go to work.

I didn't know anyone there. It meant being alone all day. I didn't want to sit around. Now I'm working because we want to save for a down payment on a house. I'll work for one or one and a half years and then stop, because we want a family in another year or so.

I had to return to work. I was supporting myself. My husband and I broke up . . . divorced.

B. Reasons for Selection of Clerical Work

My mother and father wanted me to work in an office . . . they'd like me to work in an office and not in a factory . . . she knows what it's like . . . they work hard in a factory. . . .

I wouldn't want a factory job, I got a high school diploma.

When nursing was out I figured that clerical work was something that I was capable of. That's the only course that they offered in high school besides the college course and I didn't want to go to college. . . .

145

It's the best kind of a job a girl can get. If you say you work in a factory it doesn't impress people. They say anyone can get you work like that . . . and an office is clean.

I didn't want to go any farther in school . . . I didn't really like school that much. If I went to college I'd have to take courses that I didn't like . . . clerical work seemed most interesting to me. I was always fascinated by people that could type. I wouldn't want the assembly line. It doesn't seem like the right type of job for me; no intelligence is needed in that work. I've gone through school with good marks and I wanted a job that would become a challenge to me.

For no special reason, I don't think. I knew that if I took the commercial course in school I could always get a job.

The reason I do clerical work is that I'm not trained for anything. . . . I only had a clerical course . . . a little in high school. . . . They're the only skills I can do. I'm not interested in office work, but that's all I can do now.

I think I thought I would get real working benefit out of the commercial course . . . that it would help me to get a job. If you aren't going to college this would be about the only thing I could get into. I didn't really consider anything else.

I just sort of wandered into it. One thing leads to another. You get one job working in an office and then you look for the same thing.

I like a little prestige in my job. . . . I think office work is a little more respectable for a girl. . . . no, I wouldn't think of working in a factory . . . it's too rough for me . . . both the work and the people.

My dad's not working. He was laid off in the mill. That's why he said office work or a bank or insurance company would be steadier . . . the big reason for going to the bank was security.

I don't know why I went into office work. I guess it was because that's what I took in school.

## COMMENTS

GEORGE H. HILDEBRAND, Cornell University

George Shultz underscores our lack of knowledge about the operation of nonunion labor markets, especially in the white-collar occupations.

His effort to fill the gap is highly appropriate. Such work is essential for testing and improving wage theory, for comprehending wage behavior, for evaluating union impacts and processes of transmission of wage changes, and for a better grounding of economic policies.

What kind of model, or image, of the labor market is suggested by Shultz's findings? Obviously, it lacks the over-all centralization of wage determination that might be achieved under over-all product-market unionism, an employer association, or government regulation. While the market is not competitive enough to yield a single uniform rate, the dispersion of wage rates for comparable jobs is surprisingly narrow. If, further, allowance is made for differences in personal efficiency and capacity, which Shultz says do exist, then, expressed as efficiency wages, the band of rates would be even narrower. At the same time, there is sensitive interdependence between the hiring rate for the bottom job (filing clerk, class B) and those for the upper tiers of the structure, while all the jobs are quite clear cut and uniform among firms. Moreover, the practice seems to be to hire in at the bottom and to promote from within—interesting in itself as acceptance of the qualified seniority principle, even without unionism.

Explanation of this interdependence of job rates attests to the power of competition on both sides of the market. For the employees, compression invokes discontent, lessened efficiency, and more voluntary quits at the higher levels. For the employers, these responses may be summed up as reduced labor supply. To this the obvious reaction is to increase rates across the board, adding more to total wage costs than would selective increases and at the same time substantially increasing total costs, because of the high ratio of labor costs to total expenses in this field. The employers, accordingly, are reluctant to increase wage rates, preferring where possible to resolve the problem through nonwage channels. In the end, this approach has proved permanent, although external pressures have nonetheless compelled a steady postwar rise in wage rates.

Freed though it is of centralized wage control, Shultz's market is by no means as poorly held together as that for much nonunion factory labor. Yet it has no union. Wages have risen rapidly and consistently, showing strong uniformity rather than diversity. The reason is that unionism is not the only way to introduce an organized market. In Shultz's case, what he calls "market intermediaries" serve as effective brokers to bring buyers and sellers together. Granted that the role they

*147*

play is not as effective as that exerted in the stock exchange, it contributes powerfully to the forces of mobility. In other words, competition works, and apparently works quite well, in this market. Thus wages and working conditions together strongly influence the allocation of labor among the participating firms, meaning that demand and supply relationships shape their hiring policies in a competitive manner.

In the short period, aggregative supply appears fairly inelastic, but even in the longer run it was inelastic enough relative to increasing demand to compel a substantial rise in average rates, together with many indirect responses. These latter responses include: formation or development of personnel departments and policies, increased recruiting efforts, reduced hiring standards, improved nonpecuniary attractions, formalized job and wage structures, enlargement of the labor pool, and efforts to economize labor, particularly through substitution of capital investment in laborsaving devices.

The worker population in Shultz's study is not homogeneous in quality or efficiency. To attract and to hold labor, each employer has a choice: to be a wage leader and so "advertise" a favorable market position, or to be a follower and trade inferiority for lower rates and employment costs. Interestingly enough, Shultz's evidence suggests operation of a process of introduction and transmission of wage increases like that found by Reynolds in his New Haven study. Going annual increases and orbits of coercive comparison have existed despite the absence of unionism. Equally important, tightening labor supply has even compelled the laggards to make increases to thwart the adverse effects of higher quit rates, diminished numbers and quality of new applicants, and heightened problems of discipline and performance. Clearly, too, relatively persistent full employment in the Boston area contributed strongly to tight supply—cutting down the supposed flow of entrants from other industries and increasing the propensity to migrate outward.

The conclusion that emerges from all this is that, although the simplified model of perfect competition will not do as an adequate account of wage determination and market behavior, nonetheless in the modified neoclassical version developed by Marshall and Hicks we have a satisfactory conceptual apparatus for extracting several very useful predictive implications—*for this kind of market.*

Consider the evidence. The rise in the derived demand for this kind of labor compelled a steady advance of wages in the "industry," working as it did against relatively inelastic supply. Wages did not fall, so supply could not have been negatively elastic. The theory says that wages have to rise under these conditions, because supply depends upon the ability to pull employees from competing uses in other industries and upon the annual accretion of new entrants from the schools. Further, the market is well enough organized, and the participants sufficiently lacking in power to affect price, that wages at the hiring grade showed a strong tendency to equalize, particularly in the efficiency sense. All of the employers were under strong pressure to raise wages, and all did so. Obviously, too, supply to this industry was strongly influenced by the general state of labor demand and supply. There was substantial interdependence also among occupational rates within the industry. This, too, the theory leads us to expect: if the wages for experienced and for inexperienced girls were equal, there would be a shortage of the former and a surplus of the latter. Accordingly, competition would restore a differential, responding to the difference in marginal productivities of the two grades of workers. Finally, as the cost of labor rose to these employers, they were induced to economize—by reorganizing jobs, by resort to typing pools, and by improved or new equipment.

We need not go all the way with Hicks to hold that generally this "is quite a good simplified model of the labour market," or that so far as "general tendencies are concerned, wages do turn out on the whole very much as if they were determined in this manner."[1] For, after all, this is a special kind of labor market, with underlying conditions not found everywhere. But we can agree with him that while the "labour market is not a perfect market; [and] the equalising forces do not act quickly and easily, . . . nevertheless they do act."[2]

The criticisms I have concern mainly matters I would like to have seen explored or developed more fully. Since Shultz is reporting here about only part of a large-scale inquiry, most of my comments should not be taken as adverse.

First, I think a sharp and explicit contrast should be drawn between this particular market and those with labor unions. There are marked differences, and some interesting similarities. Rates and working conditions in Shultz's market are not collectively negotiated. The employers have much more discretion, particularly in responding to changed

[1] *The Theory of Wages*, New York, Peter Smith, 1948, p. 5.
[2] *Ibid.*, p. 76.

conditions of supply. The timing of wage increases, their size and distribution, and their diffusion among firms are not affected by the duration and expiration of trade agreements. Relative to the craft-union market, there appear to be no formal restrictions upon entry, while movement within the industry is not regulated. Actually, internal movement apparently has the dual character observed in the market for unionized factory labor: up the occupational ladder within the establishment and laterally between employers, particularly for starting jobs. It is also noteworthy that, with the transition to relatively continuous full employment, these employers were compelled to borrow some of the practices of factory unionism: to replace personal rates with job rates, to design a suitable internal structure of occupational rates, to treat problems of grievances and discipline more formally, and to formulate hiring standards and to adjust them to ease or tightness of labor supply.

Second, let me consider the orbit or contour problem. Although Shultz recognizes the influence of forces external to this industry, he contends somewhat obscurely that its labor market is an internally oriented mechanism, not automatically affected by wage patterns elsewhere. As he puts it, "The personnel policy and wage changes made by the firms were stimulated by their own conditions of labor supply."

Does this mean that the forces of supply are internal to the firm, or internal to the industry? And either way, is it true? To the firm, supply is an external force, to which it must adapt. To the industry, supply is partly an internal influence, but not wholly so. Not all new entrants into the clerical market go into banking and insurance, while those already in this field are not entirely indifferent to wages for these occupations in other industries in the Boston area. If the converse were true, why then emphasize the postwar advent of a tight market as the primary cause of the many changes in employment policy noted by Shultz? Obviously the supply curve of labor to this industry has not been perfectly elastic, or it would not have raised wages as its demand for labor expanded. Should we infer that external factors have done nothing to make supply even less elastic? If wages outside the industry had not advanced postwar, would it have made no difference to the rate of increase within the industry? I do not think so.

Perhaps Shultz's point is simply that absence of unionism invokes substantial differences in timing, speed of diffusion, size, and distribution of wage increases within the industry, which should be granted.

But this goes to the process of transmission only. It is not ground for emphasizing either the isolation of this labor market or the noncompetitiveness of its labor force.

Third, I would like to see explored more fully the role of the product market in wage determination. Banking and insurance services require identical types of labor, but they involve distinct products. How did occupational rates compare as between the two? Beyond both, there are employers in other product markets who also use this kind of labor. Table 7 indicates considerable variance in these occupational rates as among different sectors in the winter of 1957-58. What is their profile for the whole postwar period? What role did differences in product markets play in effecting and possibly preserving differentials for the same occupational groups?

Fourth, I think that more intensive examination is needed regarding the structure of occupational rates within the firms in this industry. To what extent was it given by effective competition, and to what extent was it the product of administrative design? In the usual factory case, as Dunlop pointed out some time ago, the market is too blunt an instrument to provide the gradations in job rates that are normally required. Arbitrary interpolations become necessary, either through negotiation or evaluation, or some combination of the two. Is the market for clerical labor in these fields effectively competitive enough to provide each firm with a ready-made structure, or is there considerable room for administrative discretion? If there is much discretion, are there key rates and clusters to guide the administrators?

Last, one would like to know something about fringe benefits in this market. Statistical difficulties in making comparisons are extremely difficult in this field, but if benefits can be segregated as to kind, we would have additional evidence regarding the impacts of unionism upon nonunion labor markets.

Shultz has done some very useful pioneering in this study. Most of my suggestions point to possibilities for further work. Such work is essential to the attainment of his objective of increasing our knowledge of actual labor markets in order to shore up the ground for public policy. To me, his most important finding emerges in a somewhat muted way: that here is a labor market in which competition works with reasonable effectiveness, granting that its adequacy for promoting the interests of workers as workers is a question as yet left unanswered. In any case, there are other nonunion markets in which competition has not proved effective and probably never could be. If we are to make further headway in gauging the impacts of unionism, we will require more inquiries of this kind, to yield a fuller spectrum of types of labor markets, and, with this, more knowledge of their operation and their interrelations.

RICHARD A. LESTER, Princeton University

This paper involves the application to the white-collar field of the techniques of studies in the manual-worker field of employment practices, and demand and supply factors. Since Shultz participated in the Nashua study, more comparison of his results in this study with those in other studies and an explanation of differences would have been desirable.

Applied to employment in modern firms, incautious use of the term "labor market" can create misunderstanding through misleading connotations and the application of ill-suited concepts. In his paper I am not certain whether "a nonunion market" was examined. At one point it is referred to as a "submarket, a part of the general market for clerical employees. . . ." But it "may not represent the supply side of the whole market for clerical workers in Boston." Can and should one think of a single market for all clerical workers in metropolitan Boston? Or should one think in terms of submarkets by industry, by area, by occupation, or by individual firms? And to what extent do the parties themselves think and operate in market terms?

For reasons offered in the paper, market concepts may not need great modification or qualification when applied to the hiring of clerical workers by banking and insurance firms under the sort of circumstances explained in some detail. First, much of the hiring occurs in the spring through the high schools supplying newly trained entrants, under conditions of fairly wide knowledge of wage data. The situation resembles corporation recruiting of college seniors on the campus. Second, most of those employed are interested in short-term work. Seniority and promotion are not stressed; the labor turnover apparently is exceedingly high, although no figures are given. Third, there exist considerable employer exchange of wage information, and perhaps employer understandings on wages. The report states that "all the firms are now involved in efforts to develop a common pool of information about the labor market," that the large firms "were points of reference in wage surveys for all the firms studied," and that certain discussions among personnel people "no doubt served to moderate the forces of competition." More detailed information on such employer interrelationships would have been helpful.

With that much common knowledge spread by high school guidance counsellors among prospective employees and with that much cooperation among employers, it is not surprising to find that, among the six (in some years less) banks and insurance companies for which data were available for the years 1947 to 1955, the top firm's hiring rate was not over 12 per cent above the bottom firm's hiring rate, and, on the average, was under 10 per cent above.

Yet, despite all the pressures narrowing company wage differentials, it is stated that the raising of the legal minimum to 75 cents and later to $1.00 affected three companies as a sort of "mopping-up function" and that compression of the wage structure from raising the hiring rate was experienced in a number of the firms. Thus, "faithful employees with limited mobility were apparently being neglected with a generally bad effect on morale." Why did their wages lag, and what forces caused them later to rise relatively, if that did occur?

It would have been desirable to have plotted the changes in the minimum hiring rate of each of the firms studied over the nine years for which data were collected, 1947-56. In that way, it would have been possible to observe changes in interfirm differentials and the timing of the wage rate changes for different firms. With that knowledge, one could try to determine the factors that explained the results.

In this connection, perhaps the author's reference to Table 7 as showing the narrowness of the band of rates for particular jobs is somewhat ambiguous. In that table, which reproduces average weekly earnings from a BLS study of women in office jobs, considerable range of variation is shown, especially when one takes account of the fact that only the earnings averages for each of 6 industry groups (manufacturing, public utilities, wholesale trade, retail trade, finance, and services) are being compared. Nevertheless, despite a range composed of only 6 averages, the high average exceeds the low one by the following percentages for each of the 9 occupations: 23 per cent, 20 per cent, 13 per cent, 17 per cent, 30 per cent, 22 per cent, 26 per cent, and 13 per cent. Under the circumstances, those could be considered significant wage differences.

The material in this paper indicates that industrial relations policies

*153*

and governmental actions affect wage levels and structures. Part of the task of the economist is to analyze the consequences of institutional arrangements and not merely to reason as though the concepts of purely competitive and monopolistic analysis apply without qualification to employment in the workshop and the locality.

Shultz's results show that, despite differences, white-collar employment under nonunion conditions has some of the attributes and institutional influences that have been found in similar studies of manual workers. It would have been helpful to have had even more data for comparison and testing of such conclusions as the following from other studies:

1. In practice it is rare indeed to find a single "going," "market," or "competitive" wage. Only under conditions of complete unionization or complete unity of employer action is such wage uniformity likely to occur for the same quality of workers in a particular area. What one usually finds is a band of rates, often distributed without any resemblance to a bell-shaped curve.

2. Job applications do not represent labor supply. Rather, they serve a variety of purposes including a search for job information by workers, a ritual to satisfy unemployment compensation requirements or to avoid criticism at home, an act based on misinformation, a means of putting pressure on one's present employer, a form of job shopping, etc. A company tends to get the number of applications it seeks, and its volume of applications expands and contracts, not so much according to its relative wage position as with the company's actual employment—whether it is hiring people or laying them off.

3. A "rationing of jobs" occurs whenever companies are hiring. Firms usually hire only a fraction of those who apply. Companies paying below the average hiring rate in their industry still have to select or ration the available jobs among the applicants who meet the minimum standards.

In view of some remarks in the Alchian-Kessel paper, it might also be well to add that discrimination occurs against certain types of labor (Negroes, Mexicans, Jews, or other minority groups, or against females and older workers), not so much because employers gain nonpecuniary satisfactions therefrom but because of custom, social prejudice, fear of social disapproval, unfounded superstitions, etc.

Shultz neglected to investigate the hypothesis that pretty secretaries are better paid because they contribute to the nonpecuniary satisfactions of their employers and that, therefore, the level of secretarial pulchritude is considerably higher in public utilities (or possibly banks) than in so-called competitive firms. That interesting speculation is not confirmed by my limited experience of interviewing executives in their offices over a couple of decades. My guess is that public utilities and less competitive firms have just as high a proportion of "unlovelies" in their offices as do other industries, partly for reasons which are apparent to married executives and because of the image which such firms seek to project to the public.

One can sit and spin hypotheses by the hour. Some of them will be more sensible and some more nonsensical than others. Field studies, such as this one by Shultz, have the advantage that they stimulate new lines of thought and help to keep theoretical speculation from rambling without relation to the facts of employment. Examination of such studies and reflection on them can thus aid considerably in the efficient use of the scarce resources devoted to research and writing in the fields of wages and employment at the local level.

# Competition, Monopoly, and the Pursuit of Money

ARMEN A. ALCHIAN AND REUBEN A. KESSEL

UNIVERSITY OF CALIFORNIA AT LOS ANGELES AND
UNIVERSITY OF CHICAGO

## The Problem

GENERALLY speaking, the observations of economists on the subject of monopoly fall into two classes. One set of observations, which flows directly from monopoly theory, is that resources in the competitive sector of the economy would be underutilized if used by monopolists. The other, which does not arise as an implication of either monopoly or competitive theory, consists of a series of observations of empirical phenomena: that monopolistic enterprises, by comparison with competitive enterprises, are characterized by rigid prices, stodgy managements, and relaxed, easygoing working conditions. Alternatively, it is alleged that employees of competitive enterprises work harder, managements are more aggressive and flexible, and pricing is more responsive to profit opportunities.[1]

To regard this second class of observations as not an implication of either monopoly or competitive theory is only partly correct. More correctly, these observations are inconsistent with the implications of the standard profit or wealth maximization postulate. For analyzing the behavior described by Hicks, the pecuniary wealth maximization postulate is clearly inappropriate and should be replaced by a utility maximization postulate.

---

[1] Hicks concludes: "The best of all monopoly profits is a quiet life." This conclusion appears in a theoretical paper on monopoly; yet it does not flow from the theory presented.
Preceding the foregoing quotation is: "Now, as Professor Bowley and others have pointed out, the variation in monopoly profit for some way on either side of the highest profit output may often be small (in the general case it will depend on the difference between the slopes of the marginal revenue and marginal cost curves); and if this is so, the subjective costs involved in securing a close adaption to the most profitable output may well outweigh the meagre gains offered. It seems not at all unlikely that people in monopolistic positions will often be people with sharply rising subjective costs; if this is so, they are likely to exploit their advantage much more by not bothering to get very near the position of maximum profit, than by straining themselves to get very close to it. The best of all monopoly profits is a quiet life. John R. Hicks, "Annual Survey of Economic Theory: The Theory of Monopoly." *Econometrica*, January 1935, page 8.

157

## Utility Maximization, Not Wealth Maximization

That a person seeks to maximize his utility says little more than that he makes consistent choices. In order to employ this postulate as an engine of analysis, one must also specify what things are regarded as desirable. This is the class that includes all those things of which a person prefers more rather than less: money, wealth, love, esteem, friends, ease, health, beauty, meat, gasoline, etc.[2] Then, assuming that a person is willing to substitute among these variables, that is, he will give up wealth in return for more peace and quiet, or better looking secretaries, or more cordial employees, or better weather, the behavior described by Hicks can be analyzed.

Economics cannot stipulate the exchange value that these things have for any particular person, but it can and does say that, whatever his preference patterns may be, the less he must pay for an increase in one of them, the more it will be utilized. This principle, of course, is merely the fundamental demand theorem of economics—that the demand for any good is a negative function of its price. And price here means not only the pecuniary price but the cost of whatever has to be sacrificed.

For predicting the choice of productive inputs by business firms, where only the pecuniary aspects of the factors are of concern, the narrower special-case postulate of pecuniary wealth is usually satisfactory. But this special-case postulate fails when a wider class of business activities is examined. Therefore we propose to use the general case consistently, even though in some special cases simpler hypotheses, contained within this more general hypothesis, would be satisfactory.[3]

[2] The following impression is not uncommon. "To say that the individual maximizes his satisfaction is a perfectly general statement. It says nothing about the individual's psychology of behavior, is, therefore, devoid of empirical content." T. Scitovsky, "A Note on Profit Maximization and Its Implications," *Review of Economic Studies*, 1943, pp. 57-60. But this is also true of profit or wealth maximization—unless one says what variables affect profit or wealth and in what way. And so in utility maximization, one must similarly add a postulate stating what variables affect satisfaction or utility. This leads to meaningful implications refutable, in principle, by observable events. For example, an individual will increase his use of those variables that become cheaper. Utility maximization, like wealth maximization, is not a mere sterile truism.

[3] Failure to give adequate heed to the special-case properties of wealth maximization may have been responsible for some complaints about the inadequacy of economic theory and may even have led to the curious belief that people themselves change according to which postulate is used. For example, Scitovsky says (*ibid.*):
"The puritan psychology of valuing money for its own sake, and not for the enjoyments and comforts it might yield, is that of the ideal entrepreneur as he was

An example of the power of the generalized utility maximizing postulate is provided by Becker.[4] He shows that under the more general postulate a person, deliberately and even in full knowledge of the consequences for business profits or personal pecuniary wealth, will choose to accept a lower salary or smaller rate of return on invested capital in exchange for nonpecuniary income in the form of, say, working with pretty secretaries, nonforeigners, or whites. The difference in money return between what an entrepreneur could earn and what he does earn when he chooses to discriminate is an equalizing difference that will not be eliminated by market pressures. If these persisting, equalizing differences exist, their size, and consequently the extent of discrimination, will differ when institutional arrangements lead to differences in the relative costs of income in pecuniary form relative to income in nonpecuniary form. Thus, if one can determine the direction in which relative costs are affected by activities or variables that en-

---

conceived in the early days of capitalism. The combination of frugality and industry, the entrepreneurial virtues, is calculated to insure the independence of the entrepreneur's willingness to work from the level of his income. The classical economists, therefore, were justified in assuming that the entrepreneur aims at maximizing his profits. They were concerned with a type of business man whose psychology happened to be such that for him maximizing profits was identical with maximizing satisfaction.

"The entrepreneur today may have lost some of the frugality and industry of his forefathers; nevertheless, the assumption that he aims at maximizing his profits is still quite likely to apply to him—at least as a first approximation. For this assumption is patently untrue only about people who regard work as plain drudgery; a necessary evil, with which they have to put up in order to earn their living and the comforts of life. The person who derives satisfaction from his work—other than that yielded by the income he receives for it—will to a large extent be governed by ambition, spirit of emulation and rivalry, pride in his work, and similar considerations, when he plans the activity. We believe that the entrepreneur usually belongs in this last category."

Aside from the dubious validity of (1) alleged differences between the entrepreneurs of the "early days" of capitalism and those of today, and (2) the allegation that the early entrepreneur was one whose utility function had only a single variable—wealth—in it, the more general analysis obviates the urge to set up two different and inconsistent behavior postulates, as if people were schizophrenic types—utility maximizers when consumers and wealth maximizers when businessmen.

The special-case property of the wealth maximizing postulate has been noted by M. W. Reder ("A Reconsideration of the Marginal Productivity Theory," *Journal of Political Economy*, October 1947, pp. 450-458). But in suggesting alternatives he did not postulate the more general one, which includes the valid applications of the special-case postulate as well as many more, without leading to the invalid implications of the special-case postulate.

[4] Gary S. Becker, *The Economics of Discrimination*, University of Chicago Press, 1957.

hance a person's utility, then it should be possible to observe corresponding differences in behavior.

## Monopolistic Versus Competitive Behavior

The wealth-maximizing postulate seems to imply that both competitive and monopolistic enterprises pursue profits with equal vigor and effectiveness, that their managements are equally alert and aggressive, and that prices are just as flexible in competitive as in monopolized markets. Both the competitive and monopoly model imply that the assets of an enterprise, be it a monopolist or competitive firm, will be utilized by those for whom these assets have the greatest economic value. One might object to this implication of similarity between competition and monopoly by arguing that, when a monopolistic enterprise is not making the most of its pecuniary economic opportunities, it runs less risk of being driven out of business than a similarly mismanaged competitive enterprise. The answer to this is that despite the absence of competition in product markets, those who can most profitably utilize monopoly powers will acquire control over them: competition in the capital markets will allocate monopoly rights to those who can use them most profitably. Therefore, so long as free capital markets are available, the absence of competition in product markets does not imply a different quality of management in monopolistic as compared with competitive enterprises. Only in the case of nontransferable assets (human monopoly rights and powers like those commanded by Bing Crosby) does classical theory, given free capital market arrangements, admit a difference between competition and monopoly with respect to the effectiveness with which these enterprises pursue profits.[5]

The preceding argument implies that there is no difference in the proportion of inefficiently operated firms among monopolistic as compared with competitive enterprises. (Inefficiency here means that a situation is capable of being changed so that a firm could earn more pecuniary income with no loss in nonpecuniary income or else can obtain more nonpecuniary income with no loss in pecuniary income.) As Becker has shown, discrimination against Negroes in employment is not necessarily a matter of business inefficiency. It can be viewed as

[5] For a statement of this position, see Becker, *The Economics of Discrimination*, p. 38. Becker argues that, insofar as monopoly rights are randomly distributed and cannot be transferred, there are no forces operating to distribute these resources to those for whom they are most valuable. Consequently monopolists, when rights are nontransferable, would be less efficient, on the average, than competitive firms.

an expression of a taste, and one's a priori expectation is that discrimination is characterized by a negatively sloped demand curve. From this viewpoint, discrimination against Negroes by business enterprises, whether competitors or monopolists, would not lessen even if managements were convinced that discrimination reduced their pecuniary income. Presumably, the known sacrifice of pecuniary income is more than compensated for by the gain in nonpecuniary income. But if discrimination does not constitute business inefficiency, then the frequency of discrimination against Negroes ought to be just as great in competitive as in monopolistic enterprises, since both are presumed to be equally efficient. This implication is apparently inconsistent with existing evidence. Becker's data indicate that Negroes are discriminated against more frequently by monopolistic enterprises.[6] But why do monopolistic enterprises discriminate against Negroes more than do competitive enterprises? One would expect that those who have a taste for discrimination against Negroes would naturally gravitate to those economic activities that, for purely pecuniary reasons, do not employ Negroes. Free choice of economic activities implies a distribution of resources that would minimize the costs of satisfying tastes for discrimination. Consequently the managements of competitive enterprises ought to discriminate against Negroes neither more nor less than those of monopolistic enterprises.

If there is greater discrimination by monopolists than by competitive enterprises, and if it cannot be explained by arguing either that people with tastes for discrimination also have special talents related to monopolistic enterprises or that monopolists are in some sense less efficient businessmen, what, then, explains Becker's data and similar observations? More generally, what is the explanation for the contentions that monopolists pursue pecuniary wealth less vigorously, do not work as hard, have more lavish business establishments, etc.? It is to this problem that this paper is addressed.

## Monopoly and Profit Control

Stigler and others have pointed out that monopolies, both labor and product, are creatures of the state in a sense which is not true of competitive enterprises.[7] Monopolies typically are protected against the

[6] *Ibid.*, p. 40, Table II.
[7] George J. Stigler, "The Extent and Bases of Monopoly," *American Economic Review*, June 1942, Supplement Part 2, p. 1; H. Gregg Lewis, "The Labor Monopoly

hazards of competition, not simply by their ability to compete, but by the state's policy of not permitting competitors to enter monopolized markets. Laws are enacted that encourage and lead to the creation of monopolies in particular markets. Monopolies so created are beholden to the state for their existence—the state giveth, the state taketh away. Accordingly, they constrain their business policies by satisfying the requirements that they shall do what is necessary to maintain their monopoly status.

Public utilities are an example. Under this head one should include not only gas, electric, and water companies, but all franchised and licensed industries. Railroads, busses, airlines, and taxis fall in this category of business for which permission of a public authority is required, and for which rate and profit regulation exists. For many other businesses, entry regulation exists: commercial and savings banks, savings and loan associations, insurance companies, and the medical profession. All these are formally regulated monopolies, since they are licensed and operated with the approval of the state. Their cardinal sin is to be too profitable.[8] This constraint upon monopolists does not exist for firms operating in competitive markets. This difference in constraints implies differences between the business policies of competitive firms and those of monopolies. The remainder of this paper is devoted to indicating specifically the character of the constraints that are postulated and exploring the observable implications of this postulate.

Even a firm that has successfully withstood the test of open competition without government protection may manifest the behavior of a protected monopoly. Thus a firm like General Motors may become very large and outstanding and acquire a large share of a market just as a protected monopoly does. If, in addition, its profits are large, it will fear that public policy or state action may be directed against it, just as against a state-created monopoly. Such a firm constrains its behavior much in the style of a monopoly whose profit position is protected but also watched by the state. This suggests that the distinction between publicly regulated monopolies and nonregulated

Problem: A Positive Program," *Journal of Political Economy*, Aug. 1951, p. 277; C. E. Lindbloom, *Unions and Capitalism*, Yale University Press, 1949, p. 214; and Milton Friedman, "Some Comments on the Significance of Labor Unions for Economic Policy," in *The Impact of the Union*, David M. Wright, ed., Harcourt Brace, 1951, p. 214.

[8] The notorious suggestion of the medical profession that doctors not drive around town in expensive Cadillacs when visiting patients is an example of the point being made.

monopolies is a false distinction for this problem. As the possibility of state action increases, a firm will adapt its behavior to that which the state deems appropriate. In effect, state regulation is implicitly present. The cardinal sin of a monopolist, to repeat, is to be too profitable. Public regulation of monopolies is oriented about fixing final prices in order to enable monopolists to earn something like the going rate of return enjoyed by competitive firms. If monopolists are too profitable, pressures are exerted to reduce profits through lowering prices. Only if monopolists can demonstrate to regulatory authorities that they are not profitable enough are they permitted to raise prices.

## Implications

If regulated monopolists are able to earn more than the permissible pecuniary rate of return, then "inefficiency" is a free good, because the alternative to inefficiency is the same pecuniary income and no "inefficiency." Therefore this profit constraint leads to a divergence between private and economic costs. However, it is easy to be naive about this inefficiency. More properly, it is not inefficiency at all but efficient utility maximizing through nonpecuniary gains. Clearly one class of nonpecuniary income is the indulgence of one's tastes in the kind of people with whom one prefers to associate. Specifically, this may take the form of pretty secretaries, of pleasant, well-dressed, congenial people who never say anything annoying, of lavish offices, of large expense accounts, of shorter working hours, of costly administrative procedures that reduce the wear and tear on executives rather than increasing the pecuniary wealth of the enterprise, of having secretaries available on a moment's notice by having them sitting around not doing anything, and of many others. It is important to recognize that to take income in nonpecuniary form is consistent with maximizing utility. What is important is not a matter of differences in tastes between monopolists and competitive firms, but differences in the terms of trade of pecuniary for nonpecuniary income. And given this difference in the relevant price or exchange ratios, the difference in the mix purchased should not be surprising.[9]

[9] Usually in economics consumers are presumed to maximize utility subject to fixed income or wealth. What is the wealth or income constraint here? In one sense it is not merely wealth or income that is the pertinent limitation. Many people have access to the use and allocation of resources even though they don't own them. An administrator can assign offices and jobs; he can affect the way company or business resources are used. In all of these decisions, he will be

If wealth cannot be taken out of an organization in salaries or in other forms of personal pecuniary property, the terms of trade between pecuniary wealth and nonpecuniary business-associated forms of satisfaction turn against the former. More of the organization's funds will now be reinvested (which need not result in increased wealth) in ways that enhance the manager's prestige or status in the community. Or more money can be spent for goods and services that enhance the manager's and employees' utility. There can be more luxurious offices, more special services, and so forth, than would ordinarily result if their costs were coming out of personal wealth.

For the total amount of resources used, these constrained expenditure patterns necessarily yield less utility than the unconstrained. The man who spends a dollar with restrictions will need less than a dollar to get an equivalent satisfaction if he can spend it without the restriction. This constrained optimum provides the answer to the question: If a person does spend the wealth of a business as business-connected expenditures for thick rugs and beautiful secretaries, can they not be treated simply as a substitute for household consumption, since he can be regarded as voluntarily choosing to spend his wealth in the business rather than in the home? The answer is that business spending is a more constrained, even if voluntary, choice. This whole analysis is merely an illustration of the effects of restricting the operation of the law of comparative advantage by reducing the size of the market (or range of alternatives).

Employment policies will also reflect the maximization of utility. Assume that an employer prefers clean-cut, friendly, sociable employees. If two available employees are equally productive, but only one is white, native born, Christian, and attractive, the other will not get the job. And if the other employee's wages are reduced to offset this, it will take a greater cut or equilibrating difference to offset this in a monopoly. Why? Because the increase in take-home profits provided by the cost reduction is smaller (if it is increased at all) in the monopoly or state-sheltered firm. Thus one would expect to find a lower

---

influenced by the effects on his own situation. Therefore to gauge his behavior by the usual wealth or income limitation is to eliminate from consideration a wider range of activities that do not fall within the usual "wealth" or ownership limitation. By straining it is possible to incorporate even this kind of activity with the wealth constraint but we find it more convenient for exposition not to do so. In this paper, in a sense, we are discussing the institutional arrangements which determine to what extent constraints are of one type rather than another.

fraction of "other" employees in "monopolies" and other areas of sheltered competition.

What this means is that the wages paid must be high enough to attract the "right" kind of employees. At these wages the supply of the "other" kind will be plentiful. A rationing problem exists, so that the buyer, when he offers a higher price than would clear the market with respect to pecuniary productive aspects clears the market by imposing other tests, like congeniality, looks, and so on. For the right kind of employee the price is not above the market clearing price. In a competitive situation this price differential would not persist because its elimination would all redound to the benefit of the owners, whereas in monopoly it will persist because the reduction in costs cannot be transformed into equally large take-home pecuniary wealth for the owners.

The question may be raised: Even if all this is true of a regulated monopoly like a public utility, what about unregulated, competitively superior monopolies? Why should they act this way? The answer is, as pointed out earlier, that the distinction between regulated and unregulated monopolies is a false one. All monopolies are subject to regulation or the threat of destruction through antitrust action. And one of the criteria that the courts seem to consider in evaluating whether or not a firm is a "good" monopoly is its profitability.[10] It behooves an unregulated monopoly, if it wants to remain one, not to appear to be too profitable.

The owners of a monopoly, regulated or "not," therefore have their property rights attenuated because they do not have unrestricted access to or personal use of their company's wealth. This suggests that the whole analysis can be formulated, not in terms of monopoly and competition, as we have chosen to for present purposes, but in terms of private property rights. There is basically no analytic difference between the two since an analysis made in terms of monopoly and competition identifies and emphasizes circumstances that affect property rights. The same analysis can be applied to nonprofit organizations, governments, unions, state-owned, and other "non-owned" institutions, with almost identical results.

One word of clarification—the contrast here is between monopoly and competition, not between corporate and noncorporate firms. We

[10] See Aaron Director and Edward H. Levi, "Trade Regulation," *Northwestern Law Review*, 1956, p. 286 and ff.

are analyzing differences in implications for behavior that arise from factors other than the corporate structure of the firm. Although there may be differences between corporate, diffused ownership firms and single proprietorships that may affect the many kinds of behavior discussed in this paper, we have been unable to derive them from the corporate aspect. Nor are those features derived from considerations of size per se—however much this may affect behavior.[11]

The preceding propositions stated that more of some forms of behavior would be observed among monopolies. But more than what and of what? More than would be observed in competitive industries. It is not asserted that every monopolist will prefer more than every competitor; instead, it is said that, whatever the relative tastes of various individuals, all those in a monopolistic situation pay less for their actions than they would in a competitive context. And the way to test this is not to cite a favorable comparison based on one monopolist and one competitor. Rather the variations in individual preferences must be allowed to average out by random sampling from each class.

## Tests of the Analysis

What observable populations can be compared in testing these implications? One pair of populations are the public utilities and private competitive corporations. Public utilities are monopolies in that entry by competitors is prohibited. Yet, as indicated earlier, the utility is not allowed to exercise its full monopoly powers either in acquiring or distributing pecuniary wealth as dividends to its owners. The owners therefore have relatively weak incentives to try to increase their profits through more efficient management or operation beyond (usually) 6 per cent. But they do have relatively strong incentives to use the resources of the public utility for their own personal interests, but in ways that will count as company costs. Nor does the public utility regulatory body readily detect such activities, because its incentives to do so are even weaker than those of the stockholders. The regulatory body's survival function is the elimination of publicly detectable in-

[11] We were originally tempted to believe that the same theory being applied here could be applied to corporate versus noncorporate institutions, where the corporate form happens to involve many owners. Similarly the size factor could also be analyzed via the effects on the costs and rewards of various choice opportunities. Subsequent analysis suggests that many of the appealing differences between corporate, dispersed ownership and individual proprietorship proved to be superficial.

efficiencies. Furthermore, the utility regulatory board has a poor criterion of efficiency because it lacks competitive standards.

Public utility managements, whether or not they are also stockholders, will engage in activities that raise costs even if they eat up profits. Management will be rational (i.e., utility maximizing and efficient) if it uses company funds to hire pleasant and congenial employees and to buy its supplies from salesmen who have these same virtues. They cost more, of course, but how does the regulatory commission decide that these are unjustifiable expenditures—even though stockholders would prefer larger profits (which they aren't allowed to have) and customers would prefer lower product prices? Office furniture and equipment will be of higher quality than otherwise. Fringe benefits will be greater and working conditions more pleasant. The managers will be able to devote a greater part of their business time to community and civic programs. They will reap the prestige rewards given to the "statesman-businessman" class of employers. Vacations will be longer and more expensive. Time off for sick leave and for civic duties will be greater. Buildings and equipment will be more beautiful. Public utility advertising will be found more often in magazines and papers appealing to the intellectual or the culturally elite, because this is a low "cost" way of enhancing the social status of the managers and owners. Larger contributions out of company resources to education, science, and charity will be forthcoming—not because private competitors are less appreciative of these things, but because they cost monopolists less.[12]

[12] We could compare a random sample of secretaries working for public utilities with a random sample of secretaries working for competitive businesses. The former will be prettier—no matter whom we select as our judges (who must not know what hypothesis we are testing when they render their decision). The test, however, really should be made by sampling among the secretaries who are working for equal salaried executives in an attempt to eliminate the income effect on demand. Another implication is that the ratio of a secretary's salary to her supervisor's salary will be higher for a public utility—on the grounds that beauty commands a price. Other nonpecuniary, desirable attributes of secretaries also will be found to a greater extent in public utilities (as well as in nonprofit enterprises) than in private competitive firms. In a similar way, all of the preceding suggested implications about race, religion, and sex could be tested.

Another comparison can be made. Consider the sets of events in the business and in the home of the public utility employee or owner having a given salary or wealth. The ratio of the thickness of the rug in the office to that of the rug at home will be greater for the public utility than for the private competitive firm employee or owner. The ratio of the value of the available company car to the family car's value will be higher for the public utility than for the private competitive firm. And similarly for the ratios of secretary's beauty to wife's beauty, decorations in the office, travel expenses, etc.

*167*

Job security, whether in the form of seniority or tenure, is a form of increased wealth for employees. Since it makes for more pleasant employer-employee relations, it is a source of utility for employers. The incentive or willingness of owners to grant this type of wealth to employees and thereby increase their own utility is relatively strong because profits are not the opportunity costs of this choice. The owners of a competitive firm, on the other hand, would have to pay the full price either in profits or in competitive disadvantage. Therefore the viability of such activities is lower in that type of firm. The relative frequency or extent of job security should be higher in monopolies and employee turnover rates lower. Also, the incidence of tenure in private educational institutions will be less than in nonprofit or state-operated educational institutions—if the foregoing analysis is correct.[13]

The relative incidence of employee cooperatives will also provide a test. Some employee cooperatives are subsidized by employers. This subsidy often takes the form of free use of company facilities and of employees for operating the cooperative. For any given set of attitudes of employers towards employee cooperatives, costs are lower for monopolists with "excess" profits. Consequently their frequency will be greater among these enterprises.

Inability to keep excess profits in pecuniary form implies that monopolists are more willing than competitive enterprises to forego them in exchange for other forms of utility-enhancing activities within the firm. Fringe benefits, cooperatives, and special privileges for certain employees will be more common. Employees whose consumption preferences do not induce them to use the cooperatives or fringe benefits are not necessarily stupid if they complain of this diversion of resources. But their complaints do reflect their differences in tastes and their ignorance of the incentives and reward patterns that impinge upon owners and administrators. Instead of complaining, they might better seek benefits of special interest to themselves. But since this involves a power play within the firm, the senior people are likely to be the ones who win most often. Hence one would expect to find such benefits more closely tailored to the preferences of the higher administrative officials than would be observed in a competitive business.

Wage policies will also differ in monopoly and nonmonopoly enter-

[13] See Armen A. Alchian, "Private Property and the Relative Cost of Tenure," *The Public Stake in Union Power*, P. Bradley, ed., University of Virginia Press, 1958, pp. 350-371.

prises. If business should fall off, the incentive to resort to fringe or wage reductions (unpleasant under any circumstances), will be weaker for a public utility because the potential savings in profits, if profits are not below the maximum permissible level, cannot be as readily captured by the management or stockholders. One would expect to find wages falling less in hard times, and one would also expect a smaller turnover and unemployment of personnel. The fact that these same implications might be derived from the nature of the demand for the utility's product does not in itself upset the validity of these propositions. But it does make the empirical test more difficult.

Seniority, tenure, employee cooperatives, and many other fringe benefits—instead of increased money salaries or payments—can be composed of mixtures of pecuniary and nonpecuniary benefits, though the inducement to adopt them despite their inefficiency is enhanced by the relatively smaller sacrifice imposed on the owners of organizations in monopolistic situations, as defined here. The relative cost of take-home wealth for the owners is higher; hence they are more willing to utilize other consumption channels.[14]

Constraints on the opportunity to keep profits that are above the allowable limit reduce the incentive to spend money for profitable expansion of services. An upper limit on profits, with strong protection from competition but no assurance of protection from losses of over-expansion, will bias the possible rewards downward in comparison with those of competitive business. An implication of this is "shortages" of public utility services. Despite the fact that prices are above the cost of providing some services, the latter will not necessarily be available. It is better to wait until the demand is already existent and expansion is demanded by the authorities. The possible extra profits are an attentuated inducement.

But these implications hold only if the public utility is earning its allowable limit of profits on investment. If it is losing money—and there is no guarantee against it—stockholders' take-home pay will be curtailed by inefficiency. Until profits reach the take-home limit, profit-

---

[14] The other commonly advanced reasons for such benefits or "inefficiencies" are the income tax on pecuniary wealth and the influence of unions. The former force is obvious; the latter is the effect of desires by union officials to strengthen their position by emphasizing the employee members' benefits to the union administration, as is done in many fringe benefits. But whether or not these latter factors are present, the one advanced here is an independent factor implying differences between monopoly and competition.

able and efficient operations will be desirable. If the state regulatory commission is slow to grant price increases in response to cost increases, the utilities should find their profits reduced below the allowable limit during a period of inflation. As a result there should be a tightening up or elimination, or both, of some of the effects predicted in the preceding discussion.[15] One would expect the opposite to occur during periods of deflation.

The present analysis also suggests that there may be an economic rationale for the "shock theory" of wage adjustments. This theory asserts that the profit-reducing wage increases imposed by labor will shock management into greater efficiencies. Suppose that monopolies are induced to trade pecuniary wealth (because they are not allowed to keep it) for nonpecuniary forms of income financed out of business expenditures. This means that, under the impact of higher wage costs and lower profits, the monopolies can now proceed to restore profit rates. Since some of their profit possibilities had been diverted into so-called nonpecuniary forms of income, higher labor costs will make realized profits, broadly interpreted, at least a little smaller. In part, at least, the increased pecuniary wages will come at the expense of nonpecuniary benefits, which will be reduced in order to restore profit levels. Actually, the shock effect does not produce increases in efficiency. Instead, it revises the pattern of distribution of benefits. Left unchanged is the rate of pecuniary profits—if these were formerly at their allowable, but not economic, limit.

Evidence relevant for testing the hypothesis presented here has been produced by the American Jewish Congress, which surveyed the occupations of Jewish and non-Jewish Harvard Business School graduates. The data consist of a random sample of 224 non-Jewish and a sample of 128 Jewish MBA's.[16] The 352 Harvard graduates were classified by

[15] This analysis suggests that, with the decline in profitability of railroads, the principle of seniority advancement in railroad management has become relatively less viable. Similar arguments are applicable for other fringe benefits. With respect to negotiation with unions, it implies that railroad managements will more vigorously resist giving the unions extravagantly large concessions because these costs are being borne by owners.

The analysis also implies that unions do better in dealing with monopolistic as contrasted with competitive industries.

[16] The existence of these data became known to the authors as a result of an article that appeared in the New York Times on the first day of the conference at which this paper was presented. Subsequently the American Jewish Congress released a paper, "Analysis of Jobs Held by Jewish and by Non-Jewish Graduates of the Harvard Graduate School of Business Administration," which contains the data reported here.

ten industry categories: (1) agriculture, forestry, and fisheries, (2) mining, (3) construction, (4) transportation, communication, and other public utilities, (5) manufacturing, (6) wholesale and retail trade, (7) finance, insurance, and real estate, (8) business services, (9) amusement, recreation, and related services, and (10) professional and related services.

Categories (4) and (7) must be regarded as relatively monopolized. Therefore, if the hypothesis presented here is correct, the relative frequency of Jews in these two fields is lower than it is for all fields combined.[17] The relative frequency of Jews in all fields taken together, in the entire sample, is 36 per cent. These data show that the frequency of Jews—74 MBA's—in the two monopolized fields is less than 18 per cent. If a sample of 352, of whom 36 per cent are Jews, is assigned so that 74 are in monopolized and 278 in nonmonopolized fields, the probability that an assignment random with respect to religion will result in as few as 18 per cent Jews in monopolized fields (and over 41 per cent in nonmonopolized fields) is less than 0.0005. This evidence, therefore, is consistent with the hypothesis presented.

One might object to classifying all finance, insurance, and real estate as monopolized fields. This classification includes the subcategories of banking, credit agencies, investment companies, security and commodity brokers, dealers and exchanges, other finance services, insurance, and real estate. Of these, only insurance and banking are regulated monopolies. If only these two subcategories are used, then there are 6 Jews among a group of 39 or a frequency of less than 15 per cent. If a sample of 352, of whom 36 per cent are Jews, is assigned so that 39 are in monopolized and 313 in nonmonopolized fields, the probability that an assignment that is random with respect to religion will result in as few as 15 per cent Jews in the monopolized fields (and over 39 per cent in the nonmonopolized fields) is less than 0.005. This evidence is also consistent with the hypothesis presented.

## Applications to Labor Unions

This application of monopoly analysis need not be restricted to public utilities. Any regulated activity or one that regulates entry into work

---

[17] Similarly, one would expect Jews and Negroes to be underrepresented among enterprises supplying goods and services to monopolists for the same reason that they are underrepresented as employees.

should show the same characteristics. Labor unions, because of their control over entry or because of exclusive union representation in bargaining, have monopoly potential. Insofar as a union is able to use that potential to raise wages above the competitive level, unless the jobs are auctioned off, the rationing problem is a nonprice one. A "thoroughly unscrupulous" agent could, in principle, pocket the difference between the payment by the employer and the receipts to the employee, where this difference reflects the difference between the monopolistic and the competitive wage. The moral pressures and the state regulation of union monopoly operate against the existence of thoroughly unscrupulous union officers. But so long as the fruits of such monopoly are handed on to the employed members of the union, the state seems tolerant of monopoly unions. Because of the absence of free entry into the "union agent business," competitive bidding by prospective union agents will not pass on the potential monopoly gains fully to the laborers who do get the jobs.

The necessity of rationing jobs arises because the union agents or managers do not keep for themselves the entire difference between the monopoly wage and the lower competitive wage that would provide just the number of workers wanted. If they did keep it, there would be equilibrium without nonprice rationing. If any part of that difference is captured by the laborers, the quantity available will be excessive relative to the quantity demanded at the monopolized wage rate. The unwillingness of society to tolerate capture of all that difference by the union agents means that either it must be passed on to the workers, thus creating a rationing problem, or it must be indirectly captured by the union agents—not as pecuniary take-home pay, but indirectly as a utility derived from the expenditure of that difference in connection with union business.

To the extent that the monopoly gains are passed on, the preceding rationing problem and its implications exist. But to the extent that they are not, the union agents or persons in control of the monopoly organization will divert the monopoly gains to their own benefit, not through outright sale of the jobs to the highest bidder, but through such indirect devices as high initiation fees and membership dues. This ties the monopoly sale price to the conventional dues arrangement. Creation of large pension funds and special service benefits controlled by the unions redounds to the benefit of the union agents and officers in ways that are too well publicized as a result of recent hearings on union activities to need mention here.[18]

The membership of monopoly unions will tolerate such abuses to the point where the abuses offset the value of monopoly gains accruing to the employed members. We emphasize that these effects are induced by *both* the monopoly rationing problem and by the desire to convert the monopoly gains into nonpecuniary take-home pay for the union officers or dominant group. We conjecture that both elements are present; part of the monopoly gain is passed on to the workers, and part is captured as a nonpecuniary source of utility. When the former occurs the rationing problem exists, and the agents or those in the union will exclude the less desirable type of job applicants—less desirable not in pecuniary productivity to the employer but as fellow employees and fellow members of the union. Admission will be easier for people whose cultural and personal characteristics conform to the interests of the existing members.[19] And admission will be especially difficult for those regarded as potential price cutters in hard times or not to be counted on as faithful members with a strong sense of loyalty to the union. Minority groups and those who find they must accept lower wages because of some personal or cultural attribute, even though they are just as productive in a pecuniary sense to the employer, will be more willing to accept lower wages if threatened with the loss of their jobs. But these are the very types who will weaken the union's monopoly power. All of this suggests that young people, Negroes,

[18] Relevant for the analysis of monopoly power is the character of the protection afforded by the state. For utilities the state actively and directly uses its police powers to eliminate competition. For other monopolies—and this is especially relevant for union monopoly—the state permits these monopolies to use private police power to eliminate competition. The powers of the state passively and indirectly support these monopolies by refusing to act against the exercise of private police power. This suggests that there ought to exist a link between those who have a comparative advantage in the exercise of private police powers (gangsters), and monopolies that eliminate competition through "strong arm" techniques.

[19] If the employer is the nonprice rationer, i.e., if the employer does the hiring and not the union, as is true for airplane pilots, he too will display a greater amount of discrimination in nonpecuniary attributes than with a competitive wage rate. If the wage rate has been raised so that he has to retain a smaller number of employees, he will retain those with the greater nonpecuniary productivity. If the wage rate would have fallen in response to increased supplies of labor but instead is kept up by wage controls, then the supply from which he could choose is larger, and again he will select those with the greater nonpecuniary attributes—assuming we are dealing with units of labor or equal pecuniary productivity.

Jews, and other minority or unorthodox groups will be underrepresented in monopolistic unions.[20]

There exists a symmetry in effects between nonprice rationing of admission to monopolistic trade unions and the allocation of rights to operate TV channels, airlines, radio stations, banks, savings and loan associations, public utilities, and the like. In the absence of the sale of these rights by the commission or government agency charged with their allocation, nonprice rationing comes into play. This implies that Negroes, Jews, and disliked minority groups of all kinds will be underrepresented among the recipients of these rights. The symmetry between admission to monopolistic trade unions and the allocation of monopoly rights over the sale of some good or service by a government agency is not complete. The rights allocated by the government, but not by trade unions, often become private property and can be resold. Therefore this analysis implies that entrance into these economic activities is more frequently achieved by minority groups, as compared with the population as a whole, through the purchase of outstanding rights.

The chief problem in verifying these implications is that of identifying relative degrees of monopoly power. If the classification is correct, there is a possibility of testing the analysis. A comparison of the logic of craft unions with industry-wide unions suggests that the former have greater monopoly powers. Therefore if this classification is valid, the preceding analysis would be validated if the predicted results were observed.

For classic economic reasons, we conjecture that the craft unions are more likely to have monopolistic powers than industry-wide unions. Therefore we would expect to observe more such discrimination in the first type of union than in the second. And included in the category of craft unions are such organizations as the American Medical Association, and any profession in which admission involves the approval of a governing board.[21]

## Conclusions and Conjectures

This analysis suggests that strong nonrestrained profit incentives serve the interests of the relatively unpopular, unorthodox, and individualistic

[20] See Reuben A. Kessel, "Price Discrimination in Medicine," *Journal of Law and Economics*, 1958, p. 46 and ff.

[21] For evidence of the existence of discrimination, see H. R. Northrup, *Organized Labor and the Negro*, Chap. I, New York, Harpers, 1944; and Kessel, *Price Discrimination in Medicine*, p. 47 and ff.

members of society, who have relatively more to gain from the absence of restrictions. Communists are perhaps the strongest case in point. They are strongly disliked in our society and, as a matter of ideology, believe that profit incentives and private property are undesirable. Yet if this analysis is correct, one should find communists overrepresented in highly competitive enterprises. Similar conclusions hold for ex-convicts, disbarred lawyers, defrocked priests, doctors who have lost their licenses to practice medicine, and so forth.

The analysis also suggests an inconsistency in the views of those who argue that profit incentives bring out the worst in people and at the same time believe that discrimination in terms of race, creed, or color is socially undesirable. Similarly, those concerned about the pressures toward conformity in our society, i.e., fears for a society composed of organization men, ought to have some interest in the competitiveness of our markets. It is fairly obvious that the pressures to conform are weaker for a speculator on a grain or stock exchange than they are for a junior executive of A.T. and T. or a university professor with or without tenure.

## COMMENTS

GARY S. BECKER, Columbia University

### I

Sociologists, psychologists, and other social scientists have tried to explain why people differ in their prejudices or, better still, attitudes, towards others and have also tried to determine the extent of observable discrimination. There has, however, been little interaction between these investigations, so that scant attention has been paid to how attitudes get translated into actual discrimination. The economist is singularly well prepared to analyze how attitudes combine with different structural and institutional arrangements to produce actual discrimination, but, unfortunately, he has not considered this a worthwhile or manageable problem, and has made only a few contributions to its solution.[1]

In their fine paper Alchian and Kessel consider this problem worthy of attention and fill part of the void by analyzing how one important

---

[1] In this connection it is interesting to note that sociologists in the South are preoccupied with the racial question while economists there almost completely neglect it.

institutional arrangement—governmental restrictions on profits—combines with attitudes towards minority groups and with other attitudes to produce discrimination, nepotism, and other types of nonpecuniary choices. The theoretical argument showing why these restrictions on profits induce firms (or unions) to choose more nonpecuniary income is carefully laid out, and numerous empirical tests of the analysis, ranging from pretty women to seniority rules, are indicated. While they do not try to demonstrate empirically that their analysis is important, I am inclined to believe that it is sufficiently important to merit much further attention from economists.

An empirical measure of these nonpecuniary effects that yields a more quantitative estimate of their importance than do the measures suggested by Alchian and Kessel can be developed. Suppose a firm was using $100 worth of real capital and that the competitive rate of return was 5 per cent. If the firm was in a competitive industry its equilibrium income would be $5 per annum and its market value would be $100. If the firm had monopoly power its income would be greater than $5; let us assume that it would have an income of $10 in the absence of government restrictions. If the monopoly power were perfectly transferable, competition in the capital market would establish a market value for this firm equal to $200 and a market rate of return equal to 5 per cent (10/200), the competitive rate. Government regulation might limit the monopolist to receiving no more than, say, $5 of money income, and this would induce him to take some nonpecuniary income. Let it be assumed that he could get $3 worth of nonpecuniary income. The total income of the monopolist would be $8, and if this monopoly power were also perfectly transferable, the equilibrium market value of the firm would have to be $160. The market rate of return on total income would still be 5 per cent (8/160), but the observed money rate of return would only be about 3 per cent (5/160), *less* than the competitive rate. This positive difference of 2 percentage points between the competitive and monopolistic money rates of return would measure the importance of nonpecuniary income to the monopolist.[2] It would be larger the greater the monopoly power, the greater the restrictions on money income, and the greater the ease of substitution between pecuniary and nonpecuniary income.

[2] More generally, it measures the difference between the nonpecuniary income in monopolistic and competitive firms, for firms may receive nonpecuniary income even in the absence of government restrictions on money income.

The assumption of perfectly transferable monopoly power requires, among other things, that capital markets operate smoothly, and that any separation between owners and managers is limited. Dropping this assumption would affect many details of the analysis, but the principle would tend to remain the same. For example, if there were separation between owners and managers, the difference between competitive and monopolistic money rates of return would appear in the price that could be obtained for control of a firm by those in control, be they some owners or some managers. The apparent paradox of monopolists receiving less than the competitive money return would still be with us, and the difference between these returns would still tend to measure the greater nonpecuniary income in monopolies.

## II

Although the authors emphasized the effects of government restrictions on monopoly profits, many other private as well as public institutions also encourage a substitution between pecuniary and nonpecuniary income. In the remainder of this comment, I try to fit their discussion into a framework of general institutional influences on nonpecuniary behavior, with especial emphasis on discrimination.

Any restriction on the money incomes of working persons, be they employees or employers, would tend to induce a substitution of psychic for monetary income. It is well known that the ordinary income tax provides an incentive for all earners to take more psychic income since it is not taxable. It is seldom mentioned, however, that this includes an incentive to discriminate in employment against minority groups. Many private institutions also tend to limit money income and induce a substitution towards psychic income. For example, I have argued elsewhere[3] that the use of nonprice techniques to ration entry into certain unions encourages this kind of substitution and yet could not entirely be explained by government influence.

Perhaps an even more important example can be found in the separation of owners from managers in modern corporations. If managers really had *complete* control they would have little incentive to maximize profits less diligently than owners, but they would keep the profits for themselves in the form of salaries, bonuses, etc., rather than distribute them to owners. The more interesting situation arises when managers

---

[3] See my "Union Restrictions on Entry," *The Public Stake in Union Power*, Philip H. Bradley, ed.: University of Virginia Press, 1959, pp. 209-224.

do not have such complete control and when open attempts to capture profits would lead to their being turned out of office. Nevertheless, they might succeed in capturing profits if their income could be concealed, say, by complicated stock options or large expense accounts. Another way to conceal it would be to take psychic income since this is less readily observed or quantified than money income. (The argument in the Alchian and Kessel paper is really based on the same consideration, since governments want to limit the total income of monopolies but can limit the monetary part more readily.) So it would seem that much of the economic content in the separation of owners from managers lies in the impetus given to psychic income, be it from discrimination, nepotism, or corporate support of education.

It is possible to generalize the analysis still further to include a wider variety of situations by looking at the problem differently. A group would try to offset any prejudice against them by offering compensating advantages. For example, in the market place they would receive lower wages than equally productive persons not subjected to prejudice, so that the difference between these wages could be offered to offset the prejudice against them. It has been seen that restrictions placed on money incomes received, such as profit restrictions or the income tax, prevent discriminators from collecting the income difference offered them and thus make it difficult or impossible for disadvantaged groups to offset prejudices. Precisely the same situation occurs when restrictions are placed on the money income gain that can be *offered* by a disadvantaged group.

Institutions limiting the amount offered, like those limiting the amount received, appear in very different clothing. Take the "equal pay for equal work" movement which is exceedingly popular and resulted in legislation in some states and countries. The aim of the movement and legislation is to prevent various minorities, especially working women, from receiving lower wages than other apparently equally productive workers; that is, the aim is to reduce discrimination against them. But the direct[4] effect is quite different, for by preventing disadvantaged groups from offsetting the prejudice against them, the legislation tends to increase rather than decrease the observable discrimination. Legislation is not the only source of a direct restriction on the incomes of minorities. Trade unions have reduced the dispersion

---

[4] I abstract here from indirect, although possibly very important, effects of this legislation, such as the effect on attitudes.

in wages among union members and may well have reduced the dispersion between disadvantaged members and others. The important point is that, whatever the *intent* of the legislation, unions, or other institutions, the *effect* may well be to increase the observable discrimination, and in precisely the same manner as the previously discussed restrictions on the "collection" of money income.

The analysis can be further generalized by introducing the concept "cost of discrimination." The money cost of discriminating against a particular group is, at the margin, equal to the difference between the money cost of associating with this group and another equally productive one. In a private-enterprise competitive system with no controls on income it would also equal the difference between the unit wages of these groups. Controls placed on the money incomes that can be received by discriminators, such as the income tax, reduce the cost of discrimination below the difference in wages and thus encourage discrimination; controls placed on the wage difference, such as equal pay for equal work legislation, directly reduce the cost of discrimination and encourage discrimination.

All the institutions discussed so far either reduce the money incomes received by or offered to discriminators, and thereby reduce the cost of discrimination and increase discrimination. But the effects of some institutions are quite different: laws of the type administered by the Fair Employment Practices Commission, for example, tend to have just the opposite effect. Through litigation, fines, unfavorable publicity, imprisonment, etc., they increase the cost of not hiring some disadvantaged groups, which discourages discrimination against them. Thus that type of legislation has a very different direct effect on observed discrimination than equal pay for equal work legislation, although both are often strongly supported by the same persons.

I have reviewed the effects of various institutions on nonpecuniary choices, especially on discrimination against minorities. This review was motivated by the discussion by Alchian and Kessel of the effects of a government restraint on money profits. We are indebted to them not only for working out many implications of this restraint, but also for emphasizing that the phrase "nonpecuniary motive" is more than just a camouflage for ignorance; it can be given empirical content. Progress in this field has been hindered not so much by an intractable concept as by the economist's reluctance to take the concept seriously.

Martin Bronfenbrenner, Carnegie Institute of Technology

Alchian and Kessel raise the simple question: When a monopolist chooses not to maximize profits, or when regulation prevents his maximizing profits, in what ways will his behavior as a buyer of inputs differ from the behavior of a competitive firm with the same profit level?

Their answer to this question is also simple. Or rather, it involves a multiplicity of illustrations, which can be boiled down to one or two simple propositions. Let us call the sort of firm Alchian and Kessel have in mind a potential rather than an actual monopolist. Then the basic Alchian-Kessel proposition is that a potential monopolist (unless specially regulated) will run his business in such a way as to satisfy his noneconomic preferences for pretty secretaries and sumptuous offices, or his noneconomic prejudices against Jewish or Negro employees, under circumstances where a competitor would be guided by purely economic considerations. This is particularly true if the extra costs of these noneconomic preferences and prejudices can be passed on to the public on a cost-plus basis.

A second proposition, a corollary of the first, is that the potential monopolist (unless specially regulated) will pad his costs with unnecessary and inefficient employees, reputable expenditures for charity, education, publicity, and "research," fancy landscaping and interior decoration, whereas the competitor will not.

These propositions are both more or less interesting. Their interest to the labor economist is naturally concentrated on their implications for the potential monopolist's demand for labor inputs, but their interest to the general economist transcends this limitation. These propositions are also more or less obvious. Simply raising them among one's friends with or without professional training in economics will suffice to show how obvious they are. It is not a happy comment on the development of economics that they retain their interest nonetheless.

Special cases and corollaries of the Alchian-Kessel propositions are in many cases testable in principle. This adds to their interest to the empirically-minded economist. Alchian and Kessel have in fact tested only one of them here. Their paper would have been more significant if tests had not only been considered feasible in principle but had actually been carried out for a few more of the various specific statements they make.

I have no doubt that the Alchian-Kessel propositions would emerge unscathed from statistical testing of most of the special-case conclusions to which they lead. If they did not, my initial impulse would be to suspect the test procedures rather than the propositions themselves. I should, however, like to concentrate here on one important corollary which Alchian and Kessel might have to modify as a result of testing on a sufficiently large scale. This is their argument that employment of minority groups subject to racial or religious prejudice will be concentrated in competitive rather than monopolistic industry.

This argument was formulated with special reference to the Negro in America; I am not inclined to doubt its validity there. But the American Negro minority is a special kind of minority, which I should like to call a "manual labor" minority. The stereotype of the Negro makes him out too stupid, lazy, irresponsible, and shiftless for anything but unskilled manual labor. It is easy to see how this stereotype arose. Negroes were brought to a relatively advanced America as slaves from a relatively primitive Africa. They were put as slaves to manual labor jobs in which they had no interest and which they performed inefficiently. They have not yet overcome the handicaps with which they were burdened over 300 years ago. One can find plenty of similar "manual labor" minorities all over the world—the Indian "untouchables" are examples—to whom, as well as to the American Negro, the Alchian-Kessel argument applies. Excluded by prejudice from monopoly industry they congregate in the competitive sectors of the economy.

At the same time there are despised minorities aplenty with different characteristics and greater economic resources. These are the "business" minorities who are or have traditionally been more advanced economically than the majority among whom they live. The Jews are a western example; the overseas Chinese are an eastern one. Their stereotypes involve such traits as craftiness, dishonesty, clannishness, heartlessness, and scorn for physical labor. Does the Alchian-Kessel argument apply to these business minorities as well as to the manual labor ones? My suggestion is that it must be modified to take account of the "countervailing power" of these minorities to set up little monopoly enclaves of their own. Their position may accordingly be found less rather than more competitive than the position of the majority which discriminates against them.

Consider a business minority, subject to racial or religious prejudice and excluded from the more reputable monopolies and potential monopolies of their economy. These monopolies include the civil service, the public utilities, the educational system, absentee owner-ship of the land, "the Army, the Navy, the Church, and the stage." Where do such people make their living?

As owners or employees in competitive business, say Alchian and Kessel, and they are partially correct. But I should like to call your attention to another sort of business in which they congregate, which I propose to call the racial or religious cartel. Here their countervailing power is exercised. Here they themselves monopolize opportunities in their turn, excluding and exploiting members of the majority. It often happens that these racial or religious cartels, these originally despised and neglected occupations, increase in importance as eco-nomic development progresses. When this occurs, the business minori-ties often find themselves charged with stifling and strangling the entire economy for their own selfish benefit—meaning the maintenance of their monopoly power.

Gambling, banking, money lending, wholesale and retail trade are the most usual examples of racial or religious cartels in both eastern and western culture. In some cases, the service trades and "foreign" types of manufacturing also are included in the general category of middleman's services and get into minority hands. Thus barbering, tailoring, and rice milling are all characteristically "Chinese" trades throughout much of Southeast Asia. The several racial or religious cartels, moreover, are accused of interrelations which exclude the majority. In the Southeast Asian case, the Chinese banks, money lenders, wholesale traders, and retailers are allegedly in league with each other against outsiders. No Filipino or Thai or Occidental retailer can get credit from the Chinese banker or money lender on the same terms as his Chinese competitor. Nor can he get merchandise from the Chinese wholesaler on the same terms as this same Chinese competitor. The Filipino or Thai or Occidental banker or wholesaler, on the other hand, is tacitly boycotted by the whole Chinese business community. And as is well known to immigrants from Central and Eastern Europe, these charges against the Chinese of Southeast Asia have their counter-parts in charges against the European Jews. Nor, for that matter, is the overseas American community exempt from identical charges, particularly in Latin America.

It is no part of my intention to become involved here in the Chinese problem of Southeast Asia, the Jewish problem of Central Europe, or the Yankee problem of Latin America. I simply wish to present the overseas Chinese, the European Jew, and the Latin American Yankee as three examples of economic minorities who react against discrimination (or anticipate it) by forming racial or religious cartels of their own as well as concentrating in competitive industry. My suggestion as to the Alchian-Kessel argument is therefore one of limitation to a particular sort of minority—the noneconomic or manual labor sort typified by the American Negro. When it comes to the economic sort of minority, the argument should be expanded to take account of the minority's countervailing power as exercised through racial or religious cartels.

# The Economics of American Negro Slavery, 1830-1860

## ROBERT EVANS, JR.

MASSACHUSETTS INSTITUTE OF TECHNOLOGY

### Introduction

THIS study is an investigation of the economics of Negro slavery by (1) estimating the rates of return earned by slave capital in the period 1830 through 1860, (2) comparing these returns with those earned by alternative forms of capital, and (3) considering whether the industry was viable in its last years. Returns to slave capital are estimated from information on slave prices, hires (rents), and death rates between 1830 and 1860. Alternative rates of return are estimated for commercial paper, railroad stocks, and railroad capital. The viability of the slave industry is assessed by considering its demand conditions relative to those typical of a declining industry.

Negro labor, not Negro slavery, was introduced into the United States in 1619 when a Dutch ship unloaded a cargo of twenty Negroes.[1] These Negroes were sold as indentured servants under contractual conditions similar to those of their white counterparts. Even though the yearly imports of Negroes were not large, the importation combined with other factors to induce a subtle change in the attitude of white settlers toward colored servants. In 1662 Virginia passed its first law referring to Negroes as slaves. It is doubtful that by 1683 any new Negroes entered Virginia except in slavery.[2] This change in legal status did not result in any large-scale importation, and it was not until 1753 that the foreign trade in slaves became very large.[3]

In 1790 the first federal census reported 697,897 slaves (Table 1). Though concentrated in the southern states, especially in the tobacco production areas of Maryland and Virginia, slaves were reported in all

NOTE: I am indebted to the Labor Workshop of the Department of Economics of the University of Chicago for financial support for this study, and to my thesis committee, Albert Rees, H. Gregg Lewis, Earl Hamilton, and Martin Bailey, for their comments and suggestions.

[1] The exact status of these Negroes is not settled fact; for a summary of the different interpretations see: Stanley M. Elkins, *Slavery*, University of Chicago Press, 1959, p. 39.

[2] E. Franklin Frazier, *The Negro in the United States*, New York, Macmillan, 1949, pp. 3-39.

[3] James D. B. DeBow, *Statistical View of the United States . . . Being a Compendium of the Seventh Census*, Washington, Beverly Tucker, 1854, p. 84.

the states except Massachusetts. By 1810, two years after the close of the foreign slave trade, the slave population had increased to almost 1.16 million, but had declined slightly as a percentage of the white population. The next fifty years witnessed a 340 per cent increase in the

TABLE 1

SLAVE POPULATION

| Year | Slave, U.S. (1) | Slave, South (2) | Ratio of (2) to (1) (3) |
|------|-----------------|------------------|-------------------------|
| 1790 | 697,897 | 648,640 | 0.93 |
| 1800 | 893,041 | 850,942 | 0.95 |
| 1810 | 1,191,364 | 1,159,677 | 0.97 |
| 1820 | 1,538,038 | 1,514,468 | 0.98 |
| 1830 | 2,009,043 | 2,002,183 | 0.99 |
| 1840 | 2,487,455 | 2,483,721 | 1.00 |
| 1850 | 3,204,761 | 2,201,761 | 1.00 |
| 1860 | 3,953,760 | 3,951,798 | 1.00 |

SOURCE: The figures for 1850 and before are from DeBow, *Statistical View of the United States*, p. 85. For 1860, *Population of the United States in 1860 . . . The Eighth Census*, Washington, 1864, p. 595.
NOTE: The figures for the South include the populations, in the years in which they are included in the census, of Alabama, Arkansas, District of Columbia, Florida, Georgia, Kentucky, Louisiana, Maryland, Mississippi, Missouri, North Carolina, South Carolina, Tennessee, Texas, and Virginia.

slave population, a further concentration in the southern states, and a decline relative to the white population.

While the size of the southern slave population relative to the white southern population did not vary much between 1810 and 1860 (compare column 2, Table 2, with column 2, Table 1), ratios of the individual states changed a great deal as a result of the shift in the concentration of cotton production. The slave-white ratios in Mississippi, Georgia, and Virginia illustrate this movement. In 1820 the ratios of slaves to whites in these three states were approximately equal to 0.78. By 1860 the ratio had increased to 1.23 in Mississippi, remained unchanged in Georgia, and fallen to 0.47 in Virginia.

The largest southward and westward shift in the slave population took place between 1830 and 1840 and had virtually been completed by 1850 except into the southwestern states of Arkansas and Texas. The shift was accomplished by two processes, the movement of entire plantations from the relatively worn-out land of the Upper South to the richer virgin soil of the Lower South, and the sale of slaves from

TABLE 2

WHITE POPULATION

| Year | White, U.S. (1) | White, South (2) | Ratio of (2) to (1) (3) |
|---|---|---|---|
| 1790 | 3,172,464 | 1,225,178 | 0.32 |
| 1800 | 4,304,489 | 1,653,128 | 0.38 |
| 1810 | 5,862,004 | 2,153,424 | 0.36 |
| 1820 | 7,861,937 | 2,776,278 | 0.35 |
| 1830 | 10,537,378 | 3,603,157 | 0.34 |
| 1840 | 14,195,695 | 4,573,969 | 0.32 |
| 1850 | 19,553,068 | 6,151,247 | 0.32 |
| 1860 | 26,957,471 | 8,001,000 | 0.30 |

SOURCE: The figures for 1850 and before are from DeBow, *Statistical View* . . . , p. 42. For 1860, *The Eighth Census*, pp. 592-593.
NOTE: The figures for the South include the populations, in the years in which they are included in the census, of the states listed in the note to Table 1.

the plantations of the Upper South to those of the Lower South. Though estimates have been made of the relative magnitudes of these processes, none has a high degree of accuracy because of the poor quality of the available information.

The potential male slave labor force, those aged fifteen to sixty, made up about one-fourth of the slave population and about one-third of the potential southern male labor force in 1850 and 1860 (Table 3).

TABLE 3

POTENTIAL MALE LABOR FORCE IN THE SOUTH

| Year | Number of Slave Males Aged 15 to 60 (1) | Number of White Males Aged 15 to 60 (2) | Ratio of (1) to (2) |
|---|---|---|---|
| 1850 | 814,876 | 1,699,403 | 0.48 |
| 1860 | 1,016,425 | 2,180,719 | 0.46 |

SOURCE: For 1850, DeBow, *Statistical View* . . . , pp. 52-53, 56, 88-89. For 1860, *The Eighth Census*, pp. 592-595.

Because of the age distribution of the slaves imported before 1808 and the probable age distribution of white immigrants into the South, the ratios of the potential male slave labor force to the total slave population and to the potential southern male labor force were probably less in 1850 and 1860 than they were in earlier years. Unfortunately, the census age classifications in the earlier periods make it difficult to determine the number of males aged fifteen to sixty.

The majority of the actual slave labor force was engaged in agricultural work associated with the basic staple crops of cotton, hemp, rice, tobacco, and sugar cane. No precise estimates of the number of slaves employed on each type of plantation are available.[4] In addition to working as agricultural laborers, slaves found employment in most jobs requiring physical effort and minor mechanical skills. Again, no estimates of the numbers employed in these different jobs are currently available, though the 1848 census of Charleston, South Carolina, suggests a possible occupational distribution of male slaves who worked in cities (see Table 4).

This unique aspect of southern labor—slavery—elicited many contemporary comments, the informal observations of the traveler as well as the results of more formal studies on the effect of slavery on the South. A relative lack of commentary followed the Civil War, only to be followed in turn by that of twentieth century historians who reexamined slavery as a force in southern history. In the area of economics many of these students reached the conclusion that slavery was unprofitable for the owners of the slaves. In the words of Ulrich B. Phillips, the outstanding student of American slavery and a strong advocate of the hypothesis of unprofitability: ". . . By the close of the fifties it is fairly certain that no slave holders but those few whose plantations lay in the most advantageous parts of the cotton and sugar districts and whose managerial ability was exceptionally great were earning anything beyond what would cover their maintenance and carrying charges."[5] These conclusions of unprofitability have not gone unchallenged, but they have probably gained wider acceptance than has the hypothesis that slaveholding was as profitable as alternative investments in the period.

The slave industry consisted of two types of firms. One owned or rented the capital goods (slaves) and used them as factors of production to produce a marketable commodity (labor services) or combined them with other factors to produce marketable commodities (cotton,

---

[4] DeBow, *Statistical View of the United States*, p. 94. It is suggested that in 1850 about 400,000 slaves lived in cities and towns and that 2,500,000 slaves of all ages worked in agriculture with 1,815,000 in cotton, 350,000 in tobacco, 150,000 in cane sugar, 125,000 in rice, and 60,000 in hemp. DeBow does not indicate the basis for these estimates.

[5] Ulrich B. Phillips, *American Negro Slavery*, New York, Appleton-Century, 1936, p. 391.

## TABLE 4

### MANUAL OCCUPATIONS IN CHARLESTON, SOUTH CAROLINA, 1848

| Occupations | Male Slaves | Numbers of: Free Negroes | White Males |
|---|---|---|---|
| Domestics | 1,188 | 9 | 13 |
| Cooks and confectioners | 7 | 18 | 0 |
| Fruiterers and peddlers | 0 | 6 | 46 |
| Gardeners | 3 | 0 | 5 |
| Coachmen | 15 | 4 | 2 |
| Draymen | 67 | 11 | 13 |
| Porters | 35 | 5 | 8 |
| Stevedores | 2 | 1 | 21 |
| Pilots and sailors | 50 | 1 | 176 |
| Fishermen | 11 | 14 | 10 |
| Carpenters | 120 | 27 | 119 |
| Masons and bricklayers | 68 | 10 | 60 |
| Painters and plasterers | 16 | 4 | 18 |
| Tinners | 3 | 1 | 10 |
| Ship's carpenters and joiners | 51 | 6 | 52 |
| Coopers | 61 | 2 | 20 |
| Coachmakers and wheelwrights | 3 | 1 | 26 |
| Cabinetmakers | 8 | 0 | 26 |
| Upholsterers | 1 | 1 | 10 |
| Gun coopers and locksmiths | 2 | 1 | 16 |
| Blacksmiths and horseshoers | 40 | 4 | 51 |
| Millwrights | 0 | 5 | 4 |
| Bootmakers and shoemakers | 6 | 17 | 30 |
| Saddle and harness makers | 2 | 1 | 29 |
| Tailors and capmakers | 36 | 42 | 68 |
| Butchers | 5 | 1 | 10 |
| Millers | 0 | 1 | 14 |
| Bakers | 39 | 1 | 35 |
| Barbers and hairdressers | 4 | 14 | 0 |
| Cigarmakers | 5 | 1 | 10 |
| Bookbinders | 3 | 0 | 10 |
| Printers | 5 | 0 | 65 |
| Other mechanics | 45 | 2 | 182 |
| Apprentices | 43 | 14 | 55 |
| Unclassed and unskilled | 838 | 19 | 192 |
| Superannuated | 38 | 1 | 0 |
| Total | 3,520 | 245 | 1,406 |

SOURCE: J. L. Dowson and H. W. DeSaussare, *Census of Charleston for 1848*, Charleston, J. B. Nixon, 1849, pp. 31-36.

railroad services, gold, etc.). The other owned those capital goods (female slaves) which were used to produce new capital goods (slaves). Some firms, usually plantations, engaged in all three, producing labor services, agricultural products, and new slaves.

In the absence of serious market imperfections, the rate of return on slave capital will equal the market rate even though the industry is declining. Consequently, the determination of the return to slaveholding, while of interest because of the widespread uncertainty concerning its magnitude, is of little value in answering the more relevant question whether the industry was viable. The viability can be estimated by ascertaining whether it exhibited characteristics of a declining industry. Some of these are: (1) a declining demand for the unique capital employed (slaves), (2) a declining rate of production of the unique capital (slave birth rate), and (3) a declining demand for the specialized capital (female slaves) used to produce the unique capital (slaves) used in the industry.

A major error in many analyses of the American slave industry is the double counting of the cost of capital.[6] An excellent example is the following: Ralph B. Flanders[7] states that Colonel J. M. Williams of Society Hill, South Carolina, received only about 2.7 per cent from his investment in 1849.[8] The correct rate of return on Williams' investment is almost 9.7 per cent, for, before calculating the 2.7 per cent figure, a 7 per cent interest charge on $158,620 of the $161,000 invested capital was deducted from the difference between revenue and operating expenses.[9]

Other minor errors have been made, including valuing slaves at original cost rather than at market value, neglecting the depreciation of the stock of slaves because of their reproductive nature, etc. These will not be explicitly discussed, with the exception of Ulrich Phillips' error which is considered because of his stature and influence in the field of slave history. Phillips seems to have relied mainly upon the divergence late in the 1850's of the rule of thumb relationship of $100 to $0.01 between the price of prime male field hands and the price of cotton, a relationship considered appropriate by many southerners in 1850. To have used this relationship as a tool to estimate the profita-

[6] The nature of this error was recognized by some contemporaries of slavery. For a more complete discussion of it, see Thomas P. Govan, "Was Plantation Slavery Profitable?" *Journal of Southern History*, November, 1942, pp. 513-535.

[7] Ralph B. Flanders, "Planter Problems in Ante Bellum Georgia," *Georgia Historical Quarterly*, March, 1930, p. 29.

[8] Contained in an article by Solon Robinson in the *National Intelligencer* quoted in *Agricultural Section, Report of the Commissioner of Patents for 1849*, Exec. Doc. 20, H. R., 31st Cong., 1st sess., pp. 310-312.

[9] The actual rate of return was higher. These calculations are based upon a cotton price of 6 cents a pound, whereas the average price received by Williams was between 6 and 7 cents.

bility of slavery, Phillips would have been obliged to consider changes in the marginal physical productivity of the prime male field hands— a factor he neglected. A rough estimate of changes in marginal physical productivity[10] is not consistent with Phillips' implicit belief that it was roughly constant for the period 1850 through 1860.

Almost all analyses of the returns on slave capital involve use of manuscript records of actual plantations or average values of prices, production, etc., for typical plantations to estimate the return. In the absence of precise production functions, market rates of payment are estimated for the other factors, and slaves are allotted the residual income. While this type of analysis, when properly applied, yields results consistent with those I have obtained, there are strong grounds for preferring the method developed and used in this study. This method uses the net rent,[11] received by owners of slaves when they rented them out, as the estimate of the income earned by the capital good. Stated more formally, the analysis is limited to a firm with one input, a single form of capital, which produces a single output, labor services. The advantages of this method are: the income figures are estimated directly from market data rather than as residuals; and only a few variables rather than a large number need to be estimated.

## The Data

The analysis of the rate of return on slave capital is an application of the simple discount formula to the capital good, slaves. To carry forward this analysis requires four types of data: (1) the net yearly income received by the owner, (2) the price of slaves, (3) the death rate of slaves at specific ages, and (4) the rates of return on alternative investments. The rate of return on an asset is equal to the ratio of net income to the price. For an asset that wears out, this rate rises

[10] Alfred H. Conrad and John R. Meyer, "The Economics of Slavery in the Ante Bellum South," *Journal of Political Economy*, April 1958, pp. 116-119. Conrad and Meyer estimate the rate of return to slaveholding in the period 1830 through 1860. They use the capital value formula with the internal interest rate equal to the discount rate. The yearly income of the capital good is estimated as a residual using an average production function and average incomes and expenses for cotton plantations.

[11] The hires are not a random sample of all hires for the class of slaves considered. The hires are all those for that class which were found in a reasonably exhaustive search of the secondary literature and the principal archive collections of the South. It is possible that hired slaves may have been superior to average slaves. This will not bias the results unless the ratio of hire to price for the hired slaves is greater than the ratio of imputed hire to price of average slaves.

each year that the asset is held. The discount formula is used to obtain an average rate for the period the asset is held and to reduce the rate indicated by the simple ratios to allow for the decline in value of the asset over the period. The death rate is incorporated into the discount formula to allow for the fact that all slaves do not live the same number of years. The alternative rate provides a standard by which to judge the rate on slaves relative to other investments.

NET INCOME

The net yearly income received by the owner of the slave is estimated by the yearly hire of slaves rented out, i.e., slaves whose employer was not their owner. There is evidence to indicate that the hiring of slaves was a reasonably common characteristic of the slave system and that the conditions of hire were generally quite standard. Many of the characteristics of hired slave employment—size of labor force, turnover, mobility, etc.—however, cannot be quantified.[12]

The supply of slaves to the hired labor force, especially in certain industries in the Upper South[13] in the latter years, appears to have been quite large. In 1857 the Virginia and Tennessee Railroad employed 643 persons of whom 435 were hired slaves, and the Richmond and Danville Railroad employed 298 persons of whom 181 were hired slaves.[14] In April of 1858, 249 hired slaves were employed in the construction of the State House in Columbia, South Carolina.[15] In July of 1848, 81 of the approximately 300 yard laborers employed at the United States Navy Shipyard at Gosport (Norfolk), Virginia, were hired slaves.[16] An analysis of the unpublished census returns for 1860 indicates that there were at least 335 hired slaves in four counties in Tennessee.[17]

[12] The size of the hired slave labor force is discussed in Clement Eaton, "Slave-Hiring in the Upper South: A Step Toward Freedom," *Mississippi Valley Historical Review*, March 1960, pp. 673-677.

[13] The term Upper South refers to North Carolina, South Carolina, and Virginia. The term Lower South refers to Alabama, Florida, Georgia, Louisiana, and Mississippi.

[14] *Annual Reports of the Railroads to the Board of Public Works of the General Assembly of Virginia for the Year Ending September 30, 1857*, G.A. No. 17, pp. 79 and 280.

[15] State House Construction Payrolls, Voucher Three, South Carolina State Archives, Columbia, April 1858.

[16] United States Navy Bureau of Yards and Docks, Payrolls of Mechanics and Laborers . . . Gosport, Virginia, National Archives, Washington, July 1848.

[17] Chase C. Mooney, *Slavery in Tennessee*, Indiana University Press, 1957, p. 33. The counties were Davidson, Fayette, Haywood, and Lincoln. All the census

Slaves who were temporarily in excess of their owner's needs were one major source of the supply of hired slaves. Slaves who were part of estates left to widows and minor children were a second source. How common it was for other groups to hold slaves solely for hire is not clear. Some examples can be cited: the Clark Plantation during the period 1847 through 1860 regularly hired out from seven to seventeen hands.[18] A newspaper of the period (quoted indirectly) indicates that holding slaves for hire was quite common. "Negroes are a kind of capital which is loaned out at a high rate, and [in Savannah] one often meets people who have no plantation, but who keep negroes to let and receive very handsome sums for them every month."[19]

The practice of yearly re-hire suggests that there may have been a high turnover rate of individual slaves among employers. Again, only examples, not statistics, can be cited. Between 1843 and 1852 the twenty-four slaves in the estate of Henry E. Canon of Mississippi worked for a minimum of seven employers, and those hired out every year seldom worked for the same employer from year to year.[20] In 1860 the president of the Raleigh and Gaston Railroad reported: "Great labor and inconvenience is experienced in hiring new laborers. Those that are obtained are often of an inferior quality, or hard to manage . . . raw recruits unacquainted with the duties assigned to them."[21] On the other side, one group of slaves employed in the shipyard at Pensacola, Florida, worked there at least for the period 1847 through 1851 and the Tredegar Iron Works in Richmond apparently had a low turnover among its hired slave force.[22]

While there was some interstate mobility, and examples of slaves owned in Virginia working in Alabama and Florida could be cited, the impression one gathers is that most slaves were hired to work in the states in which their owners lived. There is also an indication that

marshals did not indicate hired slaves, so an exact determination of the number is not possible. There were 48,136 slaves reported in these counties of which 12,135 were males fifteen to sixty years old.
[18] Clark Plantation Book, 1825-1861, North Carolina Dept. of Archives and History, Raleigh.
[19] Frederic Bancroft, *Slave Trading in the Old South*, Baltimore, Furst, 1931, p. 146. The quotation is from *Das Ausland*, which quoted the *New York Tribune* of April 28, 1860.
[20] Charles S. Sydnor, *Slavery in Mississippi*, New York, Appleton-Century, 1933, pp. 175-178.
[21] *Tenth Annual Report of the Raleigh and Gaston Railroad*, 1860, North Carolina Dept. of Archives and History, Raleigh, pp. 9-10.
[22] Kathleen Bruce, *Virginia Iron Manufacture in the Slave Era*, New York, Century, 1931.

premium rates were paid by employers who planned to move the hired slaves across state boundaries.

Slaves were hired in three ways, (1) by personal contact between the owner and the lessee or his agent, (2) by personal contact between an agent in a major city to whom the owner had consigned his slaves and the lessee or his agent, and (3) by public auction. The first method was usually carried out by the hirer or his agent traveling through the back country picking up a few slaves at a time as he visited the various plantations. If the project involved obtaining a large number of slaves, the agent might advertise his coming and meet the owners in the local county seat. Agents in the principal cities accepted slaves on consignment and hired them out by personal contact or at public auction. Newspaper advertisements by the agents, and the payroll vouchers of the South Carolina State House construction suggest that agents were widely used. The usual charge for such services was from 6 to 8 per cent. Newspaper accounts of the practice of calling slaves at public auction, usually held on the courthouse steps around the first of January, indicate that this may have been the most popular method of hiring slaves. Its popularity may have been associated with the practice of renting out slaves belonging to estates. Of the three methods, personal contact was probably the one used in most of the cases cited in this study, with the exception of the railroads whose methods are unknown.

Slaves were employed by the day, week, month, and year. The yearly contract appears to have been the most common. The year is also the period for which one can be surest of the conditions of hire with respect to slave subsistence. Almost without exception the lessee paid for the cost of lost time (except for a runaway), paid for living quarters, food, clothing, medical care, and in many cases the taxes on the slave. Hence, the yearly hire represented a net return on the investment.[23] The following quotations illustrate these typical contract conditions:

First, the hirer shall have twelve months credit by giving Bond with two approved Securities! They will be required to furnish each negro with three suits of clothes, two homespun cotton suits for summer and one linsey suit for winter, one new pair of shoes and stockings, each man or boy with a new wool hat and each woman and

[23] The cost of hiring out the slave is considered in the section on rate of return, below. This analysis assumes that the hired slave labor market was classical rather than Keynesian in character and involuntary unemployment is not considered.

girl with a new cloth bonnet, each single negro with one new blanket and each family of negroes with two blankets and to be returned with all their bedding and clothing to this place on the second day of January.[24]

On the 25 day of December we . . . as surity, jointly and severally promise to pay to . . . or order . . . for value received. Having hired of . . . a negro . . . slave . . . from this date until the 25th of December next, we . . . as principal and as . . . surity, jointly and severally bind ourselves that said slave shall be treated humanely, furnished with competent medical aid and medicines, when necessary, furnished with good suitable and sufficient clothing during the year, and returned with good durable and sufficient clothing at the end of the time aforesaid. The hirer to pay the city taxes on said slave. This obligation is not intended to render the hirer liable for the return of the slave in the case of death or escape, further than he is by law made responsible.[25]

If a hired slave ran away or died during the contractual period, the hire usually ceased at this time. In cases where it could be shown that the lessee had been negligent or had violated the terms of the contract in a way that led to the loss of the slave, he was usually held liable for damages equal to the fair value of the slave. In the closing years of slavery some firms advertised that they would insure the lives of all the slaves that they employed—apparently not a widespread practice. Whether the probability of death was greater for hired slaves than for slaves in general would be difficult to establish. The president of the Raleigh and Gaston Railroad stated, "The risk of brakemen, trainhands, and firemen is scarcely greater than that of other employments, none having been killed on the road."[26] In 1856, however, three firemen, four brakemen, and an assistant engineer were killed and three other employees were injured on the Mobile and Ohio Railroad.[27] Of the ten, only one of the injured was a Negro, the others being white. In 1860 there were three deaths among the 400 hired

[24] Papers of Alexander H. Torrence, 1835-1915, Duke University Library, Durham, North Carolina.
[25] Contract between I. R. Jacob and I. B. O'Bannor in Louisville, Kentucky, 1857, New York Public Library, New York, Miscellaneous Slave Papers.
[26] *Tenth Annual Report*, pp. 9-10.
[27] *Ninth Annual Report of the Mobile and Ohio Railroad, 1856*, Library of the Bureau of Railway Economics, Association of American Railroads, Washington. Table 10.

slaves of Charles Fisher, a railroad contractor in North Carolina.[28] Three deaths out of 400 are fewer than would be predicted by a mortality table for slaves aged twenty to forty.

When slaves were hired for periods other than a year, it is usually not clear what the contractual conditions were regarding subsistence. It appears that when slaves were hired by the day or week their owners paid for the subsistence. Monthly hires present a mixed situation. In some cases the monthly rates are alternative methods of expressing daily or yearly ones, and the conditions of subsistence probably followed the general patterns for those rates. Where they were true monthly rates, both patterns of subsistence payments were used. The uncertainty concerning who paid for subsistence makes daily and monthly hires more useful for illustrating movements in magnitudes over time than for estimating the net income received by the owner. A more important limitation on the use of daily and monthly figures is a lack of information on number of days or months worked per year.

Data on slave hires are scattered and usually fragmentary in character. Some can be found in most twentieth century books dealing with the general subject of southern slavery or with slavery in a specific geographical area. In addition, many books and articles which treat particular aspects of the general southern economy contain some references to them, as do court cases and periodicals of the era. It is doubtful, however, that the number of useful observations from these sources exceed 500. The major sources are manuscript records and the annual reports of southern railroads.

In order to estimate correctly the net yearly income received by owners of slaves, the following information is desirable: (1) rate of hire, (2) value of slaves, (3) age, skill, and physical condition, (4) content of jobs performed. Seldom is such detailed information available. In its absence, hires were included if the context of the source indicated that it probably represented a healthy adult male performing relatively unskilled labor.

Railroad hires present a special problem, for they are often summarized into an average rate which includes the skilled train hands and the boys who swept up around the stations. The vast majority of the slaves employed by the railroads worked as track hands, and thus the use of the average rate probably does not introduce much

[28] Papers of Charles F. Fisher, 1860, Southern Historical Collection, University of North Carolina, Chapel Hill.

error. Slave rental data were included in many contemporary newspapers, usually in the form of averages or ranges with no indication of the number employed at these rates. These have been included with a weight equal to a single hire. In cases where manuscript sources used by a secondary account could be consulted, the manuscript source was used. Tables 5, 6, and 7 summarize the available data on slave hires; details and sources are included in Appendix A.

TABLE 5

AVERAGE YEARLY RATES OF HIRE FOR SLAVES

| | Upper South | | | Lower South | | |
|---|---|---|---|---|---|---|
| Period | Number of Observations | Mean | Standard Deviation | Number of Observations | Mean | Standard Deviation |
| 1830-35 | 27 | $ 62.0 | | 20 | $127.0 | |
| 1836-40 | 62 | 106.0 | $13.0 | 7 | | |
| 1841-45 | 12 | 83.0 | | 15 | 143.0 | |
| 1846-50 | 33 | 99.0 | 16.3 | 53 | 168.0 | $43.8 |
| 1851-55 | 1,195 | 141.5 | 20.9 | 96 | 167.0 | 69.8 |
| 1856-60[a] | 4,091 | 142.0 | 15.3 | 157 | 196.5 | 39.6 |

[a] After the analysis was completed, I discovered an additional 490 railroad hires of the Southside Railroad for 1859 and 1860. The average hire was $141.65. *Annual Reports of the Railroad Companies of the State of Virginia . . . Board of Public Works . . .* September 30, 1859, p. 397; 1860, p. 333.

TABLE 6

AVERAGE MONTHLY RATES OF HIRE FOR SLAVES

| | Upper South | | Lower South | |
|---|---|---|---|---|
| Period | Number of Observations | Mean | Number of Observations | Mean |
| 1830-35 | 4 | | 5 | |
| 1836-40 | 256 | $15.0 | 7 | $22.4 |
| 1841-45 | | | 18 | 14.7 |
| 1846-50 | 137 | 12.5 | 76 | 14.7 |
| 1851-55 | 36 | 13.0 | 84 | 29.5 |
| 1856-60 | 110 | 14.0 | 153 | 20.0 |

SLAVE PRICES

The slave market performed for the ante-bellum South some of the functions now performed by the New York Stock Exchange, i.e., it served in the eyes of the public as a sensitive reflector of current and future business prospects. As a consequence, the price of slaves, espe-

197

TABLE 7

AVERAGE DAILY RATES OF HIRE FOR SLAVES

| Period | Range | |
|--------|-------------|-------------|
| | Upper South | Lower South |
| 1830-35 | $0.40—0.50 | |
| 1836-40 | 0.50—0.75 | |
| 1841-45 | | |
| 1846-50 | 0.75 | $1.00 |
| 1851-55 | 0.69—0.88 | 1.00—1.25 |
| 1856-60 | 0.69—0.88 | 1.00—1.25 |

cially in other parts of the South, was often mentioned by local news-papers and by local citizens in letters and diaries, which are sources of conceptions of the general movement of slave prices. An alternative approach to a slave price series is use of actual sales recorded in bills of sale or in the accounts of planters and slave traders. The latter approach was taken by Ulrich Phillips in his studies of the prices of prime male field hands (healthy male slaves eighteen to thirty years old), which he summarized in charts of yearly slave prices for four major markets, Richmond, Charleston, mid-Georgia, and New Orleans for the years 1796 through 1860.

Phillips' estimates of slave prices are based upon more than 3,000 bills of sale which he looked at over a period of years. Bills of sale seldom list all the information desirable for constructing a price series— price, age, sex, physical condition, and skill. His method, therefore, was ". . . to select in a group of bills for any time and place such maxi-mum quotations for males as occur with any notable degree of fre-quency."[29] This method is possible because the majority of slaves sold individually rather than in groups were of prime field quality. His estimates are shown in Table 8.

Since it was not possible to duplicate Phillips' coverage of price sources, it would be desirable to have more information concerning his method of estimation, sources of prices, extent of coverage of the different markets in the different years, etc. Perhaps because he be-lieved in the illustrative use of statistics rather than in more formal statistical analysis, such information is not available. Some indication of the reliability of his estimates can be obtained from the following:

[29] Phillips, American Negro Slavery, p. 370.

TABLE 8

PRICES OF PRIME MALE FIELD HANDS, 1830-60

| Year and Period | Richmond | Charleston | Mid-Georgia | New Orleans |
|---|---|---|---|---|
| 1830 | $ 425 | $ 500 | $ 700 | $ 800 |
| 1831 | 450 | 500 | 750 | 850 |
| 1832 | 500 | 550 | 800 | 900 |
| 1833 | 550 | 600 | 850 | 950 |
| 1834 | 600 | 650 | 900 | 1,000 |
| 1835 | 650 | 750 | 1,000 | 1,150 |
| 1836 | 800 | 1,100 | 1,200 | 1,250 |
| 1837 | 1,100 | 1,200 | 1,300 | 1,300 |
| 1838 | 900 | 1,100 | 1,175 | 1,225 |
| 1839 | 1,000 | 1,150 | 1,200 | 1,250 |
| 1840 | 750 | 775 | 900 | 1,000 |
| 1841 | 600 | 650 | 775 | 875 |
| 1842 | 500 | 600 | 700 | 750 |
| 1843 | 500 | 550 | 650 | 750 |
| 1844 | 500 | 550 | 650 | 700 |
| 1845 | 550 | 600 | 650 | 700 |
| 1846 | 600 | 650 | 700 | 750 |
| 1847 | 625 | 700 | 800 | 850 |
| 1848 | 650 | 725 | 900 | 950 |
| 1849 | 675 | 775 | 950 | 1,025 |
| 1850 | 700 | 800 | 1,000 | 1,100 |
| 1851 | 725 | 825 | 1,050 | 1,150 |
| 1852 | 775 | 850 | 1,100 | 1,200 |
| 1853 | 825 | 950 | 1,200 | 1,250 |
| 1854 | 900 | 1,000 | 1,250 | 1,300 |
| 1855 | 950 | 1,025 | 1,300 | 1,350 |
| 1856 | 1,000 | 1,075 | 1,350 | 1,425 |
| 1857 | 1,025 | 1,100 | 1,450 | 1,500 |
| 1858 | 1,075 | 1,150 | 1,550 | 1,600 |
| 1859 | 1,100 | 1,200 | 1,675 | 1,700 |
| 1860 | 1,200 | 1,225 | 1,800 | 1,800 |
| 1830-35 | $ 529 | $ 592 | $ 883 | $ 942 |
| 1836-40 | 910 | 1,053 | 1,115 | 1,205 |
| 1841-45 | 530 | 590 | 685 | 745 |
| 1846-50 | 650 | 730 | 870 | 935 |
| 1851-55 | 835 | 930 | 1,180 | 1,250 |
| 1856-60 | 1,100 | 1,150 | 1,565 | 1,605 |

SOURCE: Estimated visually, to the nearest $25, from chart, "Approximate Prices of Prime Male Field Hands in Hundreds of Dollars per Head . . . ," in Ulrich B. Phillips, *Life and Labor in the Old South*, Boston, Little, Brown, 1941, p. 177.

(1) They have with one exception been accepted by other scholars.[30] (2) They are consistent with quotations in other secondary works on American slavery.[31] (3) They are, except for the Upper South 1856 through 1860, reasonably similar to observations obtained in preparing this study (Table 9). Even the Upper South 1856 through 1860, when

TABLE 9

COMPARISON OF PHILLIPS' PRICES FOR SLAVES WITH EVANS'
OBSERVATIONS OF PRICES

| Year | Phillips' Prices | Evans' Prices | | | Phillips' Prices | Evans' Prices | | |
|---|---|---|---|---|---|---|---|---|
| | | Prices | Number of Observa-tions | Standard Deviation | | Prices | Number of Observa-tions | Standar Deviati |
| | RICHMOND | | | | CHARLESTON | | | |
| 1836 | $ 800 | $ 982 | 21 | $105 | | | | |
| 1846 | 600 | 580 | 10 | 111 | | | | |
| 1860 | 1,200 | 1,478 | 14 | 120 | | | | |
| 1833 | | | | | $ 600 | $ 438 | 31 | $151 |
| 1852 | | | | | 850 | 892 | 31 | 54 |
| 1856 | | | | | 1,175 | 1,164 | 12 | 162 |
| | MID-GEORGIA | | | | NEW ORLEANS | | | |
| 1837 | $1,300 | $1,210 | 22 | $145 | | | | |
| 1859 | 1,675 | 1,500 | 27 | 0 | | | | |
| 1848 | | | | | $ 950 | $ 888 | 8 | $84 |
| 1860 | | | | | 1,800 | 1,750 | 6 | 32 |

SOURCE: Phillips' prices, Table 8.
Evans' prices: Richmond: 1836, Account Book of Whitehead and Lofftus 1835-1837, Duke University Library, Durham, North Carolina; 1846, Slave Account Book of Templeman 1846-1859, New York Public Library; 1860, Omohandro Account Book 1860, Alderman Library, University of Virginia, Charlottesville.
Charleston: 1833, Account Book of I. A. Jarratt 1833-1835, Duke University Library, Durham, North Carolina; 1852, Samuel M. Derrick, *Centennial History of South Carolina Railroad*, Columbia, State Co., 1930, p. 312; 1856, Devereaux Personal Papers, Account of Slave Sales, December 2, 1856, North Carolina Department of Archives and History, Raleigh.
Mid-Georgia: 1837, Papers of Francis P. Corbin, New York Public Library; 1859, Slave Accounts of Jeremiah Morton in Morton-Halsey Papers, Slaves Sold in Mobile in 1859, Alderman Library, University of Virginia, Charlottesville.
New Orleans: 1848, "Inventory of the Estate of Nicholas N. Destrehan," *Louisiana Historical Quarterly*, April 1924, pp. 302-303; 1860, Bill of Sale for Louisiana in Miscellaneous Slave Papers, New York Public Library.

[30] Wendell H. Stephenson, *Isaac Franklin, Slave Trader and Planter of the Old South*, Louisiana State University Press, 1938, p. 84, suggests that Phillips' New Orleans prices for 1828 through 1831 may be too high.
[31] Conrad and Meyer, "The Economics of Slavery . . . ," p. 100.

it appears that Phillips' estimates are too low, is not a clear case. Phillips gives several examples of slave sales where the means of the male sale prices are above his estimates of the prime male field price.[32]

TABLE 10

PRICES OF PRIME MALE FIELD HANDS IN VIRGINIA, 1860

| Mean Price | 75th Percentile Price |
|---|---|
| $1,478 | $1,525 |
| 1,515 | 1,595 |

SOURCE: Omohandro Account Book, 1860, Alderman Library, University of Virginia, Charlottesville; Account Book of Hector Davis of Richmond, 1860, New York Public Library, New York.

In judging the similarity of Phillips' estimates with independent observations, two things should be remembered: (1) A price differential of up to $100 is often found between prices paid and received by traders operating in a local market. (2) The independent observations, while from the general market area, are not always in the cities for which Phillips estimated his prices. It therefore seems safe to conclude that Phillips' prices can be used with confidence, except possibly for the 1856 through 1860 period in the Upper South.

The analysis will be carried out for two areas, Upper South and Lower South. Phillips' Richmond and Charleston estimates have been averaged to obtain a price series for the Upper South and his Mid-Georgia and New Orleans prices have been averaged to obtain a series for the Lower South (Table 11). I have prepared an alternative estimate of prices for the Upper South for the period 1856 through 1860 because of the uncertainty concerning the accuracy of Phillips' prices for these years. Prices for 1856 and 1860 were estimated and linear interpolation was used to obtain estimates for 1857, 1858, and 1859 prices. Phillips' 1856 price was used for 1856. An 1860 price of $1,600[33] was based upon Table 10 and the following quotations from the letters of a firm of slave traders.

Mr. Williamson says he was offered negroes at $100 per head lower in Montgomery than they are worth here. (Richmond, 1859)

[32] Phillips, *American Negro Slavery*, pp. 313-315.
[33] This is an upper limit estimate and is used to insure against overestimating the rate of return.

TABLE 11

PRICES OF PRIME MALE FIELD HANDS, 1830-60

| Year and Period | Upper South Phillips' Estimates | Evans' Estimates | Lower South Phillips' Estimates |
|---|---|---|---|
| 1830 | $ 463 | | $ 750 |
| 1831 | 475 | | 800 |
| 1832 | 525 | | 850 |
| 1833 | 575 | | 900 |
| 1834 | 625 | | 950 |
| 1835 | 700 | | 1,075 |
| 1836 | 950 | | 1,225 |
| 1837 | 1,150 | | 1,300 |
| 1838 | 950 | | 1,200 |
| 1839 | 1,075 | | 1,225 |
| 1840 | 763 | | 950 |
| 1841 | 625 | | 825 |
| 1842 | 550 | | 725 |
| 1843 | 525 | | 675 |
| 1844 | 525 | | 675 |
| 1845 | 575 | | 675 |
| 1846 | 625 | | 725 |
| 1847 | 663 | | 825 |
| 1848 | 688 | | 925 |
| 1849 | 725 | | 988 |
| 1850 | 750 | | 1,050 |
| 1851 | 775 | | 1,100 |
| 1852 | 813 | | 1,150 |
| 1853 | 888 | | 1,225 |
| 1854 | 950 | | 1,275 |
| 1855 | 988 | | 1,325 |
| 1856 | 1,038 | $1,038 | 1,388 |
| 1857 | 1,063 | 1,178 | 1,475 |
| 1858 | 1,113 | 1,318 | 1,575 |
| 1859 | 1,150 | 1,458 | 1,688 |
| 1860 | 1,213 | 1,600 | 1,800 |
| 1830-35 | 561 | | 888 |
| 1836-40 | 978 | | 1,180 |
| 1841-45 | 560 | | 715 |
| 1846-50 | 690 | | 903 |
| 1851-55 | 883 | | 1,215 |
| 1856-60 | 1,115 | 1,318 | 1,585 |

Good second rate men thirty years old can be bought at $1,000 to $1,100. (Richmond, 1859)

Sold John in South Carolina for $1,325, too low. (1859)

How can they stay at prices like these when they can't sell for $100 more further South? (Richmond, December 1859)

No. 1 men 20-26 at $1,500-1,600. (Richmond, July 1860)[34]

Because most bills of sale indicate only sex and price, it was not possible for Phillips to estimate prices for other classes of slaves. On the basis of estate valuations which list sex, age, and value, Phillips did suggest some average relationships for the prices of other classes of slaves relative to the prices of prime males. A similar procedure has been used to estimate the prices of once-prime slaves at ages forty and fifty as a percentage of prime price (Table 12). I have estimated that once-prime males at age forty were worth 78 per cent of prime price and at age fifty 52 per cent of prime price. The latter figure is similar to Phillips' estimate of 50 per cent of prime price at age fifty.[35]

### THE ALTERNATIVE RATE OF RETURN

While it is easy to describe the alternative rate of return for the investor in slaves, it is difficult to give more than an approximate estimate of the rate because of a lack of knowledge concerning risk and non-pecuniary factors involved in different types of investment.[36] The alternative rate is the real rate of interest on capital, plus or minus appropriate factors to allow for nonpecuniary returns and for the difference between the particular structure of risk attendant to investing in slaves, and some average risk involved in investment. In other words, it is that rate an investor will receive if he chooses to invest in something other than slaves, with suitable account taken of the differences in risk and nonpecuniary factors between other investment goods and slaves. It

[34] Letters of William A. J. Finney, 1848-1860, Duke University Library, Durham, North Carolina. Finney with Philip Thomas headed a firm of slave traders who bought slaves in the rural areas of Virginia and sold them in the southern markets of New Orleans and Mobile. Besides indicating that the Upper South prices were higher than Phillips' estimates, they indicate that the Upper South–Lower South differential was narrowing in this period rather than widening as shown in Phillips' charts.

[35] Phillips, *American Negro Slavery*, p. 370.

[36] In Conrad and Meyer, "The Economics of Slavery . . . ," p. 101, one finds an opposite conclusion. They argue, incorrectly in my opinion, that the alternative rate is the return on capital if the slave industry had not existed, and that this rate can be estimated from the rate of interest on short-term money in the North and South before the Civil War and in the North during the war.

## TABLE 12
### PRICES OF ONCE-PRIME SLAVES AS A PERCENTAGE OF PRIME PRICES

| Age Group | Observations | | | | | | | | | |
|---|---|---|---|---|---|---|---|---|---|---|
| | (1) | (2) | (3) | (4) | (5) | (6) | (7) | (8) | (9) | (10) |
| 20-29 | 100 | 100 | 100 | 100 | 100 | 100 | 100 | 100 | 100 | 100 |
| 30-39 | 94 | | | 92 | 97 | 84 | 86 | 100 | | 74 |
| 40 | | | | | | | | 67 | | |
| 40-49 | 79 | 50 | 80 | | 76 | 77 | 57 | | | 65 |
| 50 | | | | | | | | 47 | 50 | |
| 50-59 | 50 | | | | 35 | | | | | 31 |

SOURCE, BY COLUMN

(1) Stephenson, *Isaac Franklin, Slave Trader* . . . , pp. 168-188.
(2) *Ibid.*, pp. 157-160.
(3) William B. Hamilton and William D. McCain, "Wealth in the Natchez Region," *Journal of Mississippi History*, X, pp. 305-306.
(4) Schedule of Property of James L. Alcorn, Value of Slaves, July 4, 1860, North Carolina Department of Archives and History, Raleigh.
(5) William Clark Estate in Lewis Thompson Papers, Southern Historical Collection, University of North Carolina, Chapel Hill.
(6) Partition between Heirs of General Zachary Taylor, 1860, Library of Congress, Washington.
(7) "Estimates of the Value of Slaves," *American Historical Review*, XIX, pp. 813-836.
(8) J. Winston Coleman, Jr., *Slavery Times in Kentucky*, University of North Carolina Press, 1940, p. 121.
(9) Phillips, *American Negro Slavery*, p. 370.
(10) Devereaux Personal Papers, Division of Negroes, 1844, North Carolina Department of Archives and History, Raleigh.

is virtually impossible to estimate the alternative rate of return. Therefore, I will present several rate-of-return series for other investment goods and hope that these suggest the order of magnitude of the alternative rate.

Information on the income generated by capital or received by its owners is very limited for the period before the Civil War, except for illustrative profits of a few companies for a few years. I know of only two published series of returns for the period 1830 through 1860. These series are for returns on two-name sixty- to ninety-day bills in New York, 1831 through 1860, and for yields on railroad bonds held to maturity, 1857 through 1860.

Other estimates of returns can, with reasonable confidence, be prepared from several sources, one of the best being Martin.[37] Data on the three- to six-month bankable paper market in Boston, while not

[37] Joseph G. Martin, *One Hundred Years' History of the Boston Stock and Money Markets*, Boston, 1898.

complete, are sufficient for an estimate of the return to this class of paper for the years 1831 through 1860. From the interest rate given for many months and the beginning and ending rates for periods of change, the average monthly rate can be estimated. The yearly rates are simple averages of the monthly figures (Table 13).

Series concerning the high, low, and par stock prices and the nominal dividend rates for manufacturing and railroad companies, quoted on the Boston market, are also given by Martin. An estimate of the rate of return received by investors in railroad companies was made using these figures. It was assumed the average price of a given stock in any year was equal to the average of the high and low stock prices. The nominal dividend rate, times the par value of the stock, divided by the average yearly price gives the real dividend rate for the year. The capital gain rate of return for any given year was calculated by dividing the difference between the given year's stock price and the preceding year's stock price by the preceding year's stock price. The sum of the real dividend rate and the capital gains rate was used to estimate the yearly rate of return. This can be summarized mathematically.

$$r_1 = \frac{(D)\,(V)}{P_1} + \frac{P_1 \text{-} P_0}{P_0}$$

Where: (1) $D$ = the nominal dividend rate
      (2) $V$ = the par value of the stock
      (3) $P_1$ = the average price of the stock in year one
      (4) $P_0$ = the average price of the stock in year zero
      (5) $r_1$ = the rate of return in year one

The rates of return for Boston railroad stocks were estimated using this procedure. A sample of nineteen to twenty-three railroads was used for each year in the period 1845 through 1860. Stock prices were not deflated by a price level index because I do not consider any of them reliable enough.

A similar procedure could be used to calculate a rate of return on manufacturing stocks. This has not been done because manufacturing stocks were closely held and it is doubtful that the average stock prices are very meaningful.[38]

[38] Martin, *One Hundred Years' History* . . . , p. 126. A similar statement concerning the extent of participation in railroad and manufacturing stock markets is found in Frederick R. Macaulay, *Some Theoretical Problems Suggested by Movements of Interest Rates, Bond Yields, and Stock Prices in the United States since 1856*, New York, NBER, 1938, pp. 138-139.

## TABLE 13
Short-Term Money Rates of Interest, 1831-60
(per cent)

| Year and Period | New York 60- 90-Day Bills | Boston 3- 6-Month Bankable Paper |
|---|---|---|
| 1831 | 6.1 | 6.5 |
| 1832 | 6.3 | 6.3 |
| 1833 | 7.9 | 8.1 |
| 1834 | 14.6 | 18.5 |
| 1835 | 7.0 | 6.7 |
| 1836 | 18.4 | 20.5 |
| 1837 | 14.1 | 14.4 |
| 1838 | 9.0 | 9.0 |
| 1839 | 13.2 | 14.0 |
| 1840 | 7.8 | 7.4 |
| 1841 | 6.9 | 7.0 |
| 1842 | 8.1 | 8.2 |
| 1843 | 4.5 | 4.4 |
| 1844 | 4.9 | 4.9 |
| 1845 | 6.0 | 6.0 |
| 1846 | 8.3 | 8.3 |
| 1847 | 9.6 | 10.0 |
| 1848 | 15.1 | 15.4 |
| 1849 | 10.0 | 10.2 |
| 1850 | 8.0 | 8.0 |
| 1851 | 9.7 | 10.0 |
| 1852 | 6.6 | 6.3 |
| 1853 | 10.2 | 10.9 |
| 1854 | 10.4 | 11.6 |
| 1855 | 8.9 | 9.2 |
| 1856 | 8.9 | 9.6 |
| 1857 | 12.9 | 13.1 |
| 1858 | 5.0 | 4.8 |
| 1859 | 6.8 | 7.0 |
| 1860 | 7.0 | 8.0 |
| 1831-60 | 9.1 | 9.5 |
| 1845-60 | 9.0 | 9.3 |
| 1850-60 | 8.6 | 9.0 |
| 1857-60 | 7.9 | 8.2 |

Source: New York rates are from the Federal Reserve Bank of New York, *Monthly Review*, March 1, 1921, p. 3. Boston rates were calculated from Martin, *One Hundred Years' History*, pp. 52-53. Boston monthly rates are given in Appendix B. These series differ somewhat from similar ones in Conrad and Meyer, "The Economics of Slavery . . . ," p. 102. For New York, the difference is for the years 1831 through 1833 and results from their error in transcription from the original source. For Boston, the difference is in most of the years and results from their use of a concept of the rate sustained for a major portion of the year rather than the arithmetic average.

In addition to Martin, two other sources provide limited information on returns. Davis estimated that nine of the more prosperous Massachusetts textile firms earned returns of 16.76 per cent on total capital stock for the period 1844 through 1848 and 5.75 per cent in the period 1848 through 1853.[39] Macaulay estimated that the average yield if held to maturity of a sample of railroad bonds was 7.6 per cent for the period 1857 through 1860.[40]

Because of poor communications in the ante-bellum period, there may have been sizable imperfections in the capital markets. If this is true, rates of return estimated for the North may be of limited use as alternative rates for the slave industry. It would, therefore, be desirable to have similar series for southern money and stock markets. Returns on money are unavailable for the South, but one can estimate returns on railroad capital, though in a slightly different form than those obtained for railroad stocks traded on the Boston exchange.

A variety of sources contain information on the total capital costs incurred in building and equipping southern railroads and the yearly net incomes after paying for capital maintenance, but before payment of interest on funded debt.[41] These series have been combined to obtain two estimates of the average returns earned by capital invested in southern railroads. One estimate is the weighted average of the returns earned on capital invested in completed southern railroads. The twenty-three to twenty-seven railroads included in each year's sample (not the same in each sample) operated an average of 61.2 per cent of all southern trackage. The other estimate is the weighted average return for twelve selected southern railroads. These roads were chosen because data were available for them for almost every year of the eleven-year period 1850 through 1860.[42] The series for Boston and southern railroads are shown in Table 14. As previously indicated,

[39] Lance E. Davis, "Sources of Industrial Finance: The American Textile Industry," *Explorations in Entrepreneurial History*, April, 1957, p. 201. The figures are based upon company records in the Baker Library, Harvard Graduate School of Business Administration.

[40] Macaulay, *Some Theoretical Problems* . . . , pp. A34-A38.

[41] The data were obtained chiefly from secondary sources, but in every case the original sources are the annual reports of the railroads. Every effort has been made to assure that the capital and net income concepts defined in the text are characteristic of the data used. Detailed examination of each company's records would be required to assure that this is true.

[42] This sample includes 121 out of 132 possible railroad years. The average returns range from 5.3 per cent for the Richmond and Petersburg Railroad to 16.8 per cent for the Central Railroad and Banking Company of Georgia.

## TABLE 14
### AVERAGE RATES OF RETURN ON RAILROAD BONDS, STOCK, AND CAPITAL, 1845-60
(per cent)

| Year and Period | Boston Rails | Boston Rails, Dividend Only | Completed Southern Rails | Selected Southern Rails | Railroad Bonds |
|---|---|---|---|---|---|
| 1845 | 12.0 | 6.8 | | | |
| 1846 | 5.0 | 7.0 | | | |
| 1847 | 9.6 | 6.9 | | | |
| 1848 | 3.6 | 7.5 | | | |
| 1849 | 2.2 | 6.2 | | | |
| 1850 | 2.3 | 6.2 | | 7.6 | |
| 1851 | 9.0 | 6.5 | | 8.4 | |
| 1852 | 9.9 | 7.0 | | 8.2 | |
| 1853 | 4.2 | 6.9 | | 8.7 | |
| 1854 | −4.9 | 7.9 | | 8.5 | |
| 1855 | 4.7 | 5.7 | 8.6 | 9.2 | |
| 1856 | −3.0 | 6.2 | | 8.5 | |
| 1857 | −5.4 | 7.5 | 7.6 | 7.9 | 8.3 |
| 1858 | 14.4 | 5.0 | 8.3 | 8.4 | 7.7 |
| 1859 | 23.8 | 5.2 | 7.8 | 9.8 | 7.4 |
| 1860 | 19.0 | 4.9 | 8.4 | 9.4 | 7.1 |
| 1845-60 | 8.6 | 6.5 | | | |
| 1850-60 | 6.7 | 6.3 | | 8.5 | |
| 1857-60 | 13.0 | 5.7 | 8.0 | 8.9 | 7.6 |

SOURCE: Series for Boston were calculated as indicated in the text from information contained in Martin, *One Hundred Years' History* . . . , pp. 145-149. Data and sources for southern railroads are given in Appendix C. The information on railroad bonds is from Macaulay, *Some Theoretical Problems* . . . , pp. A34-A38.

these series do not allow one to specify the alternative rate, but they do suggest that the order of magnitude of the alternative rate may have been 6 to 10 per cent for the years 1830 through 1860.

### THE LIFE SPAN OF SLAVES

Slaves are a form of capital that both depreciates and appreciates with age. The depreciation is in two forms, death and a declining ability as a function of age to produce income. Slave appreciation results from the birth of slaves. Slave depreciation due to lessened ability to earn income and appreciation due to birth can be left out of an analysis restricted to males in the prime working ages. Slave depreciation due to death must be explicitly considered. This consideration involves knowledge about the death rates of male slaves in certain age groups.[43] Since information dealing with the death rate characteristics of populations is more often discussed in terms of life expectancy, this discussion will deal with a slave life table, though death rates will be used in the estimation of the rate of return on slave capital.

Really accurate estimates of life expectancy are a product of this century and exist for only a few countries. For the United States the earliest reasonable estimate is usually considered to be one for the state of Massachusetts in 1850.[44] Little attention has been given to slave life expectancy,[45] probably because of a lack of information rather than a lack of interest; estimates have been made for three southern states, Mississippi,[46] Maryland, and Louisiana[47] for 1850.

New estimates of the slave life expectancy have been made for this study based upon population and mortality statistics of the 1850 census. These estimates are used rather than those already calculated for the three southern states from the 1850 census, because the new estimates based upon the experience of all the southern states are preferable to those limited to only three, and because the most widely known of them,[48] for Mississippi, is in error by a factor of 1.7.[49]

[43] Conrad and Meyer, "The Economics of Slavery . . . ," in their study of the returns to slaveholding, account for deaths by summing net income produced for a period of years equal to the median life expectancy of the slaves when purchased. This will serve but only as a rough approximation. Its use introduces errors because in a physical sense the income lost due to early deaths must be made up by income gained from those who live beyond the life expectancy age. Declining ability to earn income with increasing age makes this an impossible condition. (With a life expectancy, at age twenty, of thirty-eight years it means that the income lost from the first slave death at age twenty years thirty-one days must be made up by a slave who lives to age ninety-five years and 344 days.) Even if it were physically possible, the capitalized value of extra income would be less than the capitalized value of the lost income.

[44] Louis I. Dublin, Alfred J. Lotka, and Mortimer Spiegelman, *Length of Life*, rev. ed., New York, Ronald, 1949, p. 54.

[45] For an interesting discussion of slave life expectancies in the West Indies, see George W. Roberts, *The Population of Jamaica*, Cambridge University Press, 1957.

[46] Charles S. Sydnor, "Life Span of Mississippi Slaves," *American Historical Review*, April, 1930, pp. 566-574.

[47] J. C. G. Kennedy, *Report of the Superintendent of the Census 1852*, Washington, Robert Armstrong, 1853, p. 13. This is sometimes referred to as *The Abstract of the Seventh Census*. The information is also contained in *DeBow's Review*, Vol. XXXV.

[48] This is the one used by Kenneth Stampp in *The Peculiar Institution*, New York, Knopf, 1957; and by William D. Postell in *The Health of Slaves on Southern Plantations*, Louisiana State University Press, 1951.

[49] The factor 1.7 is the ratio of my estimate to Sydnor's estimate of the life expectancy of twenty-year-old males, the only group for which Sydnor calculated

The 1850 census provides population data by age group, sex, race, condition of servitude, and state of residence. This census also supplies mortality data by age group, race, and state of residence as well as the total number of slave deaths by state. In order to obtain male slave death rates by age groups, one must estimate the percentage of Negro deaths in the southern states that accounts for male slaves. In addition, it would be desirable to have a method for estimating the degree of underreporting of deaths in the 1850 census. (Underreporting is typical of mortality data in underdeveloped areas.)

A recently published life table by Paul Jacobson[50] for whites in the United States in 1850 is used to estimate both the percentage of deaths that are male slave deaths and the reporting error.

Life expectancies in Massachusetts in 1900 through 1931 are less than those reported for the United States as a whole. This suggested to Jacobson that it would be more accurate to use an estimate for United States 1850 life expectancies which had a similar relationship to Massachusetts 1850 estimates, rather than using the Massachusetts estimates for the United States.[51] I have accepted Jacobson's new estimates for whites in 1850 as the most accurate currently obtainable for the United States and have used them to estimate the percentage of male slave deaths and the reporting error.

It seems reasonable that the relative death rates of males and females

---

an estimate. This understates his error because Mississippi death rates are lower than average death rates for the southern states.

The usual life expectation at age X is the average number of years lived beyond age X by all those alive at age X. It is calculated from the number of deaths per year at every age level in a cohort of size Y at birth. The number of deaths at any age level of the cohort is determined by the death rate for that age level in the real population under study. The cohort used to calculate the life table has the characteristic that the number of persons at any age Z + 1 is equal to the number of persons alive at age Z less the number of persons of age Z who die in a single year.

Sydnor estimated life expectancy by multiplying the number of deaths in the 1850 census year for each age group over age twenty by the average number of years lived beyond age twenty. (If 500 died between age thirty and age forty, he would have multiplied 500 by 15.) He then summed these products for all age groups and divided by the number aged twenty and older who had died in that year. This quotient he called the life expectancy at age twenty. The quotient is not the life expectancy, but the average number of years lived beyond age twenty by all those twenty and older who died in that year. The error results from his failure to relate the number of deaths in each age group to the number of persons alive in those age groups.

[50] Paul Jacobson, "An Estimate of the Length of Life in the United States in 1850," *Milbank Memorial Fund Quarterly*, April, 1957, pp. 197-201.
[51] *Ibid.*, p. 197.

at various ages were essentially the same for whites, free Negroes, and slaves. Therefore, I have used the male-female ratios in Jacobson's life table for both slaves and free Negroes. Use of these ratios in connection with the assumption that the death rates for slaves and southern free Negroes were equal allows one, by solving the following equations, to obtain estimates of the death rates for male and female slaves.

$$D = (M_x) (M) + (F_x) (F)$$
$$K = F_x/M_x$$
$$D = (K) (F) (M_x) + (M_x) (M)$$
$$M_x = \frac{D}{M + (K) (F)}$$

Where

$M_x$ is the male death rate from the census,

$M$ is the number of males,

$F_x$ is the female death rate from the census,

$F$ is the number of females,

$D$ is the total number of deaths,

$K$ is the ratio of female to male deaths from Jacobson's study.

The death rates calculated in this manner are not quite large enough to produce the recorded number of slave deaths in 1850. Each death rate was then increased proportionally so that they would produce a correct number of deaths.

By solving a similar set of equations it is possible to obtain census death rates for whites. In all cases they are smaller than those proposed by Jacobson. I have assumed that the ratios of Jacobson's death rates to the census death rates are the census reporting errors and that these errors are equal for white and slave statistics. Multiplying slave death rates by the correction factors (ratios of Jacobson's rates to census rates) yields the corrected slave death rates (Table 15) used to calculate a slave life table.

Kenneth Stampp[52] has suggested that the disparity between slave and white death rates was greater than that indicated by the 1850 census. While one could suggest various reasons why Stampp's belief was not correct, one justification for using the assumption of equality of error lies in the statement by the superintendent of the census that, if anything, the data for slaves were better than those for whites.[53]

[52] Stampp, *The Peculiar Institution*, p. 318.
[53] DeBow, *Statistical View of the United States*, p. 92.

TABLE 15

DEATH RATES FOR SLAVES AND WHITES, 1850

(deaths per 1,000 population)

| Age Group | Slave Male, Corrected | Slave Female, Corrected | Male, Jacobson | Female, Jacobson |
|---|---|---|---|---|
| 0 | 197.51 | 167.90 | 112.05 | 95.20 |
| 1- 4 | 36.75 | 33.72 | 31.83 | 29.18 |
| 5- 9 | 11.45 | 10.62 | 10.50 | 9.40 |
| 10-14 | 7.06 | 9.10 | 4.85 | 6.25 |
| 15-19 | 9.64 | 11.57 | 6.75 | 8.10 |
| 20-29 | 10.85 | 11.93 | 9.70 | 10.67 |
| 30-39 | 13.05 | 13.21 | 12.17 | 12.33 |
| 40-49 | 19.84 | 14.91 | 17.43 | 13.10 |
| 50-59 | 28.21 | 21.80 | 22.97 | 17.73 |
| 60-69 | 43.26 | 36.75 | 38.67 | 32.87 |
| 70-79 | 81.72 | 67.43 | 83.97 | 69.37 |

SOURCE: Jacobson rates are averages of figures in Jacobson, *An Estimate of the Length of Life* . . . , p. 198. The slave rates are calculated from census figures as indicated in the text.

The slave life table (Table 16) was calculated from the corrected death rates using Greville's abridged life table method.[54] There are few sources of alternative mortality data with which to

TABLE 16

LIFE EXPECTATION IN THE UNITED STATES, 1850

(years)

| Age | Slave Male | Slave Female | White Male | White Female |
|---|---|---|---|---|
| 0 | 35.54 | 38.08 | 40.4 | 43.0 |
| 1 | 44.25 | 45.73 | 47.1 | 48.4 |
| 5 | 46.96 | 48.06 | 50.1 | 51.2 |
| 10 | 44.58 | 45.54 | 47.8 | 48.6 |
| 15 | 41.09 | 42.54 | 43.9 | 44.9 |
| 20 | 37.99 | 39.92 | 40.1 | 41.7 |
| 30 | 31.72 | 34.30 | 33.6 | 35.8 |
| 40 | 25.40 | 28.40 | 27.1 | 29.1 |
| 50 | 19.82 | 22.10 | 21.2 | 23.3 |
| 60 | 14.60 | 16.20 | 15.3 | 16.7 |
| 70 | 9.79 | 11.15 | 9.6 | 10.9 |
| 80 | 6.38 | 7.32 | 5.7 | 6.6 |

SOURCE: White figures are from Jacobson, *An Estimate of the Length of Life* . . . , p. 198. Slave figures are calculated from the corrected death rates using Greville's abridged life table method (Dublin, Lotka, and Spiegelman, *Length of Life*).

[54] Dublin, Lotka, and Spiegelman, *Length of Life*, pp. 312-316.

check the accuracy of the slave and white tables. A survey of the infant death rate on fourteen plantations for the years 1817 through 1861 reported an infant mortality rate for slaves of 152.6 per 1,000 from a sample of 1,114 live births.[55] There are, however, certain tests of reasonableness and consistency which can be applied. The high infant death rate and the higher female to male death rate ratios in the child-bearing years are both consistent with what one would expect from one's knowledge of the period. Also the estimates for the United States are consistent with the reported experience of other countries of similar development in the same period (Table 17).

TABLE 17

MALE LIFE EXPECTANCIES IN THE NINETEENTH CENTURY

(years)

| | United States | | | | England | |
| Age | White | Slave | Norway | Holland | and Wales | France |
|---|---|---|---|---|---|---|
| 0 | 40.4 | 35.5 | 44.9 | 36.4 | 39.9 | 39.1 |
| 20 | 40.1 | 38.0 | 42.0 | 38.0 | 39.5 | 41.2 |
| 40 | 27.1 | 25.4 | 28.0 | 24.7 | 26.1 | 27.3 |

SOURCE: White and slave figures are for 1850 from Table 16. Norway is for 1846-65, Holland 1850-59, England and Wales 1838-54, and France 1861-65. The latter four are from Dublin, Lotka, and Spiegelman, *Length of Life*, pp. 346-348.

Estimates of slave life expectancy in 1850 of the size indicated in Table 17 have been questioned as inaccurate. "The results are of uncertain value for the figures . . . are considerably higher than those for colored persons in the Original Death Registration States half a century later, 1900-1902."[56] Several factors should be considered before accepting this view. The original death registration states consisted of New England, Indiana, New York, Michigan, New Jersey, District of Columbia plus a few major cities, while the slave figures refer to southern states, and therefore the life tables are not strictly comparable. It is probable that the majority of Negroes in the death registration area were unskilled urban workers, whereas the slaves were mostly rural agricultural workers. In 1930, the standardized death rate of gainfully occupied males aged fifteen through sixty-four engaged in agricultural employment was substantially below that of unskilled

[55] Postell, *The Health of Slaves* . . . , p. 158.
[56] Dublin, Lotka, and Spiegelman, *Length of Life*, p. 58.

workers. The standardized average death rate for the ten-state sample was 8.7 per 1,000, for agricultural workers it was 6.2 per 1,000, and for unskilled workers 13.1 per 1,000.[57] There is also evidence that the death rate for the colored population rose for at least twenty-five years after the Civil War, reaching its climax in the 1880's.[58] Even in the original death registration states, between the periods 1900 through 1902 and 1909 through 1911, when white life expectancies remained about constant, the life expectancies for colored males aged twenty and forty declined by one and one-half years.[59]

While the individual reader is free to place his own confidence limits on the slave life table for 1850, and more particularly for this study, on the corrected male slave death rates for those aged twenty to fifty, they are presented as the most reasonable and accurate estimates I can make.

## Calculation of the Rate of Return

The rates of return earned by slave capital are calculated by considering the rates of return received by owners who buy 1,000 male slaves at age twenty and hold them for periods of twenty or thirty years and sell them. By limiting the analysis to this class of slaves, twenty- to fifty-year-old males, one can neglect slave appreciation and decreased earnings due to old age. Any income from slave appreciation apparently was imputed to females.[60] Declining hire as a function of age is generally considered to begin at about age fifty or fifty-five.[61]

The rates of return received by owners of twenty- to fifty-year-old male slaves can be estimated by using the capital value equation. The form of the equation is adjusted to allow for continuous deaths among the slaves and for their re-sale value at ages forty or fifty. The adjusted form of the equation is:[62]

$$1,000\,P_{20} = \left[ \sum_{t=0}^{t=k} \frac{(H)\,(N_t)}{(1+r)^t} \right] + \frac{(P_{k+21})\,(N_{k+1/2})}{(1+r)^k}$$

[57] *Ibid.*, p. 214.

[58] S. J. Holmes, *The Negro's Struggle for Survival*, University of California Press, 1937, p. 40.

[59] Dublin, Lotka, and Spiegelman, *Length of Life*, p. 340.

[60] The ratios of female to male price were greater than the ratios of female to male hire.

[61] Conrad and Meyer, "The Economics of Slavery . . . ," p. 106.

[62] For convenience only, the calculations are based on a unit of 1,000 slaves. The analysis would not be changed in any way if the unit chosen had been one slave.

Where $P$ is the price of the slaves, the subscript indicates the age of the slaves,

$k$ is the number of years the investor holds the slaves,

$H$ is the yearly rate of hire (yearly rent) for male slaves twenty to fifty years of age,

$N$ is the number of male slaves alive at mid-year out of a group of 1,000 alive at age twenty years, zero days,

$r$ is the internal rate of interest.

Because of the limited number of observations of slave hires for any given year and because they probably reflect certain future expectations and past experience, the figures used in the calculations are averages for five-year periods, and the price figures are weighted average prices for the same five-year periods. The weight assigned to each year's price is equal to the number of observations of hire for that year relative to the total number for the five-year period. The calculation of the weighted price is illustrated in Table 18 for the

TABLE 18

SAMPLE CALCULATION OF WEIGHTED AVERAGE PRICE OF MALE SLAVES, TWENTY TO FIFTY YEARS OLD, UPPER SOUTH, 1856-60

| Year | Number, Hire Observations (1) | Per Cent of Total (2) | Average Price (3) | Weighted Price (4) |
|---|---|---|---|---|
| 1856 | 949 | 23.2 | $1,038 | $ 241 |
| 1857 | 834 | 20.4 | 1,063 | 217 |
| 1858 | 820 | 20.2 | 1,113 | 223 |
| 1859 | 927 | 22.7 | 1,150 | 260 |
| 1860 | 561 | 13.7 | 1,213 | 166 |
| Total Hires | 4,091 | 100.0 | | |
| Simple average price | | | $1,115 | |
| Weighted average price | | | | $1,107 |

SOURCE: Col. 4 is the product of cols. 2 and 3 for the individual years. The average prices are Phillips' estimates (*Life and Labor in the Old South*).

1856 through 1860 period in the Upper South. The average yearly hires and weighted average prices used in the calculations are taken from the series presented in the section on data and are summarized in Table 19.

The value of $N$ for any year is obtained by multiplying the death rate for males for the particular age by the number of slaves still alive in the preceding year out of the original cohort of 1,000, and subtracting

*215*

TABLE 19

FIVE-YEAR AVERAGES OF HIRES AND WEIGHTED
PRICES OF SLAVES, 1830-60

| Period | Upper South | | Lower South | |
|---|---|---|---|---|
| | Hire | Price | Hire | Price |
| 1830-35 | $ 62 | $ 521 | $127 | $ 948 |
| 1836-40 | 106 | 957 | | |
| 1841-45 | 83 | 529 | 143 | 722 |
| 1846-50 | 99 | 709 | 168 | 926 |
| 1851-55 | 141.5 | 935 | 167 | 1,240 |
| 1856-60 | 142 | 1,107a | 196.5 | 1,658 |
| 1856-60 | 142 | 1,294b | | |

a Based upon Phillips' estimates of slave prices (*Life and Labor in the Old South*).
b Based upon my estimates of slave prices.

this product from the number alive in the preceding year. An abridged table of the series prepared in this way is given in Table 20.

The data in Tables 19 and 20 combined with the relationships of 78 per cent of prime price for the price of forty-year-old slaves and 52 per cent of prime price for the price of fifty-year-old slaves yield estimates of the rate of return for slave capital. The nature of the capital value equation is such that it is not actually solved for the internal rate of return. Rather, an internal rate is assumed, and the equation is solved for the discounted sum of the income stream. The estimates of the rate of return on slaves are those internal rates that round to the same one-half per cent as would a rate exactly equating the discounted income stream to the original price. More accurate internal rates were not obtained because of the cost of calculation, coupled with a belief

TABLE 20

NUMBER ALIVE AT FIVE-YEAR INTERVALS OUT OF 1,000
SLAVES ALIVE AT AGE TWENTY

| Age | Number Alive at Mid-Year | Death Rate Per 1,000 | Number Dying in a Year |
|---|---|---|---|
| 20 | 994.59 | 10.85 | 10.79 |
| 24 | 952.11 | 10.85 | 10.33 |
| 29 | 901.56 | 11.95 | 10.77 |
| 34 | 845.20 | 13.05 | 11.03 |
| 39 | 791.48 | 16.45 | 12.96 |
| 44 | 718.54 | 19.84 | 14.25 |
| 49 | 650.04 | 24.03 | 15.53 |

that the accuracy of the estimating variables is not sufficient to warrant carrying the rate of return estimates to more than the nearest one-half per cent.

The rates of return in Tables 21 and 22 are the same, whether it is assumed that the slaves are held for twenty years or thirty years. The

TABLE 21

RATES OF RETURN ON SLAVES, 1830-60

(per cent)

| Period | Upper South | Lower South |
|---|---|---|
| 1830-35 | 10.5 | 12.0 |
| 1836-40 | 9.5 | |
| 1841-45 | 14.3 | 18.5 |
| 1846-50 | 12.6 | 17.0 |
| 1851-55 | 13.8 | 12.0 |
| 1856-60 (Phillips' Prices) | 11.3 | 10.3 |
| 1856-60 (Evans' Prices) | 9.5 | |

range of differences between the discounted income streams under the two assumptions is from 2 parts in 1,000 to 8 parts in 1,000. This close correspondence indicates that the results are not specific to the time period for which the slaves are held and serves to increase confidence in the generality of the conclusions concerning the rates of return.

Before accepting the estimates of the rates of return on slaves, the method of analysis should be investigated to determine if it is highly sensitive to small changes in the magnitudes of the variables used to

TABLE 22

WEIGHTED PRICES AND DISCOUNTED SUMS, FOR SLAVES, 1830-60

| | UPPER SOUTH | | | LOWER SOUTH | | |
|---|---|---|---|---|---|---|
| | | Discounted Sums | | | Discounted Sums | |
| | | Twenty | Thirty | | Twenty | Thirty |
| PERIOD | Price | Years | Years | Price | Years | Years |
| 1830-35 | $ 521 | $ 516 | $ 518 | $ 948 | $ 940 | $ 948 |
| 1836-40 | 957 | 959 | 963 | | | |
| 1841-45 | 529 | 529 | 531 | 722 | 721 | 724 |
| 1846-50 | 709 | 705 | 708 | 926 | 915 | 918 |
| 1851-55 | 935 | 929 | 933 | 1,240 | 1,241 | 1,247 |
| 1856-60 | 1,107[a] | 1,110 | 1,116 | 1,658 | 1,663 | 1,670 |
| 1856-60 | 1,294[b] | 1,284 | 1,289 | | | |

[a] Phillips' prices.
[b] Evans' prices.

217

estimate the returns. Rough estimates of the sensitivity, can, however, be obtained from results already calculated, except for the death rates where independent estimates must be made. An estimate of the effect of a change in the price of slaves can be obtained by comparing the different rates of return in periods when the rates of hire were essentially equal and prices were not equal. The periods used are those where the rates are $142.00 and $167.00. From Table 23 it can be seen that on the average a $34.00 change in the price of slaves would yield a change of 0.5 per cent in the rate of return when hires are held constant. This, with the average standard deviation in the price of

TABLE 23

Effect of a Change in the Price of Slaves on the Rate of Return

| Hire | Price[a] | Rate of Return (per cent) | Change in Price | Change in the Rate of Return (per cent) | Change in Price Per ½ Per Cent Change in the Rate of Return |
|------|----------|---------------------------|-----------------|------------------------------------------|-------------------------------------------------------------|
| $141.5 | $ 929 | 13.8 | | | |
| 142 | 1,100 | 11.3 | $181 | 2.4 | $36 |
| 141.5 | 929 | 13.8 | | | |
| 142 | 1,284 | 9.5 | 355 | 4.3 | 41 |
| 142 | 1,110 | 11.3 | | | |
| 142 | 1,284 | 9.5 | 174 | 1.8 | 48 |
| 143 | 721 | 18.5 | | | |
| 141.5 | 929 | 13.8 | 208 | 4.7 | 22 |
| 143 | 721 | 18.5 | | | |
| 142 | 1,110 | 11.3 | 389 | 7.2 | 27 |
| 143 | 721 | 18.5 | | | |
| 142 | 1,284 | 9.5 | 563 | 9.0 | 31 |
| 168 | 915 | 17.0 | | | |
| 167 | 1,241 | 12.0 | 326 | 5.0 | 33 |

a Price is the discounted sum of the income stream when the slaves are held for twenty years.

slaves of $96.00,[63] indicates that probable errors in the estimation of slave prices would not result in more than a 1.5 per cent change in the rate of return.

A similar method can be used to estimate the effect of errors in the rates of hire. The result, as is obvious from the form of the equation (Table 24), is that a given proportional error in the rate yields an

[63] Table 9.

equal percentage error in the rate of return. The average ratio of the standard deviation of the rate of hire to the rate of hire is 0.20.[64] This suggests that probable errors in the rates of hire would not result in more than a 20 per cent error in the rates of return.[65] An additional

TABLE 24

EFFECT OF A CHANGE IN THE RATE OF HIRE FOR SLAVES
ON THE RATE OF RETURN

| Price | Hire | Rate of Return (per cent) | Proportional Change in Hire | Proportional Change in Rate of Return (per cent) |
|---|---|---|---|---|
| $516 | $ 83 | 14.3 | | |
| 529 | 62 | 10.5 | 13.4 | 13.6 |
| 705 | 99 | 12.2 | | |
| 721 | 143 | 18.5 | 14.4 | 14.7 |
| 940 | 127 | 12.0 | | |
| 929 | 141.5 | 13.8 | 11.4 | 11.5 |
| 940 | 127 | 12.0 | | |
| 959 | 141.5 | 9.5 | 12.0 | 12.6 |
| 915 | 168 | 17.0 | | |
| 929 | 141.5 | 13.8 | 11.9 | 12.3 |

NOTE: Comparison is made only where the price (discounted sum of the income stream when the slaves are held twenty years) differential is less than $20.00.

error related to the rates of hire might result from a failure to net out the cost of hiring. Its maximum effect would be to lower the rate of return by a factor of 8 per cent.

There are no reliable estimates of the probable errors in the death rates. An error of 100 per cent would change the calculated rates of return by only 1.75 percentage points, which suggests that reasonable death rate errors would result in an error in the rate of return of less than 1.0 percentage point.[66]

The alternative rates summarized in Table 25 are probably reasonably accurate. They may be very poor estimates of an alternative rate to

[64] Table 5.
[65] A 20 per cent error would lower a 10 per cent return to a return of 8 per cent.
[66] The loss associated with runaways has not been considered because I have no information on their number. Successful runaways are equivalent to deaths in their effect on the rate of return. The above calculation suggests that the omission of runaways does not seriously affect the estimated returns, for it is doubtful if their number was of the same order of magnitude as the number of deaths.

slave capital because of an imperfect capital market. In the absence of more complete information, they will be used as suggestive of the range within which the alternative rate would be found. In Table 25, it appears that the probable errors of any single variable would not, except for the period 1836 through 1840, lower the rate of return on slaves below the range of the suggested alternative rates. A cumula-

TABLE 25

RATES OF RETURN ON CAPITAL, 1830-60

(per cent)

| Period | Short-Term Money | | Railroads | | | | | Slaves | | |
|---|---|---|---|---|---|---|---|---|---|---|
| 1830-35 | 8.4 | 9.2 | | | | | | 10.5 | 12.0 | |
| 1836-40 | 12.5 | 13.0 | | | | | | 9.5 | | |
| 1841-45 | 6.1 | 6.1 | | | | | | 14.3 | 18.5 | |
| 1846-50 | 12.2 | 12.4 | 4.9 | 6.7 | | | | 12.6 | 17.0 | |
| 1851-55 | 9.1 | 9.6 | 4.6 | 6.8 | 8.6 | | | 13.8 | 12.0 | |
| 1856-60 | 8.1 | 8.5 | 9.8 | 5.8 | 8.8 | 8.0 | 7.6 | 11.3 | 10.3 | 9.5 |

SOURCE: Money rates are from Table 13; railroad rates from Table 14; and slave rates from Table 21.

tion of all the probable errors would lower the 9.5 per cent return to a little above 5.0 per cent, which is just out of the range of 6 through 10 per cent suggested as the range of the alternative rate for the years 1830 through 1860. The probability of cumulated errors is low, and it thus appears that the sensitivity of the engine of analysis is not enough to destroy confidence in the conclusion that the rate of return was at least equal to alternative rates of return.

Even granted the accuracy of the analysis, the conclusion drawn would be invalid if the hires and prices do not refer to the same class of slaves, e.g., if the hires refer to a superior class of slaves and the prices to an average class. No direct test of this can be made, but the hire-price ratio of a group of slaves for whom both types of information are available for the same year suggests that differential quality is not a problem (Table 26). The average hire-price ratio for 170 male slaves in the prime working ages is 0.142, with a standard deviation of 0.036, and with 81 per cent of the observations within the ratios 0.120 through 0.179. The average of the twelve hire-price ratios used to estimate the rates of return on slave capital is 0.139, with seven of them in the range 0.120 through 0.179. (These twelve ratios can be calculated from the information given in Table 19.) Thus it appears that, if there is a differential quality problem, it has resulted in a slight underestimation of the rates of return.

In summary, the method of analysis and the related estimates of the magnitudes of the variables, allowing for reasonable errors in estimation, suggest that the rates of return on slave capital for the period 1830 through 1860 were at least equal to the rates of return being received by alternative forms of capital. This approximate equality

TABLE 26

DISTRIBUTION OF SLAVE HIRE-PRICE RATIOS

| Ratios | Number of Observations, Independent Sample | Number of Ratios Used in Estimating Rates of Return |
|---|---|---|
| More than 0.200 | 5 | 0 |
| 0.199–0.180 | 6 | 2 |
| 0.179–0.150 | 60 | 2 |
| 0.149–0.120 | 78 | 4 |
| 0.119—0.090 | 11 | 4 |
| Less than 0.090 | 10 | 0 |

suggests that previous studies, which have estimated that the pecuniary returns to slaveholding were much lower than for alternative investments, have contained errors of analysis. It also suggests that, in the absence of strong nonpecuniary returns associated with particular types of investment, the southern capital market worked surprisingly well. One cannot, however, infer from the magnitude of the rate of return, by itself or relative to any other rate, anything concerning the viability of the system. It is to this problem that we turn in the next section.

## Viability

Favorable rates of return for investors in slaves provide an answer to a major historical question, that of slave profitability. They do not answer what, to the economist, is the more relevant question, that of the viability of slavery. Viability is more relevant because theory predicts that investors will be induced to shift out of a declining industry because of capital losses on capital goods completely specialized to that industry rather than because of rates of return which are lower than market rates. Consequently, in attempting to assess the position and role of the slave industry in the United States just before the Civil War, one is primarily interested in the viability of the system and in data that suggest the probability that holders of slave capital would sustain substantial and continuing capital losses within the decision period of the average investor. Such data must be limited by the ex-ante knowledge of 1856 through 1860 and not by the ex-post knowledge of the present-day investigator.

A variety of political events of the period bear on the question of viability. Their usefulness is impaired because it is not clear exactly what their economic implications were. The controversy over new slave states may have meant that the industry was viable only if it could expand geographically; it may have been almost entirely related to the balance of political power in the Senate. The agitation for the re-opening of the foreign slave trade may have been because the industry was viable only if new slaves could be procured more cheaply, or that the industry was very viable and an increased supply of slaves was desired to limit the windfall capital gains to current owners. The movement by some slave states to prohibit manumission[67] and to allow free Negroes to become slaves may have indicated that too many slaves were being freed for economic reasons, or it may have meant that there was little concern over the power to manumit and that the laws were passed to reassure abolitionists that the South was not going to give up slavery. No attempt will be made to evaluate the implications of these events. Conclusions on viability will be drawn from information that appears to be less subject to a variety of interpretations.

Before discussing data, let us consider briefly some of the characteristics of an industry that is either nonviable or on the verge of becoming nonviable. Such an industry should exhibit some or all of the following: (1) a relative decline in the demand for its product; (2) a decline in the demand for the specialized capital used in the production of the industry's product; (3) a declining rate of production of the specialized capital used in the industry; (4) a declining demand for the specialized capital used in the industry which supplies specialized capital to the declining industry. In the case of a nonviable slave

[67] Mississippi changed its laws in 1857 to prohibit manumission under any circumstances. (Sydnor, *Slavery in Mississippi*, p. 236.) A similar law went into effect in Maryland in 1860 (Jeffrey R. Bracket, *The Negro in Maryland*, Johns Hopkins University Press, 1889, p. 171). Many states passed laws just before the Civil War to allow free Negroes to become slaves (Gray, *History of Agriculture*, Vol. I, p. 527).

industry, one should observe a decline in the demand for the labor services of slaves relative to the demand for the labor services of free men, a decline in the demand for slave capital, a falling slave birth rate, and a decline in the demand for female slaves relative to male slaves.

Because of the capital nature of the industry, one can assume that changes in the price of slaves result from shifts of the short-run demand curve along a completely inelastic short-run supply curve. (The ratio per year of new male slaves fifteen to sixty years of age to the average number of male slaves fifteen to sixty years of age is 0.022 for the period 1850 to 1860.) Therefore, in the following discussion, shifts in prices of labor services and of the capital good are presumed to illustrate the demand conditions facing the industry.

The demand for the labor services of slaves relative to the demand for the labor services of free men did not appear to be declining in the late 1850's. In the Lower South the average hire for male slaves in 1856 through 1860 was 17 per cent greater than it was in 1851 through 1855. In the Upper South the average hires in 1856 through 1860 and 1851 through 1855 were essentially equal. In the Lower South the median hire rose 25 per cent and in the Upper South it rose 8 per cent between these two periods.[68] The Virginia and Tennessee Railroad paid an average of $135.00[69] for its hired slaves in 1854 and $149.00 in 1857.[70] The Richmond and Danville Railroad paid $135.00[71] in 1855 and $139.00[72] in 1860. The Central Railroad and Banking Company of Georgia reported that the price of hire in 1859 was 20 per cent higher than it had been in 1858.[73] The ratio of slave wages to white wages in the Navy Shipyard at Gosport, Virginia, was the same in July 1860 as it had been in November 1854.[74] In Columbia, South Carolina, wage increases received in 1856-57 were, for white stone cutters 20 per

[68] White wages also rose in these periods.
[69] Annual Reports, Commonwealth of Virginia, 1853-54, p. 806.
[70] Tenth Annual Report of the Virginia and Tennessee Railroad, Library of the Bureau of Railway Economics, Association of American Railroads, pp. 210-212.
[71] Proceedings and Annual Reports of the Richmond and Danville Railroad, Library of the Bureau of Railway Economics, 1856, p. 30.
[72] Ibid., 1860.
[73] Reports of the Central Railroad and Banking Company of Georgia, No. 20-32, Library of the Bureau of Railway Economics, p. 148.
[74] National Archives, Washington, United States Navy Bureau of Yards and Docks, Payrolls of Mechanics and Labors. . . . Gosport, Virginia, November 1854 and July 1860.

cent, for white carpenters 12 per cent, and for hired slave laborers 8 per cent.[75]

There appears to have been a strong rightward shift in the demand curve for slaves as capital goods in the period 1850 through 1860. The nominal increase in the price of prime male field hands in the Lower South was 72 per cent between 1850 and 1860. The deflated (by New Orleans wholesale price index)[76] price increase was 68 per cent. In the Upper South the nominal increase was 62 or 112 per cent, depending upon which estimate of the 1860 Upper South price is used. The deflated (by Charleston wholesale price index)[77] price increases were 50 and 98 per cent.

The average increase in price of twelve railroad stocks on the Boston Stock Market between 1850 and 1860 was 13 per cent. The stock of the Hartford and New Haven Railroad increased in price 17 per cent between 1850 and 1860, and paid a higher dividend rate than any other railroad on the Boston market for that period.[78]

Some students of slavery, in later times as well as in the contemporary period, felt that the increase in slave prices was purely speculative in character. The editor of the *New Orleans Daily Crescent* disagreed with the speculative argument: "It is our impression that the great demand for slaves in the Southwest will keep up the prices as it has caused their advance in the first place, and that the rates are not a cent above the real value of the laborer."[79] One study of the marginal value productivity supports the editor's position.[80]

Whether the slave birth rate (Table 27) was a function of the price of slaves is not known, but it is not important because census data are inconclusive about the rate's increase or decrease between 1850 and 1860. It is not clear whether the demand for females rose relative to that of males. One would expect that a proved "breeder" would command a premium in the market relative to her unproved sister and that one could estimate the relative male-female demand by movements in the "breeder" premium. Despite the number of words written about a premium price for "breeders," no clear-cut evidence of a

[75] State House Construction Payrolls, South Carolina State Archives, Columbia, Negroes, April 1856, Whites, July 1856 and January 1857.
[76] Arthur H. Cole, *Wholesale Commodity Prices in the United States: 1700-1861,* Cambridge, Harvard University Press, 1938, p. 178, Table 93.
[77] *Ibid.,* p. 168, Table 80.
[78] Martin, *One Hundred Years' History . . . ,* pp. 145-149.
[79] Phillips, *Life and Labor in the Old South,* p. 180.
[80] Conrad and Meyer, "The Economics of Slavery . . . ," p. 117.

TABLE 27

SLAVE BIRTH RATES

(per cent)

| Area | Number of: Children Aged 0 Divided by Females Aged 15-44 1850 | 1860 | Children Aged 0 to 4 or 5 Divided by Females Aged 15-44 1850 | 1860 |
|---|---|---|---|---|
| Upper South | 0.120 | 0.134 | 0.163 | 0.158 |
| Lower South | 0.102 | 0.119 | 0.150 | 0.139 |
| All South | 0.115 | 0.131 | 0.154 | 0.151 |

SOURCE: Figures for 1850 are from DeBow, *Statistical View* . . . , pp. 88-89; for 1860 from *The Eighth Census*, pp. 594-595. The ratio of females 40-44 years old to those 40-49 years was estimated from figures in DeBow, p. 104.

premium has been presented.[81] One can still obtain some indication of the demand for women in their role as childbearers by observing the ratio of female to male price over a period of years (Table 28).

TABLE 28

RATIO OF FEMALE TO MALE SLAVE PRICES

| Market | Date | Ratio | Market | Date | Ratio |
|---|---|---|---|---|---|
| Richmond | Mar. 1842 | 0.78 | Richmond | July 1859 | .91 |
| Richmond | Oct. 1842 | .84 | Mobile | Oct. 1859 | .86 |
| Richmond | Nov. 1844 | .78 | Richmond | Nov. 1859 | .91 |
| Richmond | Feb. 1847 | .75 | Richmond | Dec. 1859 | .93 |
| Richmond | Nov. 1848 | .83 | Mobile | Dec. 1859 | .91 |
| Richmond | Dec. 1848 | .82 | New Orleans | Dec. 1859 | .91 |
| Richmond | Nov. 1849 | .87 | Mobile | Jan. 1860 | .88 |
| Richmond | Jan. 1858 | .85 | New Orleans | Jan. 1860 | .89 |
| Richmond | Dec. 1858 | .86 | Richmond | June, 1860 | .87 |
| Richmond | Jan. 1859 | .88 | Richmond | July, 1860 | .89 |
| Richmond | Feb. 1859 | .86 | | | |

SOURCE: Each ratio is computed from information from a single source. The observations for 1842, 1844, 1848, December 1858, and December 1859 appear to originate from the Dickinson Company of Richmond. All the collections cited are in the Duke University Library, Durham, North Carolina. Data for 1842 and 1844 are from the William Weaver papers for those years; for 1848 and December 1858, from the letters of Joseph Dickinson; for 1847 from the letters of John E. Dennis. The remainder of the data are from the letters of William A. J. Finney.

[81] Conrad and Meyer (p. 110) speak of a higher average price for proved childbearers as evident in the figures in their Appendix A. Examination of these data for 1859 and 1860 reveals that the premium is dependent upon a specific assumption concerning the ages of the children sold with their mothers.

Table 28 suggests that the demand for women as childbearers, if anything, was rising in the latter years of slavery.[82]

In addition to examining slavery in terms of the usual economic
criteria of a declining industry, one other aspect of the slave industry
must be examined. Because its capital goods are human rather than
inanimate, they might be more valuable to the individual slave than
to any other owner. It would, therefore, have been possible for the
industry to be viable by all the usual economic criteria, and yet have
been nonviable because the slaves, if given the opportunity, would
have purchased the industry out of existence.

The rates of manumission in the period 1850 through 1860 suggest
that this special form of nonviability was not present. The census estimated that there were 3,000 manumissions in the 1860 census year and
that about 20,000 had been manumitted between 1850 and 1860.[83]
Compared to the annual increase in the slave population, these rates
of manumission are quite small—about one-tenth of the increase in
the male slave population fifteen to sixty years of age in the same
period. It has been suggested that self-purchase reached its peak
in the industrialized cities.[84] At its peak it was not very large.[85]
Between 1831 and 1860, 592 Negroes were manumitted in Richmond
and Petersburg, Virginia.[86] About 296 of these manumissions may have
been promoted or instigated by Negroes.[87] Perhaps a majority of the
296 were cases of self-purchase. At a maximum then, the number of
manumissions by self-purchase in a period of thirty years is equal to
about 5.8 per cent of the number of male slaves fifteen to sixty years

---

[82] If demand was increasing, then there is little danger that the system was
nonviable because one could not afford to raise slaves at the current prices. While
a more direct test of this fact would be desirable, it has not been attempted because it would involve estimates of variables about which little is known. I have
made a few rough calculations based upon average number of children per woman
(census figures), death rates for women and children, etc., and it appears that,
as one would expect, rates of return on female slaveholding are equal to those
obtained for male slaveholding.

[83] *The Eighth Census*, p. xv.

[84] Sumner Eliot Matison, "Manumission by Purchase," *Journal of Negro History*,
April, 1948, pp. 146-167.

[85] That it was not larger is probably in great part because the majority of slaves
who earned extra money for themselves spent it for pleasure. Eaton, *Slave-Hiring
in the Upper South*, p. 669. The reader interested in this aspect of the system should
consult Stanley M. Elkins, *Slavery*, University of Chicago Press, 1959.

[86] Luther Porter Jackson, "Free Negro Labor and Property Holding in Virginia,
1830-1860" (Unpublished Ph.D. dissertation, University of Chicago), p. 240. Much
of the material in this dissertation has been published in book form.

[87] *Ibid.*, p. 227.

of age in these two cities in 1850,[88] to 5.2 per cent of the number of slaves employed in factories in Richmond in 1846,[89] and 4.7 per cent of the number employed in 1856.[90]

Thus it would appear that the slave industry did not exhibit characteristics of a nonviable industry about to wither and die under the impact of adverse economic forces, but rather gave every indication in its latter years of being a strong and growing industry.

## Appendix A

### SLAVE HIRES

The tables of this Appendix present the distribution of slave hire observations which were summarized in the text. To facilitate reference, the sources are given in groups after Table 42. Each reference includes a notation indicating the area and the years for which observations are found in it.

TABLE 29

UPPER SOUTH SLAVE HIRES, 1830-35

| | Number of Observations | | | | | | |
|---|---|---|---|---|---|---|---|
| Yearly Rate | 1830 | 1831 | 1832 | 1833 | 1834 | 1835 | 1830-35 |
| $125 | | | | | | 3 | 3 |
| 78 | | | | 1 | | | 1 |
| 70 | | 1 | | | | 2 | 3 |
| 60 | | | | 2 | | | 2 |
| 55 | | 1 | | | | | 1 |
| 50 | | 1 | | | | | 1 |
| 49 | 16 | | | | | | 16 |
| Total | 16 | 3 | 0 | 3 | 0 | 5 | 27 |
| Monthly $10 | | | | | | | 4 |

[88] DeBow, *Statistical View* . . . , p. 398.
[89] Jackson, *Free Negro Labor* . . . , p. 71.
[90] *Ibid.*

TABLE 30

UPPER SOUTH SLAVE HIRES, 1836-40

| Yearly Rate | Number of Observations | | | | | |
|---|---|---|---|---|---|---|
| | 1836 | 1837 | 1838 | 1839 | 1840 | 1836-40 |
| $133 | | | 4 | | | 4 |
| 125 | 1 | | | | | 1 |
| 120 | | | 3 | | | 3 |
| 110 | | | | | 1 | 1 |
| 107 | | | 45 | | | 45 |
| 100 | | | 2 | | | 2 |
| 85 | 1 | | | | | 1 |
| 80 | | 1 | | | | 1 |
| 75 | | 1 | 1 | | | 2 |
| 72 | | 1 | | | | 1 |
| 60 | | | 1 | | | 1 |
| Total | 2 | 3 | 56 | 0 | 1 | 62 |
| Monthly | | | | | | |
| $15 | | | | | | 238 |
| 13.5 | | | | | | 1 |
| 12.5 | | | | | | 10 |
| 12 | | | | | | 7 |
| Total | | | | | | 256 |

TABLE 31

UPPER SOUTH SLAVE HIRES, 1841-45

| Yearly Rate | Number of Observations | | | | | |
|---|---|---|---|---|---|---|
| | 1841 | 1842 | 1843 | 1844 | 1845 | 1841-45 |
| $140 | | | 1 | | | 1 |
| 80 | | | 10 | | | 10 |
| 60 | | | | | 1 | 1 |
| Total | 0 | 0 | 11 | 0 | 1 | 12 |

TABLE 32

UPPER SOUTH SLAVE HIRES, 1846-50

| Yearly Rate | Number of Observations | | | | | |
|---|---|---|---|---|---|---|
| | 1846 | 1847 | 1848 | 1849 | 1850 | 1846-50 |
| $160 | | | | | 1 | 1 |
| 130 | | 1 | | | | 1 |
| 125 | | 1 | | | 1 | 2 |
| 115 | | | | | 1 | 1 |
| 110 | | | 1 | | | 1 |
| 100 | | | 2 | 1 | | 3 |
| 96 | | | | 7 | | 7 |
| 95 | | 1 | | | | 1 |
| 94 | | 7 | | | | 7 |
| 90 | | | | | 4 | 4 |
| 85 | | | | | 4 | 4 |
| 72 | 1 | | | | | 1 |
| Total | 1 | 10 | 3 | 8 | 11 | 33 |
| Monthly | | | | | | |
| $20 | | | | | | 1 |
| 15 | | | | | | 8 |
| 12.5 | | | | | | 124 |
| 8 | | | | | | 4 |
| Total | | | | | | 137 |

229

TABLE 33

UPPER SOUTH SLAVE HIRES, 1851-55

| Yearly Rate | 1851 | 1852 | 1853 | 1854 | 1855 | 1851-55 |
|---|---|---|---|---|---|---|
| | | | Number of Observations | | | |
| $225 | | | | 11 | | 11 |
| 215 | | | | 1 | | 1 |
| 205 | | | | | 10 | 10 |
| 190 | | | | 1 | | 1 |
| 180 | | | 17 | 9 | 5 | 31 |
| 175 | | | 1 | | 26 | 27 |
| 168 | | | 6 | | | 6 |
| 167 | | | | 1 | | 1 |
| 162 | | | 1 | | | 1 |
| 160 | | 69 | 11 | 4 | 2 | 86 |
| 156 | | | | 1 | | 1 |
| 155 | | 46 | 11 | | 1 | 58 |
| 150 | | 14 | 19 | 209 | 1 | 243 |
| 140 | | | 54 | 4 | | 58 |
| 135 | | 1 | 3 | | 299 | 303 |
| 130 | | 2 | 1 | | | 3 |
| 129 | | | 10 | | | 10 |
| 127 | | | 82 | | 206 | 288 |
| 125 | 1 | | 2 | | | 3 |
| 121 | | 2 | | 2 | | 4 |
| 120 | | | 1 | | 1 | 2 |
| 115 | | 1 | | | | 1 |
| 114 | | 7 | | | | 7 |
| 112 | | | | 1 | | 1 |
| 108 | | | 1 | | | 1 |
| 104 | 7 | | | | | 7 |
| 101 | | | 1 | | | 1 |
| 100 | | 20 | | 1 | | 21 |
| 95 | | 2 | | | | 2 |
| 90 | | 2 | | | | 2 |
| 85 | | 3 | | | | 3 |
| 80 | | 1 | | | | 1 |
| Total | 8 | 170 | 221 | 245 | 551 | 1,195 |
| Monthly | | | | | | |
| $14 | | | | | | 1 |
| 13 | | | | | | 25 |
| 11 | | | | | | 7 |
| 10 | | | | | | 3 |
| Total | | | | | | 36 |

## TABLE 34
### UPPER SOUTH SLAVE HIRES, 1856-60

| Yearly Rate | Number of Observations | | | | | |
|---|---|---|---|---|---|---|
| | 1856 | 1857 | 1858 | 1859 | 1860 | 1856-60 |
| $250 | | | | | 9 | 9 |
| 240 | | | | | 11 | 11 |
| 235 | | 8 | | 7 | 3 | 18 |
| 213 | | | 1 | | | 1 |
| 200 | | 9 | | 2 | 1 | 12 |
| 190 | | | | | 1 | 1 |
| 180 | | 11 | 12 | | | 23 |
| 178 | 1 | | | | | 1 |
| 175 | | 1 | | | | 1 |
| 172 | | | 1 | 1 | | 2 |
| 165 | | | 1 | | 2 | 3 |
| 162 | | | | 3 | | 3 |
| 160 | | | 15 | 1 | | 16 |
| 155 | 18 | | | 1 | 1 | 20 |
| 150 | 276 | 5 | 261 | 154 | 122 | 818 |
| 149 | | 435 | | | 97 | 532 |
| 148 | | | | 7 | | 7 |
| 146 | | | | 392 | | 392 |
| 142 | | 109 | | 2 | | 111 |
| 140 | 1 | 2 | 341 | 1 | 1 | 346 |
| 139 | | | | | 165 | 165 |
| 138 | | | | | 22 | 22 |
| 137 | | | | 163 | | 163 |
| 136 | 360 | | | | | 360 |
| 135 | 280 | 1 | | 2 | | 283 |
| 133 | | 59 | | 176 | 1 | 236 |
| 130 | 13 | 182 | 1 | 3 | 2 | 201 |
| 127 | | | 175 | 2 | | 177 |
| 126 | | | 10 | | | 10 |
| 125 | | | | 3 | 4 | 7 |
| 122 | | | | | 4 | 4 |
| 120 | | 10 | | 3 | | 13 |
| 117 | | | 1 | | | 1 |
| 113 | | | | 3 | 2 | 5 |
| 110 | | | 1 | 1 | 103 | 105 |
| 105 | | | | | 1 | 1 |
| 103 | | | | | 1 | 1 |
| 100 | | 2 | | | 8 | 10 |
| Total | 949 | 834 | 820 | 927 | 561 | 4,091 |
| Monthly | | | | | | |
| $25 | | | | | | 17 |
| 20 | | | | | | 18 |
| 15 | | | | | | 16 |
| 14 | | | | | | 50 |
| 13 | | | | | | 9 |
| Total | | | | | | 110 |

## TABLE 35

### UPPER SOUTH DAILY SLAVE HIRES, 1830-60

| Period | Range of Rates | |
|---|---|---|
| 1830-35 | $0.40–$0.50 | |
| 1836-40 | .50 | .75 |
| 1841-45 | | |
| 1846-50 | .75 | |
| 1851-55 | .69 | .88 |
| 1856-60 | 0.69 | 0.88 |

## TABLE 36

### LOWER SOUTH SLAVE HIRES, 1830-35

| Yearly Rate | Number of Observations | | | | | | |
| | 1830 | 1831 | 1832 | 1833 | 1834 | 1835 | 1830-35 |
|---|---|---|---|---|---|---|---|
| $175 | | | | | 1 | | 1 |
| 140 | | | | 1 | | | 1 |
| 125 | | | | | 15 | | 15 |
| 116 | | | | | 3 | | 3 |
| Total | 0 | 0 | 0 | 1 | 19 | 0 | 20 |
| Monthly | | | | | | | |
| $18 | | | | | | | 1 |
| 15 | | | | | | | 2 |
| 12 | | | | | | | 1 |
| 10 | | | | | | | 1 |
| Total | | | | | | | 5 |

## TABLE 37

### LOWER SOUTH SLAVE HIRES, 1836-40

| Yearly Rate | Number of Observations | | | | | |
| | 1836 | 1837 | 1838 | 1839 | 1840 | 1836-40 |
|---|---|---|---|---|---|---|
| $130 | | | | 3 | | 3 |
| 125 | | | | | 1 | 1 |
| 100 | | | | 3 | | 3 |
| Total | 0 | 0 | 0 | 6 | 1 | 7 |
| Monthly | | | | | | |
| $32 | | | | | | 1 |
| 30 | | | | | | 1 |
| 25 | | | | | | 1 |
| 20 | | | | | | 1 |
| 18 | | | | | | 1 |
| 17 | | | | | | 1 |
| 15 | | | | | | 1 |
| Total | | | | | | 7 |

TABLE 38

LOWER SOUTH SLAVE HIRES, 1841-45

| Yearly Rate | Number of Observations | | | | | |
|---|---|---|---|---|---|---|
| | 1841 | 1842 | 1843 | 1844 | 1845 | 1841-45 |
| $184 | | 3 | | | | 3 |
| 150 | | 4 | | | 1 | 5 |
| 144 | | | | 1 | | 1 |
| 140 | 1 | | | | 1 | 2 |
| 116 | | | | | 1 | 1 |
| 100 | 1 | 1 | | 1 | | 3 |
| Total | 2 | 8 | 0 | 2 | 3 | 15 |
| Monthly | | | | | | |
| $18 | | | | | | 1 |
| 15 | | | | | | 15 |
| 12 | | | | | | 1 |
| 10 | | | | | | 1 |
| Total | | | | | | 18 |

TABLE 39

LOWER SOUTH SLAVE HIRES, 1846-50

| Yearly Rate | Number of Observations | | | | | |
|---|---|---|---|---|---|---|
| | 1846 | 1847 | 1848 | 1849 | 1850 | 1846-50 |
| $250 | | | 1 | | | 1 |
| 225 | | | | 1 | 1 | 2 |
| 220 | | | 1 | | | 1 |
| 200 | | 1 | 19 | | | 20 |
| 186 | | 1 | | | | 1 |
| 175 | | | 4 | | | 4 |
| 166 | | 1 | | | | 1 |
| 160 | | | 1 | | | 1 |
| 156 | | | 1 | 1 | | 2 |
| 150 | 1 | | 2 | | 1 | 4 |
| 140 | | | | | 1 | 1 |
| 131 | 1 | | | | | 1 |
| 129 | | | | 1 | | 1 |
| 125 | | | 3 | | | 3 |
| 120 | | | 6 | | | 6 |
| 105 | | | | | 1 | 1 |
| 80 | | | 2 | | | 2 |
| 72 | | | | 1 | | 1 |
| Total | 2 | 3 | 40 | 4 | 4 | 53 |
| Monthly | | | | | | |
| $30 | | | | | | 2 |
| 15 | | | | | | 67 |
| 10 | | | | | | 7 |
| Total | | | | | | 76 |

*233*

## TABLE 40
### LOWER SOUTH SLAVE HIRES, 1851-55

| Yearly Rate | Number of Observations | | | | | |
|---|---|---|---|---|---|---|
| | 1851 | 1852 | 1853 | 1854 | 1855 | 1851-55 |
| $225 | 1 | | | 32 | | 33 |
| 200 | | 1 | | | | 1 |
| 195 | | | | | 2 | 2 |
| 191 | 1 | | | | | 1 |
| 180 | | 1 | 2 | 1 | 1 | 5 |
| 175 | | 1 | 1 | | | 2 |
| 170 | | 1 | | | | 1 |
| 158 | | | | | 15 | 15 |
| 155 | | | | 16 | | 16 |
| 152 | 1 | | | | | 1 |
| 135 | 1 | | | | | 1 |
| 125 | 15 | | | | | 15 |
| 120 | 1 | 1 | | | | 2 |
| 100 | | | | | 1 | 1 |
| Total | 20 | 5 | 3 | 49 | 19 | 96 |
| Monthly | | | | | | |
| $30 | | | | | | 81 |
| 20 | | | | | | 1 |
| 15 | | | | | | 1 |
| 13 | | | | | | 1 |
| Total | | | | | | 84 |

## TABLE 41
### LOWER SOUTH SLAVE HIRES, 1856-60

| Yearly Rate | Number of Observations | | | | | |
|---|---|---|---|---|---|---|
| | 1856 | 1857 | 1858 | 1859 | 1860 | 1856-60 |
| $329 | | | | | 6 | 6 |
| 250 | | | | 1 | | 1 |
| 225 | | | | 30 | | 30 |
| 215 | | | | 18 | 23 | 41 |
| 200 | | | 11 | 4 | 5 | 20 |
| 180 | | | | | 1 | 1 |
| 171 | | | | | 1 | 1 |
| 166 | | | | | 1 | 1 |
| 160 | | | 16 | 1 | | 17 |
| 150 | 15 | | 1 | 2 | 2 | 20 |
| 147 | | 16 | | | | 16 |
| 139 | | | | | 1 | 1 |
| 138 | | | | | 1 | 1 |
| 124 | | | | | 1 | 1 |
| Total | 15 | 16 | 28 | 56 | 42 | 157 |
| Monthly | | | | | | |
| $27 | | | | | | 1 |
| 20 | | | | | | 151 |
| 8 | | | | | | 1 |
| Total | | | | | | 153 |

## TABLE 42
### LOWER SOUTH DAILY SLAVE HIRES, 1830-60

| Period | Range of Rates |
|--------|----------------|
| 1846-50 | $1.00 |
| 1851-55 | $1.00- 1.25 |
| 1856-60 | 1.00- 1.25 |

SOURCE, TABLES 29-42

Data on Yearly and Monthly Slave Hire

Frederic Bancroft, *Slave Trading in the Old South*, Baltimore, Furst, 1931.
Upper South: 1852, 1855, 1858, 1859
Kathleen Bruce, *Virginia Iron Manufacture in the Slave Era*, New York, Century, 1931.
Upper South: 1845, 1846, 1848, 1849, 1853
Helen T. Catterall, ed., *Judicial Cases concerning American Slavery and the Negro*, Vols. I-III, Carnegie Institution of Washington, 1926-32.
Lower South: 1833, 1834, 1836, 1837, 1839, 1841, 1842, 1848, 1849, 1850, 1851, 1852, 1853, 1854, 1855, 1856, 1858, 1860
Upper South: 1837, 1838, 1843, 1847, 1850, 1853, 1854, 1855, 1857, 1858, 1859
E. Merton Coulter, *Aurarie*, University of Georgia Press, 1956.
Lower South: 1834
James D. B. DeBow, ed., *The Commercial Review of the South and West* (DeBow's Review), 1847, 1853, 1860.
Lower South: 1847, 1860
Upper South: 1853
Ralph B. Flanders, "Plantation Slavery in the State of Georgia," unpublished Ph.D. dissertation, Duke University, 1929.
Lower South: 1856
*Idem*, "Farish Carter, a Forgotten Man of the Old South," *Georgia Historical Quarterly*, June 1937, pp. 142-175.
Lower South: 1850
Lewis C. Gray, *History of Agriculture in the Southern United States to 1860*, 2 vols., Carnegie Institution of Washington, 1933.
Upper South: 1837, 1838, 1851, 1857
Fletcher Green, "Gold Mining, a Forgotten Industry in Ante Bellum North Carolina," *North Carolina Historical Review*, Jan. and Apr. 1937, pp. 1-19, 135-155.
Upper South: 1850
William R. Hogan and Edwin A. Davis, eds., *William Johnson's Natchez*, Source Studies in Southern History, Vol. I, Louisiana State University Press, 1951.
Lower South: 1841, 1842, 1843, 1845
Weymouth T. Jordan, *Hugh Davis and his Alabama Plantation*, University of Alabama Press, 1948.
Lower South: 1848
John S. Kendall, "New Orleans Peculiar Institution," *Louisiana Historical Quarterly*, July 1940, pp. 864-886.
Lower South: 1837
E. M. Lander, "Slave Labor in South Carolina Cotton Mills," *Journal of Negro History*, 1953, pp. 161-173.
Upper South: 1837, 1847

Frederick L. Olmsted, *A Journey in the Seaboard Slave States*, 2 vols., New York, Putnam, 1904 (1856).
Upper South: 1853, 1854
Lower South: 1853, 1854

*Idem, The Cotton Kingdom*, 2 vols., New York, Mason, 1861.
Upper South: 1859

Ulrich B. Phillips, "The Economic Cost of Slaveholding in the Cotton Belt," *Political Science Quarterly*, June 1905, pp. 257-275.
Lower South: 1833, 1848

*Idem, American Negro Slavery*, New York, Appleton-Century, 1936.
Lower South: 1838, 1840, 1849, 1850
Upper South: 1854, 1855

Paul E. Postell, "John Hampton Randolph, a Planter," *Louisiana Historical Quarterly*, January 1942, pp. 150-217.
Lower South: 1837

Phillip M. Rice, "Internal Improvements in Virginia, 1775-1860," unpublished Ph.D. dissertation, University of North Carolina, 1948.
Upper South: 1837

Wendell H. Stephenson, *Isaac Franklin, Slave Trader and Planter of the Old South*, Louisiana State University Press, 1938.
Lower South: 1848

Charles S. Sydnor, *Slavery in Mississippi*, New York, Appleton-Century, 1933.
Lower South: 1844-52, 1854-58

Rosser H. Taylor, *Slaveholding in North Carolina*, James Spruit Historical Publications, Vol. XXVIII, University of North Carolina Press, 1926.
Upper South: 1851

James K. Turner, "Slavery in Edgecomb County," *Trinity College Historical Series*, 1910, pp. 5-36.
Upper South: 1856

GOVERNMENT REPORTS

*Report of the Commissioner of Agriculture*, H. R., Ex. Doc. 91, 40th Cong., 1st sess., 1867 (Upper South, 1860; Lower South, 1860).
*Report of the Commissioner of Patents*, H. R., Ex. Doc. 59, 30th Cong., 2d sess., 1848 (Upper South, 1848; Lower South, 1848).
*Annual Reports of the Board of Public Works*, Virginia General Assembly, 1853-54, 1855 (Upper South, 1852, 1853, 1855).

REPORTS OF SOUTHERN RAILROADS

Library of the Bureau of Railway Economics of the Association of American Railroads, Washington
Central Railroad and Bank Company of Georgia, 1834, 1851 (Lower South: 1834, 1849, 1850).
Louisa Railroad of Virginia, 1838 (Upper South: 1838).
Charlotte and South Carolina Railroad, 1854 (Upper South: 1854).
Virginia and Tennessee Railroad, 1854-59 (Upper South: 1854-59).
Richmond and Danville Railroad, 1856-60 (Upper South: 1856-60).
Petersburg Railroad, 1857, 1860 (Upper South: 1857, 1860).
Virginia Central Railroad, 1858 (Upper South: 1858).
Norfolk and Petersburg Railroad, 1859 (Upper South: 1859).
North Carolina Department of Archives and History, Raleigh
Raleigh and Gaston Railroad, 1840, 1841, 1860 (Upper South: 1840, 1841, 1860).

North Carolina Railroad, 1856, 1858 (Upper South: 1856, 1858).
Petersburg Railroad in North Carolina, 1858 (Upper South: 1858).
Atlantic and North Carolina Railroad, 1860 (Upper South: 1860).
South Carolinian Library, South Carolina University, Columbia
Louisville, Cincinnati and Charleston Railroad, 1840 (Upper South: 1840).
Department of Archives, Louisiana State University, Baton Rouge
Clinton and Port Hudson Railroad, 1839 (Lower South: 1839).

REPORTS OF PERSONS HIRED

National Archives, Washington, War Department, Office of the Quartermaster General:
Augusta Arsenal, 1833; Fort Howard, 1832; Key West, 1832; Port of New Orleans, 1832; Cedar Keys, 1842; Tampa, 1850; Fort Meade, 1850 (Lower South: 1832, 1833, 1842, 1850); Fort Mallory, 1832 (Upper South: 1832).

PAPERS, ACCOUNTS, LETTERS, DIARIES

Duke University Library, Durham, North Carolina
William Weaver Papers, 1830-35, 1853, 1854, 1858, 1860 (Upper South: 1830-35, 1853, 1854, 1858, 1860).
J. Rutherford Letters, 1842 (Upper South: 1843).
Francis Harper Papers, 1853 (Upper South: 1853).
Alex Torrence Papers, 1853, 1856, 1857, 1860 (Upper South: 1853, 1856, 1857, 1860).
John Buford Papers, 1854-57 (Upper South: 1854-58).
Francis Anderson Papers, 1853, 1855, 1858 (Upper South: 1853, 1855, 1858).
Wm. Clark Grasty Papers, 1858, 1859 (Upper South: 1858, 1859).
Southern Historical Collection, University of North Carolina, Chapel Hill
Hawkins Account Books, 1838, 1851, 1853, 1856, 1858 (Upper South: 1838, 1851, 1853, 1856, 1858).
High Shoal Gold Mine Account Book, 1848, 1851 (Upper South: 1848, 1851).
Guardian's Accounts, Bertie County, North Carolina, 1850 (Upper South: 1850).
Hawkins Papers, 1851, 1853, 1857, 1859, 1860 (Upper South: 1851, 1853, 1857, 1859, 1860).
Charles F. Fisher Papers, 1856-1860 (Upper South: 1856-1860).
William L. Mitchell Papers, 1848 (Lower South: 1848).
H. A. Ellison Slave Records, 1848, 1858-60 (Lower South: 1848, 1858-60).
Lewis Thompson Papers, 1851 (Lower South: 1851).
New York Public Library, New York
Francis P. Corbin Papers, 1853 (Lower South: 1853).
Department of Archives, Louisiana State University, Baton Rouge
Andrew and Ellen McCollam Diaries, 1842, 1844 (Lower South: 1842, 1844).
James H. Dakin Diary, 1848 (Lower South: 1848).
Alderman Library, University of Virginia, Charlottesville
Graham Time Book, 1852 (Upper South: 1852).
Dr. George W. Elment Slave Papers, 1852 (Upper South: 1852).

237

Jeremiah Morton Correspondence, 1854, 1857 (Upper South: 1857, Lower South: 1854).
Jeremiah Morton Slave Account, 1859 (Lower South: 1859).
Virginia State Library, Richmond
    Walker Diaries, 1853 (Upper South: 1853).
    Estate of J. Watson, 1856, 1857 (Upper South: 1856, 1857).
North Carolina Department of Archives and History, Raleigh
    Clark Plantation Book, 1847-49, 1851-60 (Upper South: 1847-49, 1850-60).
    Whitford Collection, 1855 (Upper South: 1855).

## NEWSPAPERS

*Register*, Raleigh, North Carolina, Jan. 1853 (Upper South: 1853).
*Argus*, Norfolk, North Carolina, Jan. 1854 (Upper South: 1854).
*Daily Alabama Journal*, Augusta, Georgia, Dec. 1851 (Lower South: 1851).

## DATA ON DAILY SLAVE HIRE

North Carolina Department of Archives and History, Raleigh
    Capital Pay Records, State Treasurer's Office, 1833-1840 (Upper South: 1833-40).
South Carolina State Archives, Columbia
    State House Payrolls, 1856-60 (Upper South: 1856-60).
National Archives, Washington, Navy Department, Bureau of Yards and Docks, Payrolls of Mechanics and Laborers
    Pensacola, Florida, 1844-59 (Lower South: 1846-59).
    Gosport (Norfolk), Virginia, 1847-60 (Upper South: 1847-60).

## Appendix B

### TABLE 43

AVERAGE MONTHLY RATES OF INTEREST ON THREE- TO SIX-MONTHS BANKABLE PAPER IN BOSTON, 1831-60

| Year | Jan. | Feb. | Mar. | Apr. | May | June | July | Aug. | Sep. | Oct. | Nov. | Dec. | Average |
|---|---|---|---|---|---|---|---|---|---|---|---|---|---|
| 1831 | 5.5 | 5.7 | 5.9 | 6.1 | 6.3 | 6.5 | 6.7 | 6.9 | 7.0 | 7.0 | 7.0 | 7.0 | 6.5 |
| 1832 | 7.0 | 6.5 | 6.0 | 6.5 | 7.0 | 6.0 | 6.0 | 6.0 | 6.0 | 6.0 | 6.0 | 6.0 | 6.3 |
| 1833 | 6.0 | 5.5 | 5.8 | 6.0 | 6.2 | 6.5 | 8.0 | 8.0 | 8.0 | 10.0 | 12.0 | 15.0 | 8.1 |
| 1834 | 19.5 | 24.0 | 20.0 | 20.0 | 20.0 | 20.0 | 20.0 | 20.0 | 20.0 | 16.0 | 14.0 | 9.0 | 18.5 |
| 1835 | 9.0 | 8.0 | 7.0 | 6.0 | 5.0 | 5.0 | 5.0 | 5.0 | 6.0 | 7.0 | 8.0 | 9.0 | 6.7 |
| 1836 | 10.0 | 11.0 | 12.0 | 15.0 | 18.0 | 20.0 | 22.0 | 24.0 | 24.0 | 36.0 | 27.0 | 27.0 | 20.5 |
| 1837 | 15.0 | 18.0 | 27.0 | 30.0 | 32.0 | 6.0 | 6.8 | 7.5 | 7.5 | 6.7 | 6.0 | 10.0 | 14.4 |
| 1838 | 11.0 | 12.0 | 15.0 | 15.0 | 8.5 | 6.5 | 6.5 | 6.5 | 6.5 | 6.5 | 6.5 | 8.0 | 9.0 |
| 1839 | 7.5 | 7.5 | 7.5 | 7.5 | 7.5 | 7.5 | 11.5 | 15.0 | 21.0 | 30.0 | 36.0 | 9.0 | 14.0 |
| 1840 | 9.0 | 10.5 | 10.5 | 7.0 | 7.0 | 7.0 | 5.0 | 6.5 | 6.5 | 6.5 | 6.5 | 6.5 | 7.4 |
| 1841 | 6.5 | 6.5 | 6.5 | 6.5 | 6.0 | 6.0 | 6.0 | 6.0 | 6.9 | 8.0 | 9.0 | 10.5 | 7.0 |
| 1842 | 10.5 | 10.5 | 10.5 | 8.0 | 8.0 | 8.0 | 8.0 | 8.0 | 7.0 | 6.0 | 6.0 | 7.5 | 8.2 |
| 1843 | 6.0 | 5.5 | 5.5 | 5.5 | 4.5 | 3.0 | 3.7 | 3.8 | 3.7 | 3.8 | 3.7 | 3.8 | 4.4 |
| 1844 | 4.0 | 4.5 | 5.0 | 5.0 | 5.0 | 5.0 | 5.0 | 5.0 | 5.0 | 5.0 | 5.0 | 5.0 | 4.9 |
| 1845 | 5.0 | 5.5 | 5.5 | 5.5 | 5.5 | 5.5 | 5.5 | 5.5 | 6.0 | 7.0 | 8.0 | 8.0 | 6.0 |
| 1846 | 8.0 | 9.0 | 7.0 | 10.0 | 10.0 | 10.0 | 10.0 | 8.5 | 6.0 | 6.0 | 7.0 | 8.0 | 8.3 |
| 1847 | 10.0 | 12.0 | 9.0 | 8.0 | 7.0 | 6.0 | 7.0 | 8.0 | 9.0 | 10.5 | 15.0 | 18.0 | 10.0 |
| 1848 | 18.0 | 16.0 | 13.5 | 13.5 | 16.5 | 16.5 | 13.5 | 13.5 | 15.0 | 18.0 | 16.5 | 13.5 | 15.4 |
| 1849 | 12.0 | 10.5 | 13.5 | 13.5 | 10.5 | 7.0 | 8.0 | 8.0 | 9.0 | 9.5 | 10.0 | 10.5 | 10.2 |
| 1850 | 9.7 | 8.5 | 8.5 | 7.7 | 7.8 | 7.7 | 6.5 | 7.7 | 9.0 | 7.5 | 7.5 | 7.5 | 8.0 |

(continued)

TABLE 43 (concluded)

AVERAGE MONTHLY RATES OF INTEREST ON THREE- TO SIX-MONTHS BANKABLE PAPER IN BOSTON, 1831-60

| Year | Jan. | Feb. | Mar. | Apr. | May | June | July | Aug. | Sep. | Oct. | Nov. | Dec. | Average |
|------|------|------|------|------|-----|------|------|------|------|------|------|------|---------|
| 1851 | 7.2 | 7.8 | 7.8 | 8.0 | 6.5 | 8.8 | 11.0 | 11.0 | 15.0 | 16.0 | 10.5 | 10.5 | 10.0 |
| 1852 | 9.0 | 7.2 | 6.0 | 6.0 | 6.0 | 5.5 | 5.5 | 5.5 | 6.5 | 6.0 | 6.0 | 6.0 | 6.3 |
| 1853 | 7.0 | 9.5 | 12.0 | 10.0 | 8.0 | 9.5 | 9.5 | 10.8 | 12.0 | 15.0 | 18.0 | 9.0 | 10.9 |
| 1854 | 9.0 | 7.0 | 10.0 | 12.0 | 12.0 | 9.0 | 9.5 | 12.0 | 11.0 | 14.0 | 16.0 | 18.0 | 11.6 |
| 1855 | 15.0 | 10.0 | 7.0 | 10.0 | 6.5 | 8.0 | 7.0 | 7.0 | 7.0 | 9.0 | 12.0 | 12.0 | 9.2 |
| 1856 | 11.0 | 9.5 | 8.0 | 9.5 | 9.5 | 9.5 | 9.5 | 9.5 | 9.5 | 9.5 | 9.5 | 10.5 | 9.6 |
| 1857 | 9.5 | 8.8 | 9.5 | 7.5 | 7.5 | 9.5 | 9.5 | 9.5 | 24.0 | 30.0 | 19.5 | 12.0 | 13.1 |
| 1858 | 8.2 | 5.5 | 5.0 | 4.5 | 4.2 | 4.3 | 4.3 | 4.2 | 4.3 | 4.0 | 4.0 | 5.0 | 4.8 |
| 1859 | 5.5 | 6.2 | 6.3 | 6.2 | 7.3 | 7.5 | 7.5 | 7.5 | 7.5 | 7.5 | 7.5 | 7.8 | 7.0 |
| 1860 | 8.0 | 8.0 | 7.0 | 6.5 | 6.5 | 6.0 | 5.7 | 7.5 | 7.3 | 7.0 | 11.0 | 15.0 | 8.0 |

SOURCE: Estimated from data in Joseph G. Martin, *One Hundred Years' History of the Boston Stock and Money Markets*, Boston 1898, pp. 52-53.

## Appendix C

### TABLE 44

COST OF CAPITAL AND NET INCOME OF SELECTED SOUTHERN RAILROADS, 1850-60
(current dollars)

| | Year 1850 | | 1851 | | 1852 | |
|---|---|---|---|---|---|---|
| Railroad | Cost | Income | Cost | Income | Cost | Income |
| A | 941,195 | 37,677 | 945,137 | 37,242 | 945,822 | 42,750 |
| B | 2,400,000 | 147,561 | 2,420,000 | 219,964 | 2,440,000 | 184,129 |
| C | 798,317 | 100,438 | 1,238,996 | 110,112 | 1,276,422 | 150,331 |
| D | 6,649,205 | 528,680 | 7,002,396 | 609,711 | 6,853,327 | 671,230 |
| E | 3,848,303 | 398,525 | 4,064,900 | 426,486 | 4,241,779 | 440,303 |
| F | 2,996,117 | 325,355 | 3,133,740 | 406,797 | 3,378,132 | 507,625 |
| G | 3,737,853 | 66,015 | 3,831,927 | 102,319 | 4,087,919 | 48,671 |
| H | | | | | 1,126,000 | 16,178 |
| I | | | | | | |
| J | | | 996,087 | 64,986 | 1,315,307 | 74,902 |
| K | 1,509,959 | 164,041 | 1,531,238 | 123,584 | 1,531,238 | 93,991 |
| L | | | | | 743,525 | 71,535 |
| | 1853 | | 1854 | | 1855 | |
| A | 983,335 | 42,273 | 1,095,812 | 68,805 | 1,167,000 | 73,234 |
| B | 2,460,000 | 220,592 | 2,480,000 | 191,620 | 2,500,000 | 173,176 |
| C | 1,339,931 | 149,062 | 1,407,460 | 149,062 | 1,472,214 | 193,375 |
| D | 7,141,215 | 659,742 | 7,133,848 | 798,862 | 7,298,977 | 883,399 |
| E | 4,276,185 | 456,468 | 4,416,991 | 342,214 | 4,174,491 | 306,395 |
| F | 3,465,879 | 509,348 | 3,465,879 | 534,526 | 3,694,210 | 739,654 |
| G | 4,309,700 | 239,601 | 4,578,537 | 341,160 | 4,903,079 | 438,066 |
| H | 1,126,261 | 37,917 | 1,135,451 | 103,393 | 1,162,000 | 101,145 |
| I | 1,242,209 | 42,648 | 3,545,256 | 63,155 | 4,211,000 | 126,330 |
| J | 1,707,539 | 103,538 | 2,392,215 | 99,077 | 3,503,980 | 122,534 |
| K | 1,531,238 | 115,795 | 1,690,618 | 116,685 | 1,767,669 | 119,226 |
| L | 983,692 | 76,807 | 1,223,860 | 121,605 | 1,288,441 | 141,168 |

(continued)

TABLE 44 (concluded)

| | *Year* | | | | | |
|---|---|---|---|---|---|---|
| | 1856 | | 1857 | | 1858 | |
| Railroad | Cost | Income | Cost | Income | Cost | Income |
| A | 1,205,030 | 73,234 | 1,202,960 | 74,746 | 1,205,411 | 85,180 |
| B | 2,592,135 | 205,454 | 2,684,270 | 199,177 | 2,776,404 | 198,065 |
| C | 1,500,000 | 142,116 | 1,500,000 | 130,706 | 1,500,000 | 164,407 |
| D | 7,588,037 | 766,269 | 7,588,037 | 740,535 | 7,588,037 | 820,512 |
| E | 4,174,491 | 357,689 | 4,174,491 | 389,464 | 4,174,495 | 326,175 |
| F | 3,750,000 | 694,696 | 3,750,000 | 542,310 | 3,750,000 | 755,614 |
| G | 5,142,387 | 421,074 | 5,517,828 | 467,485 | 5,901,488 | 406,264 |
| H | 1,170,845 | 76,668 | 1,170,845 | 108,541 | 1,170,846 | 102,149 |
| I | 5,469,780 | 165,076 | 6,582,370 | 190,907 | 6,765,154 | 213,237 |
| J | 4,681,621 | 270,364 | 5,022,940 | 220,239 | 5,364,260 | 295,776 |
| K | 1,864,408 | 106,017 | 1,921,105 | 129,203 | 1,985,179 | 143,713 |
| L | 1,615,402 | 202,265 | 1,942,363 | 199,897 | 2,269,323 | 208,711 |
| | 1859 | | 1860 | | 1850-60 | |
| A | 1,250,186 | 82,485 | 1,106,903 | 84,881 | 12,048,791 | 702,201 |
| B | 2,586,238 | 235,201 | 2,632,737 | 174,826 | 27,971,784 | 2,149,765 |
| C | 1,500,000 | 209,785 | 1,500,000 | 279,498 | 15,033,340 | 1,728,892 |
| D | 7,588,037 | 804,286 | 7,588,037 | 701,943 | 80,019,153 | 7,975,169 |
| E | 4,174,492 | 544,363 | 4,156,000 | 528,044 | 45,876,618 | 4,516,306 |
| F | 3,750,000 | 851,211 | 4,366,800 | 764,574 | 39,500,757 | 6,631,710 |
| G | 6,088,245 | 448,184 | 6,115,571 | 390,375 | 54,214,534 | 3,369,214 |
| H | 1,240,241 | 101,001 | | | 9,302,489 | 646,984 |
| I | 6,342,802 | 278,863 | 6,833,734 | 347,957 | 40,992,305 | 1,428,173 |
| J | 5,362,910 | 382,696 | 5,493,950 | 359,130 | 35,840,809 | 1,993,242 |
| K | 1,985,557 | 145,385 | 1,985,579 | 152,217 | 19,303,788 | 1,409,857 |
| L | | | 3,165,000 | 423,521 | 12,247,914 | 1,445,569 |

SOURCE TO TABLE 44

NOTE: Keys to selected southern railroads are: A, Richmond and Petersburg; B, Wilmington and Weldon; C, Macon and Western; D, South Carolina; E, Georgia Railroad and Bank Company; F, Central Railroad and Banking Company of Georgia; G, Western and Atlantic; H, Raleigh and Gaston; I, Virginia and Tennessee; J, Virginia Central; K, Richmond, Fredericksburg, and Potomac; L, Southwestern.

*Data on Selected Southern Railroads*

*American Railroad Journal*, Vols. 24, 1850, to 34, 1861 (used for 1859-60). James D. B. DeBow, ed., *The Commercial Review of the South and West*, Vol. 28, 1859 (*DeBow's Review*).

Harold D. Dozier, *A History of the Atlantic Coast Line*, Cambridge, Houghton Mifflin, 1920.
Freeman Hunt, ed., *The Merchants' Magazine and Commercial Review*, Vol. 25, 1851 (*Hunt's Merchants' Magazine*).
James H. Johnston, comp., *Western and Atlantic Railroad of the State of Georgia*, Atlanta, Stein Printing Co., 1931.
Ulrich B. Phillips, *History of Transportation in the Eastern Cotton Belt to 1860*, New York, Columbia University Press, 1908.
F. H. Stow, *Capitalist's Guide and Railway Annual for 1859*, New York, Callahan, 1859 (used for 1857-58).

RAILROAD REPORTS

Raleigh and Gaston Railroad, 1852-60.
Virginia and Tennessee Railroad, 1859.

GOVERNMENT REPORTS

*Report of the Secretary of the Treasury on the State of the Finances for the Year Ending June 30, 1856*, Senate, 34th Cong., 3d sess., 1857 (used for 1855).
*Annual Reports of the Board of Public Works*, Virginia General Assembly, 1853-54, 1860.

## COMMENTS

THOMAS P. GOVAN, New York University

My role in this discussion of Robert Evans' paper is an ambiguous one. I am an economic historian, not an economist, and I have little understanding of the language and techniques you employ. This ignorance extends even to the problems with which you are concerned, and if my comments are obscurantist in nature, I apologize in advance, for as a student of American history who is particularly concerned with the nation's economic growth and development I find the present study confusing rather than helpful. I agree entirely with the conclusion "that the slave industry did not exhibit the characteristics of a nonviable industry about to wither and die under the impact of adverse economic forces, but rather gave every indication in its latter years of being a strong and growing industry." But the evidence presented by Evans in his paper has little relevance to this conclusion.

The subject of the study, as well as its title, is the economics of Negro slavery between 1830 and 1860, but nowhere does the author discuss the institution of slavery as it actually was. Instead he uses twentieth century concepts and terms, drawn essentially from manufacturing, as a description of something quite different. "The slave industry," he writes, "consisted of two types of firms. One owned or rented the capital goods (slaves) and used them as factors of production to produce a marketable commodity (labor services) or combined them with other factors to produce a marketable commodity (cotton, railroad services, gold, etc.). The other owned those capital goods (female slaves) which were used to produce new capital goods (slaves). Some firms, usually plantations, engaged in all three, producing labor services, agricultural products, and new slaves." Such a description may be useful, but I fail to see its use. It is obvious that Evans knows that human beings do not reproduce by parthenogenesis, and that the owner of female slaves would have to have the aid of at least one male in order to produce new slaves unless—if I may be ribald—he performed this function himself. But the more serious and important objection is that no such firm existed, at least, if it did, no record has been found. The natural increase of slaves was a source of profit within the system but no one, so far as has been ascertained, had as his principal object and effort the raising of slaves for sale.

Slavery itself was not an industry; it was an institution, a social practice sustained by law and custom through which labor was procured, organized, controlled, and directed. Owners of slaves employed them as household servants, in agriculture, in manufacturing, in mining, in construction, and rented their services to others. The object was profit, slaves were sold and bought, but to call slavery itself an industry confuses the problem rather than helping to clarify it.

My objections so far have had solely to do with statements in the introduction to the study, and, though I have others, we must get on to the central arguments advanced by Evans. His purpose is to investigate "the economics of Negro slavery by (1) estimating the rates of return earned by slave capital in the period 1830 through 1860, (2) comparing these returns with those earned by alternative forms of capital, and (3) considering whether the industry was viable in its last years." The rate of return "is of little value in answering the more relevant question whether the industry was viable," but it is raised and discussed "because of the widespread uncertainty concerning its magnitude." The author, nevertheless, devoted his major time and attention to this less relevant problem, but in estimating the rate of return of capital invested in slaves, he eliminates from consideration plantations and farms, the principal users of slaves, because of the inconclusive and fragmentary nature of the evidence. Instead he confines his study to the single and, on the whole, minor aspect of the economics of slavery, the renting of slaves, for the reason, he says, that these "income figures are estimated directly from market data rather than as residuals" and involve "only a few variables." But when he comes to gather data on slave hiring he finds that they, too, "are scattered and usually fragmentary in character," and though "to estimate correctly the net yearly income received by the owners of slaves, one would like the following information: (1) rate of hire, (2) value of slaves, (3) age, skill, and physical condition, (4) content of jobs performed. Seldom is such detailed information available."

This leaves the author in the position of guessing on the basis of incomplete evidence what the net yearly income received actually was, and this guess is related to another as to the price of slaves. For this information he relies essentially on estimates made by Ulrich B. Phillips, concerning which he says, "it would be desirable to have more information concerning his method of estimation, sources of prices, extent of coverage of the different markets in the different years, etc.," but, unfortunately, this too is not available since, Evans correctly says, Phillips "believed in the illustrative use of statistics rather than in more formal statistical analysis." A similar uncertainty is found in the third kind of datum, the death rate of slaves, for here we are told, "really accurate estimates of life expectancy are a product of this century and exist for only a few countries."

We now have three guesses (intelligent, critical guesses, but still guesses) as to net yearly income, the price of slaves, and the death rate of slaves, which the author uses to establish the rate of return earned by, he says, slave capital. But he does this by creating a purely imaginary situation, an abstract problem that has no connection with history, nor does it, in my opinion, say anything about the economics of slavery from 1830 to 1860. No person in the slaveholding states ever purchased 1,000 male slaves at age 20 to hire them out for periods of 20 to 30 years before selling them, and, if he had, all of the figures used by the author, except perhaps his estimate of the death rate, would have been substantially different. The purchase of 1,000 slaves in any one year for such a purpose would have raised prices, and the existence of so large a number in the hire market would have altered the rate paid.

We now enter a realm in which I am not qualified to comment. These various estimates (I still would prefer to call them guesses used in an imagined situation) are combined in a "capital value equation," the usefulness of which as a tool for economists I am unable to evaluate.

*245*

But the results from this equation seem to me truly astonishing. From 1830 to 1835, a most prosperous period except for the winter of 1833-34, the rate of return on capital invested in slaves is said to be 12%, but in the period from 1841 to 1845, when operators of plantations, businesses, and factories in the United States were barely getting by, the rate of return is said to be 18.5%. With the return of general prosperity from 1846 to 1860, the rate of return in the lower South drops first to 17%, then to 12%, and finally to 10.3% in the three five-year periods. At the risk once again of being ignorant and obscurantist I cannot see the value of a method of economic analysis which indicates that the rate of return is higher in bad times than in good.

I am bothered and confused also by the use Evans makes of the short-term money rate in Boston and New York to arrive at the alternative rate of return on capital from 1830 to 1860. Short-term money—bank credit—is not capital, it is more nearly a commodity, the price of which (interest rate) is determined in large part by its availability and the need for it. The interest received for the loan of this money is not net income to the banks or the merchants who lend it; rather it is gross profit from which must be deducted all the expenses of operation. To take a very narrow example, I doubt seriously whether the Boston banks and merchants were making as large a rate of return in October, 1836, when the short-money rate was 36 per cent as they had been the previous January when it was 10 per cent. The reason for the high rate in October was the issuance of the specie circular which meant that the banks could not afford to lend at a moment when merchants were in dire need of money.

My more fundamental objection to this total procedure is the one I have referred to earlier, that, as a historian convinced somehow of not only the importance but also in some ways of the sacredness of what actually happened, it seems to me to be wrong to use such a title as the Economics of Negro Slavery, 1830 to 1860 for a study that has little or no concern either for the actual profitableness of the enterprises using slaves or for the other economic aspects of this historical institution. I somehow resent also the use of mathematical equations to give an aspect of exactness and accuracy to what, at best, are intelligent and critical guesses, though as I stated when I began this commentary, I am as certain as I can be of any judgment concerning the past that Evans is correct when he says that slavery was a viable and profitable institution.

John E. Moes, University of Virginia

At the end of his paper Robert Evans concludes: "Thus it would appear that the slave industry did not exhibit characteristics of a nonviable industry about to wither and die under the impact of adverse economic forces, but rather gave every indication in its latter years of being a strong and growing industry." As against this, I intend to show that *economic forces*—to the extent that they can be separated from other forces—are always adverse to the perpetuation of a system of slavery, except if new slaves can be obtained by force from outside the economic system, as in the Western Hemisphere before the abolition of the overseas trade. By this I do not mean to imply that in the ante-bellum South slavery was withering and dying—obviously it was not, since the slave population was growing at a rate equal to the rate of increase of the free population—but that the impact of economic forces proper was diverted in the social and political environment of the South. While the self-interest of the two parties directly concerned, the slaves and their owners, would have led to a termination of the system had these parties been free and unimpeded to transact their business accordingly, there were other influences at work in the South that interfered with this process.

One criterion that has been applied to determine the viability of slavery in the ante-bellum South is whether the rate of return on investment in slaves was generally less than that in other types of investment. Conrad and Meyer adopt this criterion explicitly and then proceed to show that returns were about as high on slave capital as on nonslave capital.[1] The outstanding proponent of the opposite view, U. B. Phillips, is quoted by Evans to the effect that by the close of the fifties keeping slaves had become unprofitable in terms of returns on investment in slave capital. Evans himself devotes the bulk of his paper to refuting the notion that returns on slave capital were relatively small, although he recognizes that nothing at all can be inferred from the magnitude of the rate of return, by itself or relative to any other rate, concerning the relevant question—the viability of slavery. This is so because, as Evans points out, capital values adjust to expected returns. Confirmation of this proposition by means of calculations like those carried out by Evans involves an impressive amount of work,

[1] Alfred H. Conrad and John R. Meyer, "The Economics of Slavery in the Ante Bellum South," *Journal of Political Economy*, April 1958, pp. 95-130.

but is, in my estimation, hardly required. Besides, for various reasons these calculations can scarcely be called convincing.

In the first place, the available data upon which the computations must be based are thoroughly incomplete. Given the nature of these data, some of the assumptions that have to be made in the calculation process are far more heroic than the assumption that people will attempt to maximize the returns on their investments. Yet, from the latter assumption, the conclusion follows that "pure" returns will tend to be equal on all types of investment.

Secondly, there is the personal preference of individuals for more or less risky types of investment and their evaluation of riskiness. Suppose that people always act in their best pecuniary interest as they see it when making investment decisions. Certainly we could not on that basis predict what differentials in rates of return would prevail in the market.

A third objection to this procedure is that we have no way of determining to what extent actual and expected returns deviated from each other for the various types of investment used in the comparison. Differentials in returns on investment are caused by a number of factors, and the quantitative influence of any one of them cannot in practice be separated from that of the others. This, in my opinion, disqualifies any attempt to assess the rationality in an economic sense of the people who paid the prices they did for slaves by comparing the returns on that type of investment with the returns on other types. A study of the motives of slaveowners, general knowledge of human nature, and even introspection provide for this purpose empirical material of much better quality than data obtained in the market.

It may be objected that the purpose of comparing returns on slave capital with returns on other capital is not to test the rationality hypothesis but, for instance, to determine in an ex post sense the profitability of investment in slaves. While in one place Evans seems to be saying that this is the question he has answered, it is hardly consistent with his dictum (upon which my considerations developed above are based) that one would expect the rate of return on slave capital to equal the market rate, even though the "slave industry" was declining. It is also inconsistent with his subsequent discussion of capital losses as a separate issue—one that would have a bearing upon the problem of viability, while the comparison between rates of return would be irrelevant. Clearly, the issue of the profitability of investment in slaves in an ex post sense cannot be determined without taking into consideration capital gains and losses resulting from changes in price; and, in fact, in Evans' calculations attempts are made to take into consideration the effect of changes in the price of slaves. I must admit that I am a little puzzled by all this. It is just not clear whether Evans is discussing expected returns, or returns that were actually realized, or perhaps the latter as an approximation to the former.

Next consider the bearing of the movement in slave prices upon the problem of viability. The data indicate that in the ante-bellum period slave prices were rising, but suppose this was the result of unwarranted speculation—as Phillips and others have argued, a crash of the slave market being inevitable. Why should this have led to a termination of slavery? The price of slaves would simply have fallen to a more realistic level, for which there was plenty of room; downward adjustment of slave prices in fact occurred frequently. Not until the price of any type of slaves settled near zero could one expect slaveowners to abandon their property voluntarily without compensation. And even this is conceivable only when we assume that, restrained by ethical considerations, the owner would not contemplate the alternative always open to him of working his slave to death in a relatively short period without providing adequate maintenance. In the latter case slavery would decline through excessive mortality rather than emancipation, at least in the absence of new importations. With new importations available, a system of slavery can be maintained indefinitely in this inhumane manner. In fact, this was done in the British and French West Indies where, before the abolition of the slave trade, the natural rate of decrease in some islands was said to be in excess of 5 per cent per annum,[2] and where the life expectancy of a slave employed in the sugar industry was no more than seven years. In Barbados, because of the density of the slave population relative to the extent of arable land, the marginal revenue product of labor fell so low that white settlers who did not own extensive property were reduced to a condition said to be the most degraded seen anywhere, and between 1676 and 1712 their number fell from 21,000 to 12,000.[3]

But in North America, where arable land was unlimited, labor pro-

[2] Herbert Heaton, *Economic History of Europe*, rev. ed., New York, 1948, pp. 333-34.

[3] W. L. Mathieson, *British Slavery and its Abolition, 1823-1838*, London, 1926, pp. 39 and 44.

ductivity was high and, as a result, slaves were maintained under much better material conditions. The slave system under such circumstances develops along different lines. If a decline in labor value sets in, an ethical code sustained by a considerable degree of mutual affection between master and slave may prevent lowering the standard of living of the slave to a level in accordance with the pecuniary interest of his owner. To a decent family, slaves may then become a burden instead of an asset. Of course, the unscrupulous might still be able to make a profit out of a slave and offer a price, but by the same token a "good" master might hesitate to sell (although this might possibly be easier on his conscience than administering harsh treatment himself). Thus, while market prices are still positive, in reality to most slaveowners the value has become zero or negative. At such a time, when the cost of customary maintenance of adult slaves can no longer be covered out of the revenue the slaves produce—at least at the margin—and raising slave children does not seem profitable, manumission may become a frequent occurrence, and even abolition without compensation by legal decree may meet with relatively little opposition. The situation is similar to one that, in a free labor market, causes unemployment when the demand for labor declines and wages are relatively inflexible in the downward direction. However, the analogous contingency in the slave market is much less likely to occur. For one thing, there is no money illusion that may aggravate the situation but, more basically, it requires a shift in the demand for labor sufficient to wipe out normally existing property rents. I think that those who write as if any decline in the demand for labor would have spelled the end of the slave system in the ante-bellum South, where property rents were very high, forget this.

Nevertheless, at one time in the history of slavery in this country the contingency did occur. During a period of disrupted trade connections and agricultural transition in the old South, George Washington and everyone else were grumbling about their slaves devouring them.[4] As a result, Americans have generally thought in these terms when contemplating the possible termination of slavery under the impact of adverse economic forces. But for slavery to come to an end in this fashion has been the great exception in the world history of slavery. In fact, I am not aware of a single instance except in the U.S., and here it only happened "almost." Yet, when we view the history

[4] Lewis Cecil Gray, *History of Agriculture in the Southern United States to 1860*, Washington, 1933, Vol. II, p. 911.

of slavery in the world as a whole, we are immediately struck by the fact that a slave system of any economic importance (i.e., comprising more than a relatively small number of domestic servants maintained by the wealthy as a sign of conspicuous consumption) is a very great rarity. To this I shall return. First, let us briefly look at the other items on Evans' list of things he would expect to observe if slavery had been a "declining industry." In addition to a fall in the prices of slaves in general, these include a falling birth rate, a fall in the price of female slaves relative to male slaves, and a fall in the rates of hire of slaves relative to those of free workers.

I would not expect a decline in the demand for slave labor to lead to a fall in the birth rate, so long as demand did not decline to the point where the value of a slave, at an age at which he would begin to cover his maintenance, would be less than the expense of raising him (including time off for the mother during and after pregnancy). Even then, one would not expect a fall in the birth rate because to achieve this one would have to separate male and female slaves (and also keep the latter away from their masters), which is practically impossible unless one is willing to treat the slaves very harshly in all other respects also. It is a fact of life that, in general, not having children is much more difficult than having them, which is also the reason why slave-owners did not need to resort to the device of "breeding" in any other sense than just allowing the slaves to get together.

Even if the price of female slaves in general had been falling, one would hardly expect a fall in the price of female slaves relative to male slaves. Both embody labor services that will become available in the future, the only difference being that the female slave embodies labor services of her offspring in addition to her own, so that on the average the labor services a female slave represents become available later than those of a male slave of the same age. The relative value of the two will depend, therefore, upon the expected value of labor services at different points in the future. Only if people came to believe that in the remote future (say, twenty years later) the hitherto accepted value of labor services would fall relative to the current value would there be a relative decline in the price of female slaves. But this would obviously be a rather minor matter. The value of as yet unborn babies can hardly have been great, given the long period over which the value of their future services would have to be discounted and the uncertainty at that time of an infant's ever reaching maturity.

Moreover, babies are more or less a joint product of a man and woman. The institution of slave marriage was, in practice, widely respected although not officially sanctioned, and man and wife were rarely separated. If, therefore, in a display of scientific detachment, we start using the slightly repulsive term "breeding," we should be cautious lest we be carried away by our analogy. The family, to a large extent, was a unit, and if that is so, there is hardly any reason to expect a relative fall in the price of female slaves when future labor services were expected to decline in value relative to current labor services. The value of a man as a mate to a woman would decline by about the same amount.

Finally, I would expect a fall in the rate of hire of slaves relative to that of free workers only when slaves were becoming less productive relative to free labor doing the same work. Evans, however, says: when an industry is declining, one would expect to observe a relative decline in the demand for its product. In the case of a nonviable slave industry, the product being slave labor, one would therefore expect the price of slave labor to decline relative to that of free labor. But this reasoning is not admissible, for the product of slaves and free workers is the same—labor. The price paid for a given quantity of slave labor will therefore always be equal to the price paid for the same quantity of free labor—the market will see to that. Inasmuch as rates of hire are quoted per time unit rather than per quantity of labor performed, these rates may of course differ between slaves and free workers, but by the same token these hourly or daily rates are not properly the price of labor.

In the following remarks I shall discuss from a different point of view the prospects of the institution of slavery at the eve of the Civil War. The argument is based upon a comparison between the productivity of a slave who is given the opportunity to earn his own freedom and of one who has no hope of altering his status. Experience indicates that in the former case the slave would work well and hard to an extent that no manner of compulsion can bring forth, and thus his master would benefit until the slave has accomplished his purpose. To accumulate savings in order to buy his own freedom at market price, the slave was given some time to himself in which he could work for someone else or for his own master and keep the wages, or he was allowed to produce commodities that he could sell in the market. In the remainder of the time, in which he still worked for his master, he performed better than he otherwise would. The master might also set a manumission price higher than the slave's market value so as to make a capital gain when replacing the freed slave with another.[5] Under an alternative arrangement, the slave paid his master a rental price for his time, was allowed to seek employment or follow a trade independently, saved, and accumulated his ransom. In Rome, slaves were frequently freed in anticipation of the payment of their ransom, often continuing to work for their former masters for wages. In many other instances, the master supplied the capital for a freed man to set himself up in business. There are, of course, innumerable variations on this theme.[6]

I use the word ransom deliberately, for in this view slavery is essentially a transitional stage in a person's life from the time he enters captivity (which may be at his birth) until he pays a price for his freedom, which is the expected thing. It was the experience of antiquity that holding slaves under such conditions was more profitable than when the outlook was for a man to remain in bondage for life. As a consequence, manumissions by self-purchase were always numerous, and when, because of the establishment of the Pax Romana by Emperor Augustus, slaves ceased to stream into Italy in the form of captives of war, while piracy and banditry, the other major sources of slave supply, were vigorously suppressed, slavery was doomed to virtual extinction. This transition was accomplished in rural areas as well as in the cities. It was by no means a phenomenon restricted to an urban society or to slaves that were particularly talented. On the land, the chained slave gangs (which in the time of the Roman Republic, when slave prices were low and the treatment of slaves accordingly harsh, had worked the *latifundia*) disappeared. The estates came to be occupied by free tenants, descendants of slaves who against a consideration had been voluntarily emancipated by their masters. And since the times were prosperous, all this occurred in a period in which slave prices were high and rising. The institution of slavery itself was transformed beyond recognition. Family life among slaves was now encouraged and women were given premiums and sometimes freedom for bearing numerous children. Under the influence of the higher prices the slaves

[5] Manumission prices in ancient Greece were in excess of the usual market prices of slaves, according to William L. Westermann, *The Slave Systems of Greek and Roman Antiquity*, Philadelphia, 1955, p. 36.

[6] See A. M. Duff, *Freedmen in the Early Roman Empire*, Oxford, 1928, especially Chaps. I and II.

were treated more humanely, and this in turn created a setting in which arrangements could be worked out for the slave to earn his freedom.[7]

It is in this manner that one would expect slavery eventually to have ended in this country, if economic forces could have had free sway. To entertain for a moment the notion that in the South, if the Civil War had not intervened, slavery might have become unprofitable in any other way except that it might have been more profitable to sell the slave his freedom than to keep him is simply ludicrous. The South was a prosperous and rapidly growing region where in the decade preceding the war the output of the primary staple crops doubled. The war and its aftermath interrupted this progress, but the long-run picture has of course been one of rising labor productivity. Already before the war it had been demonstrated that slave labor could be used in virtually any occupation. If nowadays slavery still were to exist, slave prices would be higher and the institution more profitable than ever, because the discrepancy between what a worker can earn and what would be necessary for the reasonable maintenance of a slave has never been so great. Nor is there any reason to believe that this would have been different if slavery had not been abolished. (It is true that the expansion of a privately owned labor force absorbs savings that otherwise would be available for investment in nonhuman capital, but any detrimental effect on economic growth that this may have in a closed system was virtually eliminated in the case of the South through the free flow of capital into the region.)[8] Every sensible discussion of the possible termination of slavery under the impact of economic forces, therefore, should be an inquiry into the prospects for the slaves to acquire their freedom by self-purchase. Yet this whole matter is summarily dismissed by Evans in one brief paragraph, where he observes that in the South manumission by self-purchase was infrequent. Sometimes, however, a phenomenon is important for what it spells rather than for what it is. When we look into the history of slavery in other parts of the world, and especially in the Roman Empire,

---

[7] See: Duff, *Freedmen* . . . ; Westermann, *The Slave Systems* . . . , pp. 72, 76-77; R. H. Barrow, *Slavery in the Roman Empire*, London, 1928, pp. 54, 83, 89-90; Tenney Frank, *An Economic History of Rome*, 2d ed., Baltimore, 1927, pp. 327, 436-439.

[8] On this question see John E. Moes, "The Absorption of Capital in Slave Labor in the Ante Bellum South and Economic Growth," *American Journal of Economics and Sociology*, Oct. 1961, pp. 535-541.

we cannot fail to recognize the potential importance of manumission by self-purchase in the American setting. The similarity in motivation and methods used is striking, and so is the fact that enormous gains could be obtained by southern slaveowners who were alert enough to seize this opportunity.[9] Indeed, to me, there is no doubt that the tendency for slavery to be concluded by self-purchase of the slaves, if in no other way, is of universal dimensions, for the forces that lead to it are deeply rooted in human nature. These forces are the profit motive (of the masters) and the desire for freedom (of the slaves).[10] Bring these two elements together in a setting where a man, when given a motive to apply himself, can earn more than his keep, and a contract between slave and master leading to self-purchase is the result. And these are in truth economic forces, since they spring from the self-interest of individuals as it can be served by material means. However, other forces may interfere. To make sure of being understood, allow me to present a crude analogy. The law of markets says that in the market a price will be established at which the quantities supplied and demanded are equal. I am not bothering here with qualifications. The forces that lead to this I would call economic forces. But suppose that the government interferes and sets a price by statute lower than the market equilibrium (or one higher than the equilibrium price, as governments often do in the labor market). Respect for the law, fear of punishment, etc. may then be effective countervailing forces that prevent the law of markets becoming manifest in the price. Or, as in the labor market, a social convention regarding what constitutes a decent minimum price may impose an effective floor and interfere with the law of markets when a decline in demand occurs. These interfering forces we would then have to designate as noneconomic.

This terminology is of course open to legitimate objections. An entrepreneur who refuses to hire workers at less than the customary minimum rate, even though he could get them at a lower rate, acts in his self-interest. It is by no means clear where the line between economic and noneconomic forces should be drawn. With regard to the slavery problem, racial prejudice, for instance, would certainly have to be

[9] See Sumner Eliot Matison, "Manumission by Purchase," *Journal of Negro History*, April, 1948; also U. B. Phillips, *American Negro Slavery*, New York, 1918, pp. 412-414; William Allan, *Life and Work of John McDonogh*, Baltimore, 1886, p. 49.

[10] The great desire for freedom among the slave population is brought out convincingly in Kenneth M. Stampp, *The Peculiar Institution*, New York, 1956.

classified as a noneconomic force, and yet racial feelings may well be influenced unconsciously or even consciously by considerations of economic self-interest. But the slavery question has traditionally been discussed in this manner and, in a rough way, so long as it does not create misunderstanding, this may even be useful. At any rate, Evans has followed the tradition, and I must answer him in his own terminology. I would say, then, that economic forces in the ante-bellum South clearly tended toward voluntary emancipation. That for the time being this did not become manifest in a number of manumissions large relative to the slave population must be explained in terms of countervailing social and political forces. Among these, one thinks in the first place of the feeling that the Negro race was inferior, which caused the whites to contemplate with concern the prospect of a sizeable population of free Negroes. As a result, manifold social and legal obstacles to manumission existed. All this was greatly reinforced by the reaction in the South against northern abolitionism. Precisely how these factors interfered with the law of manumission should be spelled out further, but time is lacking.[11] However, I wish to submit that in the long run the prospects may be dim for an institution that has to be maintained against the self-interest of the parties immediately concerned (*in casu* masters and slaves). We must remember that in the ante-bellum South there was hardly a long run, the abolition of the external slave trade being less than fifty years old when the Civil War started. Rome, too, enacted laws against manumission and knew social prejudice against freed slaves; and there, also, it took considerably more than fifty years for slavery to wither away after the large-scale influx of slaves had ceased.

[11] I have attempted this elsewhere. See John E. Moes, "The Economics of Slavery in the Ante Bellum South. Another Comment," *Journal of Political Economy*, LXVIII (April, 1960) 183-87.

# Wage Differentials: Theory and Measurement

## MELVIN W. REDER

STANFORD UNIVERSITY

THIS paper reports an investigation of certain aspects of wage differentials. The array of earnings of individuals from work may be arranged in many ways: in this paper we consider only two arrangements, by skill (or occupation) and by industry. In analyzing the behavior of wage differentials, it is difficult to avoid drastic simplification in their measurement; we frequently treat the number of workers at each level of skill and in each industry as though it were a quantity, and either their mean or their median wage as though it were a price.

The violence this does to a very complicated set of facts is obvious. Though some of the appropriate warnings are given where needed, others are not; therefore it may be helpful if, at the outset, a few precautionary remarks are made.

1. As usually measured, wages exclude the pecuniary value of fringe benefits. This may well distort interindustry or interoccupational wage comparisons for the postwar period. However, an appropriate set of corrections is not at hand, and, willy-nilly, we have written as though we believed fringe benefits were distributed more or less proportionately to wages. This could affect some of our results; all we can do is hope that the necessary amendments would not prove catastrophic.

2. When we speak of the wage level of an occupation or an industry, we refer indifferently (unless otherwise specified) to straight-time average hourly earnings; average hourly earnings, including overtime premiums; mean or median weekly or annual earnings. These various concepts of earnings do not vary proportionally from one industry or occupation to another, and we must take care not to make statements, based on data referring to one concept of earnings, as though they were necessarily applicable to data pertaining to other concepts.

3. We indicate whole frequency distributions of industrial or occupational wage payments by a single measure of central tendency, a mean or a median. This leaves completely unexplored the effect of industry or occupation on other characteristics of earnings distributions.

NOTE: This paper is part of a longer study on wage differentials, which has been financed by a grant from the Ford Foundation to the Economics Department of Stanford University.

4. Finally, in treating the mean or median of an industry's or occupation's earnings distribution as an indicator of the price of a particular kind of labor, we abstract from all variations in hiring requirements—labor "quality" as judged by the employer, and all variations in job attractiveness as judged by the worker. However, these variations reflect an important aspect of labor-market behavior.

Certainly we attempt to take these various factors into account at places where they are especially pertinent. But there are places, particularly in the section on industrial differentials, where paucity of data and the usages of an existing literature lead us to speak of "average wages" in an industry as though it were much more closely related to the "price of a factor of production" than it actually is. Obviously, in individual cases where the consequences of abstraction are known, they are taken into account. However, there are many cases where these consequences are not known and we proceed to apply economic theory without, each time, mentioning all the necessary reservations. For this one can only point to the need for reasonable brevity, and explain in advance.

## Occupational Wage Structure

Since J. S. Mill invented the concept of noncompeting groups, if not before, economic theorists have tended to explain occupational differences in wages by differences in costs of training or other obstacles to supply. But this explanation is, at most, supposed to account only for long-run differences. In the short run, as usually defined, the number of persons in one occupation is assumed to be virtually fixed, and earnings are therefore presumed to be affected by recent changes in labor demand and wage rigidities, as well as by supply influences. It will therefore be convenient to separate the long- and short-run aspects of the matter and discuss them separately, though giving their interrelation due attention.

In discussing occupational or skill differentials, we adopt a particular, though customary, definition of the wage recipients whom we designate as skilled and unskilled. Here, the skilled workers are usually some sort of manual craftsmen, e.g., carpenters, millwrights, electricians, etc., while the unskilled are laborers, sweepers, watchmen, and the like. The records of the wages paid in the specific occupations chosen suffer from the usual limitations of samples and, in addition, the occupations used to represent skilled and unskilled workers are themselves samples of skilled and unskilled occupations generally. The existence and relative increase of intermediate grades of skill create problems of demarcating skilled from unskilled occupations. One study, Keat's, measures skill differentials by the coefficient of variation of the ratio of the wage rates in 141 specific occupations to the average hourly earnings in all manufacturing; this largely overcomes the aforementioned difficulties except for those resulting from the limitations of manufacturing as a sample of the whole economy.

We measure the skill differential as the *percentage* difference between the hourly earnings of workers designated as skilled and those designated as unskilled. This is not the only possible measure that could be used; an alternative would be to measure the *absolute* differential—the dollar amount of the differential. We have chosen to measure the differential in percentage terms because we are primarily interested in the skill differential as one indicator of the relative economic well-being of two groups of earners. Though neither the absolute, the percentage, nor any one-dimensional measure of the earnings differential will be completely satisfactory for the purpose, we believe that changes in the percentage differential far more closely approximate that by which economists and others judge relative economic well-being than changes in the absolute differential do.

In an unpublished study, Gary S. Becker (properly) argues that the percentage differential is not always relevant in analyzing resource allocation. He contends that it is appropriate when we are attempting to explain variations in relative demand for skilled and unskilled workers. But if we should be interested in explaining variations in the resources devoted to investment in "human capital"—to education and training—as compared with those devoted to other uses, then it is the absolute difference that is relevant. This is because the percentage return on a given dollar investment in human capital is identified with the skill differential.

This view implies that if the dollar (i.e., absolute) skill differential between occupations A and B declined from $t_0$ to $t_1$, but in proportion with a decline in the difference in training costs, the skill differential (as measured) would be unchanged. However, we would still be interested, from a "welfare-distribution" point of view, in the differential earnings of the *persons* engaged in these occupations as well as in the return on the differential (dollar) investments they embody. Since we have, *inter alia*, this welfare-distributive interest, we concentrate upon the behavior of percentage differentials.

Now let us turn to a consideration of the long-run characteristics of the wage structure.

### SECULAR BEHAVIOR OF THE OCCUPATIONAL WAGE STRUCTURE

Most writers, including the present one, have contended that occupational relative (i.e., percentage) wage differentials, on an hourly basis (hereafter called the "skill margin"), have shown a secular tendency to diminish.[1] One important reason for this belief is empirical; the available evidence has seemed to support this view.[2] But, as we shall see, the facts do not tell a completely unambiguous story. If they did, we should expect to find that close substitutes of unskilled *urban*[3] workers would also have experienced a relative increase in hourly earnings—and some have not done so. For example, we should expect that the hourly wages of farm workers, who are closer substitutes for urban unskilled and semiskilled than for urban skilled workers,[4] would

---

[1] M. W. Reder, "The Theory of Occupational Wage Differentials," *American Economic Review*, Dec. 1955, pp. 833-852, especially n. 1, contains a fairly extensive bibliography of the literature before that date. The more important contributions since then are L. G. Reynolds and C. H. Taft, *The Evolution of Wage Structure*, New Haven, 1956; *Economic Survey of Europe in 1955*, United Nations, 1956, pp. 153-157; M. Rothbaum, "National Wage-structure Comparisons," *New Concepts in Wage Determination*, G. W. Taylor and F. C. Pierson, eds., New York, 1957, pp. 299-327; *The Theory of Wage Determination*, J. T. Dunlop, ed., London, 1957, especially the papers of Clark Kerr and Lloyd Reynolds; R. Perlman, "Forces Widening Occupational Wage Differentials," *Review of Economics and Statistics*, May 1958, pp. 107-115; M. Yanowitch, "Trends in Soviet Occupational Wage Differentials," *Industrial and Labor Relations Review*, Jan. 1960, pp. 166-191; William Goldner, "Labor Market Factors and Skill Differentials in Wage Rates," *Proceedings of the Industrial Relations Research Association*, 1957, pp. 207-216; and an unpublished doctoral dissertation by P. G. Keat, "Changes in Occupational Wage Structure, 1900-1956," at the University of Chicago, 1959. An article by Keat, "Long-run Changes in Occupational Wage Structure, 1900-1956," *Journal of Political Economy*, Dec. 1960, pp. 584-600, is based on his thesis.

[2] The best data summaries are in Reynolds and Taft, *The Evolution*, pp. 32-38; 59-63; 92-96; 108-128; 213-218; 240-242; 269-275; 293-298; and 319-327; and in Keat, "Changes in Occupational." Perlman, "Forces Widening," also contains some useful discussion of the data.

[3] The data on skill differentials refer almost exclusively to urban workers.

[4] Since one critic has challenged this assertion, we submit the following data from the 1950 Census: Among employed persons (both sexes) who resided in urban or rural nonfarm locations in March 1950 and were employed in nonfarm occupations, but had resided on farms in 1949, 55.8 per cent were occupationally classified as operatives and kindred workers; laborers except farm and mine or service workers—these are what are usually considered unskilled or semiskilled jobs. Classified as craftsmen, foremen, etc.—i.e., as skilled manual workers—were 13.8 per cent. For all other employed persons, the corresponding percentages were 40.3

rise relative to skilled earnings, but it is not clear that they have done so. The data in Table 1 clearly imply that in 1956 the ratio of their earnings to average hourly earnings in manufacturing was well below what it was in 1929, which was less than it had been in 1914. How-

TABLE 1

AVERAGE GROSS HOURLY EARNINGS IN MANUFACTURING, LAUNDRIES, AND AGRICULTURE, SELECTED DATES, 1929-58

| | All Manufacturing | Index | Laundries | Index | Agriculture | Index |
|---|---|---|---|---|---|---|
| 1929 | $0.566 | 100 | n.a. | | $0.241 | 100 |
| 1934 | 0.532 | 94 | $0.378 | 100 | 0.152 | 63 |
| 1939 | 0.633 | 112 | 0.422 | 112 | 0.166 | 69 |
| 1940 | 0.661 | 117 | 0.429 | 113 | 0.169 | 70 |
| 1941 | 0.729 | 129 | 0.444 | 117 | 0.206 | 86 |
| 1945 | 1.023 | 181 | 0.648 | 172 | 0.472 | 196 |
| 1948 | 1.350 | 239 | 0.817 | 216 | 0.588 | 241 |
| 1955 | 1.88 | 332 | 1.01 | 267 | 0.675 | 280 |
| 1956 | 1.98 | 350 | 1.05 | 268 | 0.705 | 292 |
| 1957 | 2.07 | 366 | 1.09 | 277 | 0.728 | 302 |
| 1958 | 2.13 | 376 | 1.13 | 299 | 0.757 | 314 |
| 1959 | 2.22 | 392 | 1.17 | 310 | 0.798 | 331 |
| 1960 | 2.29 | 405 | 1.22 | 323 | 0.818 | 339 |

SOURCE: Department of Labor and Department of Agriculture.

ever, these data are not beyond challenge: H. G. Lewis has shown me some unpublished computations of average hourly compensation in agriculture and manufacturing which show that with the ratio, $\frac{\text{average hourly earnings in agriculture}}{\text{average hourly earnings in manufacturing}}$, put equal to 100 in 1929, its value stood at 118 in 1956; i.e., contrary to the implication of Table 1, agricultural hourly compensation rose relatively to manufacturing. Fortunately, for the purposes of this paper, it is not necessary to choose between the two sets of estimates or even attempt to reconcile them.[5]

per cent in the various unskilled and semiskilled categories, and 15.7 per cent in the craftsmen, etc., group (data from *1950 Population Census*, Special Report P-E, No. 4C, *Population Mobility—Farm-Nonfarm Movers*, Table 3, p. 4C-14). In other words, recent rural-urban migrants were more prone to be employed as unskilled or semiskilled manual workers, and less likely to be employed as skilled—at least in 1950—than the remainder of the labor force.

[5] The main source of difference between Lewis's data and those cited in Table 1 is in the figures on agricultural earnings. The series in Table 1 is derived directly from the Department of Agriculture surveys, while Lewis's compensation data come from the Department of Commerce and from some unpublished hours-per-

But despite their differences, both series reveal a marked decline (about 20 per cent) in the above ratio during the 1950's, when the skill margin was about constant. This implies either that rural and urban labor markets are somewhat insulated from one another or that their interrelation is subject to a prolonged lag. In either event, there arises the possibility that the observed behavior of skill differentials in part of the economy may be a misleading guide to what has happened in other parts.

Laundry workers, like farm workers, are far better substitutes for unskilled than for skilled workers. And, in the absence of a competing series, we shall assert that their hourly earnings have declined relative to those in manufacturing from 1929 to 1957. Hence, if the trend toward reduced skill differentials is genuine, it is necessary to explain the growing gap between hourly earnings in manufacturing and in laundries, as well as the questionable relation between agricultural and manufacturing earnings.

One explanation of the growing wage disadvantage of the laundry workers is that, in terms of employment, laundering is a declining industry. From 1947 through 1958, employment in this industry fell 14 per cent (from 365,000 to 313,000). Thus it might be possible to rationalize the behavior of laundry wages as that of a declining industry in which some older workers are trapped but from which the more mobile are escaping; such an explanation is an entirely conventional application of short-run equilibrium analysis. No doubt there is validity in this explanation, but it is hard to believe that it is the whole story. For, in the postwar period, employment opportunities have usually been adequate to permit the escape of most workers into low-skilled jobs in manufacturing. A further explanatory factor that we believe should be taken into account is the probable relaxation of

---

year data supplied by John Kendrick. The disagreement between the two sets of data lies mainly in their trends in hourly agricultural compensation: in Lewis's series the average rate of increase between 1929 and 1956 is about 1½ times as great as in that of Table 1. However, both series show (1) an appreciable (over 30 per cent) decline in the ratio of average hourly compensation in agriculture to that in industry during the early 1930's; (2) a very sharp rise in this same ratio during World War II; and (3) a sharp fall in this ratio from 1950-51 through (at least) 1957.

In fairness to Lewis, it should be noted that he does *not* claim his series to be superior to that in Table 1; he merely believes that, on available information, there is not an adequate base for choosing.

hiring standards to accept increasingly less eligible workers,[6] and some related phenomena to be discussed.

The declining industry hypothesis—i.e., relative declines in hourly earnings in an industry result from an uncompleted adjustment to a reduction in employment—could also be applied to explain the behavior of agricultural earnings, if such earnings have shown a relative decline. But, once again, the opportunities for interindustry mobility have raised a question as to whether there has been a differential change in hiring standards as between agriculture and the rest of the economy.

It might seem that the declining industry hypothesis, with a slight modification, could account for the relative wage behavior in both agriculture and laundries. That is, the conventional short-run analysis of a declining industry's relative wages implies that they will fall because some workers cannot or will not shift industries, though when they retire they will not be replaced. As the immobile workers disproportionately represent the older segment of the industry's labor force, it is to be expected that in the short run there will be a decline in the quality of the labor force as well as in employment; this will appear as a change in hiring standards.

The main factors which this analysis leaves out of account are such "institutional" ones as the differential effect of minimum wage laws, trade union pressure, curbs on child labor, etc. Clearly, minimum wage laws affect far larger segments of manufacturing than of either laundering or agriculture. Consequently, the relative decline of hourly earnings in the latter two industries may simply indicate the fact that market forces were free to set low wages in many of these industries' local markets but were prevented from doing so in manufacturing.

In other words, the usual measures of skill margins refer to differences in hourly earnings of different occupational groups in a large section of the economy, but do not reflect events in another part which is of some importance. The available statistics refer to urban areas and are collected disproportionately from large firms which are fairly long-lived; conversely, they underrepresent firms with the opposite characteristics. This creates the possibility that divergent movements

---

[6] It is difficult to test this surmise on census data since the Census Bureau does not publish detailed characteristics of laundry workers separately, but combines them with those of persons employed in cleaning and dyeing establishments. However, the matter can surely be investigated further.

in the "premium for skill" in these two parts of the economy may render data from either sector a misleading guide to skill margins in the economy as a whole.

Did this possibility materialize in the United States and elsewhere during the past twenty-five to fifty years? In our judgment, the answer is probably not. The compression of differentials in annual earnings since 1929, noted by Kuznets, Goldsmith, and others, would imply that this distribution behaved as though there had been a contraction in the margin for skill. Moreover, from 1939 to 1949 (at least), the dispersion of the medians of annual earnings of (full-year) wage and salary workers in different occupations declined during that period; this would suggest the same conclusion, though for a shorter period.[7]

There is further evidence, though of a different kind, which also suggests that there was secular shrinkage in the skill margin. It will not be seriously disputed that persons engaged in what are normally called skilled occupations generally have a higher level of education (more years of schooling) than those in unskilled trades. It will also be agreed that, whatever the causal pattern, variations in years of school attendance are associated with variations in occupational levels. Clearly, in the past fifty years, if not longer, there has been a marked cumulative increase in the median number of years of school completed by members of the American labor force. This would, *ceteris paribus*, have the effect of increasing the fraction of the labor force able to hold skilled jobs. Since the fraction of the labor force in skilled employment has increased secularly,[8] it is tempting to relate this fact and the decline in the skill margin by a conventional application of price theory.

This argument is as follows: there has been a secular increase in the relative supply of skilled as compared with unskilled workers which has led—because of a failure of relative demand for skilled workers to increase as much (at relevant ratios of skilled to unskilled wage rates)—to a decline in the skill differentials. The relative increase in the number of skilled workers is thus consistent with the above theory and with a decline in the skill margin; therefore it would seem to pro-

[7] H. P. Miller, *Income of the American People*, New York, Wiley, 1955, Chap. 9, especially pp. 120-21 and Table 67.

[8] From 1900 to 1950, craftsmen, foremen and kindred workers (roughly, skilled manual workers) increased from 10.5 per cent to 14.2 per cent of the labor force. Operatives, etc. (the semiskilled) increased even more (in percentage terms) during that period, but laborers, both farm and nonfarm (the urban unskilled and their substitutes) decreased sharply (see D. J. Bogue, *The Population of the United States*, Glencoe, Illinois, 1959, Table 17-1, p. 475).

vide an additional reason for believing that the skill margin really has declined secularly.

But this argument is not free from difficulty: it is possible that the secular increase in the relative number of skilled workers is due mainly to changes in relative demand rather than supply. We do not have any independent measure of changes in relative demands for skilled and unskilled workers, and we cannot deny that the spreading of education may have been partly a response to relative changes in labor demand.[9] If this possibility is accepted as an "important" cause of the relative increase in the number of skilled workers, we cannot buttress the finding of a declining skill margin by the behavior of the relative numbers of skilled and unskilled workers.

However, we are inclined to deny that there have been important changes in relative demand for the following reasons: (1) below the college level—and it is with this range that we are concerned—increased schooling has been due in good part to laws compelling school attendance; (2) a substantial role in the relative decline of unskilled labor has been the sharp reduction in child labor (under legal pressure) and, in the United States, the reduction in immigration. Both of these developments tended to reduce the relative supply of the unskilled at the same time that they raised the median years of schooling of the labor force. (3) Of the increase in private expenditure for education that has occurred, the major explanatory factor has been the increased income (of parents); i.e., private educational expenditure *below the college level* has been viewed as a consumer luxury good rather than as a producer good. (4) Those ambitious persons who respond to the lure of higher incomes by increasing their training—at least in the United States—have not gone into skilled manual work but into business or the professions. Consequently, their effect on the supply of skilled labor would have been small.

While we believe that these assertions can be supported with empirical evidence (1 and 2 easily, 3 with a little effort, and 4 with considerable effort), for the present consider them merely as assertions. If all were true, they could not prove that changes in relative demand

[9] This possibility is indicated very clearly in G. S. Becker's unpublished manuscript, "Investment in Human Capital." For the purpose of our paper, delayed (supply) response to an initial skill differential in excess of the (long-run) equilibrium level would yield the same price-quantity behavior as a shift in the supply function with instantaneous adjustments; i.e., the relative quantity of the skilled will increase and their differential wage advantage will shrink. Hence, we shall not bother to distinguish this from a downward shift in the long-run supply function.

265

had no part, or even a smaller part than changes in relative supply, in narrowing the margin for skill. All they are intended to do is indicate the evidence that could be marshalled in support of the claim that supply factors are adequate to explain the secular decline in the skill differential. But it cannot be denied that an adequate alternative explanation stressing demand factors might yet be offered.

The explanation of a secular decline in the skill margin offered here would strongly suggest that the decline will continue. However, not everyone agrees: one recent writer[10] has argued that because of the possibility of relaxing hiring standards, it is likely that in the future skill differentials will be widening rather than narrowing. That is, employers will relax hiring standards for the unskilled more than for the skilled, thereby causing a widening of the skill margin. Moreover, as he contends, it is possible that technical progress will have the effect of increasing the ratio, $\frac{\text{DEMAND FOR SKILLED WORKERS}}{\text{DEMAND FOR UNSKILLED WORKERS}}$, more than broadened educational opportunities will increase the ratio, $\frac{\text{SUPPLY OF SKILLED WORKERS}}{\text{SUPPLY OF UNSKILLED WORKERS}}$, at a given set of relative wages.[11] This possibility could manifest itself by drawing an increasing fraction of full-time adult male earners toward skilled trades, with their places being taken (in part) by "the transient, the very young, the very old, and the physically, mentally and socially handicapped."

However, this "labor reserve" has always been available and, moreover, was in the past bolstered by elements no longer available, e.g., children and immigrants. Perlman offers no reason to suppose that the net result of these various factors should be a different secular trend in the skill margin than has existed hitherto. Nevertheless, it is possible that technical progress in transportation (e.g., the automobile) and in household appliances has shifted downward the supply schedule of the typical housewife's labor services.[12] In considering this possibility, it is necessary to recognize that many housewives, wishing employ-

---

[10] R. Perlman, "Forces Widening Occupational Wage Differentials," *Review of Economics and Statistics*, May 1958, pp. 107-115.

[11] This statement, and the one following, is my interpretation of Perlman's argument on p. 113.

[12] The secular rise in the fraction of the female population in the labor force is, of course, no evidence for or against this possibility; at least part of this rise has been simply a movement along a given supply function in response to increased demand; on this point the reader should see the paper of Jacob Mincer in this volume.

ment at going wage rates, have often been frustrated by employer hiring requirements or legal restraints on hiring, or both.[13] Relaxation of either of these restraints clearly may lower unskilled wage rates relative to others.[14]

Another possibility is that with rising family incomes it is possible that secondary earners will tend to substitute lower-paying, but pleasanter, jobs for jobs with the reverse characteristics. This would, *ceteris paribus*, reduce the wage rates on what have traditionally been considered pleasant jobs, and raise them on jobs traditionally considered unpleasant. If we assume unskilled manual labor to be "unpleasant," and white-collar jobs to be "pleasant," this would imply a decline in the relative earnings of white-collar to manual jobs. It seems likely that something of this sort has happened over the last half-century.[15]

In short, it is possible that the concomitants of economic progress will, as Douglas once surmised, transform the occupational wage structure so that the jobs at the bottom will be comparatively pleasant and their low remuneration a "compensating" differential. Whether this comes to pass will depend more upon employer hiring standards concerning part-time workers, especially married women, etc., and upon legal and customary restraints upon hourly wages, than upon the relative costs of educating such workers.

In other words, the secular behavior of skill differentials reflects not only variations in relative costs of "producing" skilled and unskilled workers, but also the restraints upon the labor market imposed by legal action (e.g., minimum wage laws, restrictions on child labor, etc.) and the variations in relative labor supply of skilled and unskilled labor services consequent upon rising real incomes. The operation of these latter factors *could* alter the trend in skill differentials and make it widen in the future; however, in our judgment there is no reason for thinking that these forces will be more powerful in the future than they have been heretofore.

So far in our discussion we have deliberately ignored the alleged influence of inflation on the skill differential. One writer (Perlman)

[13] For example, minimum wage laws, laws against industrial homework, etc.
[14] I have discussed this point elsewhere: "Theory of Occupational Wage Differentials," pp. 838-840.
[15] Cf. K. M. McCaffree, "The Earnings Differential Between White Collar and Manual Occupations," *Review of Economics and Statistics*, Feb. 1953, pp. 20-30, especially pp. 20-21; also P. H. Douglas, *Real Wages in the United States, 1890-1926*, Boston, Houghton Mifflin, 1930, pp. 367-368.

contends that "our inflation-conscious public, government, and monetary authorities will exert every effort to stabilize prices, thus removing the strongest force in narrowing the differential—inflation."[16] Let us put aside the prognostication about the future of the price level and concentrate on the analytical issue—the relation of wage structure and inflation. Perlman's contention is that unskilled workers "need" larger percentage increases in hourly wages than skilled and, therefore, exert "more urgent upward pressure on wages."[17]

This argument is not peculiar to any one author,[18] but despite its currency, we find it simply implausible. Our objection to the argument does not refer to its use as an ad hoc explanation of events in a specific (short-run) situation; in such applications, one must judge it as best one can, case by case. The following remarks are directed solely to its use as an explanation of a secular trend in wage differentials.

As we have argued elsewhere, there is, in nearly every community, a minimum real hourly wage below which the hiring of labor services is not permitted.[19] The minimum is closely related to unskilled wage rates (but not to skilled rates) and variations in it may therefore have a marked—and possibly permanent—effect on skill differentials. The argument we are considering goes further: it alleges (in effect) that this minimum is subject to a money illusion; i.e., the relative value of the minimum rises with the price level in such a way that the greater the secular rise of the latter, the greater the secular decline in the skill margin. Testing this contention would not be difficult if we were free to assume that both the skilled and the unskilled labor markets were in equilibrium. However, the existence of a minimum real wage has frequently caused unemployment of the unskilled; this is one of the strongest arguments to support the hypothesis of a minimum real wage. This makes the hypothesis of labor market equilibrium doubtful, which, in turn, puts the above-mentioned money-illusion thesis beyond reach of simple tests.[20] For the present, one is free to accept it if he chooses; but there is no reason for doing so.

---

[16] Perlman, "Forces Widening," p. 115.

[17] This is a dubious contention for periods of full employment which frequently coexist with inflation. For with full employment, families whose principal earner has deficient wages can remedy the deficit by supplying secondary earners. That is, since unemployment hits the unskilled more than the skilled, full employment benefits them proportionately more.

[18] For example, it is also expressed by Knowles and Robertson, "Differences between the Wages of Skilled and Unskilled Workers, 1880-1950," *Bulletin of the Oxford Institute of Statistics*, Apr. 1951, pp. 109-127.

[19] Reder, "Theory of Occupational," pp. 839-840.

[20] What is needed, as a minimum, are data measuring excess demand or unem-

THE PATTERN OF SHORT-RUN FLUCTUATIONS IN SKILL MARGINS

It is generally agreed that in the short run skill margins change relatively little during "normal" periods, but contract sharply during periods of over-full employment. It is also possible that they widen during major depressions, though this is not clear.[21] We have attempted elsewhere to account for the sharp reduction in skill margins during the two World Wars when there was excess demand for all types of labor.[22] What is not accounted for is why the sharp narrowing of occupational wage rates that has occurred during war periods has been only partially reversed subsequently.

If we grant that there is a secular decline in the skill margin, and that little or no decline occurs in "normal" periods, it is a matter of arithmetic that wartime declines must exceed postwar increases. The analytical question is why a trend that presumably reflects more or less steady changes in supply should manifest itself in short violent movements followed by long periods of comparative quiescence. There may be many possible explanations of this phenomenon; let us consider two.

The first of these is as follows: the relative supply of skilled and unskilled workers is only indirectly affected by the educational attainment of the labor force. Having more schooling does not automatically fit a man for a more skilled job; it merely increases his ability to absorb the specific training that qualifies him for such a job. To obtain this training it is necessary to serve an apprenticeship, attend a trade school, or get it on the job. In some cases (e.g., where training must come through a union-influenced apprentice program), availability of training may be limited by the current employment situation. In others, workers seem uninterested in taking advantage of training programs unless they are connected with the imminent prospect of promotion or unless they involve on-the-job training. This lack of interest largely reflects the apparent reluctance (or inability) of employers

---

ployment for skilled and unskilled workers, separately, under conditions of secular inflation; i.e., we need long-time series or at least a few observations well separated in time.

[21] Keat ("Changes in Occupational," Chapter II) finds evidence of this in both the 1920-21 and 1929-32 depressions. P. W. Bell ("Cyclical Variations and Trends in Occupational Wage Differentials in American Industry since 1914," Review of Economics and Statistics, Nov. 1951, pp. 329-337), however, found a widening of the differential only in the 1920-21 contraction. Knowles and Robertson ("Differences Between the Wages," especially p. 111) found that skill differentials did not widen in Great Britain during 1929-32, though they did in the early 1920's.

[22] Reder, "Theory of Occupational," pp. 840-845.

to accept inexperienced or partially skilled workers merely in order to reduce the wage premium on skilled jobs. According to this piece of speculation, in "normal" times, supply and demand for skilled workers is kept more or less in balance at current skill margins by the various obstacles (and discouragements) to acquiring requisite skill.

To elaborate a bit: Much of the difference between a highly competent skilled worker and one less competent lies in the greater range of tasks that the more competent worker can perform. Assuming, realistically, that labor turnover involves expense,[23] the differential advantage of the more competent skilled worker to his employer will become greater the more varied are the tasks that the firm's output pattern imposes on him. Conversely, long runs of one particular product minimize variation in a skilled worker's productive role, and hence in his differential advantage.

During a war period, huge orders create the possibility of producing long runs of one particular product. This makes it possible to keep partially trained workers continuously occupied at a narrow range of tasks; consequently, it may—though it need not—absolutely reduce the demand for the broadly trained. Put differently, the elasticity of substitution between partially (narrowly) and fully (broadly) skilled workers is increased. Furthermore, in wartime the premium on speed of delivery makes it more profitable than normally to hire workers whose limited skills compel them to be idle—"unproductive"—for part of the time spent on the job. The relatively short and simple training needed to learn one or a few specific skills further encourages training and use of partially skilled workers.[24]

In short, in a war period, there is a relative shift in labor demand from more to less broadly skilled workers, with the less broadly skilled tending to acquire the titles but only part of the functions of those more fully trained. The effect is (1) to increase the supply of workers able to fill jobs with skilled titles and (2) to curb the increase in demand for workers with specific high-level skills. While (1) acts as a brake upon wage increases to those holding jobs with skilled titles,[25] (2) curbs wage increases to those who have broad skills.

[23] The importance of this point is brought home by an unpublished doctoral dissertation of W. Y. Oi of the University of Chicago.

[24] This statement implies that firms become short-run monopsonists with regard to fully trained workers, but not with regard to the partially trained (see fuller discussion below).

[25] Which is what the data reflect.

After the war, labor demand reverts, more or less, to its prewar composition in response to the relative decline in large orders which require long runs and permit the use of limited skill workers. However, the partial training acquired during the war reduces the prime cost of becoming fully trained, as compared with starting from scratch. Furthermore, many of the workers promoted during the war display such industry and aptitude that they are offered continued employment on skilled jobs if only they acquire the full range of skills needed for peacetime employment; sometimes employers will even defray the training costs involved. The effect of a job promise, combined with successful experience, is greatly to reduce the uncertainty of getting employment which is a real, though nonpecuniary, cost of training. Thus, the relative supply of skilled workers is increased, which tends to prevent a return to the prewar skill margin.

A second explanation is suggested by the behavior of "experience differentials." By experience differentials I refer to the wage differentials that are associated with length of service in a given firm or organization. There is a very extensive overlap of skill and experience; in many cases skill, and the reward thereof, is simply a by-product of long experience in a particular line of work, and is acquired more or less by osmosis. Often, when an employer specifies that he wants an "experienced" worker, what he means is that he wants a relatively skilled one, and considers successful experience as an indication of skill. Consequently, it is not surprising that skill and experience should be confused, both in practical and theoretical discourse.

For reasons that will become apparent, we believe that the wages of unskilled or inexperienced workers or both are apt to be more sensitive to the state of the labor market than those of workers with the reverse characteristics. In support of this proposition, let us consider a rather rare type of data: the behavior of earnings data classified by years of experience of the earner. Such data are quite rare: one of the few good sources is the data for engineers presented by Blank and Stigler.[26] These data are the monthly salaries of engineers, classified by years of

---

[26] D. M. Blank and G. J. Stigler, *The Demand and Supply of Scientific Personnel*, New York, National Bureau of Economic Research, 1957; see Appendix Tables A-3 (p. 117), A-9 (pp. 133-134), A-14 and A-15 (pp. 140-141).

Since this section was written, an excellent study by Robert Evans, Jr. ("Worker Quality and Wage Dispersion: An Analysis of a Clerical Labor Market in Boston," *Proc. Industrial Relations Research Association*, Dec. 1961, pp. 246-259) has appeared. In his paper, Evans presents strong evidence of experience differentials among Boston stenographers (see pp. 250-251).

experience, for selected years in the period from 1894 to 1953; they reveal a pronounced upward trend in the ratio (1) of the salaries of starting engineers[27] to those of experienced engineers and (2) of the salaries of less experienced engineers to those of more experienced. What is more to our present purpose, these ratios rose especially rapidly in periods when the over-all demand for engineers rose with unusual speed but then subsequently declined, contrary to trend, when the demand for engineers declined. For example: during World Wars I and II and during the Korean episode (periods of sharp increase in demand) the salaries of inexperienced engineers rose markedly relative to those of engineers with more experience.[28] And, in each case,

[27] That is, those with less than one year of experience. Years of experience refers to years elapsed since start of first professional job, though in some cases this is estimated (imperfectly) by the difference between an engineer's age and the median age at which graduate engineers receive their first degree. Thus defined, experience is not length of experience with one firm as the argument requires; however, it is likely to be strongly correlated with it.

[28] As Blank and Stigler summarize the data for the World War I period, "the increase in earnings at the starting level and at one and two years experience ranged between 61 and 80 per cent between 1914-1916 and 1919-1921, while the increase for engineering graduates with 10, 15 and 20 years experience ranged between zero and 20 per cent" (*The Demand and Supply*, pp. 124-125, and Table A-5).

For the World War II period, the data in Table A-8 (p. 130 of Blank and Stigler) show that the median salary for engineers with less than 1 year of experience rose by 80 per cent between 1939 and 1946, but rose by only 58 per cent (during the same period) for those with 9-11 years of experience and by only 27 per cent for those with 30-34 years experience. (Tables A-10 and A-11, pp. 135-136, show that a similar relation existed within each field of engineering.)

During the Korean War, average monthly salaries for engineers of varying levels of experience behaved as indicated in the following table, which shows the annual percentage changes in average monthly salaries of research engineers and scientists with B.S. degrees, by years of experience, 1948-55. The relevant pairs of years are 1951-52 and 1952-53.

*Percentage Changes, by Years of Experience*

|  | 0 | 1 | 9 | 10 | 11 |
|---|---|---|---|---|---|
| 1948-49 | −3.2 | −0.3 | 2.8 | 1.1 | 0.9 |
| 1949-50 | 1.8 | 1.7 | 2.0 | 3.5 | 3.2 |
| 1950-51 | 6.9 | 5.0 | 7.6 | 6.7 | 6.9 |
| 1951-52 | 11.3 | 12.7 | 8.2 | 9.4 | 8.1 |
| 1952-53 | 6.8 | 6.7 | 3.8 | 4.0 | 4.4 |
| 1953-54 | 3.7 | 5.5 | 1.6 | 2.1 | 3.4 |
| 1954-55 | 7.2 | 5.0 | 16.6 | 8.9 | 8.0 |

SOURCE: National Survey of Professional Scientific Salaries, Los Alamos Scientific Laboratory of the University of California, 1949 through 1955. Each set of percentages derived from data collected in a single survey, to avoid the effects of changes in coverage. Taken from Blank and Stigler, Table A-15, p. 141.

soon after the demand for engineering service slackened, the salaries of inexperienced engineers underwent a relative decline.[29] Furthermore, during the depressed 1930's (1929-39), the salaries of inexperienced engineers declined relative to those with more experience.[30]

It is possible that this argument rests upon a statistical mirage. That is, the tendency for the experience differential among engineers to diminish in periods of sharp increase in demand might be due mainly to the fact that in such periods demand is concentrated on certain newly developed specialties (e.g., in the early 1950's, the strong demand was for electronic engineers, aeronautical engineers, and so forth) in which there is literally no stock of experienced practitioners. If so, the relative increase in wages of the inexperienced has occurred only because the pressure of increased demand has been greatest in those specialties where the number of experienced engineers was extremely small relative to demand. If this were the whole story, we would expect that there would be no tendency for the experience differential, within given categories of engineers (especially those little affected by tem-

[29] In the post-World War I period, from 1919 to 1924, the median monthly starting salary for engineers rose by 14 per cent, while that of engineers with 9-11 years experience rose by one-third (Table A-6, Blank and Stigler, *The Demand and Supply*, p. 126).

Data for the post-World War II period are given in the table in footnote 28. These data show that in each of the pairs of years between 1948 and 1951 (with the exception of new graduates as compared with those of 10 and 11 years experience in 1950-51) the salaries of engineers with zero or one year of experience declined relative to those with 9, 10, or 11 years of experience. In the post-Korean period, 1953-54 and 1954-55, the wages of the engineers with zero and one year of experience declined relative to those with 9 or more years. This decline does not appear in 1953-54, but it is marked in 1954-55 and also in the two-year period 1953-55.

[30] Between 1929 and 1932, the median salary of engineers with less than one year's experience declined relatively more than that of all engineers; salaries for those with one year's experience fell 26.5 per cent as compared to 18.7 per cent for all engineers. For the decade 1929-39, the median for beginning engineers declined 14.1 per cent; for all engineers the decline was 4.2 per cent.

From 1932 to 1934 the median salary of new engineers declined less than for all engineers (Blank and Stigler, *The Demand and Supply*, Table A-8, p. 130). This accompanied a marked decline in the ratio of the interquartile difference to the median from .43 to .35 for engineers with less than 1 year of experience, while the corresponding ratio for those with 9-11 years of experience was virtually unchanged (.45 in 1932 and .44 in 1934) and increased from .72 to .75 for those with 30-34 years of experience (Blank and Stigler, Table A-3, p. 117). I would suggest that this reflects the upward pressure upon very low wages that stemmed from the National Industrial Recovery Act and related phenomena; this interpretation is supported by the fact that, between 1932 and 1934, the lowest quartile of salaries for engineers with less than 1 year of experience rose from $89 to $91 per month, while the median fell from $111 to $110 and the highest quartile fell from $137 to $129. For experienced engineers, all quartiles fell from 1932 to 1934.

porary "shortages"), to contract. However, the available data are inconsistent with this surmise; during World War II, at least, the "margin for experience" contracted in each of the five specialties for which data are available.[31]

Therefore, for the present we shall assume that the behavior of the experience differential is not entirely due to a statistical mirage and, in part, reflects other factors. One of these may be that the relative demand for inexperienced (as against experienced) engineers increases when total demand for engineers increases, and vice versa.

One possible explanation of why it is more profitable, given the initial difference in salaries, to train and promote inexperienced engineers to senior positions than to recruit experienced engineers *in a tight labor market*, but that it is more profitable to do the reverse in other kinds of markets, is as follows.

In a normal labor market, the individual firm can hire both experienced and inexperienced engineers in the quantities it desires from the unemployed resulting from normal labor turnover. But in a tight labor market, experienced engineers cannot be hired from the ranks of the unemployed, but must be bid away from their current employers. (The reverse is true of newly graduated and, by definition, inexperienced engineers.) There are two reasons why this is more costly than hiring comparable engineers who are currently unemployed: (1) it is time-consuming to find an appropriately skilled and experienced engineer who is currently employed and "pirate" him and (2) it is costly to induce him to leave a situation where he has known and favorable prospects for advancement, good personal relations, etc. and, where done, it is usually at a substantial increase over his current salary. Both

---

[31] Blank and Stigler, *The Demand and Supply*, p. 136.
Despite these facts, there may be a connection between the sharp rise in demand for certain specialties, and the contraction in the experience differential. Consider: the sharp rise in the entrance rates for certain types of engineers may have led to a switch to those specialties by students—which could occur within two years—thereby decreasing the relative supply of graduates in other fields and (*ceteris paribus*) causing a rise in their entrance rate. Whether such a shift took place during (say) the Korean episode is not easy to determine: the data on percentage of engineering degrees awarded in various fields reveal a suspicious tendency for the percentage in "other" to rise from 1950 to 1953. (Cf. Blank and Stigler, Tables C-5, C-6, C-7, and C-8, pp. 160-165. "Other" is other than civil, mechanical, electrical, chemical and mining; specifically it includes aeronautical and electronic engineers.) However, it is obvious that a more detailed analysis is necessary to see if the data will bear this interpretation; but even if they do, it is far from clear that this "mirage argument" provides a complete explanation of the behavior of the experience differential.

of these factors make the *marginal cost* of hiring *additional* experienced engineers rise substantially when the labor market tightens, but do not affect the wage rate that must be paid to those experienced engineers already hired, provided no new ones are added. And they do not apply to new engineering graduates. Hence, the marginal cost of recruiting experienced engineers rises relative to that of hiring inexperienced ones, even though their relative wage rates remain unchanged.[32] This tends to reduce the demand for additional experienced engineers (relative to that for inexperienced) at given relative wage rates, thereby (given the supply functions) driving up the relative wages of the inexperienced.[33]

Conversely, when the market for engineers loosens, it becomes easier for an employer who needs an experienced engineer to find one currently looking for a job so that the marginal cost of hiring him is no greater than the wage paid those already employed. Thus, when the over-all demand for engineers falls, the marginal cost of hiring an experienced one falls relatively (to that of hiring an inexperienced one), if relative wage rates are unchanged; therefore there is a tendency for the relative demand for and wages of the inexperienced to decline.

This explanation applies directly to the case of engineers. Superficially, at least, it also seems consistent with the behavior of teachers' salaries. And we believe it is applicable to a wide variety of labor market situations. Indeed, whenever a firm has an incentive to prefer previously hired workers to new ones—either because of a desire to minimize the costs of labor turnover or because it has made an investment in training its workers—it will try to keep its present employees from desiring to leave. Since it does not have a parallel incentive for the newly hired, it may follow the market for that group, but maintain a given wage rate for each job among the more experienced.[34] This

[32] That is, in a tight labor market, the supply curve of experienced engineers to a firm develops a discontinuity at the quantity currently hired. However, this discontinuity disappears—or is greatly reduced—in a "normal" or "loose" market; this is a species of monopsonistic behavior.

[33] One would expect that the (few) experienced engineers who do get onto the labor market when it is tight would receive higher wages than those who do not. Perhaps they do, but two contrary possibilities must be considered: (1) that the experienced engineers appearing on the market may be an inferior sample of the relevant population and (2) that, because of the market situation, employers have made such *short-run* arrangements that they cannot effectively use additional experienced men. Furthermore, it is notoriously difficult to discriminate in favor of newcomers without creating grave discontent among old employees. The need to extend the "recruitment price" to those already hired may be a serious deterrent to recruiting experienced personnel; this is typical of monopsony.

[34] To do this a firm need not juggle its starting rate continuously. It will suffice

will generate a pattern of fluctuations in experience differentials in response to labor demand similar to that which students have observed. Given the association between skill and experience, which is implied by the practice of promotion from within, the skill differential is likely to move with the experience differential.

## Interindustry Differentials

### LONG RUN[35]

Most discussions of interindustry wage differentials proceed without much explicit consideration of economic theory. The literature abounds in ad hoc hypotheses, some of which are consistent with neoclassical price theory but many of which are not. However, these various hypotheses are usually treated as being equally plausible, a priori; consistency with the implications of price theory has counted for very little in appraising the merits of a theory. Our attitude is somewhat different; we believe that if a theory is inconsistent with the implications of price theory it is cause for concern, and that an explanation is in order. Consequently it will be helpful if we begin our discussion by spelling out what is implied by price theory for interindustrial differentials.

In the long run, under competitive conditions,[36] any industry will pay the same price for a given grade of labor as any other industry hiring in the same location. This remark must be qualified for differences in the nonpecuniary attractions of different industries and locations, but let us abstract from these at first. Therefore, in the long run, real wage differentials among industries will reflect differences in the skill mix. Money wage differences among locations, for given skill, should be no greater than can be rationalized by differences in living costs.

---

simply to have two or more similar entering job titles with different rates, and hire for the job title consistent with the current market rate.

[35] In this section, the distinction between long and short run is drawn very sharply. The theoretical basis of the distinction is the usual Marshallian one. In practice, we interpret a period as long, for the purpose in hand, if shifting the initial or terminal date to any other year in the same reference cycle would not alter the argument. Specifically, we regard 1899-1953 or 1909-53 or even 1929-53 as "long periods," but not 1929-38.

In the Methodological Appendix, the argument of this section concerning the relation of long run and short run, the "competitive hypothesis," and related matters is stated in more detail.

[36] We shall assume, except when the contrary is specifically stated, that competitive conditions exist.

This means that there should be no association of industry wage levels either with the amount of labor employed or with the amount of capital employed (total or per worker) except insofar as either of these quantities is correlated with the skill mix. This absence of association between industry wage level and quantity of labor utilized is an important distinguishing characteristic between long- and short-run situations (see Appendix). In the short run, the greater the increase in employment over the recent past, the more likely is an industry to encounter rising wages because of short-run inelasticities of labor supply; hence the theory implies a positive association of increase in labor quantity used and wage increase in short periods, but not in long periods. Moreover, it seems reasonable to suppose that it will be more likely that skilled labor will become relatively scarce[37] to an expanding industry than nonskilled. Therefore, in the short run, skill differentials should be positively associated with changes in employment.[38]

That is, we interpret price theory as saying that in the long run each industry's wage level will, ceteris paribus, vary in the same direction as its skill and locational mix (see below) and, in particular, will not be related to changes in the quantities of labor or capital employed. Now if ceteris were exactly paribus, and our sample were large enough, the correlation coefficient (among industries) between long-run changes in wage levels and those in (any) factor quantity would be exactly zero. But our samples are limited and ceteris is never exactly paribus; hence the theory will be considered "not inconsistent with the evidence" if the above mentioned correlation coefficients are approximately zero. Inconsistency with the evidence will emerge if ceteris is insufficiently paribus in the sense that forces affecting long-run relative wage changes are significantly correlated with long-run relative changes in factor quantities.[39]

[37] That is, it will take longer to train workers with skills peculiar to the industry than unspecialized workers and hence, for a time, their elasticity of supply will be less.

[38] This is analogous to Clark Kerr's contention that, "The lesser the degree and the greater the rate of industrialization, the wider will be the occupational differentials and the greater the premiums for skill." (See "Wage Relationships—The Comparative Impact of Market and Power Forces," in The Theory of Wage Determination [cited in footnote 1], p. 187, especially no. 2.)

[39] Now a word about the nonpecuniary attraction of different industries. It is hard to believe—though imaginable—that industries as such have differing degrees of nonpecuniary attractiveness to labor force members. Most of the apparent nonpecuniary differences among industries would seem to boil down to differences in the relative attractiveness of different locations and of the specific jobs offered. For example, we submit that a job as bookkeeper in the New York office of a coal

Now, how do these inferences square with available evidence? One body of evidence is presented by Fabricant[40] in a study of average growth rates of real hourly wages, labor employed, and capital utilized in 33 industries from 1899 to 1953.[41] Let us suppose that in a period of 54 years the long-run forces that affect the relative levels of industries' wages make changes sufficiently large to permit us to treat differences between 1899 and 1953 as reflecting mainly these forces and, only to a minor degree, random and short-run forces.[42] That is, the differences between 1899 and 1953 are assumed to be explicable on the hypothesis that they are, save for random disturbances, positions of comparative statics. If so, there should be no association between either the relative growth in the quantity of labor utilized, or the relative growth in the stock of capital employed in a given industry, and the relative growth in wages (measured by average hourly earnings) in that industry. The rank correlation coefficients between (a) wages and labor employed and (b) wages and tangible capital owned,[43] with each industry taken as a single observation, are +.21 between wages and labor quantity and +.29 between wages and capital quantity. The standard error of the rank correlation coefficient with 33 observations is .17, and hence neither coefficient is statistically significant at the 5 per cent level.[44]

---

mining firm is no less attractive than a similar job in the same location in an electronics firm. However, coal mining will offer proportionately more jobs in mining towns, and underground, than (say) electronics manufacturing and therefore might well face a higher *pecuniary* supply price for its labor.

It would not be correct, conceptually, to identify unskilled jobs with unattractive ones, but historically there has been a strong positive association. In general, as industries have shifted away from unskilled labor they have also improved working conditions and reduced nonpecuniary disutilities. And since it is obviously very difficult to measure or indicate the relative nonpecuniary attractiveness of different industries, we have assumed that the *rank* of the various industries with respect to nonpecuniary utilities varies with the percentage of its workers employed in unskilled jobs. Clearly, this is a rough approximation which must later be improved upon.

[40] S. Fabricant, *Basic Facts on Productivity Change*, New York, NBER, Occasional Paper 63, 1959, especially pp. 29-37.

[41] These data are presented in extended form in J. W. Kendrick, *Productivity Trends in the United States*, Princeton for NBER, 1961.

[42] See Methodological Appendix.

[43] Perforce, we use the Kendrick-Fabricant definitions of labor, capital, and output. The data used are contained in Table B, pp. 46-47, of Fabricant, *Basic Facts*. "Wages," "labor," and "capital" mean here percentage change in each of these variables between 1899 and 1953.

[44] It might be contended that, because we have two coefficients differing from zero, and with the same sign, the two coefficients together differ significantly from

These findings are compatible with the competitive hypothesis.[45] Indeed, the fact that both of the correlation coefficients are positive, as well as small, is what might be expected because of the tendency for rapidly growing industries to locate (as of 1953) in relatively high-wage urban centers. There is, moreover, further evidence that is also favorable to the competitive hypothesis.

(1) Contrary to much of the recent literature, there was only a slight correlation between productivity[46] and average hourly labor compensation among 33 industry groups during the period 1899-1953. The rank correlation during that period was +.24 (insignificant at the 5 per cent level); in various shorter periods the coefficient was appreciably higher.[47] Confirming this is the fact that during 1899-1947, among 80 manufacturing industries, the rank correlation coefficient between output per man-hour and average hourly labor compensation was 0.26—not quite significant at 5 per cent; during individual decades of that period, the coefficient was invariably higher than this.[48]

It would be possible to hide behind the insignificance of the above coefficients and say that the competitive hypothesis is not disconfirmed. However, it seems more plausible to suppose that the two coefficients (noted above) together indicate the operation of some rather weak force systematically correlating average hourly labor compensation and productivity. One explanation of this that would not be incom-

---

zero (to which theory implies they are both equal). However, output, capital, and labor are all highly correlated so that we cannot suppose the two coefficients to be independent, and combining the tests is therefore extremely difficult.

[45] By "competitive hypothesis," I mean the hypothesis that prices and quantities behave as though they were in long-run equilibrium under conditions of pure competition. When we speak of the short-run competitive hypothesis we mean the same hypothesis except for the modifications introduced by the substitution of Marshallian short-run equilibrium for long run (see Appendix).

[46] "Productivity" is total productivity as defined by Kendrick; i.e., output per unit of input of both labor and capital. However, output per unit of labor input is highly correlated with total productivity (rank correlation coefficient among 33 industry groups is +0.94) and, as Kendrick says, "Thus analysis of productivity change based on output-per-manhour measures should give results comparable to analyses based on total factor productivity" (p. 155). Therefore, we shall consider Kendrick's results, where "total productivity" is interchangeable with man-hour productivity.

The competitive hypothesis implies that there will be no correlation *in the long run* between (average) productivity and wages. That is, industries in which average productivity grows relatively to others will show an increasing ratio of average to marginal (labor) productivity because all industries must pay the same for given grades of labor *in the long run*. This, of course, is not true in the short run.

[47] Kendrick, *Productivity Trends*, Table 55, p. 198.
[48] *Ibid.*

patible with the competitive hypothesis is that there is a tendency for industries with a greater than average increase in productivity to experience a greater than average "improvement" in skill mix[49] and, therefore, to have a greater than average increase in hourly labor compensation. Though not directly testable, this explanation seems to have considerable plausibility. Another possibility consistent with the competitive hypothesis is that increases in productivity are weakly associated with a tendency toward urbanization and higher wages. Last, but not least, in the short run a positive correlation between relative wages and employment is to be expected (see below). This coefficient may approach zero in the long run, but it may remain positive and finite for a very long time—long enough to generate (at least) some of the positive coefficients reported in this section.[50] Obviously, failing empirical tests of these and rival hypotheses, there is room for doubt and debate.

(2) Another finding consistent with the competitive hypothesis is that the ratio of capital compensation per unit of capital service is only slightly correlated with changes in average hourly labor compensation among 33 industries in the period 1929-53; the rank correlation coefficient was only +.12.[51] The competitive hypothesis implies that this coefficient be zero. Though the coefficient is insignificant at the 5 per cent level, we are inclined to take its positive sign seriously and rationalize it as follows: in industries with a higher than average rate of increase in productivity, there is a slight tendency for both labor and capital "quality" to increase more than the average.[52] A further finding that tends to support this conclusion is the very slight positive correlation (+.05) between (1) factor compensation (of both labor and capital) per unit of input, and (2) productivity among 33 industries in 1899-1953.

[49] That is, a greater than average increase in the percentage of high-earning and presumably skilled workers employed. "Skill mix" is defined more precisely below.

[50] This possibility is discussed in more detail in the appendix. The point was raised in discussion by both M. J. Bailey and H. G. Lewis.

[51] Kendrick, *Productivity Trends*, Table 55.

[52] By "capital quality," I refer to the intangible (and unmeasured) inputs that add to the nonlabor income of an enterprise, but are not included in its measured capital stock. Included in these would be entrepreneurial skill and investment in research and development. In this connection, Kendrick reports (Ch. VI, p. 183) a rank correlation coefficient of +.68 between research and development expenditures, as a per cent of sales in 1953, and the average annual rate of change in total factor productivity in 1948-53.

Contrasted with these slight positive correlations is the very sub-stantial negative rank correlation coefficient, during 1899-1953, between unit prices of output and factor productivity, —.55, which is significant at 5 per cent.[53] The sign of this coefficient is what the competitive hypothesis would lead one to expect. Combined with the other findings cited it bears out the view that, as between industries, the relative gains of factor productivity are passed on to buyers and none accrue to the factors employed.

(3) Still a third finding that bears upon the competitive hypothesis is the behavior of the interindustrial wage structure itself. We have seen that there has been a secular decline in skill differentials in the economy as a whole. What has been said of skill differentials also applies to geographical differentials.

We also know that the ranking of industries with respect to their level of earnings per worker is quite stable over long periods of time. That is, the rank correlation of an industry's position in the industrial wage hierarchy in one year (or period) with another very distant in time is "quite high." For example, Cullen[54] found a rank correlation coefficient of +.66 for 76 manufacturing industries between ranks of per-worker annual earnings in 1899 and 1950. In Kendrick's data, the rank correlation between average hourly earnings in 1899-1909 and 1948-53 was +.46.[55] Slichter found a coefficient of rank correlation of +.7289 between the average hourly earnings of male unskilled labor among 20 manufacturing industries in 1923 and 1946.[56]

Because of the secular decline in skill margins and in regional differ-entials, the competitive hypothesis implies that there would have been a secular decrease in interindustry relative wage dispersion if the skills and geographical mix had remained more or less unchanged.[57] The evidence that there has been a secular decrease in interindustry rela-tive wage dispersion is far from conclusive; and Cullen's scepticism of this evidence as proof of secularly[58] reduced dispersion seems fully

[53] Kendrick, *Productivity Trends*, Table 57.
[54] D. E. Cullen, "The Inter-industry Wage Structure, 1899-1950," *American Economic Review*, June 1956, pp. 353-69, especially Table II, p. 359.
[55] Kendrick, *Productivity Trends*, computed from Table 54.
[56] S. H. Slichter, "Notes on the Structure of Wages," *Review of Economics and Statistics*, Feb. 1950, pp. 80-91, especially p. 88 and Table 7.
[57] Kerr ("Wage Relationships," pp. 189-191) argues this very strongly, though without indicating the crucial role of the competitive hypothesis.
[58] The very marked and undisputed declines since the late 1930's are irrelevant for long-run analysis, as it seems clear that at that time these differentials were abnormally large.

warranted.[59] It is possible that further investigation will show that dispersion has indeed been reduced. But if it does not, certain more or less alternative inferences may be drawn: (1) despite the general decline in skill margins, the relative wage premiums that must be paid by industries that are expanding their labor forces rapidly were as great in the late 1940's as at the turn of the century;[60] (2) there was an increasing dispersion in the "richness" of industrial skill mixes[61] which offset the reduced skill margins; (3) there were offsetting inter-industry changes in skill mixes, locational mixes, etc.; and (4) the competitive hypothesis is wrong. These inferences are not mutually

[59] Cullen, "The Inter-industry Wage Structure," p. 361. Further evidence to the same general effect is provided by correlating the percentage wage change between 1899 and 1953 (from Kendrick's data) with the index of "richness of skill mix" by industry, in 1950 (see n. 63). If the relative richness of skill mix of the various industries had been unchanged over time, the percentage wage increase should have been the smaller, the richer the skill mix, because of the secular decline in skill margins. However, the rank correlation coefficient was only −.086 (between richness of skill mix in 1950 and percentage change in wages between 1899 and 1953). The sign is in accord with the hypothesis of no change in relative skill mix, but far too small to be taken seriously.

[60] That is, the industries that are "very high" wage payers in any given year include a disproportionate number of those expanding rapidly, and therefore trying to increase their total labor force; the converse applies to those industries that are "very low" wage payers. Industries at either end of the rankings include a disproportionate fraction of those in temporary disequilibrium. Naturally, those industries need not be the same ones in 1899 and 1950.

[61] By "richness of the skill mix," I refer to the relative numbers of skilled, semi-skilled, and unskilled workers employed. An industry's skill mix is richer, the greater the fraction of the first, and the smaller the fraction of the last in the work force.

We can measure the richness of the skill mix of different industries in 1950 from the statistics of *Occupation by Industry* which, so far as we are aware, has not been published for any other Census. The measure of the richness of an industry's skill mix is defined as the following weighted average:

$$R_i = \frac{\sum\limits_{j=1}^{n} a_{ji} W_j}{E_i} \text{ (males)} + \frac{\sum\limits_{j=1}^{n} a_{ji} W_j}{E_i} \text{ (females)}$$

This weighted average refers to the $i$ th industry; $W_j$ is the median annual earnings of persons in the $j$ occupation throughout the economy; $a_{ji}$ is the number of persons of given sex employed in the $i$ th industry, and the $i$ th occupation; and $E_i$ is the number of persons employed in the $i$ th industry. $R_i$ is a weighted average of the nation-wide median occupational earnings of the employees in the $i$ th industry with the fraction of the $i$ th industry employment in the various age-sex classes serving as weights.

Sex, as well as occupation, is treated as a determinant of skill mix because women, even in the same occupational category and industry, tend to be paid less than men (for whatever reason). It would have been better to have corrected our weights for degree of unemployment, but we were unable to do so. The richness of skill mix in 1950 was rank correlated with median industrial annual earnings in 1949 by a coefficient of +.613.

exclusive, and they could all be true to a degree; however, none of the first three has yet been tested, though it is far from impossible to do so.

We have already presented some evidence which tends to reject (4); i.e., which tends to support the competitive hypothesis. And there is some further evidence to the same effect: both Cullen and Woytinsky find evidence of diminishing secular dispersion of interindustrial earning among the particular industries that happened to be at the upper and lower extremes of the distribution in a particular year.[62] This means that, although the over-all interindustry dispersion among a collection of industries may not have diminished appreciably over time, the spread among the group of industries that happened to be paying very high and very low wages in a given base year (e.g., 1899 or 1929) diminished. In other words, the particular industries that are toward the high and low extremes in the interindustrial earnings hierarchy in a given year tended to regress toward the mean with the passage of time.

This is what the competitive hypothesis implies will happen; for, in any given year, part of the interindustry dispersion of wages is due to disequilibrium of industries expanding and contracting employment more than the average, and this source of interindustry wage dispersion is reduced over time by the operation of the price system. The competitive hypothesis implies nothing concerning the long-term trend in interindustrial wage dispersion among a particular group of industries as a whole, except that it should depend solely upon variations in skill and locational differentials and random disturbances.

One further hypothesis, not strictly of a long-run variety, should be mentioned. The rise of an economy from a less- to a more-full utilization of its labor force (including its reserves) may cause a reduction in interindustry differentials, as happened when the economy emerged from the depression of the 1930's to the full employment of

[62] Cullen ("Inter-industry Wage," Table III, p. 361) found a reduction between 1899 and 1947-50 of 8-12 per cent in the difference between the median annual earnings in industries in the upper and lower quartiles of the distribution of 84 manufacturing industries, in 1899. W. S. Woytinsky (*Employment and Wages in the United States*, New York, Twentieth Century Fund, 1953, Chap. 39, pp. 460-462 and 507-509) found a tendency for low-wage industries in 1929 to have climbed relatively to high-wage industries by 1950.

Cullen (pp. 364-365) notes that most of the narrowing in dispersion in his data occurred before 1921. This, of course, would suggest that the short-run disturbances had been washed out before that date. This interpretation of Cullen's findings is different from (and possibly inconsistent with) his own.

the 1940's.[63] Such behavior would follow from the narrowing of skill differentials during such periods. Whether this limited experience can be generalized to a proposition relating level of employment, or growth rate in labor demand, to the interindustry dispersion of wage rates is not clear. However, it is a possibility.

Several other hypotheses concerning the long-run equilibrium industrial structure of wage rates have been advanced by Slichter:[64]

(1) "The average hourly earnings of male unskilled labor (U) tend to be high where the average hourly earnings of male semiskilled and skilled labor (S) are high." Slichter found, in 1939, a rank correlation coefficient of $+.7098$ (among 20 manufacturing industries) between U and S. If this correlation is interpreted as resulting from a tendency for industries using relatively expensive types of skilled labor also to use expensive types of nonskilled, then it is compatible with the competitive hypothesis. Slichter accepts this interpretation in part,[65] but also contends that the correlation is partly due to company wage policy, which presumably is independent of market forces; on this point, see below. It should be noted that it is also possible that Slichter's observation reflects short-period and not long-period forces; i.e., expanding industries are more likely than others to encounter increasing supply prices (as a function of rate of increase of employment) for all kinds of labor.[66]

(2) "The hourly earnings of male common labor (M) have some (not pronounced) tendency to be low where the percentage of women (W) among wage earners is high." The coefficient of rank correlation between M and W in 1939 (for 19 manufacturing industries) was $+.4491$, and in 1929, $+.5224$.[67] This, as Slichter (in effect) argues, may well reflect the operation of the competitive mechanism; i.e.,

---

[63] This has been stressed in two studies of English data: P. Haddy and N. A. Tolles, "British and American Changes in Inter-industry Wage Structure under Full Employment," *Review of Economics and Statistics*, Nov. 1957, pp. 408-414; and P. Haddy and M. E. Currell, British Inter-Industrial Earnings Differentials, 1924-1955," *Economic Journal*, Mar. 1958, pp. 104-111. This tendency also appears in Cullen's data ("Inter-industry Wage") for World War II; however, it does not appear during World War I.

[64] Slichter, "Notes on the Structure of Wages." Slichter does not distinguish carefully between long- and short-run relations; consequently, the interpretation placed on his findings is entirely our own.

[65] *Ibid.*, p. 84.

[66] This possibility would seem less likely in 1939, to which Slichter's data refer, than in the 1920's, 1940's, or 1950's. It is also possible that the correlation reflects the common effect of locational factors.

[67] Industries are ranked in inverse order of male common labor earnings.

women are hired mainly in low-wage industries and men, in order to compete with them, must accept less than the average male wage. That is, the correlation is presumed to reflect competition for similar jobs, and not osmosis. If this explanation is correct, then the industries where women are most highly concentrated should be those in which the unfavored (by the market) males, e.g., Negroes, are also concentrated; and this seems to be the case.[68]

(3) Slichter also found substantial rank correlation between net income after taxes, as a percentage of sales, $\pi$, and average hourly earnings both of unskilled and of skilled and semiskilled workers.[69] Slichter interpreted $\pi$ as an index of profitability. Accepting this interpretation, we could easily rationalize the observed rank correlations as short-period phenomena resulting from the short-run association between increased labor demand and profitability. However, Slichter, like many other writers, contends that this phenomenon "reinforces the view that wages, within a considerable range, reflect managerial discretion, and that where managements are barely breaking even, they tend to keep wages down."[70] This interpretation is incompatible with the competitive hypothesis.

We believe that the importance of this possibility can easily be exaggerated. Nonetheless, the field work on our study of interfirm wage differentials has confirmed the oft-expressed view that large and profitable firms will often ignore local labor market situations by overpaying on certain jobs in certain areas in order to avoid undesired intercompany differentials. Such firms also manifest a desire to be toward the top of any labor market in which they hire, both for reasons of prestige and quality selection.

To be sure, there is a tendency for out-of-line wages to be corrected "as soon as the opportunity presents itself," but it is also true that large firms are more dilatory about correcting overpayment (e.g., red circle rates) than correcting underpayment. This, together with a preference for selective recruitment policies, creates an upward bias in wage level relative to the market as of any given moment. Thus, we would be inclined to agree that large and profitable firms do tend to pay more

[68] The rank correlation coefficient between percentage of women and percentage of Negroes (among males) employed (from 1950 Census data) for 14 industries was +.386; when finance and agriculture are excluded, the coefficient is raised to +.662. However, the osmosis hypothesis requires further investigation.

[69] Slichter, "Notes on the Structure of Wages," p. 88.

[70] Ibid., see also p. 90.

at any one time than could be explained by the competitive hypothesis. However, this cannot explain *movements* in relative wages; at most, it can explain relative wage levels as of a given moment.

These remarks pertain directly to individual firms, and not to entire industries. Their relation to the industrial wage structure results from the fact that in some industries the percentage of workers employed in large firms is greater than in others. Industries concentrating relatively large fractions of their labor forces in large firms should tend to exhibit relatively high concentration ratios;[71] hence there might well be an association between high concentration ratios and high wages at a *given moment of time.*

However, this is no reason to suppose there would be an association between *changes* in relative industrial wage levels over time and the index of concentration as of a given moment, as some writers have argued.[72] These writers contend that the index of concentration is a rough (inverse) indicator of the relative degree of competitiveness of an industry;[73] and that noncompetitive industries tend to raise wages more than others. But, since it is not alleged that the indexes of concentration for different industries have changed during the relevant time period, it cannot be permanent differences in industry structure that are responsible for differential wage behavior; it must be differential *changes* in industry behavior. That is, what must be explained are differential changes in the willingness or ability or both of highly concentrated industries (relative to others) to grant wage increases; to our knowledge this has never been attempted. It should also be noted that to relate *levels* of concentration with *increases* (in favor of concentrated industries) in wages implies a secular increase in wage dispersion which is grossly inconsistent with known facts.

Because the hypothesis that interindustrial differences in degree of monopoly are an important factor in explaining the interindustrial differences in wage behavior has had wide currency, and is obviously a rival to the competitive hypothesis, we have attempted one rather simple test of it. We have taken Nutter's data on the relative extent

[71] As measured by (say) the percentage of the industry's employment concentrated in the four or eight largest firms.

[72] For example, H. M. Levinson, "Post-war Movement in Prices and Wages in Manufacturing Industries," *Study Paper No. 4*, Joint Economic Committee, Congress of the United States, 1960, pp. 2-5 and 21; also J. W. Garbarino, "A Theory of Inter-industry Wage Structure," *Quarterly Journal of Economics*, May 1950, pp. 282-305, especially pp. 299-300.

[73] This is highly debatable but, for the sake of argument, let us concede it.

of monopoly in 1899 and 1937 by major industry groups,[74] and correlated the change in the rankings between those dates with the change in the rankings of wages paid by those groups.[75] The correlation coefficient of these rank changes was —.05, indicating a slight (negligible) tendency for a decrease in monopoly to accompany an increase in wages—inconsistent with the hypothesis.[76]

(4) Slichter alleges a strong inverse association between hourly earnings of unskilled labor and the ratio of payrolls to sales. He explains this by saying: "Managements naturally are more concerned about the rates which they pay for labor when payrolls are large in relation to the receipts of the enterprise than when payrolls are small."[77] One (slightly astonishing) implication of this is that vertical disintegration, per se, leads to high wages. But leaving this aside, let us concede that, in the absence of competition, a low ratio does make it easier for a benevolent employer or an aggressive union to raise wages than otherwise. However, before accepting this as an important determinant of industrial wage differences, we would urge consideration of the following alternative: high ratios of payrolls to sales are more likely to be found in industries that specialize in fabricating operations, and are associated with low wages because the likelihood of such specialization is greater where the fabrication can be performed by low-wage labor.

But at the very most, the above relation obtains only at a given instant. It provides no warrant for a long-run interpretation of Dunlop's contention that "wage and salary rates would be expected to increase most . . . where labor costs are a small percentage of total costs."[78]

[74] G. W. Nutter, The Extent of Enterprise Monopoly in the United States, 1899-1939, University of Chicago Press, 1951, Tables 10 and 11.
[75] The wage figures were obtained as follows: 1953 (annual average) hourly wages were extrapolated back to 1899 by means of Kendrick's data, and ranks were obtained; these were compared with the ranks of median annual earnings per worker in 1939 as reported in the 1940 Census (see H. P. Miller, "Changes in the Industrial Wage Distribution of Wages in the United States, 1939-1949," An Appraisal of the 1950 Census Income Data, Studies in Income and Wealth, Vol. 23, Princeton for NBER, 1958, Table B-2. It is assumed that the 1937 and 1939 rankings would be virtually the same.
[76] David Schwartzman ("Monopoly and Wages," Canadian Journal of Economics and Political Science, Aug. 1960, pp. 428-38) reaches a similar conclusion on the basis of comparing United States and Canadian industries with varying concentration ratios.
[77] Slichter, "Notes on the Structure of Wages," p. 87.
[78] J. T. Dunlop, "Productivity and the Wage Structure," Income, Employment and Public Policy, Essays in Honor of A. H. Hansen," New York, Norton, 1948, p. 360. In fairness to Dunlop, it should be noted that he has not indicated whether

So far as we are aware this contention has never been substantiated *for the long run.*

(5) One determinant of an industry's place in the interindustry wage hierarchy at a given moment is the relative richness of its skill mix. For 1950, we ranked industries by richness of skill mix and correlated this with rank in the interindustry wage hierarchy; the rank correlation coefficient was +.612.[79] This cross-sectional relationship reflects departures from long-run equilibrium, crudeness of industrial classifications, etc. Nonetheless it indicates a substantial degree of relation between the two sets of rankings.

SHORT RUN

Let us begin our discussion of the short-run behavior of the interindustry wage structure by considering the relation of its variations to those in employment. The competitive hypothesis explains such variations as due to wages rising in industries where employment is expanding because of short-run inelasticities of labor supply, and falling in industries where employment is shrinking because of labor immobility. In the short run, *differential* changes in skill mix are assumed to be uncorrelated with differential changes in employment.[80]

There has been a number of studies of the relation of variations in the interindustry wage structure to changes in employment. Unfortunately, not all of their findings are mutually consistent. For example, Garbarino[81] found a rank correlation coefficient of +.48 between percentage changes in hourly earnings and employment (for 34 manufacturing industries) in 1923-40; Ross and Goldner found that in three of four periods studied there was a strong positive association of percentage increases in hourly earnings and percentage increases in employment.[82] Ostry found that in Canada there had been

---

he intended this relationship as long or short run. The short-run version is discussed below.

[79] This coefficient was computed from an analysis of 14 major industry groups.

[80] See Appendix.

[81] Garbarino, "Theory of Inter-industry Wage Structure," p. 304.

[82] A. M. Ross and W. Goldner, "Forces Affecting the Inter-industry Wage Structure," *Quarterly Journal of Economics,* May 1950, pp. 254-281, especially Table VI, and pp. 272-276. The four periods studied were 1933-38, 1938-42, 1942-46, and 1933-46; the deviant period was the wartime interval 1942-46. The authors present no correlations but merely place industries into four quartiles in accordance with the percentage increase in employment.

F. C. Pierson (*Community Wage Patterns,* University of California Press, 1953, Chap. VI) also finds a positive rank correlation between average hourly earnings

an appreciable correlation between percentage changes in hourly earnings and in employment; among 36 industries, the correlation coefficient in 1945-49 was $+.44$; in 1949-56 it was $+.53$, and for 1945-56, $+.56$.[83]

Moreover, Hansen and Rehn, in a study of wage differentials from 1947 to 1954 among eight industries in Sweden,[84] found substantial interindustry correlation between wage drift[85] and excess demand[86] for labor, which is consistent with the hypothesis that short-run wage differentials result mainly from differing rates of increase in labor demand. They found virtually no correlation of wage drift with gains in average man-hour productivity, but were unable to use Swedish profit data for interindustry analyses.

But the data do not all point to one conclusion: Slichter found among 20 industries, during 1923-39, a coefficient of rank correlation (between percentage changes in hourly earnings and percentage changes in employment) of only $+.2812$.[87] Eisemann found that in 1939-47, percentage increases in manufacturing wages were negatively correlated with percentage increases in employment; however, the absolute increase in average hourly earnings was positively correlated with percentage increases in employment.[88] Levinson[89] has found that in 4 of the 11 year-to-year changes between 1947 and 1958 there was

and employment for manufacturing industries among several cities between 1929 and 1939, but not during the war period, 1940-48.

[83] S. W. Ostry, "Inter-industry Earnings Differentials in Canada, 1945-1956," *Industrial and Labor Relations Review*, Apr. 1959, pp. 335-352, especially pp. 341-343.

[84] B. Hansen and Gosta Rehn, "On Wage-Drift: A Problem of Money-Wage Dynamics," *Twenty-five Economic Essays in Honour of Erik Lindahl*, Stockholm, 1956, pp. 87-133, especially pp. 105-106 and 128-133.

[85] That is, wage increase in excess of what was implied in collective bargaining agreements.

[86] That is, unfilled vacancies minus unemployment.

[87] Slichter ("Notes on the Structure of Wages," p. 90) argues very explicitly that the relation between hourly earnings and profits is due to wage policy and not labor-market pressure. He found a small *negative* coefficient of rank correlation between changes in employment and changes in average hourly earnings in 1923-39 for *unskilled* workers (as contrasted to the positive coefficient for all workers). Somehow, this argument is not very impressive. (1) As argued above, one would expect the supply of unskilled workers to a given industry to be more elastic in the short run than that of semiskilled and skilled. (2) Slichter's period is almost identical with that of Garbarino ("Theory of Inter-industry Wage Structure"), who found evidence of a stronger relationship than Slichter, and with better data.

[88] Doris M. Eisemann, "Inter-Industry Wage Changes, 1939-1947," *Review of Economics and Statistics*, Nov. 1956, p. 446.

[89] Levinson, "Post-war Movements," Table 1, p. 3.

a negative correlation among 19 manufacturing industries between percentage changes in straight-time hourly earnings and percentage changes in production worker employment. He also found a negative partial correlation coefficient between this pair of variables for 1947-53 and a negligible positive one ($+.0046$) for 1953-58.[90]

Bowen[91] computed correlation coefficients between percentage changes in average hourly earnings, $w$, and percentage changes in employment, $e$, during six subperiods of the interval 1947-59. These various coefficients reflect the association between $w$ and $e$ among 20 two-digit manufacturing industries. Bowen computed both simple and partial correlation coefficients. The partial coefficients between $w$ and $e$ held constant some or all of the following: (1) average level of profits in the industry; (2) the concentration ratio (in 1954); and (3) the percentage of the production workers unionized (in 1958). All possible first and second order partial correlation coefficients between $w$ and $e$ (holding constant the other variables, both singly and in pairs) are presented. The coefficients show a positive correlation between $w$ and $e$ in the three subperiods when unemployment was relatively low,[92] and this relation is generally stronger in the partial than in the simple coefficients. In the three subperiods in which unemployment was relatively high, the coefficients showed a different pattern: in two of these three subperiods the simple coefficients were negative; in one of them all of the partials were negative; and in another, half of them were negative.

Thus Bowen's findings (on this point) tend to support the competitive hypothesis for periods of "low unemployment," but not for those of higher unemployment. That the relation between $w$ and $e$ should be stronger in periods of low unemployment is in the spirit of the competitive hypothesis (though not its letter);[93] i.e., in periods of low unemployment, short-run elasticities of labor supply to indus-

[90] *Ibid.*, Table 2, p. 4. A. H. Conrad ("The Share of Wages and Salaries in Manufacturing Incomes, 1947-1956," *Study Paper No. 9*, Joint Economic Committee of Congress, Washington, 1959) obtained similar results on *Census of Manufactures* data for all 61 three-digit industries, for the period 1949-56.

[91] W. G. Bowen, *The Wage-Price Issue: A Theoretical Analysis*, Princeton University Press, 1960, pp. 59-66 and Table E-1, pp. 134-135.

[92] The subperiods of low unemployment are characterized by an unemployment percentage (of the civilian labor force) that was "generally below 4.3." The subperiods of high unemployment are those where the unemployment percentage was always above 4.3. Bowen, pp. 24-29.

[93] The letter of the competitive hypothesis makes no provision for unemployment as a variable in supply or demand functions.

tries are likely to be smaller, and differential increases in employment therefore more likely to produce differential wage changes. But if Bowen's findings are accepted, then the competitive hypothesis is uninformative, if not invalid, as an explanation of short-run wage movements in the presence of "appreciable"[94] unemployment.

In short, the evidence does not give unqualified support to the view that short-run variations in labor demand are a major cause of variation in straight-time hourly earnings. Some of the contrary evidence can be "explained away." The adverse findings of Ross and Goldner for 1942-46 and of Eisemann for 1939-47 may well be due to the fact that the war industries which expanded most rapidly were the very ones where dilution of the skill mix was greatest. However, it is harder to explain away the findings of Levinson, Conrad, and especially Bowen. Let us now turn to alternative explanations.

PROFITS, CONCENTRATION, AND RELATED VARIABLES

Levinson suggests that relative industry wage levels have varied either with (industry levels of) current profits or with profits lagged one year.[95] He measures profits as return on stockholders' equity both before or after taxes. This alleged relation is not, of itself, inconsistent with the competitive hypothesis, for the level of current profits would be expected to be associated with recent increases in employment. However, Levinson computes partial correlation coefficients between percentage wage changes, $w$, and percentage increases in employment, $e$ (average profit level, $P$, constant), for 1947-53 and 1953-58 and also between $w$ and $P$ ($e$ constant) for the same interval. In 1947-53, the coefficient between $w$ and $e$ was negative, while that between $w$ and $P$ was positive; in 1953-58, the latter coefficient substantially exceeded the former though both were positive.[96]

These findings were similar to those of Bowen, who finds a consistent positive correlation (among 20 manufacturing industries) between percentage change in average hourly earnings and percentage change in average level of profits.[97] This positive relation is found in the

[94] Using Bowen's 4.3 per cent as a criterion for distinguishing years of appreciable unemployment from others, 33 of the first 58 years of this century were years of "appreciable unemployment." Even if we exclude the 11 years, 1930-40, 22 out of 47 years showed appreciable unemployment. (These figures are Stanley Lebergott's as quoted by Bowen in Appendix A, pp. 99-101.)
[95] Levinson, "Post-war Movement," pp. 2-7.
[96] Levinson, "Post-war Movement," Table 2, p. 4.
[97] Bowen, Wage-Price Issue, pp. 67-69 and 134-135.

simple correlation coefficients in all of Bowen's subperiods; it is also found among the partial coefficients (save for three small negative ones).

What are we to make of these findings? Barring some unperceived differential change in hiring requirements (among industries), we would seem driven to accept Slichter's judgment that "wages, within a considerable range, reflect managerial discretion, that where managements can easily pay high wages they tend to do so, and that where managements are barely breaking even, they tend to keep wages down."[98] This judgment is, of course, incompatible with the competitive hypothesis for the short run.

It is important to distinguish sharply between levels and movements. It is entirely in keeping with the competitive hypothesis that more profitable firms should find it advantageous to demand superior personnel, and pay more to get it. This is essentially what Slichter, Reynolds, and others have contended. What is more difficult to accept is the finding that differences in profit levels also explain *movements* in interindustry differentials.

For certain periods, the *level* of current profits may well be related to the *change* in wage rates. One such period seems to have been 1947-58, and perhaps there have been others. But unless we are to infer a secular trend toward increasing wage dispersion in favor of the high-profit industries—a trend which no one has alleged and which would be inconsistent with the available evidence—we are left with the problem of explaining why the profit-wage relation is so intermittent. To say that the relation may well hold for one period but not for another is merely to state the facts. The problem of theory is to indicate the differential characteristics of the periods when it does hold and those when it does not. Let us consider a possible explanation.

Despite the evidence he presents on the association of wage change and profit level, Bowen distrusts differentials in profit levels as an explanatory factor of differential in wage changes among industries.[99] He does so mainly because he feels that the partial correlations in the 1954 and 1958 recessions were very small, and that the dominant factor in the simple correlation was the high intercorrelation among wage changes, concentration ratios, and degree of unionization.

Because of the behavior of the partial correlation coefficients Bowen

[98] Slichter, "Notes on the Structure of Wages," p. 88.
[99] Bowen, *Wage-Price Issue*, p. 68.

(rightly) rejects the possibility of a consistent *ceteris paribus* relation between wage changes and either concentration or unionization, taken separately. However, he contends that when we consider the combined effect of concentration and unionization (which are strongly inter-correlated in his sample), we find a stable relationship.[100] In discussing this, Bowen abandons correlation analysis and instead divides his industries into two groups: a "market power" sector (consisting of industries that are both highly concentrated and highly unionized) and a "competitive" sector in which the industries have the reverse characteristics. He argues that, with one exception,[101] the percentage change in average hourly earnings was greater in the market-power sector in all of the subperiods between 1947 and 1959. Although recognizing that the average level of profits was generally higher in the market-power sector, he says "that the importance of profits in this picture ought not to be exaggerated."[102] He also rejects the possibility that different rates of growth in employment are a differentiating characteristic of the two sectors.[103]

Bowen does not allege that what he has observed is part of a secular trend, but neither does he attempt to indicate what special characteristics of the period, 1947-59, are responsible for the unusual behavior observed, or why such behavior cannot persist indefinitely.[104] However, one possible explanation seems to be fairly obvious: the market-power sector contains a relatively large number of firms that respond to market stimuli rather slowly as compared with firms in the competitive sector. This relative sluggishness reflects the fact that *investment* decisions are expensive; can be made only infrequently and cannot easily be reversed. This would seem to be most characteristic of those sectors of the economy where "productive capacity" per unit of output is relatively expensive and long lived. Firms with these characteristics typically produce durable goods and are disproportionately found in

[100] *Ibid.*, pp. 74-81.
[101] The period January 1949-October 1950.
[102] Bowen, *Wage-Price Issue*, p. 78.
[103] Whatever the validity of this contention, it is not consistent with his own data. From Table 13, p. 77, we can compute (putting initial employment in Jan. 1947 = 100) that employment in June 1959 was 102.5 in the market-power sector but only 97.7 in the competitive sector.
[104] Bowen does offer an explanation, in spirit similar to what follows, of wage behavior in the 1954 and 1958 recessions (pp. 82-84). However, he does not recognize that if there is growth in differentials in recessions, there must be either (1) contraction of the differentials in periods of high employment or (2) a secular trend (in the differentials).

Bowen's market-power sector. Investment and output decisions in these firms respond not so much to current profits, as in the competitive sector, but to (moving) averages of current and past sales and profits which serve (along with other indicators) as a guide to the future.

On this view, the wage behavior described by Bowen is explained thus: at the end of World War II both sectors were confronted with situations of strong demand and high profits. The competitive sector acted to eliminate its excess demand faster than the market-power sector where long gestation periods of capital goods combined with a cautious outlook to hold back the investment program. This made the market-power sector's period of high profits, full capacity operation, and "strength" in product prices last longer than the competitive sector's period did. This, in turn, facilitated the payment of relative increases in earnings (in the market-power sector) during most of the 1950's.

If this explanation is correct, the growth of excess capacity and price weakness in the market-power sector during the late 1950's will soon end its relative wage gains, if it has not already done so. Also, if true, there should have been similar periods to the 1950's in the past—e.g., in the 1920's, as an aftermath of World War I. This particular hypothesis implies the same response pattern of wage changes to current profits or to current labor market conditions in Bowen's two sectors; it requires (1) that the two sectors both start from initial positions of excess product demand; (2) that the response mechanism of the market-power sector to excess product demand be slower, so that it takes a longer period to reach equilibrium; and (3) that relative wages in the competitive sector be high enough to obviate the need for short-run adjustments under pressure of a growing relative labor scarcity. It is quite possible that the wage adjustment mechanism in the market-power sector is also more sluggish; the differential incidence of long-term contracts with automatic deferred wage increases would suggest this.

We also suspect that, in the above explanation, the role of product prices is crucial. That is, when firms believe that cost increases can be passed on to buyers, they are more inclined to grant wage increases than when the reverse is the case. This is consistent with some findings of Dunlop on the relation of changes in wages and product prices,[105]

[105] J. T. Dunlop, *Wage Determination under Trade Unions*, 2nd ed. New York, Kelley, 1950, Chap. VII. Dunlop found a strong positive association (among industries) between declines in wage rates and product prices during the recessions of 1929-32 and 1937-38, and presents substantial evidence to support this observa-

which should be investigated further and brought up to date, especially the interrelation among changes in wages, product prices, and profits.

But if there is anything to the idea that there are two important sectors of the economy in which the ratio of *current* wages to the *current* marginal productivity of labor[106] behaves differently, it is incompatible with the competitive hypothesis as an explanation of wage behavior in the short run. This is because shifts in the ratio of current wages to current marginal productivity of labor can always be expressed as changes in the elasticities of (imagined) supply of factor or demand for product curves or both, whose alleged shifts are the staple of noncompetitive explanations of relative wage and price behavior. Such short-run shifts are simply the obverse side of a pattern of delayed response to market stimuli; it may also be true that a pattern of delayed response—especially in adding to productive capacity—requires some restriction upon entry and a substantial degree of concentration. Failure of either of these conditions to obtain may make it impossible for any one firm to hold off on expansion because of its inability to keep communicating with—or even to keep track of—all its potential rivals. The reader will understand that this is to suggest an hypothesis; testing it is another and far more difficult matter.

There are a number of other ad hoc short-period hypotheses concerning the behavior of industry wage levels. For example, it has been suggested that changes in industry wage levels tend to be more closely related in absolute than in percentage terms. While more careful writers have usually agreed that neither percentage nor absolute measures of changing differentials was ideal, the argument is that, because of union or governmental pressure, or both, industries tend to obtain equal absolute wage increases rather than equal percentage hikes.[107] This argument has been widely discussed in recent years, and appears to have had considerable validity for the period 1933-45, when

---

tion for the two depressions in question. However, Levinson ("Post-war Movement," p. 15) found that from 1947 through 1951-52 "price changes were unrelated to changes in gross hourly earnings—after that point, however, the correlation became very much stronger."

[106] That is the value of the marginal physical product as reflected in the output records for the *same* accounting period to which the wages are imputed. The reason for this rather narrow view of the competitive hypothesis is indicated in the Appendix.

[107] A very large number of writers have argued in this fashion. One of the earliest was A. M. Ross, *Trade Union Wage Policy*, University of California Press, 1948, Chap. VI.

interindustry (like other) differentials were narrowing. However, for the period since 1947, the hypothesis does not seem so plausible.[108] It is worth noting that this hypothesis implies, contrary to the competitive hypothesis, that in the short run relative wage levels are altered by variations in supply determinants (union and government policies) rather than by variations in demand determinants.

To argue that movements in relative wage levels are strongly correlated with levels of relative profits or changes in relative product prices is not to contradict the competitive hypothesis, per se. For both of the aforementioned independent variables may be correlated with variations in the level of employment and reflect only the influence of this variable on relative wage levels. Moreover, industries with high current profits might well be industries in process of an unusually marked tendency to be hiring workers to operate new processes or to work in newly developing high-wage areas, or both. Either or both of these tendencies could create (upward) labor market pressure on wage rates despite a tendency for over-all employment to decline. None of the studies to which reference has been made has attempted to control against these possibilities.

### PRODUCTIVITY

Some writers have found that the increase in average hourly earnings was greater in industries where the increase in physical production per man-hour was greater; e.g., Dunlop[109] and Garbarino.[110] Barring a correlation of skill mix and/or location with productivity, such a relationship is incompatible with the competitive hypothesis in the long run; whether it is compatible in the short run depends upon whether increases in man-hour productivity are positively correlated with increases in employment via correlation with the *value* of labor's marginal physical product.

The alleged factual relation between man-hour productivity and wages has itself been disputed by Levinson,[111] Meyers and Bowlby,[112] and Perlman.[113] These authors, especially the last, rightly stress the

[108] For example, Levinson's data would not seem consistent with it.
[109] Dunlop, "Productivity and the Wage Structure."
[110] Garbarino, "Theory of Inter-industry Wage Structure," pp. 298-300.
[111] "Post-war Movement," Table 1, p. 3.
[112] F. Meyers and R. L. Bowlby, "The Inter-industry Wage Structure and Productivity," *Industrial and Labor Relations Review*, Oct. 1953, pp. 93-102.
[113] R. Perlman, "Value Productivity and the Inter-industry Wage Structure," *Industrial and Labor Relations Review*, Oct. 1956, pp. 26-39.

importance of product price movements in determining the relative average value productivity of labor in different industries. Despite the dispute about whether the various correlation coefficients are significant, and which periods should be studied, it seems that the coefficients are usually positive,[114] which suggests the existence of a positive short-run association, but one which is disturbed by extraneous factors whose intensity varies from one period to another.

How one is to interpret this association is another matter. Garbarino found that in Dunlop's data (where the correlation between increases in man-hour productivity and wages was strong), the coefficient of rank correlation between increases in employment and in man-hour productivity was only +.08.[115] Obviously this militates against the short-run competitive hypothesis that there is a positive association between changes in hourly earnings and changes in man-hour productivity, because of an empirical association of the latter with rising output and employment. Another possible explanation, of pertinence in the long run as well as the short, is that industries in which man-hour productivity increases most are those in which the skill mix is likely to improve most. Yet another possible explanation of this phenomenon posits the existence of a link between wage increases and rises in productivity via profits and ability to pay, à la Slichter, Levinson, et al. But there is no good reason, either in theory or fact, for accepting any of these hypotheses.[116]

UNIONS

Our discussion of interindustry wage differentials has obviously left out unions; the omission is intentional. The main reason for exclusion is the failure of previous research to obtain very satisfactory results in relating them either to the levels or movements in interindustry wage differentials. The well-known conclusion of Douglas and of Ross and

[114] But not always: Meyers and Bowlby turned up some negative coefficients ("Inter-industry Wage Structure," p. 98) and so did Levinson.

[115] "Theory of Inter-industry Wage Structure," p. 285.

[116] In a recent paper, L. Johansen ("A Note on the Theory of Inter-industrial Wage Differentials," *Review of Economic Studies*, Feb. 1958, pp. 109-113) concludes that "we may expect not changes in wage differentials, but wage differentials themselves to be correlated with the changes in productivity." This result, however, refers only to differentials that reflect labor market disequilibrium; i.e., his results depend on labor market disequilibrium embodied in his equation (4) on p. 110. For the short run, his conclusion is identical in empirical content with the conventional Marshallian one, where productivity is reflected in a parameter of the industry labor demand fraction.

Goldner[117] that new unionism is associated with differential percentage wage gains to an industry, but long-established unionism is not, was about as far as anyone had been able to go before the work reported on by H. G. Lewis in this volume. We shall not attempt to appraise this work here but only note its relevance to our discussion.

One possibility of detecting the influence of unionism is to analyze the association among industries between wage changes and profit levels, holding employment changes constant. If unionism is effective in making wages higher than they would have been in its absence, this should be reflected in a forced sharing of profits[118] which should be, in the short run, over and above the influence of labor market conditions. That is, the positive partial association between wage changes and profit levels should increase with the strength of unionism— however measured. Of course, the influence of extraneous factors such as changes in skill and locational mix must be somehow taken into account.

## Conclusion

This paper's point of departure is that relative wage levels, both by skill and industry, behave more or less as though they were market prices reflecting predominantly the interplay of changing tastes, techniques, and resources—the competitive hypothesis. The implications of this hypothesis, however, are not so simple as they might seem because tastes, techniques, and resources interact in peculiar and complicated ways. Moreover, the basic hypothesis has required amendment to allow for the effect of changes in minimum wage laws, etc., for secular rural-urban migration, and for the gradual broadening of educational opportunities.

The competitive hypothesis is at its best, both in explaining skill margins and interindustry differentials, when it is used to explain variations over long periods of time. It can hardly be said to be firmly established as an explanation of wage phenomena even for long periods;

[117] P. H. Douglas, *Real Wages in the United States*, p. 564; Ross and Goldner, "Forces Affecting," p. 267.

[118] To test our hypothesis, it is necessary that unions be not "too strong"; i.e., unions must compel relatively more profitable firms to *share* their "excess profits" with wage earners (but not obliterate them), so that there are still greater than average profits to be observed. It is conceivable—though not likely—that unions could be so effective in raising wages that all potential supernormal profits were transferred to wages, completely obscuring the hypothesized relation.

but it has at least survived (reasonably well) the tests to which it has so far been put.

For the short run the competitive hypothesis does not appear very reliable. There are a number of findings concerning interindustry differentials which simply are not consistent with its short-run implication that relative industry wage rates vary in the same direction as relative changes in employment, in any given short-time interval (see Appendix). We are not without alternative short-run hypotheses; but these either break down during one time interval or another, or still are in a primitive state of formulation and testing.

In this paper we have discussed only skill and industrial differentials. No attempt has been made to analyze interfirm, interplant, and interregional differentials which, incidentally, may be associated with skill or industry differentials. However, this task will be attempted in the near future.

## Appendix on Methodology

This brief appendix was written because of numerous criticisms and misunderstandings of my remarks on the "competitive hypothesis," its implications and their tests. This statement is not intended as original, in any fundamental sense; and obviously it is cursory. The views expressed, or similar ones, have been in the atmosphere for some time. Though the spirit of the exposition is similar to that of Milton Friedman's famous essay on the methodology of positive economics,[119] its content is different. In short, all of the blame for possible misstatement must rest here; much of whatever credit is due should go elsewhere.

When we speak of the "competitive hypothesis" we are referring to a hypothesis which states that the behavior of relative prices and quantities can be explained as though these prices and quantities were equilibrium values in a static economic model,[120] in which all pur-

NOTE: I am very grateful to my colleagues K. J. Arrow and Marc Nerlove for their criticism of an initial draft.

[119] Milton Friedman, *Essays in Positive Economics*, Chap. I, University of Chicago Press, 1952.

[120] This is not the entire content of static general equilibrium theory, but it is the part with which we are concerned. In particular, we are abstracting from those aspects connected with the determination of money prices.

In private discussion, objections have sometimes been made that the competitive hypothesis is not—or ought not to be—defined so as to apply only to cases where concurrent (unlagged) relations obtain among the variables. There can, of course, be no quarrel with a definition, but if the competitive hypothesis is defined so as

chases and sales are made by units bent on maximizing satisfaction[121] subject to individual budgetary restraints, having access to the same technology, and treating prices as parametric constants, independent of the quantities they (individually) purchase or sell. The prices in question, when taken as a set, make all excess demands equal to zero. As this argument is very well known, it is not considered necessary to spell out its details. The competitive hypothesis discussed here could be called, with propriety, the long-run static competitive hypothesis.[122] (The short-run version is mentioned briefly below.)

The utility functions of the households in our model shift with the tastes of the individuals who compose them; i.e., changes in a household's tastes are reflected in shifts of one or more parameters of its utility function. Similarly changes in the technology available to a firm are reflected in shifts of one or more parameters of its transformation function. Consequently, we may write the excess demand function for the $j$ th kind of labor by the $i$ th industry as

$$q_{ij} = D_{ij}\left(p_1 - p_n; v_{i1} - v_{im}; a_{i1} - a_{iz}; \beta_{i1} - \beta_{ih}; \gamma_{i1} = \gamma_{id}\right)(1),$$

For simplicity, we assume each of these industries to produce only one commodity; hence we have $n$ prices and the subscript of the $p_i$'s runs from 1 to $n$.[123] $v_{ij}$ is the wage rate of the $j$ th kind of labor in the $i$ th industry, and $j = 1, 2 - - m$. Because our argument will be concerned not with the $v_{ij}$'s, but with their ratios, let us define $w_{ij} = v_{ij}/v_{tj}$, where $v_{tj}$ is the wage paid the $j$ th kind of labor in the $t$ th industry. This means that in long-run equilibrium, $w_{ij} = 1$; i.e., all industries

---

to permit lagging relations then, in the short run, there are no generally applicable theorems concerning concurrent price-quantity relations. The character of the concurrent relations will vary both with the structure of the lagged system and the time period. Because we prefer that the competitive hypothesis have some specific short run implications, we define it as applying solely to static relationships.

Kenneth Arrow has said he believes widely applicable theorems on price-quantity relations involving lags can be deduced from individual behavior functions which include weighted lags. That is, with only "reasonable" restrictions on the weights, theorems can be deduced which will apply almost as widely as do those of comparative statics in the long run. When these results are published it will be possible to push further the argument of this appendix; but they will not invalidate what is stated.

[121] Profit maximization is clearly a special case of this.

[122] This statement applies either to an economy in stationary equilibrium or to one always on its growth path. Some of the relative prices will vary from a stationary state to a situation of balanced growth, but not those discussed in this appendix.

[123] Capital goods are treated as outputs of particular industries and their prices are included in the $p$'s.

must pay the same wage rate for a given kind of labor. $a_{i1} - a_{iz}$ are parameters reflecting changes in the tastes of the households; $\beta_{i1} - \beta_{ih}$ are other parameters reflecting changes in the technologies of the firms and $\gamma_{i1} - \gamma_{ir}$ reflect the resources owned by each decision-making unit. (For simplicity, when there is no danger of confusion we shall refer to the set, $a_{i1} - a_{iz}$, by $a$ — without subscript; similarly, for the sets $\beta_{i1} - \beta_{ih}$ and $\gamma_{i1} - \gamma_{rd}$.)

Barring corner solutions, static equilibrium requires that $q_{ij} = 0$ ($i = 1, 2 - n; j = 1, 2 - m$). It also requires that $v_{ij} = v_{rj}$ and $w_{ij} = 1$, where $r$ is any industry other than $i$. Obviously, these are not sufficient conditions for equilibrium; however, they are necessary, and they are the only ones with which we shall work. Let us designate the value of $w_j$ at which $w_{ij} = w_{rj}$ ($i = 1, 2 - n$) as $w_j{}^*$ — the equilibrium value of $w_j$. (As we have seen, $w_j{}^* = w_f{}^* = 1$, where $f$ is a kind of labor other than $j$. However, to avoid confusion, we shall not utilize this fact and write the equilibrium value of $w_j$ as $w_j{}^*$.) Let us also designate $q_{ij}{}^* = 0$ as the value of $q_{ij}$ corresponding to $w_j{}^*$ and $Q_{ij} = F(q_{ij})$ as the equilibrium quantity of $j$ employed in the $i$ th industry. ($Q_{ij}$ is the observed employment of the $j$ th kind of labor in the $i$ th industry, and $Q_{ij}{}^*$ is its equilibrium value.[124]) Neither $w_j{}^*$ nor $Q_{ij}{}^*$ is observable; they are intellectual constructions whose *raison d'être* is to explain the behavior of the observed $w_{ij}$ and $Q_{ij}$. The competitive hypothesis, in effect, states that the behavior of $w_{ij}$ and $Q_{ij}$ is "approximately" the same as that implied by static economic theory concerning the behavior of $w_j{}^*$ and $Q_{ij}{}^*$.

$w_{ij}$ and $Q_{ij}$ vary both from time to time and place to place. (For the sake of exposition, let us speak only of variation from one date to another, remembering that date and place are, in this discussion, interchangeable.) At any given date,

$$\log w_{ij} = \log w_j{}^* + \log \epsilon_{ij} \qquad (2)$$

[124] To avoid formal indeterminacy let us suppose that workers are not indifferent about the industry in which they work, at given relative wages, and that in equilibrium the industry of each worker is determined. However, to preserve the equilibrium condition, $v_{ij} = v_{tj}$, let us assume that workers' nonpecuniary preferences for industries are such that, *at equal wages*, the number preferring to work in a particular industry is proportional to the demand of that industry.

This assumption is, of course, restrictive and unrealistic. But to relax it would greatly complicate the exposition and obscure the point of the appendix. Moreover, to do so would not generate any interesting new possibilities; it would merely embody in the model the nonpecuniary preferences from which compensating wage differentials arise.

where $\epsilon_{ij}$ is a "disturbance" term whose log is assumed to be uncorrelated with log $w_j^*$ and which reflects all the forces bearing upon log $w_{ij}$ except those affecting log $w_j^*$; i.e., $w_{ij} = w_j^* \, \epsilon_{ij}$.

We assume that $E \; (\log \epsilon_{ij}) = 1$ and that $\sigma_{\log \epsilon_{ij}} = \lambda w_j^*$, where $\lambda < 1$; i.e., the standard deviation of the disturbance term is proportional to the equilibrium value. (Hereafter, for brevity, we shall write $\overline{w}_{ij}$ for log $w_{ij}$, $\overline{\epsilon}_{ij}$ for log $\epsilon_{ij}$, etc. for all logarithms; we shall also assume all variables to be measured as deviations from their mean values.) The assumption embodied in (2) is, of course, arbitrary. Its only defence is that it is similar to those usually made in econometric research, and that some arbitrary assumption of this kind must be made to begin any argument relating theory and observation.

The movement of $\overline{w}_{ij}$ between any two dates (0) and (1) is represented by $\Delta\overline{w}_{ij}$; i.e., $\Delta\overline{w}_{ij} = \overline{w}_{ij}^{(1)} - \overline{w}_{ij}^{(0)}$. Similarly, we define $\Delta\overline{\epsilon}_{ij} = \overline{\epsilon}_{ij}^{(1)} - \overline{\epsilon}_{ij}^{(0)}$, and will adopt analogous conventions for all other variables. This gives us, by substitution in (2)

$$\Delta\overline{w}_{ij} = \Delta\overline{w}_j^* + \Delta\overline{\epsilon}_{ij}. \tag{2a}$$

We also have

$$\Delta\overline{Q}_{ij} = \Delta\overline{Q}_{ij}^* + \Delta\overline{\zeta}_{ij} \tag{3}$$

where $\overline{\zeta}_{ij}$ is a disturbance term. The analogue of each relation among $\overline{w}_{ij}$, $\overline{w}_j^*$ and $\overline{\epsilon}_{ij}$ that has been posited, is assumed to hold among $\overline{Q}_{ij}$, $\overline{Q}_{ij}^*$ and $\overline{\zeta}_{ij}$, and

$$E(\Delta\overline{w}_{ij} \, \Delta\overline{Q}_{ij}) = E[(\Delta\overline{w}_j^* + \Delta\overline{\epsilon}_{ij}) \; (\Delta\overline{Q}_{ij}^* + \Delta\overline{\zeta}_{ij})] =$$
$$E(\Delta\overline{w}_j^* \, \Delta\overline{Q}_{ij}^*) + E(\Delta\overline{w}_j^* \, \Delta\overline{\zeta}_{ij}) + E(\Delta\overline{Q}_{ij}^* \, \Delta\overline{\epsilon}_{ij}) +$$
$$E(\Delta\overline{\epsilon}_{ij} \, \Delta\overline{\zeta}_{ij}). \tag{4}$$

Since $\overline{w}_j^*$ is the same in all industries it is a constant which implies, because we are measuring all variables as deviations from their means, that the first two terms in (4) vanish. And, as we interpret the competitive hypothesis, it implies that the second two terms vanish also. This means that the competitive hypothesis implies that $E(\Delta\overline{w}_{ij} \, \Delta\overline{Q}_{ij}) = 0$; i.e., that it implies an absence of correlation between percentage changes in wage rate and percentage changes in employment among industries *when the positions compared are those of long-run equilibrium*.

Crucial to this contention is the assumption that $E(\Delta\overline{Q}_{ij}^* \, \Delta\overline{\epsilon}_{ij}) = E(\Delta\overline{\epsilon}_{ij} \, \Delta\overline{\zeta}_{ij}) = 0$. To assert $E(\overline{Q}_{ij}^* \, \Delta\overline{\epsilon}_{ij}) = 0$ is to say that the percentage change in the long-run equilibrium volume of employment of the $j$ th type labor in the $i$ th industry is uncorrelated with the percentage change in the disturbance component in the wage rate paid it. In a literal sense, there is nothing in economic theory that implies this statement. But if it were not true, economic theory would be very different than it is or ever has been. It would have to be so constructed that transient disturbances to the parameters of the excess demand functions for factors would have permanent effects (i.e., would change long-run equilibrium values). This would mean that *equilibrium* prices and quantities would reflect not only the states of tastes, techniques, and resource endowments but also the whole history of prices including the effects of accidental disturbances. I doubt that one could construct useful economic models from such premises, and certainly no one has seriously tried to do so. Consequently, I shall interpret the competitive hypothesis as implying $E(\Delta \overline{Q}_{ij}{}^{*} \Delta \overline{\epsilon}_{ij}) = 0$. For similar reasons, we assume $E(\Delta \overline{Q}_{ij}{}^{*} \Delta \overline{\zeta}_{ij}) = 0$.

In the short run there is good reason to suppose that $E(\Delta \overline{\epsilon}_{ij} \Delta \overline{\zeta}_{ij}) > 0$. That is, the short-run disturbances that make measured employment exceed long-run equilibrium levels (e.g., unanticipated increases in demand) will also tend to make factor prices exceed long-run equilibrium levels. As $\overline{\epsilon}_{ij}$ and $\zeta_{ij}$ are disturbance terms, and there is no reason to suppose that disturbances become smaller with the passage of time, it follows that in the long run, as well as in the short,

$$E(\Delta \overline{\epsilon}_{ij} \Delta \overline{\zeta}_{ij}) > 0.$$

For concreteness let us assume that $E(\Delta \overline{\epsilon}_{ij} \Delta \overline{\zeta}_{ij}) > 0 = $ constant in any time period. This assumption is arbitrary, but necessary; to assume that the expression increased indefinitely with time would open the possibility that actual prices or quantities, or both, might deviate ever further from equilibrium ones—i.e., a long run might never be reached. To assume that the expression diminishes with time would add to the strength of long-run forces, but such an assumption would be unwarranted and unnecessary. In fact, all we need assume is that the expression does not increase so fast as to upset the following argument; to assume constancy is to impose—for simplicity of statement—a somewhat stronger condition than necessary.

If the competitive hypothesis is true, then $E(\Delta \overline{w}_{ij} \Delta \overline{Q}_{ij})$ will behave as $E(\Delta \overline{w}_{j}{}^{*} \Delta \overline{Q}_{ij}{}^{*})$ when $\Delta$ is so chosen as to generate a long run. As we have seen, $E(\Delta\overline{w}_j{}^* \, \Delta\overline{Q}_{ij}{}^*)$ is zero, but $E(\Delta\overline{w}_{ij} \, \Delta\overline{Q}_{ij})$ is not because of $E(\Delta\overline{\epsilon}_{ij}\,\Delta\overline{\zeta}_{ij})$. But the correlation coefficient between $\Delta\overline{w}_{ij}$ and $\Delta\overline{Q}_{ij}$ will, under competitive conditions, approach zero asymptotically in the long run. By the usual argument, the closer the approach to zero, the smaller is the relative importance of $E(\Delta\overline{\epsilon}_{ij}\,\Delta\overline{\zeta}_{ij})$ in explaining the behavior of $E(\Delta\overline{w}_{ij} \, \Delta\overline{Q}_{ij})$. The correlation coefficient is

$$ r = \frac{E(\Delta\overline{w}_{ij} \, \Delta\overline{Q}_{ij})}{\sigma_{(\Delta\overline{w}_{ij}{}^* + \Delta\overline{\epsilon}_{ij})} \, \sigma_{(\Delta\overline{Q}_{ij}{}^* + \Delta\overline{\zeta}_{ij})}} = \frac{E(\Delta\overline{\epsilon}_{ij} \, \Delta\overline{\zeta}_{ij})}{\sigma_{\Delta\overline{\epsilon}_{ij}} \sqrt{\sigma^2_{\Delta Q_{ij}{}^*} + \sigma^2_{\Delta\overline{\zeta}_{ij}}}} $$

The equality of the numerators follows from our argument concerning (4) which showed all its terms to be zero except $E(\Delta\overline{\Sigma}_{ij} \, \Delta\overline{\zeta}_{ij})$. The denominators are equal because $\sigma_{\Delta\overline{w}_{ij}{}^*} = 0$ *ex hypothesi*, and the expression under the radical sign is simply the expanded form of the standard deviation of a sum of two variables which are assumed to be uncorrelated.

Now in the long run $\sigma^2_{\Delta\overline{Q}_{ij}{}^*}$ increases indefinitely (see below). Since $\sigma_{\overline{\zeta}_{ij}} = \mu\overline{Q}_{ij}{}^*$, it is conceivable that it could shrink despite the rise in $\sigma^2\Delta\overline{Q}_{ij}{}^*$ if the predominant direction of movement in the $\overline{Q}_{ij}{}^*$'s was downward; i.e., if the relative importance of the error component in observed quantities secularly increased. In the data discussed in this paper, most of the $\overline{Q}_{ij}$'s increased markedly. This does not prove that the $\overline{Q}_{ij}{}^*$'s (not observable) also increased, but for the sake of the argument we shall assume that they do. (A complete treatment must consider other possibilities.) Therefore, given our assumptions, the denominator of the correlation coefficient grows with time, but the numerator remains unchanged, so that the quotient eventually approaches zero.

To reach this conclusion—that the correlation between $\Delta\overline{w}_{ij}$ and $\Delta\overline{Q}_{ij}$ diminishes (algebraically) over time to approach zero asymptotically—in the long run—requires an hypothesis about how the $\Delta\overline{Q}_{ij}$'s behave in the long run. The hypothesis is that the $\overline{Q}_{ij}{}^*$'s, predominantly, have long-run monotonic trends and that their variance increases with the length of the interval considered. This hypothesis would be satisfied, for example, if each $\overline{Q}_{ij}{}^*$ increased at a constant percentage rate and the variance at any given moment was non-zero.

This hypothesis implies that $\sigma_{\Delta\overline{Q}_{ij}{}^*}$ will increase with the passage of time and that, provided the covariance of the disturbances is not "perversely" correlated with time, the correlation between $\Delta \overline{w}_{ij}$ and $\Delta \overline{Q}_{ij}$ will eventually approach zero. How much time must elapse before we have any specified degree of approximation to a long run depends upon the divergence in the rates of trend movement among the $\overline{Q}_{ij}$'s; the greater the divergence, the less time required. If there is no predominant tendency toward monotonic trends among the $Q_{ij}^{\circ}$'s, then the long-run forces may never dominate the behavior of $E(\Delta \overline{w}_{ij} \Delta \overline{Q}_{ij})$.

R. H. Strotz has suggested a very useful simile to explain this point: if a pair of rifle targets is far apart, the difference in the locus of observed shots may be explained by the difference in aim of the rifleman. But if they are close together, the error component may make it impossible to infer at which target a given shot was aimed, and force us to ignore the difference in targets as an explanatory variable.

Now let us suppose that the correlation coefficient between $\Delta \overline{w}_{ij}$ and $\Delta \overline{Q}_{ij}$ shows no signs of approaching zero with an increase in the length of the period, casting doubt on the competitive hypothesis. How should this eventuality be interpreted? It would *not* mean that we should reject price theory as invalid; rather we should say that the assumptions of price theory were violated in such a way as to make the competitive hypothesis inapplicable to the data in question. To say this would not, in any sense, "save" the hypothesis; a hypothesis is valued according to its fruitfulness, and one that is frequently found to be inapplicable is inferior to another which is inapplicable less frequently.

If the competitive hypothesis is found inapplicable, there is a variety of possible alternatives:

1. It is frequently argued that the absence of pure competition invalidates the competitive hypothesis. Surely it is possible that there is correlation—in either direction—between $\Delta Q_{ij}$ and $\Delta \epsilon_{ij}$ because of a correlation of $\Delta Q_{ij}$ with changes in the parameters of (1). The competitive hypothesis asserts that these parameters reflect only tastes, techniques, and resources;[125] but if the hypothesis is found inapplicable, one reason might be that the parameters also reflect, *inter alia*, the ratio of the value of a factor's marginal product to its rate of reward.

[125] Put in a slightly different way, the competitive hypothesis asserts that the $\Delta w_j^{\circ}$'s reflect only changes in parameters reflecting tastes, techniques, and resources, and from no other forces. Among the forces thus excluded are changing union wage policies which might alter the supply functions of given grades of labor differently in different industries.

It should be noted that the competitive hypothesis can be applied successfully, even though there is monopoly in one or more markets. It suffices for the argument of this paper that there should be no *changes* in the degree of monopoly power;[126] i.e., for the present purpose, the competitive hypothesis does not say that observed prices are approximately those that would obtain under pure competition,[127] but only that *changes* in these prices are the same as those that would have occurred if the degree of monopoly power in every market had been (approximately) constant. That is to say, in terms of equation (1), there are parameters which reflect changes in the degrees of monopoly power, but for the period in question they are approximately constant. Indeed, for the purpose of this paper, it is not necessary that there should be *no* changes in the degrees of monopoly power, but only that these changes should be uncorrelated with $\Delta Q_{ij}$ (or other variables whose covariance with $\Delta w_j$ is being studied). On this last interpretation of the competitive hypothesis, monopoly could be an important factor in explaining changes in any individual price, but this would not imply that it would be useful in explaining the relative long-run changes among any "fairly large" group of prices.

2. The test of the competitive hypothesis we have been discussing is not a very powerful instrument for discriminating between monopolistic and nonmonopolistic situations because—at the level of industry data[128]—the price-quantity behavior which is characteristic of a changing degree of monopoly power is often consistent with two or more very different interpretations. For example, (1) if industries have quantity responses to price changes that involve interindustrial differences in the "true lags" of price behind quantity (or vice versa) and (2) if these lags are subject to change, then the recorded concurrent association of prices and quantities will be identical with what it would have been had there been a changing pattern of monopoly behavior.[129] To say the same thing in a different way: if one is given a set of prices and quantities, it is always possible—in the absence of knowledge about costs or imagined demand elasticities or both—to invent a set of imagined demand elasticities which vary (if necessary) from one

[126] The degree of monopoly power of any seller or buyer is the ratio of price to marginal revenue or marginal expenditure, as the case may be.

[127] This remark applies only to the particular aspect of the competitive hypothesis discussed here. In other contexts—e.g., discussions of relative economic efficiency—the competitive hypothesis implies that observed prices actually approximate competitive ones.

[128] As distinguished from the data for individual firms.

[129] That is, a changing degree of monopoly power, as defined in footnote 126.

period to the next that will "explain" the price-quantity relations perfectly and without reference to any lags.

If firms do not consistently attempt to maximize profits, then variations in the strength of their "propensity to maximize" also could simulate the effects of a changing degree of monopoly power. Yet another possibility arises where there are technological lags of output behind inputs; variations of these lags (either because of changes in technology or in interest rates) will simulate the effect of a changing degree of monopoly power on concurrent price-quantity data.

All of these possibilities are known to have materialized in varying (and disputed) degrees. To disentangle their separate effects in the event the competitive hypothesis is rejected is often very difficult and, in this appendix, we shall make no attempt to discuss the problems that arise.

At this point, it would be well to emphasize that in this discussion of the competitive hypothesis we are considering only those aspects that are relevant to explaining the behavior of a set of industrial wage rates and employment quantities, or, more generally, industry prices and quantities. As such, it is a useful test to apply to historical records of wages, prices, and related quantities of the sort that can be obtained from censuses and which have recently been extensively utilized by by Kendrick and others. Its utility lies mainly in the fact that it requires no data beyond series of prices (factor or product) and quantities— data that are comparatively easy to obtain. But it is a test that is biased in favor of accepting the hypothesis.

Consider: we have, in effect, proposed accepting the competitive hypothesis if the correlation coefficient between $\Delta \bar{w}_{ij}$ and $\Delta \bar{Q}_{ij}$ does not differ significantly from zero. The reason is that, if the coefficient were zero, $E(\Delta \bar{Q}_{ij}^* \, \Delta \bar{\epsilon}_{ij}) = E(\Delta \bar{\epsilon}_{ij} \, \Delta \bar{\zeta}_{ij}) = 0$. But $(\Delta \bar{\epsilon}_{ij} \, \Delta \bar{\zeta}_{ij})$ reflects the effect of all forces acting on industry wages and employment except those implied in the competitive hypothesis. Suppose that, contrary to the hypothesis, $E(\Delta \bar{Q}_{ij}^* \, \Delta \bar{\epsilon}_{ij}) \neq 0$, but is small relative to the variance of $E(\Delta \bar{\epsilon}_{ij} \, \Delta \bar{\zeta}_{ij})$, whose mathematical expectation is zero; in this event, we might well accept the hypothesis despite its falsehood. To put the matter in another way: what the hypothesis asserts is also what the absence of correlation between the disturbance terms implies; therefore, increases in the variance of the covariance of the disturbances increases the probability of accepting the hypothesis even though every term in (4) is unchanged.

Nevertheless, when we have only industry averages for wages (prices) and quantities at two dates, this test is the only one available. As the number of dates for which data are available increases, at least one other test becomes possible. Because $E(\Delta\bar{\epsilon}_{ij} \, \Delta\bar{\zeta}_{ij}) > 0$, we should find the correlation between $\Delta\bar{w}_{ij}$ and $\Delta\bar{Q}_{ij}$ tending to be positive, but (as we have seen) steadily diminishing as the period considered becomes longer. This test is not subject to the aforementioned bias. Further tests are also possible, but they require additional data. Some of them have been discussed in the text above. However, these tests usually relate relative industry wage levels, or changes therein, to the skill-mix or other aspects of the composition of the industries' labor forces and do not directly involve the methodological issues raised in this appendix. There are still other implications of the competitive hypothesis, and other types of tests; it is not suggested that these are less important than those discussed here.

3. If, on any particular set of data, the competitive hypothesis is rejected, it is sometimes plausible to suppose that the dates to which the data refer are insufficiently separated to constitute a long run; i.e., the hypothesis may be valid for the long run, but the particular period studied should not be considered as such. But if such an approach is not to render the hypothesis inaccessible to empirical confrontation, it is necessary to specify how long a period must be before it is considered a long run.

A rough and ready answer to this question is as follows: a time period is a long run, for the purpose of a particular hypothesis, if extending it further without limit or reducing it slightly[130] does not alter the outcome of any relevant test. In the context of this paper, this criterion means that we have reached a long-run situation when the series of correlation coefficients between $\Delta\bar{w}_{ij}$ and $\Delta\bar{Q}_{ij}$ generated by extending the length of the period from (0) to (1), by increasing (1) indefinitely or by reducing it slightly or both, becomes indistinguishable from a random sample from a normal universe with a zero mean.[131]

---

[130] Put differently, a long-run relation is one that holds irrespective of the time interval chosen, provided the interval is picked from an admissible set of intervals. Given (0), defining a long-run is akin to choosing the lower bound of the set of admissible dates for (1)—a set for which there is no upper bound.

[131] If the series of coefficients "stabilizes" around a non-zero value, this would suggest that a long run has been reached and the competitive hypothesis disconfirmed. However, the possibility of a spurious long run should never be neglected.

The importance of distinguishing between short- and long-run relationships arises from the fact that in the short run, *ceteris paribus*, there is likely to be a correlation between $\Delta w_{ij}$ and $\Delta Q_{ij}$. That is, when (0) and (1) are close together, industries for which $\Delta Q_{ij}$ is relatively large will almost certainly be those which are growing relatively rapidly at (1). And, because of short-run inelasticity of labor supply to individual industries, the wage rate in the $i$ th industry will tend to rise more, the greater the increase in employment; this induces positive correlation between $\Delta \epsilon_{ij}$ and $\Delta Q_{ij}$. Also, rapidly growing industries tend to experience (temporary) high profits, bursts of growth in productivity, capital stock, etc. However, as (0) and (1) become further removed, the relative size of $\Delta Q_{ij}$ becomes decreasingly correlated with its relative growth rate at (1); i.e., industries that experienced great relative growth between 1899 and 1953 are not, to any appreciable degree, those that were experiencing great relative growth in 1953. Moreover, the correlation between $\Delta \epsilon_{ij}$ and the growth rate of $Q_{ij}$ at (1) tends to disappear as we lengthen the period over which differential rates of employment growth are compared; this is because the main reason for short-run inelasticity of factor supply to an industry is failure to anticipate demand accurately. And if an industry's employment has been growing at a more or less steady rate for a fairly prolonged period, both sides of the market will have time to adjust, thereby eliminating the correlation; i.e., $E(\Delta \epsilon_{ij} \Delta \zeta_{ij})$ tends to zero.

In short, lengthening the period between (0) and (1) tends to reduce the correlation between $\Delta \epsilon_{ij}$ and $\Delta Q_{ij}$ until for some length—and all longer ones—it becomes approximately zero. How long such a period may be, or if it is finite, can be determined only empirically, and ad hoc. As we have seen, the length of the period will depend upon the variance among the trends in $Q_{ij}^*$ as compared with the intercorrelations of $\Delta \epsilon_{ij}$ and $\Delta \zeta_{ij}$. The appearance of a set of (small) positive correlations[132] may well provoke a suspicion that we have been studying a period shorter than that necessary to apply long-run theory. However, it must be remembered that there is no guarantee that lengthening the period, even indefinitely, will eliminate the correlation; i.e., the competitive hypothesis may be inapplicable even in the long run.

[132] Generated by varying the length of the period (0)—(1).

The reader will note that in discussing the competitive hypothesis, long-run version, we have hardly mentioned *ceteris paribus*. This is deliberate; as we interpret it, the competitive hypothesis does not assert that certain relations hold, *ceteris paribus*; this is what economic theory asserts. The competitive hypothesis says that other things *are* sufficiently equal for the implications of competitive price theory to apply. If these implications do not hold, then there is need for an alternative hypothesis—possibly including the competitive hypothesis as a special case.

So far, we have been considering only the long-run version of the competitive hypothesis. The short-run version of the competitive hypothesis is in a somewhat different position (from the long run). This is because the short-run version is, as we interpret it, supposed to apply to any and all periods.[133] Therefore, because there is a number of variables associated (for short periods) with relative increase in an industry's wages, the relationship implied by the competitive hypothesis[134] is not the only one that will be found. Hence, the competitive hypothesis may be interpreted in (at least) two ways: (1) In the strong form, it states—parallel to the long-period version—that the relationship it implies is the only one that will be found consistently.[135] The repetitive finding of any other relation is inconsistent with the theory. (2) In its weak form the competitive hypothesis does not state that there is a simple positive correlation between $\Delta w_{ij}$ and $\Delta Q_{ij}$ but merely that this relationship exists *ceteris paribus*; i.e., appropriate partial correlations will have positive signs. Intermediate versions of the hypothesis—e.g., that the *ceteris paribus* relation between $\Delta w_{ij}$ and $\Delta Q_{ij}$ is stronger than that between $\Delta w_{ij}$ and any other variable— can also be formulated.[136]

So far all our remarks in this appendix have referred to one specific kind of labor employed in a number of different industries and whose wage (in each industry) was recorded.[137] In practice, much of the

[133] It should be emphasized that this is one writer's conception. Other economists may—and some surely will—define terms differently.

[134] That is, that supply price of a factor to an industry, occupation, etc. is a nondecreasing function of quantity; and for quantities "large enough" it is a monatomically increasing function.

[135] That is, evidence of any other relationship will be explicable as a result of random disturbances or sampling fluctuations.

[136] However, it would seem reasonable to insist that the short-run competitive hypothesis be stated so as to imply that the partial correlation coefficients (with all other relevant variables constant) between $\Delta w_{ij}$ and $\Delta Q_{ij}$ are positive.

[137] A further implicit restriction is that all employment occurred in one location

data with which we deal are industry averages of wages in various occupations or of individuals working in different places. Consequently, as the text indicates, much of the explanation of changes in relative industrial wages runs in terms of changes in the composition of the items affecting these averages. The argument of this appendix does not apply directly to these averages, but only to their components and the relationships of substitution and complementarity among them. Where the competitive hypothesis is found to hold for industrial averages, it implies either that the relative changes among the components are unimportant or that they cancel one another.[138]

## COMMENT

DONALD E. CULLEN, New York State School of Industrial and Labor Relations, Cornell University

I should like to direct most of my remarks to Melvin Reder's treatment of interindustry wage differentials, for I find his defense of the competitive hypothesis less persuasive in that area than in the case of the

---

or some unvarying set of locations, thus eliminating interlocational variations in excess demand functions.

[138] It has been argued (privately) by H. G. Lewis that there is a priori reason to suspect long-run correlation between $\Delta w_i{}^*$ and $\Delta Q_{ij}{}^*$. As I interpret the argument, such correlation might arise in several ways, one being the following. Suppose some industries require two or more kinds of labor. Also suppose, for simplicity, that the long-run supply curve of each kind of labor is an increasing function of its price, and that some or all of the industries are sufficiently important as users of some (or all) of the kinds of labor they hire for the long-run equilibrium price of any one kind (which is the same for all industries) to increase with the amount the industry hires. Then, *ceteris paribus*, industries growing relatively more (or declining less) than others will tend to create higher relative prices for the kinds of labor they use most intensively, and hence in their average wage rates. The pressure to substitute against the kinds of labor that have become relatively more expensive mitigates, but does not eliminate, this tendency. *Ceteris paribus*, this factor would lead to a positive correlation in the relative average wage of an industry and its relative employment. Its practical importance will depend on the size of the industries considered; the smaller the industries, the less the importance.

There are other strong forces relating these two variables, e.g., some industries utilize relatively large quantities of man-hours of dirty, rough work which tends to have a negative income elasticity of supply. Consequently, these industries tend to face secular increases in relative (average) supply price of the labor employed per unit of output, which tends (*ceteris paribus*) both to raise relative product prices and therefore to reduce employment, and to increase average wages; this introduces a correlation opposite in sign to that discussed above. The net correlation between employment and wages, even in the long run, will obviously depend upon the relative strength of these and possibly other linkages between the variables. In the text we assumed, *faute de mieux*, that this net correlation was zero. However, this is an assumption that may prove misleading.

skill margin. Orthodox theory, as he points out, would lead one to predict that occupational differentials will be narrowed as educational opportunity is equalized; this narrowing has certainly occurred, and to a very marked degree, in most Western countries; and since he has shown that the spasmodic nature of this secular trend can also be explained in competitive terms, I agree that there is no reason to search for an alternative theory of occupational differentials. When Reder turns to a consideration of interindustry differentials, however, he does not offer such decisive evidence in support of the competitive hypothesis; in fact, the available data suggest that these differentials have not narrowed much at all. Much of his analysis therefore turns upon the question of whether anyone has come up with a better explanation of this wage structure than that offered by the competitive model, and while he inflicts some mortal wounds upon some of the alternatives which have been put forth, that in itself is not a positive confirmation of his model.

We now have a great deal of information on three aspects of interindustry wage differentials: (1) the structure of these differentials in local labor markets over short periods of time; (2) the dispersion of these differentials on a national level over both the short run and, within manufacturing, the long run; and (3) the relation of short-run changes in the national structure to several other factors, such as productivity and employment changes, concentration, etc. Reder concentrates upon the last two of these aspects and offers several valuable insights to which I shall return. First, however, I should like to consider the problems posed by interindustry differentials in local markets.

The competitive hypothesis, he points out, predicts that "In the long run, under competitive conditions, any industry will pay the same price for a given grade of labor as any other industry hiring in the same location." But if all labor economists agree on anything (which is doubtful), it is that a wide diversity of rates for the same jobs characterizes the average local labor market, and that a uniformity of rates is usually a sure sign that the market in question is not "free" but rather is dominated by either organized labor or organized management.

It is this apparent failure of local rates to equalize which has long been seized upon by critics of competitive theory as their prime exhibit. You will recall that Marshall referred to the "naive" assertions of this nature by Cliff Leslie and other critics of that day, and that he retorted that differences in money rates (for the same job in the same market) were actually evidence of the effectiveness of competitive forces, since workers of different efficiency must necessarily receive different money wages in a competitive market.[1] As our discussion yesterday showed, this argument continues unabated today. On the one hand, the inter-firm differentials examined by Shultz were not widely dispersed and appeared to be closely related to quality differences. On the other hand, it was pointed out that this market more closely approached the competitive "norm" than most others which have been studied, and that the narrowness of these largely intraindustry differentials should not be taken as evidence of a similar narrowness of *inter*industry differentials for the same type of labor.

Since no one has been able to measure labor quality differences with any degree of precision, nearly every set of wage data we use to test the competitive hypothesis is subject to conflicting interpretations on this crucial score. I would agree, however, with the view that many of these local wage differentials for the same jobs are so large—50 to 100 percent—that they cannot be explained away as reflections solely of quality differentials. If you grant this, then haven't you denied the validity of the competitive hypothesis? No, says Reder quite properly, since the hypothesis would predict wage variations arising from dis-equilibrium situations in the short run. To test this possibility, he then examines the several studies that have compared wage and employment changes over the short run but justifiably concludes that the evidence on this point is as conflicting as the evidence adduced to test alter-native models stressing concentration, profits, productivity, and union organizations.

One way of resolving this question might be to apply to the local-market level the type of analysis, comparing wage changes with several variables, which to date has largely been employed at the national, industry-wide level. Unlike the gross industry averages used in most studies, local wage data are often available for identical jobs, are obviously not affected by interindustry differences in location, and afford a good test of whether variations within industries (e.g., be-tween large and small firms) are not more revealing than those between industries.

For example, consider the provocative data which Dunlop cites to

---

[1] Alfred Marshall, *Principles of Economics*, 8th ed., London, Macmillan, 1936, pp. 548-549.

illustrate his concept of wage contours: in Boston in July 1953, the union rate for truck drivers ranged among twenty-two industries from $1.27 to $2.494.[2] Dunlop argues persuasively that this great disparity in the rates paid for the same job in the same market, particularly when organized by the same union, cannot be satisfactorily explained either by orthodox theory or by models which emphasize market frictions or union power. Similar data can be found in other local market studies and in various BLS publications, and these data in some ways pose the issues involved in interindustry wage differentials more sharply than the national, all-worker industry averages. Unfortunately, perhaps for lack of data on the nonwage variables, there has been little if any attempt made to analyze these local wage data with the rigorous, quantitative methods employed in most of the interindustry wage studies.

Also, in keeping with the make-work-for-authors spirit of this conference, I would suggest that the local market has advantages as the setting for the long-run test that Reder correctly points out is the most fitting for his purposes: the determination of whether the differentials existing between the high- and low-wage industries in a given base year narrow over the long run. I don't know if any of the Census or Labor Department occupational and industry data from the turn of the century could be followed through for a single city, but this procedure, if at all feasible, would naturally avoid the problems posed by long-run shifts in skill mix and location.

Difficult as such a test would be, I nevertheless suggest that something more persuasive is needed as a proof of the long-run validity of the competitive model than the evidence Reder can now offer. As he notes, we mildly disagree about the interpretation of my own findings on this point. In analyzing annual earnings data for workers in 84 manufacturing industries over the 1899-1950 period, I found that the percentage differential between the industries which were at the top and the bottom of the structure in 1899 narrowed only from 162 per cent in 1899 to 149 per cent in 1950. While it is true that this slight narrowing "tends to support" the competitive model, it is hardly overwhelming as evidence of the leveling effects of competition over a fifty-year period, and certainly it is not as convincing as the drop in the skill margin from 200 per cent to 138 per cent over a comparable

---

[2] John T. Dunlop, "The Task of Contemporary Wage Theory," in *New Concepts in Wage Determination*, Taylor and Pierson, eds., New York, McGraw-Hill, 1957, p. 135.

period—a drop, incidentally, which in itself could have produced a narrowing of interindustry all-worker differentials (assuming little change in skill mix) without narrowing the "real" differentials between wages for comparable jobs.

Of course, all-worker data can greatly overstate interindustry differentials because of the effect of skill mix. One of the few sources of wage data by industry and occupation over time is the Conference Board figures for unskilled rates by industry for 1923-46. My impression is that these data are derived from a sample of highly dubious value, but for what they are worth they show the percentage differential between the unskilled rates in the high- and low-wage industries in 1923 to have been 134 per cent in 1923, 133 per cent in 1939, and 121 per cent in 1946.[3] Perhaps better data of this nature over a longer period would show the substantial narrowing necessary to support Reder's argument, but the available evidence is weak indeed.

When he turns from this "positive" test to considering the alternatives offered by others, however, I feel he makes at least two very significant contributions. The first is his vigorous reminder to fellow economists that there is, after all, a difference between the short and long run, a first principle frequently forgotten by some of us in our absorption with the turbulent labor markets of the 1930's and 1940's. Second, he points out that some of the studies of one aspect of this wage structure— short-run wage changes compared with several variables—proceed quite oblivious to the results of studies of a different aspect, the structure's dispersion over time. If I read him correctly on this point, he is the first to warn that many studies have suggested in effect that wages increase most rapidly *over time* in those industries that tend to be the highest-paying *at any point in time*—which would result in a steadily expanding structure, although all the evidence is against this. Thus, the data seem to indicate that, at least in some recent periods, wages increased most rapidly in industries such as iron and steel, petroleum refining, rubber, and automobiles, which have long been high-wage industries in an absolute sense, and the laggards are such industries as cotton textiles and boots and shoes, which are low-wage industries to begin with.

But might this be simply a short-run phenomenon—that, as Reynolds

[3] Median earnings of the top quarter of the wage structure divided by median earnings of the bottom quarter. For the NICB data, see Sumner H. Slichter, "Notes on the Structure of Wages," *Review of Economics and Statistics*, Feb. 1950, p. 89.

and Taft suggest,[4] most industries pass through a "life cycle" in which they rank at the top of the structure in their growth years and are then supplanted by other, newer industries? This possibility has not been adequately tested, but again the burden of my own findings is to the effect that the high-wage industries of fifty years ago tenaciously maintained their position against most comers.

And here we can return to the local market studies. Imperfect as our evidence now is, most of it is consistent in suggesting that: (1) substantial interindustry wage differentials exist for the same jobs in local markets and tend to persist in the short run, and (2) to a lesser extent, all-worker differentials exist between industries on the national level and these tend to persist even over the long run. If this is true, the explanation can lie in a combination of the competitive hypothesis *and* the findings of local market studies. That is, local differentials arise for a variety of reasons—frictions, monopsony, the entry of new industries, union pressure, management philosophy, etc., and once established, these differentials tend to persist, partly for "noneconomic" reasons (for instance, the practical difficulty of abolishing differentials accepted as customary) and partly for the "economic" reason that, as Reynolds and Taft put it, "the wage structure never gets a chance to approach static equilibrium."[5] If the poor do not get poorer, that is, the rich certainly get richer; they do not sit by idly until the low-wage industries catch up with them, and consequently the state of the arts is not frozen for any substantial length of time.

For example, Reynolds and Taft suggest that the persistence of regional differentials over time is the result not only of the growth of labor supply in the South but also of the continuing industrial expansion in the North and West, which has served to offset the "eroding effect of labor and capital migration."[6] Reder suggests that the failure of agricultural wages to catch up with manufacturing wages is also the result of a continuing disequilibrium over the long run. Can this not also be true of many other interindustry differentials? If it is true, however, it is difficult to isolate statistically the effects of the competitive hypothesis, and it also loses much of its predictive value at this particular level.

[4] Lloyd G. Reynolds and Cynthia H. Taft, *The Evolution of Wage Structure*, Yale University Press, 1956, pp. 356-357.

[5] Reynolds and Taft, *Evolution*, 369.

[6] *Ibid.*, p. 370.

To sum up: With respect to interindustry differentials, the competitive hypothesis has not been validated in the short run—nor, as Reder shows so well, has it been conclusively disproved. However, neither has it yet been proved or disproved for the long run.

Finally, two footnotes. First, it is to be devoutly hoped that we can soon incorporate fringe benefits in interindustry wage studies, for I share the suspicion that these have served to widen this type of differential during the very period when the structure of *rates* alone appears to have narrowed (and, of course, during the period when unions have greatly increased in strength).

Second, I hope someone will tackle the problem of our overreliance upon manufacturing data in these studies. Perhaps this is not a serious problem, since manufacturing industries certainly do vary greatly among themselves in certain respects. Yet, in view of the decreasing relative importance of manufacturing, I am uneasy over the studies in which the wage patterns among the 30 or 40 or 80 manufacturing industries for which we can get detailed data overpower the wage movements among a few nonmanufacturing industries. In spite of the hazards obviously involved, the relation of all-manufacturing wages to wages in agriculture, construction, mining, and particularly the service industries deserves more attention than it has received.

# The Effects of Unions on Industrial
# Wage Differentials

H. GREGG LEWIS

UNIVERSITY OF CHICAGO

## 1. Scope of the Paper

THE purpose of this paper is to estimate the impact of unionism on relative (percentage) wage differentials among industries in the United States. The estimates are based chiefly on evidence obtained from earlier studies of unionism and wage differentials.

The effect of unionism on the interindustrial relative wage structure at any date consists of a set of numbers, one number for each detailed industry in the United States.[1] Estimation of these numbers for each industry at each of several dates in the last three or four decades is an enormous undertaking, only a small part of which has been completed in research done to date. Nevertheless this research does provide evidence for estimating some of the global characteristics of the complete set of numbers for all industries in this period. This paper considers mainly these global numbers rather than estimates of the effects of unionism on relative wages of particular industries.

Let $w_t$ be the weighted geometric mean wage observed in a particular industry at date $t$ in the presence of unionism; $w_{0t}$ is the weighted geometric mean, with the same weights as in $w_t$,[2] that would

---

[1] If there are $n$ industries, there are only $(n\text{-}1)$ *independent* numbers in the set, since the all-industry average effect of unionism on relative wages is always zero.

[2] Both $w_t$ and $w_{0t}$ are weighted geometric means of the wages of the various grades of labor employed in the industry, with the same set of weights in $w_t$ as in $w_{0t}$. The relative weight for each grade is the ratio of the aggregate compensation per unit period of time of employees in the grade to the total compensation per unit period of time of all employees in the industry, the compensation ratios being calculated in the presence of unionism. (The compensation data that are directly available in historical records are those in the presence of unionism.)

If the aggregate production function in the industry were a Cobb-Douglas function of the rates of employment of the various grades of labor and other productive services and were independent of unionism, then the set of relative compensation weights would be the same in the presence of unionism as in its absence and the ratio of $w_t$ to $w_{0t}$ would be the "true" index of the effect of unionism on the absolute level of wages in the industry. In the more general case in which the elasticities of substitution among the productive services are not unity, the relative compensation weights in the presence of unionism will differ from those in the absence of unionism and $w_t/w_{0t}$ may be a biased index of the effect of unionism on the wages of the industry.

have been observed in the absence of unionism. (The total effect of unionism on the average wage of an industry consists of the direct effect of any unionism that is present in the industry and the indirect effect of unionism present elsewhere in the economy. Thus the "unionism" that I refer to in the expression "in the presence of unionism" is *all* of the unionism present in the economy. Similarly "in the absence of unionism" means "in the absence of any unionism in the economy.") The all-industry counterparts of $w_t$ and $w_{0t}$ are $\overline{w}_t$ and $\overline{w}_{0t}$ respectively.

The industry's *relative wage* in the presence of unionism is $v_t = w_t/\overline{w}_t$ and in the absence of unionism is $v_{0t} = w_{0t}/\overline{w}_{0t}$. The weighted all-industry geometric mean relative wage is unity both in the presence of unionism and in its absence.

The index of the effect of unionism on the relative wage of the industry is $I_t = v_t/v_{0t}$.[3] The weighted all-industry geometric mean of the $I$'s is always unity.

What I seek to estimate are two different aspects of the differences among industries in the relative wage effects of unionism:

1. The dispersion (standard deviation) among industries at various dates of the $I$'s: $\sigma_{I_t}$. (Here and elsewhere in this paper the symbol $\sigma$ denotes the standard deviation of the variable indicated in the subscript.) Because the $I$'s are ratios, it is sometimes simpler analytically to deal with the logarithms of the $I$'s, than with their absolute values. For values of $I$ close to unity there is little difference between $(I-1)$ and the natural logarithm of $I$. (For example, log $1.25 = 0.223$.) Thus for values of $\sigma_I$ of the size of those estimated in this paper, $\sigma_I \cong \sigma_{\log I}$.

---

[3] In defining relative wages I have not distinguished between relative *money* wages and relative *real* wages. The effects of unionism on relative money wages are the same as the effects of unionism on relative real wages only if the effects of unionism on the cost of living of employees in different industries are the same for all industries. I assume that any differences among industries in the effects of unionism on the cost of living of their employees are negligible and, therefore, interpret the relative wage findings of this paper as applying equally to relative money wages and relative real wages.

Let $A_t = w_t/w_{0t}$ be the index of the effect of unionism on the *absolute* (money or real as the case may be) wage level of a particular industry. The weighted all-industry geometric mean of the $A$'s is the index of the effect of unionism on the general wage level. It follows from these definitions and that of $I_t$ that $I_t = A_t/\overline{A}_t$. Thus the indexes $I$ of the effects of unionism on relative wages can be deduced from the set of indexes $A$ of the effects of unionism on absolute wages. The converse proposition, however, does not hold—the effects of unionism on absolute wages cannot be deduced from the effects of unionism on relative wages. Of course, if unionism has no effect on the general wage level, then $I_t = A_t$. However, not even the algebraic sign of $(\overline{A}_t - 1)$ can be deduced from knowledge only of the relative wage effects of unionism.

2. The effect of unionism on the relative dispersion of wages among industries at various dates as measured by $D_t = (\sigma_{\log v_t} - \sigma_{\log v_{0t}})$. The standard deviation $\sigma_I$ directly measures the extent to which the relative wage effects of unionism differ among industries. Furthermore, it is likely that the larger is this standard deviation, the larger is the impact of unionism on the distribution of employment and output among industries—the resource allocation effect of unionism.

If $\sigma_I$ is not zero, the effect $D$ of unionism on relative wage dispersion among industries must be positive unless the relative wage effects of unionism are sufficiently negatively correlated among industries with their relative wages. There is rather strong evidence that this correlation is positive (though less than unity) rather than negative and, therefore, that

(1) $$0 < D < \sigma_{\log I}.$$

If estimates of $I$ and of $v$ were available for one or more dates for a random sample of detailed industries, then both $\sigma_I$ and $D$ could be estimated for these dates from such sample data. Unfortunately, the numbers that emerge from presently available studies of unionism and wage differentials rarely are estimates of $I$ by detailed industry and date. The sample of such estimates provided by the studies is both small and nonrandom. Therefore, I have used a less direct approach.

The relative wage effect estimates that may be drawn from the empirical literature on unionism and wage differentials in numerous instances are for categories that are not industries. Hence in this and the following paragraph interpret the index $I$ as pertaining to any category of the labor force. Let $p$ be the ratio in the category of the total employee compensation of union labor—labor covered by collective bargaining arrangements—to the total compensation of all labor. I term $p$ the "extent of unionism" of the category. I denote the extent of unionism in the labor force as a whole by $\bar{p}$. The quantity $U = p - \bar{p}$ is the excess extent of unionism of the category. The all-category average of the $U$'s is zero.

The numbers that I have derived from the studies of unions and wage differentials are of two similar types:

A. For a pair of categories (denoted by subscripts 1 and 2) the logarithmic or percentage difference in the relative wage effects of unionism per percentage point difference in extent of unionism:

$$\frac{\log I_1 - \log I_2}{p_1 - p_2} \cong \frac{I_1 - I_2}{I_2(p_1 - p_2)} \cong \frac{I_1 - I_2}{p_1 - p_2}$$

B. For more than two categories the regression coefficient among the categories of log I (or I) on p. The dimension of the regression coefficient also is in per cent per percentage point difference in extent of unionism. Indeed, the type A numbers are similar regression coefficients in the two-category case.

Return now to the distribution of the relative wage effects of unionism among industries. Let $\beta$ denote the regression coefficient of log I (or I) on p among all industries. Then,

$$(2) \qquad\qquad \log I = \beta U + \lambda,$$

where $\lambda$ is the residual from the regression. It follows from equation (2) that

$$(3) \qquad\qquad \sigma^2{}_{\log I} = \beta^2 \sigma_p{}^2 + \sigma_\lambda{}^2.$$

I have gauged the order of magnitude of $\beta$ from the type A and B numbers derived from the earlier studies. I have estimated the standard deviation of extent of unionism among industries for the late 1920's and the 1950's from a wide variety of data, chiefly those on union membership and employment by industry.

It follows from equation (3) that $\beta\sigma_p$ cannot exceed $\sigma_{\log I}$. (The ratio $\beta\sigma_p/\sigma_{\log I}$ is the simple correlation coefficient between log I and $p$; the correlation between these two variables among industries surely is considerably less than unity.) Thus I regard my estimates of $\beta\sigma_p$ as underestimates of the corresponding values of $\sigma_{\log I}$.

It is much more difficult to estimate the residual variance $\sigma_\lambda{}^2$. For a few industries, all relatively highly unionized, I have been able to derive estimates of the index $I$. For these industries I have used equation (2) to calculate approximations of $\lambda$ from the estimates of $I$, $U$, and $\beta$. The standard deviation of these residuals is a crude estimate of $\sigma_\lambda$

I turn now to the problem of estimating the effect of unionism on relative wage dispersion among industries as measured by $D = \sigma_{\log v} - \sigma_{\log v_0}$. $D$ may be approximated from the inequality $|D| < \sigma_{\log I}$. More precise estimation of $D$ requires knowledge of the correlation between relative wages and the relative wage effects of unionism among industries. Since $\log I = \log v - \log v_0$,

$$(4) \qquad\qquad \sigma^2{}_{\log v_0} = \sigma^2{}_{\log v} + \sigma^2{}_{\log I} - 2r_{Iv}\,\sigma_{\log v}\,\sigma_{\log I}$$

where $r_{Iv}$ is the simple correlation between log I and log $v$.

Data are available for estimating the correlation between relative wages, $v$, and extent of unionism, $p$. In estimating $D$ in section 4, I have assumed that $r_{Iv} = r_{pv}$.

## 2. Summary of the Relative Wage Effect Estimates Derived from Earlier Studies

Our knowledge of the relative wage impact of unionism in the United States stems almost entirely from research reported in the last decade and a half. Before World War II there were, to be sure, many serious studies of wages and of unionism containing statements regarding the effects of unions on wage differentials. However, in none of these studies, to the best of my knowledge, are there numerical estimates, with supporting data, of the relative wage effects of unions. Since the war, on the other hand, there has been an outpouring of empirical research on unions and wage differentials. Table 1 summarizes the estimates of the relative wage effects of unionism which I have drawn from this research.[4]

The effect of unionism on the relative wage differential between a pair of industries cannot be estimated simply from: the percentage difference between the two industries in their average hourly or weekly earnings or compensation or similar measure of average wages and the difference between the two industries in extent of unionism. The gross (unadjusted) differentials among industries in the common measures of average wages reflect not only effects of unionism but also the effects of differences among industries in:

1. The composition of their working forces by such characteristics as skill, age, sex, race, and so on
2. The distribution of their employment by size of community and in the attractiveness of the work and working conditions they offer employees
3. The rates of change over time of underlying demand and supply

[4] In constructing Table 1, I have endeavored to cover all the reports of empirical research on unionism and wage differentials from which I could take directly or compute numerical estimates of relative wage effects of unionism or of directions of change in these effects. (The table, however, does not cover the three recent studies mentioned below in note 6.) Unfortunately, a considerable part of the postwar research on unions and wage differentials is available only in unpublished papers and doctoral dissertations some of which, no doubt, are not known to me. The table also excludes a good many published studies in which there is evidence that unionism may have caused relative wage changes, but the evidence was of such nature that I could not estimate the size of the wage effects.

conditions and in the responsiveness of wages to these changes in conditions

## TABLE 1

ESTIMATES OF RELATIVE WAGE EFFECTS OF UNIONISM DERIVED FROM EARLIER STUDIES

(in per cent per percentage point difference in extent of unionism)

| Year | Author and Study Number | | | | |
|---|---|---|---|---|---|
| | Levinson (1) | Sobotka (2) | Greenslade (3) | Lurie (4) | Rayack (5) |
| 1914-18 | — | — | 0.40 | — | — |
| 1919 | — | < in 1914 | 0.30 | — | 0.24 |
| 1920 | < in 1914 | — | 0.57 | ≅ 1925 | — |
| 1922 | > in 1914 | — | 1.17 | — | 0.20 |
| 1923 | — | > in 1919 | — | ≅ 1925 | — |
| 1924 | — | — | 0.58—0.60 | — | 0.17 |
| 1925 | — | — | — | 0.15—0.20 | — |
| 1926 | — | — | 0.55—0.61 | — | 0.21 |
| 1928 | — | — | — | — | 0.30 |
| 1929 | > in 1922 | ≅ 1939 | 0.33—0.43 | 0.15—0.19 | — |
| 1930 | — | — | — | — | 0.34 |
| 1931 | > in 1929 | > in 1929 | 0.45—0.48 | — | — |
| 1932 | — | — | — | — | 0.39 |
| 1933 | > in 1931 | — | 0.56—0.58 | 0.22—0.24 | — |
| 1935 | — | < in 1929 | — | — | — |
| 1937 | — | — | ⎫ | 0.12 | — |
| 1938 | 0.16 | — | ⎬ 0.31 | 0.03—0.06 | — |
| 1939 | — | 0.25; 0.05 | ⎭ | — | 0.20 |
| 1941 | 0.17 | — | — | — | — |
| 1944 | 0.09 | < in 1939 | < in 1939 | — | — |
| 1945 | 0.07 | — | — | — | — |
| 1946 | 0.05 | — | — | — | ≅ 0.00 |
| 1948 | — | — | — | 0.07—0.18 | — |
| 1950 | — | > in 1944 | 0.50[a] | — | — |
| 1957 | — | — | — | ≅ 1948 | ≅ 0.00 |

| Study Number and Author | Estimated Effect and Date |
|---|---|
| 6. Ross | 0.08-0.09 (Jan. 1945) |
| 7. Ross and Goldner | 0.04 (1946) (1946 < 1938-42) |
| 8. Tullock | < 0.25 (1948-52) |
| 9. Goldner | 0.14-0.20 (1951-52) |
| 10. Garbarino | 0.15 (1940) |
| 11. Sobotka and others | 0.22-0.29 (1956) |
| 12. Scherer | 0.00 (1939); 0.06-0.10 (1948) |
| 13. Craycraft | 0.01 (1948); 0.19 (1954) |
| 14. Rees | 0.00 (1945-48); (1939 > 1945-48) |
| 15. Rapping | 0.08-0.35 (1950's) |
| 16. Friedman and Kuznets | < 0.25 (1929-34) |
| 17. Lewis | 0.00 (1948-51) |

[a] 1949-51 average.

## COVERAGE OF THE ESTIMATES, BY STUDY

*Study No.*                                *Coverage*

1.  1914-33: wage earners, by industry (and in some industries, by skill level), in selected mining, construction, manufacturing, transportation, and public utility industries.

    1938-46: wage earners, by industry, in selected mining and manufacturing industries.

2.  1939: 0.25 estimate is for composite of five skilled building crafts (carpenters, masons, painters, plasterers, plumbers), by city, in 32 large cities; 0.05 is for common construction labor, by city, in 32 large cities.

    Other years: given group is skilled building craftsmen; bench-mark group is all employees in economy.

3.  Given group: production workers in bituminous coal mining.
    Bench-mark group: all employees in economy.

4.  Given group: unionized motormen in local transit industry.
    Bench-mark group: nonunion motormen in local transit industry.

5.  1919-32: given group is unionized production workers in manufacturing of men's and boys' suits and coats; bench-mark group is nonunion production workers in same industry.

    Other years: given group is production workers in manufacturing of men's and boys' suits and coats; bench-mark group is all employees in economy.

6.  Wage earners, by industry, in selected mining and manufacturing industries.

7.  Wage earners, by industry, in selected mining, manufacturing, transportation, and public utility industries.

8.  Wage and salary employees, by industry, economy-wide.

9.  Wage earners in selected occupations, by standard metropolitan area, in 39 such areas.

10. Wage earners, by industry, in selected manufacturing industries.

11. Given group: commercial airline pilots. Bench-mark group: chemical engineers.

12. Given group: employees of year-round hotels in large cities in which these employees were relatively highly unionized.

    Bench-mark group: similar employees in large cities in which few of these employees were unionized.

13. Barbers, by city, in 20 large cities.

14. Given group: production workers in basic steel manufacturing.
    Bench-mark group: all employees in economy.

15. Given group: seamen in Atlantic coast ocean shipping.
    Bench-mark group: all employees in economy.

16. Given group: nonsalaried physicians.
    Bench-mark group: nonsalaried dentists.

17. Given group: civilian physicians.
    Bench-mark group: civilian dentists.

## STUDIES COVERED IN TABLE 1

*Study No.*

1.  Harold M. Levinson, *Unionism, Wage Trends, and Income Distribution, 1914-1947, Michigan Business Studies,* June 1951.

2.  Stephen P. Sobotka, "The Influence of Unions on Wages and Earnings of Labor in the Construction Industry," unpublished Ph.D. dissertation, University of Chicago, June 1952; "Union Influence on Wages: The Construction Industry," *Journal of Political Economy,* April 1953, pp. 127-143.

STUDIES COVERED IN TABLE 1 (concluded)

*Study No.*
3. Rush V. Greenslade, "The Economic Effects of Collective Bargaining in Bituminous Coal Mining," unpublished Ph.D. dissertation, University of Chicago, December 1952.
4. Melvin Lurie, "The Measurement of the Effect of Unionization on Wages in the Transit Industry," unpublished Ph.D. dissertation, University of Chicago, December 1958.
5. Elton Rayack, "The Effect of Unionism on Wages in the Men's Clothing Industry, 1911-1955," unpublished Ph.D. dissertation, University of Chicago, December 1957.
6. Arthur M. Ross, "The Influence of Unionism upon Earnings," *Quarterly Journal of Economics*, February 1948, pp. 263-286. This paper is Chapter VI in his *Trade Union Wage Policy*, University of California Press, 1950.
7. Arthur M. Ross and William Goldner, "Forces Affecting the Inter-industry Wage Structure," *Quarterly Journal of Economics*, May 1950, pp. 254-281.
8. Gordon Tullock, *The Sources of Union Gains*, Research Monograph 2, The Thomas Jefferson Center for Studies in Political Economy, University of Virginia, June 1959.
9. William Goldner, "Labor Market Factors and Skill Differentials in Wage Rates," *Proceedings of Tenth Annual Meeting of Industrial Relations Research Association*, 1958, pp. 207-216.
10. Joseph W. Garbarino, "A Theory of Interindustry Wage Structure Variation," *Quarterly Journal of Economics*, May 1950, pp. 282-305.
11. Stephen Sobotka and others, "Analysis of Airline Pilot Earnings," unpublished mimeographed manuscript, The Transportation Center at Northwestern University, March 1958.
12. Joseph Scherer, "Collective Bargaining in Service Industries: A Study of the Year-Round Hotels," unpublished Ph.D. dissertation, University of Chicago, August 1951; "The Union Impact on Wages: The Case of the Year-Round Hotel Industry," *Industrial and Labor Relations Review*, January 1956, pp. 213-224.
13. Joseph L. Craycraft, "A Cross-Section Analysis of the Effect of Unionism on the Relative Earnings of Barbers," unpublished M.A. paper, University of Chicago, Summer 1957.
14. Albert E. Rees, "The Effect of Collective Bargaining on Wage and Price Levels in the Basic Steel and Bituminous Coal Industries, 1945-1948," unpublished Ph.D. dissertation, University of Chicago, September 1950; "Postwar Wage Determination in the Basic Steel Industry," *American Economic Review*, June 1951, pp. 389-404; "The Economic Impact of Collective Bargaining in the Steel and Coal Industries during the Post-War Period," *Proceedings of the Third Annual Meeting of Industrial Relations Research Association*, 1950, pp. 203-212; Lloyd Ulman, "The Union and Wages in Basic Steel: A Comment," *American Economic Review*, June 1958, pp. 408-426; Rees, "Reply," *American Economic Review*, June 1958, pp. 426-433.
15. Leonard Rapping, "The Impact of Unionism and Government Subsidies on the Relative Wages of Seamen," unpublished Ph.D. dissertation, University of Chicago, 1961.
16. Milton Friedman and Simon Kuznets, *Income from Independent Professional Practice*, New York, National Bureau of Economic Research, 1945, Chapter 4.
17. H. Gregg Lewis, unpublished paper.

Because the studies covered in Table 1 are numerous and dissimilar in their details, I cannot provide here[5] a study-by-study description of either the data used in the studies or of the techniques employed to separate the effects of unionism from those of other statistical and economic factors. Speaking broadly, however, two different approaches have been used to estimate the relative wage effects of unions.

1. The *cross-section* approach compares the average wage of a given, usually highly unionized, category of labor at a given date with the corresponding average wage of a less highly unionized bench-mark group of labor. The gross wage differential between the two groups is adjusted to eliminate the effects of some of the factors listed above that would produce a difference in average wages between the two groups in the absence of unionism. It is this adjusted or residual difference in average wages that is attributed to unionism.

Two difficulties arise in the use of this method. First, if the two groups differ substantially in characteristics other than unionism, it is often very costly, given available data, to adjust the gross wage difference more than crudely, if at all, for some of the factors other than unionism. The residual wage difference attributed to unionism then contains not only the effects of unionism and of the errors of measurement in the underlying wage data, but also the errors of omission and commission in adjusting the gross wage difference. Moreover, it is likely, I think, that the errors resulting from incomplete adjustment of the gross wage difference more frequently lead to overestimation than to underestimation of the effect of unionism. In this paper "relative wage effects of unionism" are the effects of unionism on the relative wages *of labor of given relative quality*. If relative quality differences between given and bench-mark groups of labor typically were uncorrelated with the true effects of unionism on the relative wage differentials between the two groups, failure to adjust gross wage differences fully for the quality differences would not lead to overestimation, on the average, of the relative wage effects of unionism. However, unionism itself may cause relative quality differences that are positively correlated with its relative wage effects.

For example, a 25 per cent greater relative wage for commercial airline pilots than would be true in the absence of unionization of

[5] In a forthcoming monograph, *Unionism and Relative Wages in the United States: An Empirical Inquiry*, I review in detail the relevant portions of the studies covered in Table 1 and in other respects document fully the data and procedures underlying the estimates given in Table 1.

these pilots, with pilot quality only loosely specified in collective bargaining, probably would be accompanied by substantial increases in the hiring standards of new pilots by the airlines. New pilots would have to meet higher standards of physical fitness, flight training and experience, and the like. The average quality of pilots employed thus would rise, reducing the true relative wage effect of unionism below 25 per cent.

Union rules may restrain employers from taking full advantage of collectively bargained higher relative wages to raise the average quality of their working forces. In some cases, the rules may be so restrictive as to cause average quality to fall. Nevertheless, I doubt that on the average the union rules have completely prevented increases in relative quality from taking place.

The difficulties of adjusting gross wage differences, when the given and bench-mark groups differ considerably in their labor force characteristics, provide an incentive to restrict the wage comparisons to groups of labor that resemble each other closely except with respect to unionism: union and nonunion employees in the same detailed industry, occupation, locality, size of establishment, of the same sex, race, work experience, etc. The imposition of such strong comparability criteria, however, tends to confine the estimates of the relative wage effects of unionism to small and highly selected samples of union and nonunion employees, whose services may be highly substitutable in demand. The resulting estimates of the relative wage impact of unionism may have little relevance for gauging the effects of unionism on wage differentials *among* industries, occupations, localities, etc.

Several authors have used a variant of the cross-section method in which more than two groups of labor differing in extent of unionism were considered simultaneously. The variant adjusts the wages of each of the groups for factors other than unionism and correlates the adjusted wages with extent of unionism to estimate the wage differential effect of unionism per percentage point difference in extent of unionism. The adjustment and the correlation, of course, may take place simultaneously in a multivariate analysis of wages, extent of unionism, and variables reflecting factors other than unionism.

2. The *time-series* approach adjusts the *change* from a base date to a given date in the gross wage differential between the given group and the bench-mark group for factors other than unionism, and attributes the adjusted or residual *change* in wage differential to the *change*

in unionism from the base date to the given date. This method involves difficulties similar to those of the cross-section method. Furthermore, the adjusted change in the wage differential is an estimate of the level at the given date (as well as the change in the level from the base date to the given date) of the effect of unionism on the wage differential between the two groups only if the corresponding effect at the base date was negligible.

There is also a variant of the time-series method comparable to that of the cross-section method in which the adjusted changes in wages for more than two groups of labor are correlated with the corresponding changes in the extent of unionism of these groups.

Really thorough review of any of the studies covered in Table 1 would go far beyond tabulating summary numbers derived from the study to inquiry into the accuracy and relevance of the evidence used in the study, assembly of relevant data not brought to bear on the findings, and critical analysis of the specific techniques used to isolate unionism from other factors affecting wage differentials. I have not attempted such thorough review of any of the studies covered in Table 1. However, few of the figures in the table are precise copies of numerical estimates made in the studies. In the first place, the statistical work in some of the studies was not carried to the point of providing *numerical* estimates of the relative wage effects of unionism. Secondly, in some other studies the numerical estimates were not in the same dimensions as those in Table 1. For both groups of studies I have made the additional calculations, data permitting, required to reach numerical estimates of the relative wage effects of unionism in per cent per percentage point difference in extent of unionism. Thirdly, in a number of instances I have made alternative estimates that were prompted by disagreements with procedures used in some of the studies or by the ready availability now of data superior to some of those used in the studies. Although in the main I have performed these calculations on the data and within the analytical framework presented in each study, the responsibility for the numbers emerging from these calculations clearly is mine rather than that of the authors of the studies.

In interpreting Table 1, it is important to recognize that there is some statistical dependence among the estimates from the separate studies. The dependence among the figures for the mid-1940's derived from the Levinson, Ross, and Ross and Goldner papers is almost perfect. There is also some dependence between the 1938 and 1941 estimates derived from Levinson and the 1940 estimate derived from Garbarino. Moreover, the six studies with broad coverage (Levinson, Ross, Ross and Goldner, Tullock, Goldner, and Garbarino), of course, overlap in varying degree the other studies in the table.

Though I show the numbers in Table 1 to two decimal places, the individual estimates undoubtedly contain errors that in some cases may be quite large. Thus, though comparison of the figures for bituminous coal mining (Greenslade, study number 3) and for the skilled building trades (Sobotka, study number 2), for example, with other figures in the table appears to confirm the popular view that the unions representing coal miners and skilled building craftsmen have been exceptionally effective in raising the relative wages of these workers, I do not regard the evidence in the table as establishing this view conclusively. Furthermore, the data in the table and in more detail in the works underlying it are too meager, in my judgment, to settle the differences among economists regarding the comparative effectiveness of craft and industrial unionism and the significance of degree of product monopoly (output concentration) as a factor producing differences in relative wage effects of unionism.

On the other hand, Table 1 does support two general empirical findings.

1. The effects of unionism on relative wages have varied substantially from one date to another in what appears to be a systematic fashion. The evidence is strongest for the period beginning in the late 1930's and ending at the end of the war or shortly thereafter. Five of the seven studies (counting the Levinson and Ross-Goldner studies as one study) that provided data for that period show declines in the relative wage effects of unionism from the beginning to the end of the period. There is less information for the comparable World War I period, but what there is points to a similar decline in relative wage effect. Both 1914-20 and 1939-48 were marked by rapid inflation of the general price level. Furthermore, there is some evidence of decline in relative wage effects from 1933 to 1939.

In contrast, three of the four studies that span the 1920-22 deflation and all five of the studies covering the deflation following 1929 show increases in the relative wage effects of unionism. Moreover, though the period since 1948 was not one of deflation, the rate of inflation generally was much lower than during and immediately following

World War II, and Table 1 indicates that the relative wage effects of unionism may have risen considerably since 1948.[6]

Thus the data in Table 1 suggest that unionism has tended to make money wages of union labor somewhat rigid against movements of the general price level in the short run. There are two reasons for suspecting that the information in Table 1 may give an erroneous impression of the amount of money wage rigidity attributable to collective bargaining:

First, the wage rigidity finding rests chiefly on the data from the five studies summarized at the top of Table 1. Part of the data in the Levinson study (for 1933 and earlier years) consists, however, of minimum wage rates specified in union agreements and such contract minima probably are more rigid than wage rates actually paid in the short run. The time series data on skilled building trades wages in Sobotka's study (number 2) also may be defective in this respect.

Second, the adjustments of the wage data for factors that might have produced wage rigidity in the absence of unionism, in the estimates derived from the data in the Levinson, Sobotka building trades (except the estimates for 1939), Greenslade, and Rayack (after 1932) studies were crude. Hence the appearance of union money wage rigidity in Table 1 may reflect in part errors in the estimates of the relative wage effects of unionism.[7]

[6] Three recent studies, not covered in Table 1, contain information, I judge from my first reading of them, from which it may be possible to estimate the changes since 1948 in the relative wage impact of unionism. They are:
Yossef Attiyeh, "Wage-Price Spiral versus Demand Inflation: United States, 1949-1957," unpublished Ph.D. dissertation, University of Chicago, Dec. 1959. Harold M. Levinson, "Postwar Movement of Prices and Wages in Manufacturing Industries," Study Paper No. 21, *Study of Employment, Growth, and Price Levels*, Joint Economic Committee, 86th Congress, 2d sess., 1960. William G. Bowen, *Wage Behavior in the Postwar Period*, Industrial Relations Section, Princeton University, 1960.
In the larger study from which I have drawn this paper I plan to make use of the data in these three studies.

[7] I have nearly completed research in which I am attempting to estimate the extent to which changes over time in the rate of inflation have led to changes in the opposite direction in the relative wage effects of unionism. Let $y$ be a measure of the rate of inflation of money wages or prices and $U$ the excess of the extent of unionism of an industry over the extent of unionism in the economy as a whole. The distinguishing feature of the statistical economic models that I have used is that they include among the variables determining the relative wage of an industry not only $U$, but also $y$ and the product of $U$ and $y$. I have fitted a variety of models incorporating these variables to time-series data (annual, 1920-58) for two large industry groups, one consisting of the most extensively unionized industries and the second of almost completely nonunion industries. The results to date rather

2. Throughout the last twenty-five years and very likely also in earlier years (except those of rapid deflation), the *average* relative wage effect of unionism, as measured by the coefficient $\beta$ in per cent per percentage point difference in extent of unionism, probably at no time exceeded 0.25 and may have been 0.05 or less at the end of and just following World War II.

Except for bituminous coal mining (study number 3), men's clothing (study number 5) in 1930 and 1932, and, uncertainly, Atlantic Coast seamen (study number 15), none of the numerical estimates in Table 1 is as large as 0.30. Furthermore, I suspect that the biases in Table 1 are toward overestimation rather than underestimation of $\beta$, not only because of inadequate control over the labor quality factor discussed in the preceding section, but also because of bias in the coverage of Table 1. I judge from my experience as an onlooker and, sometimes, adviser in several of the studies covered by the table that the industries and occupations selected for study consisted disproportionately of those in which the relative wage effects of unionism were believed to be exceptionally large. These beliefs, of course, may have been wrong, but if they were right, the sample of estimates in the table has an upward bias on this account. For these reasons I put the upper limit estimate of $\beta$ at 0.20, except possibly during periods of rapid deflation of the general price level.

On the other hand, it is difficult to put the central tendency of the estimates in the table below 0.10 except in the years near the end of World War II. Thus I estimate that, apart from periods of unusually rapid inflation or of deflation, the average relative wage effect of unionism, $\beta$, was 0.10 to 0.20 per cent per percentage point difference in extent of unionism.

### 3. Estimates of the Dispersion among Industries in Relative Wage Impact of Unionism

Return now to equation (3) of section 1:

$$(3) \qquad \sigma^2_{\log I} = \beta^2 \sigma^2_p + \sigma^2_\lambda$$

where $\sigma^2_{\log I}$ is the variance among industries in the logarithms of the relative wage effect indexes $I$, $\sigma^2_p$ is the corresponding variance of extent

---

consistently show negative partial correlations between relative wages and $Uy$, indicating that the relative wage effects of unionism (per percentage point difference in extent of unionism) have tended to move in the opposite direction to the rate of inflation.

of unionism, and $\sigma^2_\lambda$ is the residual variance—that is, that part of $\sigma^2_{\log I}$ not accounted for by dispersion among industries in extent of unionism. In this section I estimate $\sigma_p$ and, much more roughly, $\sigma_\lambda$.

Despite the widespread interest in unionism and collective bargaining in the last half-century, there is no source to which one can turn for the distributions by industry, with substantial industry detail, of either the total compensation or the number of workers covered by collective bargaining agreements in recent years. I was forced, therefore, to make my own estimates of extent of unionism by industry from fragmentary information. Table 2 contains these estimates.

TABLE 2

NUMBER OF UNION WORKERS AS A PER CENT OF NUMBER OF
PERSONS ENGAGED IN PRODUCTION, BY INDUSTRY
GROUP, 1929 AND 1953

| | Per Cent | |
| Industry Group | 1929 | 1953 |
| --- | --- | --- |
| Farms | a | a |
| Agricultural services, forestry, and fishing | a | 12 |
| Metal mining | 3 | 68 |
| Anthracite mining | 80 | 75 |
| Bituminous and other soft-coal mining | 30 | 86 |
| Crude petroleum and natural gas | 1 | 13 |
| Nonmetallic mining and quarrying | 12 | 30 |
| Contract construction | 31 | 51 |
| Food and kindred products | 4 | 44 |
| Tobacco manufactures | 12 | 57 |
| Textile-mill products | 3 | 30 |
| Apparel and other finished fabric products | 28 | 52 |
| Lumber and timber basic products | 12 | 20 |
| Furniture and finished lumber products | 3 | 29 |
| Paper and allied products | 2 | 45 |
| Printing, publishing, and allied industries | 23 | 37 |
| Chemicals and allied products | a | 39 |
| Products of petroleum and coal | a | 67 |
| Rubber products | a | 54 |
| Leather and leather products | 12 | 39 |
| Stone, clay, and glass products | 9 | 44 |
| Iron and steel and their products, including ordnance | 5 | 57 |
| Nonferrous metals and their products | 4 | 46 |
| Miscellaneous manufacturing | 3 | 18 |
| Machinery, except electrical | 13 | 45 |
| Electrical machinery | 12 | 56 |
| Transportation equipment, except automobiles | a | 52 |
| Automobiles and automobile equipment | a | 80 |
| Wholesale trade | a | 4 |

(continued)

TABLE 2 (concluded)

| Industry Group | Per Cent 1929 | Per Cent 1953 |
|---|---|---|
| Retail trade and automobile services | 1 | 11 |
| Banking | a | a |
| Security and commodity dealers, brokers, and exchanges | a | 3 |
| Finance, n. e. c. | a | a |
| Insurance carriers | a | a |
| Insurance agents and combination offices | a | 8 |
| Real estate | 2 | 11 |
| Railroads | 33 | 95 |
| Local railways and bus lines | 36 | 74 |
| Highway passenger transportation, n. e. c. | a | 58 |
| Highway freight transportation and warehousing | 25 | 63 |
| Water transportation | 16 | 74 |
| Air transportation | a | 51 |
| Pipeline transportation | a | 50 |
| Services allied to transportation | 22 | 59 |
| Telephone, telegraph, and related services | 1 | 68 |
| Radio broadcasting and television | a | 50 |
| Utilities: electric and gas | a | 41 |
| Local utilities and public services, n. e. c. | a | a |
| Hotels and other lodging places | 2 | 20 |
| Personal services | 6 | 19 |
| Private households | a | a |
| Commercial and trade schools, employment agencies | a | a |
| Business services, n. e. c. | a | a |
| Miscellaneous repair services and hand trades | a | a |
| Motion pictures | 15 | 21 |
| Other amusement and recreation | 21 | 23 |
| Medical and other health services | a | a |
| Legal services | a | a |
| Engineering and other professional services | a | 1 |
| Educational services, n. e. c. | a | a |
| Nonprofit membership organizations | a | a |
| Federal general government, civilian | 11 | 15 |
| Federal government enterprises | 65 | 79 |
| Public education | a | 2 |
| State and local general government, nonschool | 1 | 11 |
| State and local government enterprises | a | 30 |

SOURCE: See accompanying text.
a Less than 0.5 per cent.
n. e. c. = not elsewhere classified.

The denominators of the percentages in Table 2, except for nine industry groups in 1953, are the Department of Commerce estimates of the number of persons engaged in production.[8] The numerators

[8] *National Income*, 1954 ed., supplement to *Survey of Current Business*, 1954,

of the percentages are estimates of the number of employed persons covered by collective bargaining arrangements. The 1929 numerators are based on Leo Wolman's estimates of union membership by industry[9] and on information obtained from union journals and proceedings and studies of trade unionism in the 1920's. The 1953 numerators were estimated from information from a wide variety of sources: unpublished tabulations of the membership of individual trade unions by Leo Wolman and Leo Troy;[10] the Bureau of Labor Statistics surveys of trade union membership,[11] its *Current Wage Development* series, its *Wage Structure* studies, and articles in its *Monthly Labor Review*; trade union proceedings and periodicals, and correspondence with some of the unions whose membership distributions by industry proved most difficult to estimate; business and popular periodicals; correspondence and interviews with economists who have studied unionism in particular industries; articles and book-length studies of particular unions and of unionism in particular industries; and such standard statistical sources as the *U.S. Census of Population* and the BLS monthly, *Employment and Earnings*.

I constructed Table 2 mainly in order to estimate the standard deviation among the industry groups used in the table of the per cent of workers covered by collective bargaining arrangements, rather than to provide myself and others with data on the extent of collective bargaining coverage in particular industries. Thus, though I believe

---

Table 28; *U.S. Income and Output*, supplement to *Survey of Current Business*, 1958, Table VI-16.

Because of changes in industry definitions, Commerce has not published estimates for the following manufacturing industries, for the years 1948 to date, that are strictly comparable to those for 1929-47:

| | |
|---|---|
| Lumber and timber basic products | Furniture and finished lumber products |
| Chemicals and allied products | Products of petroleum and coal |
| Iron and steel and their products, including ordnance | Machinery, except electrical |
| | Electrical machinery |
| Miscellaneous manufacturing | Nonferrous metals and their products |

(The industry classification scheme followed in Table 2 is that of the Department of Commerce in its series for 1929-47.) For the nine industry groups listed above I have extrapolated the Commerce series for 1929-47 using data from the Bureau of Labor Statistics, the Bureau of Employment Security, and the Bureau of the Census.

[9] Leo Wolman, *Ebb and Flow in Trade Unionism*, New York, National Bureau of Economic Research, 1936, Appendix Tables V, VII, VIII, and IX.

[10] Leo Wolman and Leo Troy, unpublished mimeographed tables revised as of August 1959, from a forthcoming monograph on trade union membership to be published by NBER.

[11] Bureau of Labor Statistics, Bulletin Nos. 1127, 1185, 1222, and 1267.

that the standard deviation of the 1953 figures in the table differs by less than 5 percentage points from the true standard deviation among the industry groups of the per cent of workers covered by collective bargaining arrangements, I suspect that some of the individual figures in the table may err by as much as 20 percentage points.[12]

The weighted (by number of persons engaged in production) standard deviations of the figures in Table 2 are 12.4 percentage points for 1929 and 24.7 percentage points for 1953. These standard deviations differ conceptually, however, from the standard deviation, $\sigma_p$, of extent of unionism among industries in two respects. First, the extent of unionism in an industry, as I have defined this concept, is not the per cent of total employment (number of persons engaged) covered by collective bargaining arrangements, but the per cent of total employee compensation going to persons covered by such arrangements. Fragmentary data indicate that for the economy as a whole the error on this score is quite small. Second, the classifications in Table 2 are for broad industry groups rather than detailed industries. There were many hints in the materials used that there was rather large dispersion in extent of unionism among industries within some of the industry groups of the table, especially in the manufacturing industry division. Since the standard deviations computed from Table 2 exclude this within-group dispersion, I put the estimated value of $\sigma_p$ at closer to 15 than to 12 percentage points for 1929 and nearer to 30 than 25 percentage points for 1953.

The data from which I estimated Table 2 indicate that the dispersion of extent of unionism among industries varied little during the decade 1923-33 and from about 1945 to date. Hence I estimate that $\sigma_p$ was approximately 15 percentage points in 1923-33, rose to about 30 percentage points by the end of World War II, and then stabilized at approximately 30 points.

In the preceding section, I estimated that $\beta$, the average relative wage effect of unionism per percentage point difference in extent of unionism, was approximately 0.10 to 0.20 in the latter part of the 1920's, the late 1930's and early 1940's, and again in recent years. This range and the estimates of $\sigma_p$ imply that $\beta\sigma_p$ was approximately 1½ to 3 percentage points in the late 1920's, 3 to 6 percentage points recently, and between these two ranges in and near 1940.

---

[12] I have least confidence in the figures for 1953 for the lumber, furniture, paper, stone-clay-glass, electrical machinery, and miscellaneous manufacturing industry groups.

The quantity $\beta\sigma_p$ is that part of the dispersion, $\sigma_I$ (or $\sigma_{\log I}$), of the relative wage effect indexes that is correlated among industries with extent of unionism. There is much less information for calculating the approximate value of the dispersion, $\sigma_\lambda$, of the $I$'s that is not correlated with extent of unionism. For the following six industries or industry groups I have calculated approximate values of $I$ and of $U$ (the excess of extent of unionism in the industry over extent of unionism in the economy) chiefly from data in the studies indicated:

Contract construction (Sobotka, study number 2, estimate of $I$ from 1939 data)

Bituminous coal mining (Greenslade, study number 3, estimate of $I$ from 1949-1951 data)

Local transit (Lurie, study number 4, estimate of $I$ from 1948 data)

Men's clothing (Rayack, study number 5, estimate of $I$ from 1957 data)

Hotels (Scherer, study number 12, estimate of $I$ from 1948 data)

Water transportation (Rapping, study number 15, estimate of $I$ for the 1950's).

I then calculated the residual $\lambda$ for each industry by means of equation (2) in the first section of this paper, with $\beta$ set equal to 0.20. The weighted (by number of persons engaged) standard deviation of these residuals was close to 5 percentage points—about the same size as the estimate of $\beta\sigma_p$ for recent years (at a value of $\beta$ of 0.20).

I do not hold this estimate of $\sigma_\lambda$ in high esteem. It is based on imprecise information for a nonrandom sample consisting of six industry groups employing a small fraction of the labor force. On the other hand, the estimate does suggest that the residual dispersion $\sigma_\lambda$ is roughly the same in size as the dispersion $\beta\sigma_p$ correlated with extent of unionism, and thus that the total dispersion $\sigma_I$, is about half again as large as $\beta\sigma_p$. I conclude that in the late 1920's the standard deviation of the relative wage effects of unionism among industries was approximately 2 to 4 percentage points and recently about 4 to 8 percentage points.

## 4. Estimates of the Effects of Unionism on Interindustrial Relative Wage Dispersion

In the preceding section, I estimated the amount of dispersion, $\sigma_I \cong \sigma_{\log I}$, among industries of the relative wage effects of unions. In this section, I estimate the amount, $D = \sigma_{\log v} - \sigma_{\log v_0}$ of the effect of unionism on relative wage dispersion among industries. Although these two measures of the relative wage impact of unionism are related, they are not the same. In particular, the second cannot exceed the first numerically: $|D| \leq \sigma_{\log I}$. My estimates of $\sigma_I$ imply, therefore, that unionism changed the amount of interindustrial relative wage dispersion by no more than 2 to 4 percentage points in the late 1920's and no more than 4 to 8 percentage points recently.

Table 3 shows the standard deviation of relative average annual full-time compensation among the industry groups (except military and work relief) for which the Department of Commerce reports employment and employee compensation of wage and salary employees.[13] (The industry groups are the same as those in Table 2.)

TABLE 3

STANDARD DEVIATION OF RELATIVE AVERAGE ANNUAL FULL-TIME
COMPENSATION AMONG INDUSTRIES, 1929-58

(per cent)

| Year | Standard Deviation | Year | Standard Deviation | Year | Standard Deviation |
|------|--------------------|------|--------------------|------|--------------------|
| 1929 | 29.6 | 1939 | 31.9 | 1949 | 25.4 |
| 1930 | 29.9 | 1940 | 32.1 | 1950 | 26.5 |
| 1931 | 32.1 | 1941 | 32.0 | 1951 | 27.7 |
| 1932 | 35.1 | 1942 | 33.1 | 1952 | 28.0 |
| 1933 | 34.4 | 1943 | 31.7 | 1953 | 28.7 |
| 1934 | 33.4 | 1944 | 29.4 | 1954 | 28.9 |
| 1935 | 33.1 | 1945 | 26.6 | 1955 | 29.7 |
| 1936 | 33.0 | 1946 | 24.1 | 1956 | 30.5 |
| 1937 | 31.8 | 1947 | 24.2 | 1957 | 30.9 |
| 1938 | 32.4 | 1948 | 24.9 | 1958 | 31.5 |

SOURCE: See note 13.

[13] The data underlying Table 3 are largely from the following national income reports of the Office of Business Economics, Dept. of Commerce: *National Income*, 1954, *U.S. Income and Output*, 1958, and *Survey of Current Business*, July 1959, pp. 3-43.

For each industry group and year, I computed average annual full-time compensation by dividing total employee compensation by the number of full-time equivalent employees. The numbers in Table 3 are fixed weighted coefficients of variation of these average annual compensation figures. The fixed weight for each industry group is the group's average number of full-time equivalent employees over the period 1929-57.

For the nine industry groups mentioned in note 8, Commerce employment and employee compensation data for 1948-58 are not "strictly comparable" to those for 1929-47. I have extended the 1929-47 series for these groups through 1958

Throughout the whole period covered by the table the amount of relative wage dispersion among industries was quite large.[14] Furthermore, only a small part of the dispersion was transitory. In general, the industries whose relative wages were high in any one of the thirty years also had high relative wages in the other years: the standard deviation among the industry groups of their thirty-year average relative wages was 28.6 per cent, which is only slightly lower than the thirty-year average (30.1 per cent) of the figures in the table. Thus the interindustrial relative wage structure was a highly stable one in the sense that the correlations among industries between relative wages in one year and relative wages in another year in the period were very high. The structure was also relatively stable in a second sense: there is no trend to speak of in the figures in Table 3. On the other hand, some of the short-run changes in relative wage dispersion were large: the standard deviation rose by 5.5 percentage points from 1929 to 1932 and declined by 9.0 percentage points from 1942 to 1946.

As already noted, $\sigma_I$ is an overestimate of the magnitude of the effect of unionism on relative wage dispersion among industries, unless the relative wage effects of unionism are perfectly correlated among industries with relative wages. Nevertheless, though my estimates of $\sigma_I$ are not negligible compared to the figures in Table 3, it is quite clear that, unless I have badly underestimated $\sigma_I$, the level of relative wage dispersion among industries must be accounted for largely in terms of factors other than unionism. There is some tendency for the *movements* in the series in Table 3 to correlate positively with the changes in relative wage effects of unionism in Table 2. Thus it is quite possible

---

using the national income reports data and data from the Bureaus of Employment Security, Labor Statistics, and Census.

It was also necessary to allocate wage supplement totals for the Commerce "general government" headings among the industry groups within these headings. I allocated the wage supplements as follows: (1) zero wage supplements to "work relief," (2) wage supplements to the remaining groups in proportion to their total wages and salaries.

[14] It is likely that the standard deviations in Table 3 contain some upward bias resulting from errors of measurement in the relative wage figures from which they were computed. On the other hand, the standard deviations surely are biased downward by their exclusion of relative wage dispersion among detailed industries within the broad industry headings used by the Department of Commerce.

The standard deviations may also be affected by differences among industries in relative "full-time" hours worked per man per year. I suspect that in most of the years covered by the table the standard deviation of average hourly compensation would not have differed much from the standard deviation of average annual compensation.

that unionism may account for an important part of the difference between the level of the series in the late 1930's and early 1940's, and again in 1956-58, and the level in 1929-30. The changes in relative wage dispersion from 1929 to 1932, 1942 to 1946, and 1946 to 1958, however, are too large to be explained mainly in terms of unionism.

For the two years, 1929 and 1953, for which I have estimated extent of unionism for the industry groups in Table 2, I have attempted to make more precise estimates of the effect of unionism on interindustrial relative wage dispersion. These estimates take into account, at least roughly, the correlation among industries between relative wages and the relative wage effects of unionism. The procedure followed is that discussed at the end of section 1. For each industry group in Table 2, the estimates of relative wages $v$, in the presence of unionism for 1929 and 1953, are those underlying the standard deviations for those years in Table 3. The formula used for calculating relative wages, $v_0$, in the absence of unionism is:

$$v_0 = v/(1 + U\sigma_I/\sigma_p)$$

where $U$ is the excess of the extent of unionism $p$ in the industry group over the average extent of unionism $\bar{p}$ in all industries. My estimates of $\sigma_I$ and $\sigma_p$ imply that in both years the ratio $\sigma_I/\sigma_p$ was approximately 0.2, and this is the figure that I used in the computations. The extent of unionism figures in Table 2 refer to all persons engaged in production in each industry group. The relative wage estimates underlying Table 3, however, cover only wage and salary employees on a full-time equivalent basis. To make the extent of unionism figures comparable with the relative wage figures, I multiplied each figure in Table 2 by the ratio for the industry group and year of the number of persons engaged in production to the number of full-time equivalent employees.[15]

For 1929, the estimated standard deviation of relative wages in the absence of unionism was 29.5 per cent, negligibly lower than the actual dispersion, 29.6 per cent, shown in Table 3. The estimate for 1953 of the standard deviation of relative wages in the absence of unionism was 26.4 per cent, 2.3 percentage points lower than the actual standard deviation of 28.7 per cent. Thus though unionism apparently explains the slightly higher level of relative wage dispersion in recent years than in 1929-30, it can account for only a small part of the actual

[15] See notes 8 and 13 for sources of these employment data.

dispersion in relative wages during the period 1929 to 1958. Further-more, these more precise estimates make it very likely that the large changes in relative wage dispersion from 1929 to 1932, 1942 to 1946, and 1946 to 1958 stemmed mostly from factors other than unionism.

## 5. Summary

In this paper I have brought together information from a rather large number of studies of unionism for the purpose of estimating for the economy as a whole (1) the extent to which unionism has affected in different proportions the wages paid by different industries and (2) the amount of the effect of unionism on relative wage dispersion among industries. These estimates are easily summarized:

a. The standard deviation among industries of the percentage effects of unionism on relative wages, I estimate, was of the order of magnitude of 2 to 4 percentage points in the latter half of the 1920's, about 4 to 8 percentage points recently, between these two ranges in the late 1930's and early 1940's, but may have been as low as 2 percentage points or even lower at the end of and immediately following World War II. The data in Tables 1 and 2 indicate that a standard deviation of relative wage effects of unionism as large as 4 to 8 per cent surely involves for some industries relative wage effects that, I judge, few economists would describe as either "small" or "economically insignificant."

b. The role of unionism as a factor explaining relative wage dispersion among industries surely was minor compared to that of factors other than unionism. During the period 1929-58 the standard deviation of relative wages among industries ranged from 24 to 35 per cent and averaged 30 per cent. In 1929 the dispersion was about 30 per cent, in 1953 about 29 per cent. I estimate that in the absence of unionism the dispersion would have been only slightly lower: by less than one-half percentage point in 1929 and by roughly 2 to 3 percentage points in 1953.

## COMMENT

JOHN T. DUNLOP

(1) The effects of combinations of workmen, trade unions or collective bargaining have been a persistent problem to economists from the earliest days of the discipline in Great Britain. The many recent attempts to measure or to estimate the magnitude of these effects is in keeping

with the quantitative developments of our discipline. Gregg Lewis is concerned with only one dimension of the effects of unions, that on interindustry wage differentials. He is not concerned with the effects of unions (or collective bargaining) on the level of wages nor with its impact on occupational or geographical differentials or other aspects of the structure of wages. But he does provide a useful summary and interpretation of seventeen studies of interindustry differentials, although since his paper was prepared a number of additional articles have appeared.

(2) Lewis' general results will not surprise students of the problem. He concludes that the relative wage effect of unionism among industries was approximately 2 to 4 percentage points in the late 1920's and about 4 to 8 percentage points in the late 1950's; that the interindustry wage structure tends to be highly stable; that unionism tended to make money wages somewhat rigid against price decreases in the Great Depression and against price increases in the post-World War II inflation, and that relative wage dispersion among industries must be accounted for largely in terms of factors other than unionism.

(3) In view of the growing number of statistical studies of the impact of unions on wages, it is unfortunate that more attention has not been paid to a number of basic questions concerning the significance and fruitfulness of this use of scholarly resources. There are a number of problems with the whole line of inquiry which need to be raised, and the present conference is an appropriate occasion.

(4) On general intellectual grounds one should suspect that it would be well-nigh impossible to measure the specific impact on wage rates, and more specifically, the effects on the interindustry wage structure, of so complex an institutional change as the introduction of collective bargaining. To separate out the independent effect of unionism from all the other factors influencing wage-rate structures implies a higher degree of confidence in our statistical data and methods and a simpler view of the workings of collective bargaining than is warranted.

One must seek a reason for this persistent concern with the impact of unionism. There appears to be no similar concern to measure the independent effect of the corporate form of organization on industrial prices, or the independent effects of the banking sytem or the savings banks on the structure of interest rates. No one estimates what prices would be or what the price structure would look like with a different size distribution of enterprises, or with a greater or lesser degree of concentration in business. No one attempts to give a figure for the effect of insurance companies or investment trusts or personal finance companies on the structure of interest rates. The persistent concern with the impact of unionism as an institution perhaps reflects a preoccupation with defending or condemning the institution as a whole. The institution is here and is likely to stay. The factors influencing wage structure and wage levels are a significant area of investigation, but the institution itself is hardly to be included in equations alongside profits, employment, productivity, the degree of competition, and other variables.

(5) All we know about collective bargaining suggests that the most important effects involve fundamental changes in an enterprise and its surrounding product and labor markets. It is really not possible to leave the enterprise and its markets alone, introduce a union, and then see what happens to the wage structure. The introduction of unionism typically involves a wholesale transformation. Lewis recognizes one facet of this change when he points to changes in what he terms the quality of the work force. But there are many more aspects to the problem. The content of jobs and the division of one from another is frequently altered. The method of wage payment may be changed. The division of compensation between wage rates and fringes and benefits is altered. Working rules change the meaning of the services supplied. Even greater significance should be placed on the point that virtually every determinant of wages in an enterprise and its surrounding markets may be altered, and often is changed, with the introduction of collective bargaining. The physical productivity of labor including its skill, training, and morale may be changed. The information on jobs and the workings of the labor market may be altered. The whole internal management of an enterprise is almost certain to be drastically altered to confront or deal with a labor organization. Aside from substitution, technology may be different. Product-market competition has been decisively affected in many cases. It is unrealistic and improper to pose the problem in terms of comparing wages with or without a union, assuming all other wage-setting factors are unchanged. Collective bargaining changes most of the wage-setting variables.

(6) The fashion to measure union power by the proportion of an industry governed by collective bargaining agreements or by the proportion of employees in an industry in labor unions involves some serious difficulties. This measure does not distinguish between equally

well-organized unions, some of whom operate in favorable markets and others who confront unfavorable environments. Consider the differences in wage movements in the last decade between the steel industry and the men's clothing industry. The difficulty with the measure of union power may be most clearly seen if one considers a fully unionized labor force; the measure then ceases to have meaning as any index of union power to interpret the wage structure. The measure also fails to acknowledge the difference between an initial impact of collective bargaining and the long-term consequences, a distinction which has been noted by many observers from Paul H. Douglas on. Moreover, the measure constitutes an implied negation of the whole field of union (or collective bargaining) policy making. The intellectual problem is to explain the different policies developed by different parties. Contrast, for example, the various policies of the coal and railroad unions, each equally well organized and confronted with autonomous decreases in demand in their product markets. There are different effects on wages (also employment, technical change, etc.) in accordance with different policies of the parties.

(7) Brief mention should be made of at least one statistical difficulty common to these studies. The use of standard industrial classifications of industries involves divisions of the economy that may be of little significance for wage-setting purposes. The industrial classifications of "stone, clay, and glass products," "products of petroleum and coal" or "chemical and allied products," for instance, involve mixtures of product markets and local or national wage-setting contours which are not likely to reveal the forces determining wage rates. Wage rates are determined in these separate contours, and ideally the wage data and the variables thought to influence wage rates should be presented for such contours or sectors of the economy.

# SUBJECT INDEX

Barber licensing, *see* Licensing, occupational

Clerical workers, number, 109-112
   *See also* Female labor force

Competitive enterprises, 160, 168, 176-177; and discrimination, 160-161
   *See also* Discrimination in employment; Monopoly

Competitive hypothesis, 279-284, 299-311
   *See also* Wage differentials

Discrimination in employment:
   Chinese, 181-183
   cost of, 179
   Jews, 170-171, 173-174, 181-183
   Negroes, 160-161, 173-174, 181-183
      *See also* Competitive enterprises; Monopoly

Dispersion of wages, 320-321, 332-339
   effect of unionism on, 321-324, 339-340
      *See also* Labor unions; Wage differentials

Engineers, salaries of, 271-275
      *See also* Wage differentials, by skill

Fair Employment Practices Commission. 179

Female labor force:
   clerical workers:
      earnings, 113-117, 119
      hours of work, 117
      number, 109
      personnel policies affecting, 121-124
      recruitment of, 139-143, 152-153
      turnover of, 137-139, 143
      wage policies affecting, 124-129, 142-143, 147-149, 152-154
      unionization, 118
   married women, labor force rates of:
      and age, 91
      and ages of children, 91-92
      and education, 88
      and family consumption, 97, 100
      and family income, 65-66, 69-79
      and husband's age, 77-84; earnings, 73-74, 77-84, 87-89; education, 77-84, 89; employment status, 90

labor-force rates of Negro, 103-104
   secular changes in labor-force behavior of, 92-96
   time, moment-of-time and overtime relationships, 99-104
   variations in turnover of, 68
   work preferences of, 67-68

Jews, jobs held in ten occupations, 170-171
   *See also* Discrimination in employment

Labor unions:
   as monopolies, 172-174
   production workers in, 333-334
   and relative wage differentials, 319-324, 329-332
   cross-section approach, 327-328
   time-series approach, 328-329
   and wages, 293, 297-298
      *See also* Monopolies; Wage differentials

License laws, 4-6
Licensing, business, 3, 5
Licensing, occupational:
   barber, 14-20
   effect of entry cost, 6-8, 12-13
   funeral directors and embalmers, 9-10
   restrictions on, 11-12

Married women, *see* Female labor force, married women

Monopoly, 160-163, 171
   and discrimination, 160-161, 165, 170-171
   and labor unions, 172-174
   personnel practices of, 168-169, 180
   potential monopolist, 180
   and profit control by government, 161-166, 176-178
   racial or religious cartels, 182-183
      *See also* Discrimination in employment; Labor unions; Public utilities

Negro slaves, *see* Slaves, Negro
Nonpecuniary income, 158-161, 176-179

Occupational licensing, *see* Licensing, occupational

Pecuniary vs. nonpecuniary gains, 158-161, 176-179

# AUTHOR INDEX

Alchian, Armen A., 168 n.
Allan, William, 255 n.
Attiyeh, Yossef, 331 n.

Bailey, M. J., 280 n.
Bancroft, Frederic, 193 n., 235
Bancroft, Gertrude, 72, 75 n., 87 n.
Barrow, R. H., 254 n.
Becker, Gary S., 159 n., 160 n., 161, 259, 265 n.
Becker, Howard, 45 n.
Bell, P. W., 269 n.
Bendix, Richard, 40 n.
Blank, D. M., 271 n., 272 n., 273 n., 274 n.
Bogue, D. J., 264 n.
Bowen, William G., 120 n., 122 n., 290-294, 331 n.
Bowlby, R. L., 296
Bracket, Jeffrey R., 222 n.
Bradley, Philip H., 177 n.
Bruce, Kathleen, 193 n., 235

Catterall, Helen T., 235
Cole, Arthur H., 224 n.
Cole. G. D. H., 41 n., 48 n.
Coleman, J. Winston, 204
Conant, Eaton Hall, 107 n., 137 n., 139 n.
Conrad, Alfred H., 191 n., 200, 203 n., 206, 209 n., 214 n., 224 n., 225 n., 247, 290 n., 291
Coulter, E. Merton, 235
Craycraft, Joseph L., 324, 326
Cullen, D. E., 281-283
Currell, M. E., 284 n.

Davis, Edwin A., 235
Davis, Lance E., 207 n.
DeBow, James D. B., 185 n., 186-187, 188 n., 211 n., 225, 227 n., 235, 242
Derrick, Samuel M., 200
DeSaussare, H. W., 189
Director, Aaron, 165 n.
Dorfman, Joseph, 33 n.
Douglas, Paul H., 63 n., 71, 73 n., 267 n., 297, 298 n., 344
Dowson, J. L., 189
Dozier, Harold D., 243
Dubin, R., 23 n.
Dublin, Louis I., 209 n., 212-213, 214 n.
Duff, A. M., 253 n., 254 n.

Dunlop, John T., 25 n., 36 n., 53, 144 n., 287 n., 294 n., 296-297, 313-314
Durand, John D., 63 n., 91 n.

Eaton, Clement, 192 n., 226 n.
Eisemann, Doris M., 289 n., 291
Eisner, R., 71 n.
Elkins, Stanley M., 185 n., 226 n.
Engels, Friedrich, 31 n., 33 n.
Evans, Robert, Jr., 271 n.

Fabricant, Solomon, 278 n.
Flanders, Ralph B., 190 n., 235
Forchheimer, K., 51 n.
Frank, Tenney, 254 n.
Frazier, E. Franklin, 185 n.
Friedman, Milton, 69 n., 88 n., 100, 162 n., 299, 324, 326

Garbarino, J. W., 286 n., 288 n., 296-297, 324, 326, 330
Gellhorn, Walter, 3 n., 6 n.
Gerschenkron, Alexander, 36
Goldner, William, 260 n., 288, 291, 298, 324, 326, 329-330
Govan, Thomas P., 190 n.
Gray, Lewis G., 222 n., 235, 250 n.
Green, Fletcher, 235
Greenslade, Rush V., 324, 326, 331, 337

Haddy, P., 284 n.
Hamilton, William B., 204
Hansen, Alvin H., 51 n.
Hansen, B., 289
Harbison, Frederick H., 25 n., 26 n., 36 n., 53
Hartman, Paul T., 51 n.
Heaton, Herbert, 249 n.
Hicks, John R., 157-158
Hobson, J. A., 33 n.
Hogan, William R., 235
Holmes, S. J., 214 n.
Homan, Paul T., 33 n.
Houthakker, H. S., 88 n.
Hunt, Freeman, 243

Irwin, Donald, 51 n.

Jackson, Luther Porter, 226 n., 227 n.
Jacobson, Paul, 210 n., 212
Johansen, L., 297 n.
Johnston, James H., 243
Jordan, Weymouth T., 235

*347*